The Philosophy of
Heidegger

Continental European Philosophy

This series provides accessible and stimulating introductions to the ideas of continental thinkers who have shaped the fundamentals of European philosophical thought. Powerful and radical, the ideas of these philosophers have often been contested, but they remain key to understanding current philosophical thinking as well as the current direction of disciplines such as political science, literary theory, social theory, art history and cultural studies. Each book seeks to combine clarity with depth, introducing fresh insights and wider perspectives while also providing a comprehensive survey of each thinker's philosophical ideas.

The Philosophy of Agamben
Catherine Mills

The Philosophy of Derrida
Mark Dooley and Liam Kavanagh

The Philosophy of Foucault
Todd May

The Philosophy of Gadamer
Jean Grondin

The Philosophy of Habermas
Andrew Edgar

The Philosophy of Heidegger
Michael Watts

The Philosophy of Hegel
Allen Speight

The Philosophy of Husserl
Burt C. Hopkins

The Philosophy of Kierkegaard
George Pattison

The Philosophy of Merleau-Ponty
Eric Matthews

The Philosophy of Nietzsche
Rex Welshon

The Philosophy of Schopenhauer
Dale Jacquette

The Philosophy of Heidegger

Michael Watts

Routledge
Taylor & Francis Group

LONDON AND NEW YORK

With thanks to my parents and all the family for their considerable support.

First Published 2011 by Acumen

Published 2014 by Routledge
2 Park Square, Milton Park, Abingdon, Oxon OX14 4RN
711 Third Avenue, New York, NY 10017, USA

*Routledge is an imprint of the Taylor and Francis Group,
an informa business*

ISBN: 978-1-84465-263-1 (hardcover)
ISBN: 978-1-84465-264-8 (paperback)

British Library Cataloguing-in-Publication Data
A catalogue record for this book is available from the British Library.

Typeset in Classical Garamond.

Contents

Preface

No Western philosopher since Socrates has attracted such varied, often totally opposed, views as Heidegger. In a popular history of philosophy by Bertrand Russell, the entry on Heidegger comprises only one short paragraph. The first line reads: "Highly eccentric in its terminology, his philosophy is extremely obscure. One cannot help suspecting that language is here running riot" (1989: 303). The analytic philosopher A. J. Ayer once accused him of charlatanism (1984: 228); Roger Scruton, a contemporary conservative British philosopher, described Heidegger's most important work *Being and Time* as "formidably difficult – unless it is utter nonsense, in which case it is laughably easy" (2001: 270). Against these dismissals, the American philosopher Richard Rorty (1981: 5) rates Heidegger as one of the three most important philosophers of the twentieth century, along with John Dewey and Wittgenstein.

Heidegger also, frequently, has been damned both as a man and as a thinker for his brief but enthusiastic support of the Nazis. This was symbolized by his acceptance of the post of rector of Freiburg University in 1933, where he proved a passionate advocate of subordinating the university to the new Nazi regime. Although he resigned the rectorship after only a year, and became increasingly critical of the direction taken by the Nazi party, he never uttered a full apology for his support of National Socialism, nor admitted guilt for having done so, during the thirty-one years he lived after 1945. If Heidegger could not, even with hindsight, accept that he had been wrong, many have questioned how much value should be placed on his work, particularly because his philosophy stresses the importance of a life lived as an experience in time and place, rather than as a collection of abstract theories.

For the English-speaker, such biographical problems are not the only drawbacks. Heidegger wrote a distinctive, notoriously dense prose that, when translated, can appear impenetrably Teutonic. Unsurprisingly, therefore, for a long time he was ignored in the Anglo-American world. But he was hailed as one of existentialism's founding fathers in continental Europe from the 1940s. Since his death in 1976 he has become almost as famed in the anglophone world, despite further controversies over his links with the Nazis and over his exploitative relationship with Hannah Arendt when she was his student. Some critics have seen him as both a Nazi and an unscrupulous seducer of a vulnerable teenager; for others, he appears a covert critic of Nazism and an intellectual mentor to Arendt as well as her lover. Above all, he is now held to have had vital insights into the central problems of modern life, including the uses and abuses of technology, literature, poetry, theatre, sociology and even architecture.

Deeply concerned with the way that language shapes human thought, Heidegger made a vital contribution to the development of phenomenology, founded by his teacher Edmund Husserl. But Heidegger outstripped his mentor's achievement, finally passing beyond phenomenology to create a wholly new approach to thinking that profoundly influenced German philosophers such as Jürgen Habermas and Hans-Georg Gadamer, English-speaking philosophers such as Charles Taylor and Rorty, and French philosophers such as Jacques Derrida, Michel Foucault and Maurice Merleau-Ponty. Indeed, he inspired Jean-Paul Sartre to create the twentieth century's perhaps most famous philosophical school: existentialism. (This was despite Heidegger's letter to Jean Beaufret in 1947 "Letter on Humanism", in which he distanced his own philosophy from French existentialism.) For many, Heidegger is finally the ultimate "philosopher of Being", who pursued the question of the "meaning of Being" relentlessly until death ended his quest.

Heidegger was remarkably prescient about some of the current ecological problems. Strongly opposed to many trends in industrial society, with its emphasis on technology and mass consumption, he attacked the mistreatment of livestock and the misuse of the planet's resources. When even leading scientists (such as Martin Rees, one of Britain's most respected astronomers) now give humanity a less-than-even chance of surviving the century, Heidegger's declaration "Only a god can save us", made in 1966, seems uncannily prophetic about the deepening ecological crisis. He now appears a timely philosopher, whose deep ontological thinking, revealed in *Being and Time*, his masterpiece of 1927, is still pressingly pertinent.

Although Heidegger remains the most controversial philosopher of the twentieth century, it is possible to chart a middle way between conflicting explanations of his thought. Here his ideas are presented as unambiguously as possible, with his innovative but often-obscure language explained clearly in the text and in the glossary. The book is intended to be read, with relative ease, both by postgraduate students and by complete newcomers to philosophy, setting out clearly the central ideas of what can appear the most complex and obscure of all philosophers. But to explain Heidegger's ideas more comprehensibly within and between chapters, the book does not always follow the development of Heidegger's thought strictly chronologically.

While Heidegger's thought can appear exceptionally convoluted, it is also an exhilarating intellectual challenge. This book can be used as a "launch pad", providing a solid foundation of understanding to give readers the confidence, inspiration and basic tools for further explorations of Heidegger's own writings.

Abbreviations

Publication details can be found in the Bibliography. Works in the *Gesamtausgabe* (Collected Works) are cited by volume number and page number in the original German edition.

BPP   *The Basic Problems of Phenomenology*, Hofstadter (trans.) (1982). GA 24.

BT   *Being and Time*, Macquarrie & Robinson (trans.) (1962).

BW   *Basic Writings*, Krell (ed.) (1993).

CTP   *Contributions to Philosophy (From Enowning)*, Emad & Maly (trans.) (1999). GA 65.

DT   *Discourse on Thinking*, Anderson & Freund (trans.) (1966).

EGT   *Early Greek Thinking*, Krell & Capuzzi (trans.) (1975).

EH   *Elucidations of Hölderlin's Poetry*, Hoeller (trans.) (2000).

FCM   *The Fundamental Concepts of Metaphysics: World, Finitude, Solitude*, McNeill & Walker (trans.) (1995). GA 29/30.

GA   *Gesamtausgabe* (Collected Works) (Frankfurt: Klostermann, 1975–).

GA 4   *Erläuterungen zu Hölderlins Dichtung*, von Herrmann (ed.) (1981).

GA 5   *Holzwege*, von Herrmann (ed.) (1978).

GA 7   *Vorträge und Aufsätze*, von Herrmann (ed.) (2000).

GA 9   *Wegmarken*, von Herrmann (ed.) (1976).

GA 10   *Der Satz vom Grund*, von Herrmann (ed.) (1997).

GA 12   *Unterwegs zur Sprache (1950–1959)*, von Herrmann (ed.) (1985).

GA 15   *Seminare (1915–1973)*, Ochwadt (ed.) (2005).

GA 18   *Grundbegriffe der aristotelischen Philosophie* (2002).

GA 20   *History of the Concept of Time: Prolegomena*, Kiesel (trans.) (1985); originally published in the *Gesamtausgabe* as *Prolegomena zur Geschichte des Zeitbegriffs* (1979).

GA 21   *Logik: Die Frage nach der Wahrheit* (1976). Quotations are from translations in Inwood (2000b).

GA 31   *The Essence of Human Freedom: An Introduction to Philosophy*, Sadler (trans.) (2002); originally published in the *Gesamtausgabe* as *Vom Wesen der Menschlichen Freiheit. Einleitung in die Philosophie*, Tietjen (ed.) (1983).

GA 33   *Aristotle's Metaphysics θ, 1–3: On the Essence and Actuality of Force*, Brogan & Warnek (trans.) (1995); originally published in the *Gesamtausgabe* as *Aristoteles, Metaphysik θ, 1–3: Von Wesen und Wirklichkeit der Kraft*, Hüni (ed.) (1981).

GA 34   *Vom Wesen der Wahrheit: Zu Platons Hohlengleichnis und Theatet* (1988)

GA 38   *Logik als Frage nach dem Wesen der Sprache*, Seubold (ed.) (1998).

GA 39   *Hölderlins Hymnen "Germanien" und "Der Rhein"*, Ziegler (ed.) (1980; 2nd edn 1989).

GA 46   *Nietzsches II. Unzeitgemässe Betrachtung*, Friedrich (ed.) (2003).

GA 49   *Die Metaphysik des deutschen Idealismus* (Schelling), Seubold (ed.) (1991).

GA 51   *Basic Concepts*, Aylesworth (trans.) (1933); originally published in the *Gesamtausgabe* as *Grundbegriffe* (1981).

GA 52   *Hölderlins Hymne "Andenken"* (1976).

GA 54   *Parmenides*, Schuwer & Rojcewicz (trans.) (1992); originally published in the *Gesamtausgabe* as *Parmenides* (1982).

GA 55   *Heraklit* (1979).

GA 56/57   *Zur Bestimmung der Philosophie*, Heimbuchel (ed.) (1987).

GA 61   *Phänomenologische Interpretationen zu Aristoteles: Einführung in die phänomenologische Forschung*, Bröcker & Bröcker-Oltmanns (eds) (1985).

GA 63   *Ontology and the Hermeneutics of Facticity*, van Buren (trans.) (1999).

GA 65   *Beitrage zur Philosophie (Vom Eriegnis) [Contributions to Philosophy (From Enowning)]*, von Herrmann (ed.) (1989).

GA 77   *Feldweg-Gespräche* (1995).

GA 87   *Nietzsche Seminare 1937 und 1944* (2004).

HCT   *History of the Concept of Time: Prolegomena*, Kiesel (trans.) (1985). GA 20.

HEP   "Holderlin and the Essence of Poetry", Scott (trans.) (1949).

ID   *Identität und Differenz* (1990). GA 11.

IM   *An Introduction to Metaphysics*, (i) Manheim (trans.) (1959), (ii) Fried & Polt (trans.) (2000). The Mannheim translation is quoted unless otherwise indicated.

Logica   *Logica: lecciones de M. Heidegger (semester verano 1934) en el legado de Helene Weiss*, Farías (trans.) (1991) [German and Spanish].

MFL   *The Metaphysical Foundations of Logic*, Heim (trans.) (1984). GA 26.

Ni   *Nietzsche I: The Will to Power as Art*, Krell (trans.) (1979).

Nii   *Nietzsche II: The Eternal Recurrence of the Same*, Krell (trans.) (1984).

Niii   *Nietzsche III: The Will to Power as Knowledge and as Metaphysics*, Stambaugh *et al.* (trans.) (1987).

Niv   *Nietzsche IV: Nihilism*, Capuzzi (trans.) (1982).

OGSU   "Only a God Can Save Us: *Der Spiegel's* Interview with Martin Heidegger", Alter & Caputo (trans.) (1976).

OM   "Overcoming Metaphysics" (2003).

OT   *On Time and Being*, Stambaugh (trans.) (1972).

OWA   *The Origin of the Work of Art* (1975).

OWL   *On the Way to Language*, Hertz (trans.) (1971).

P   *Pathmarks*, McNeill (trans.) (1998).

PIA   "Phenomenological Interpretations in Connection with Aristotle: An Indication of the Hermeneutical Situation" (2002).

PLT   *Poetry, Language, Thought,* Hofstadter (trans.) (1975).

PR   *The Principle of Reason*, Lilly (trans.) (1991).

PRL   *The Phenomenology of Religious Life*, Gosetti-Ferencei & Fritsch (trans.) (2004).

PS   *Plato's* Sophist, R. Rojcewicz & A. Schuwer (trans.) (1997). GA 19.

QB   *Zur Seinesfrage/The Question of Being*, Kluback & Wilde (trans.) (1959). Cited by page number in this edition, but translations in Inwood (2000b).

QCT   *The Question Concerning Technology and Other Essays*, Lovitt (trans.) (1977).

US   *Unterwegs zur Sprache* (1965).

WCT   *What is Called Thinking?*, Wieck & Gray (trans.) (1968).

WIP   *What is Philosophy?*, Kluback & Wilde (trans.) (1958).

WT   *What is a Thing?*, Barton & Deutsch (trans.) (1967).

Zollikon   *Zollikon Seminars: Protocols – Conversations – Letters*, Boss (ed.), Mayr & Askay (trans.) (2001).

ZSD   *Zur Sache des Denkens*, 3rd edn (1988).

CHAPTER ONE

Heidegger's life

In the small town of Messkirch in the Black Forest region of Baden-Wurttemberg, southwest Germany, lies St Martin's, a small Catholic church. In its quiet hilltop graveyard there is a tombstone inscribed "Martin Heidegger, 1889–1976". It is not marked with a cross, but with a star, recalling a line written by the philosopher in 1947: "To think is to confine yourself to a single thought that one day stands still like a star in the world's sky" (PLT: 4). The grave marks the final return of Heidegger, the great philosopher, to his roots.

Heidegger was born in Messkirch, then a pious, very conservative agricultural town, to a poor lower-middle-class, devoutly religious Catholic family. The local church employed his father Friedrich as bellringer, gravedigger and caretaker of the vestments and sacred vessels, so Heidegger's childhood was steeped in Catholicism, a religion that long dominated his life and thinking. The simple, still rustic, world in which Heidegger grew up left him with an enduring sympathy for the life of the traditional German countryside. He came from a social class whose lives for centuries had been filled with the daily round of hard labour and he felt a part of the cultivated farmland. He also loved to hike and ski through the wild mountainous landscape of the Black Forest.

His early experiences of nature and craftsmanship, combined with a typically Catholic sense of guilt – for he also grew up in an atmosphere saturated with Christian doctrines of sin and redemption – became central to his later philosophy. In 1933 he refused to leave Freiburg University to teach in Berlin, explaining that his "philosophical work … belongs right in the midst of the 'peasants' work" (Sheehan 1981: 28).

How relevant are such biographical details to understanding a philosopher's work? Heidegger's own views on this are ambiguous. At the start of a lecture on Aristotle he states: "The only thing of interest regarding the person of a philosopher is this: He was born on such and such a date, he worked, and he died" (GA 18: 5; Davis 2010b: 2). And in 1955, during a memorial address in Messkirch, he proclaimed: "The greater the master, the more completely his person vanishes behind his work" ("Memorial Address", in DT: 44). Yet later on in the same speech he quotes from a local poet, Johann Peter Hebel: "We are like plants which – whether we like to admit it to ourselves or not – must with our roots rise out of the earth in order to bloom in the ether and to bear fruit" (DT: 47). And in a lecture course in 1920 he asserts: "philosophy arises from factical life experience. And within factical life experience philosophy returns back into factical life experience" (PRL: 6–7).

More importantly, in his later thinking he views the historical existence of the individual as located within an epoch of the "history of Being" itself. In the case of the great philosophers, they actually *influence* the shifts between epochs. Heidegger viewed his own thought as crucially positioned at the conclusion of the history of philosophy as metaphysics and at the beginning of what he termed "the task of thinking" (BW: 431ff.). Thus, if one agrees with Heidegger on this matter, it would seem reasonable to conclude that to understand in depth the thinking of a great philosopher it is essential that we also have knowledge of the particular epoch in the history of Being in which the philosopher's thinking is situated.

Education

From an early age Heidegger displayed a keen interest in religion and seemed destined for the priesthood. In 1903 he gained a scholarship to the *Gymnasium* (grammar/high school) in Konstanz, where he lived in a Catholic boarding house. Three years later he transferred to another *Gymnasium* in Freiburg. The Catholic Church continued to provide him with free board and lodging while he simultaneously trained for the priesthood at the Freiburg Jesuit Seminary. It was here, in the summer of 1907, that Martin Heidegger, now a seventeen-year-old high-school student, received a book from Conrad Grober, a pastor and friend of his father. Written by the Catholic thinker Franz Brentano and entitled *On the Manifold Meaning of Being according to Aristotle* (1862), it served to catalyse Heidegger's lifelong relation with philosophy.

In 1909 he left school to become a Jesuit novice at the Society of Jesus in Tisis, Austria, only to quit after a couple of weeks because of severe chest pains that were attributed to heart trouble. (The pains were probably psychosomatic in origin, however, as he lived to a robust eighty-six.) But his interest in religion remained strong, and for the next two years a church scholarship paid for his studies at the seminary of Albert-Ludwig University in Freiburg, where he studied Catholic theology and medieval Christian philosophy in preparation for the priesthood.

He then encountered his next major philosophical influence: *On Being: An Outline of Ontology* (1896). The author of the work, Carl Braig, was a theology professor who taught at Freiburg University. This book marked the start of Heidegger's deep commitment to exploring what he considered the single most important question of existence: what is Being? "The following question concerned me in quite a vague manner: If Being is predicated in manifold meanings, then what is its leading fundamental meaning? What does Being mean?" (OT: 74). The attempt to provide answers to this became Heidegger's central preoccupation, one that was to grip him right up to his death.

In 1911, owing to asthma and further suspected heart problems, he abandoned his training for the priesthood and transferred from the seminary to become officially a philosophy student. Although he never completely lost his interest in theology, it became far less central to his life and academic pursuits. He now immersed himself in the works of Aristotle while also studying mathematics. He was increasingly attracted to writers who explored the extremes of human emotion and experience: Dostoyevsky, Nietzsche and Kierkegaard. The latter two, although in many areas deeply opposed in their ways of thinking, held the same view with regard to the philosophical tradition preceding them, which they felt overemphasized the value of *cognition* while providing little insight pertaining to the actual life of the individual.

Further, both of these "existentialist" thinkers viewed the everyday life that most people lead as superficial and inauthentic, a distortion of a deeper and potentially distressing underlying truth that, when revealed, can serve to inspire an authentic existence liberated from the influence of the masses. The two thinkers, however, who perhaps *most* influenced the methodology that Heidegger used to investigate and interpret the significance that everyday life both embodies and conceals were Wilhelm Dilthey (1833–1911) and Edmund Husserl (1859–1938). Heidegger's philosophy in many ways creatively combines the ideas and methods of both men. Dilthey, with his theory of *hermeneutics*, asserted that we cannot effectively employ the techniques used in the natural sciences to understand meaningful human behaviour, with its linguistic expressions and symbols, because the former seeks to provide general laws that are universally applicable at all times to explain natural events, whereas human behaviour is "place and time sensitive", and can only be understood within a concrete social and historical context. Indeed, in *Being and Time*, Heidegger asserts that our mode of Being makes sense only in terms of this historical, social and cultural context, and, importantly, it also only *is* what it is *in terms of* that context.

3

After gaining his doctorate from Freiburg University in July 1913 on "The Doctrine of Judgement in Psychologism", and completing a thesis on the medieval theologian Duns Scotus in 1915 that allowed him to teach in German universities, Heidegger was conscripted into the German army in 1915. However, after only two months he was discharged on health grounds. Early in 1917 he was again called up into the army, assigned to the military postal service. In the same year he married a north German Protestant, Elfride Petri. In 1918 he was sent to a meteorological station on the Western Front near Verdun, where he served until the Armistice, but he never saw actual combat. In 1919 and 1920 his two sons, Jörg and Hermann, were born. In January 1919 he wrote a letter to a friend, Father Krebs, in which he said that various philosophical insights made orthodox Catholicism unacceptable to him. This break with the Catholic Church – which may have been partly due to his failure to gain the chair in Catholic scholastic philosophy at Freiburg University for which he had hoped – was essential to his intellectual development. Like Husserl and many others, Heidegger strongly believed that philosophy is only done properly by a thinker freed from all theological assumptions.

Academic career

In February 1919 Heidegger began lecturing in philosophy at Freiburg as a *privatdozent* (assistant lecturer) under the guidance of Husserl. Husserl held the chair of philosophy at the university, where Heidegger soon became his most trusted assistant, helping develop phenomenology, the movement pioneered by Husserl. The personal relationship between Husserl and Heidegger soon became a quasi-parental one; Mrs Husserl was reported to have introduced Heidegger to Karl Jaspers, another philosopher, as her husband's "phenomenological child". Heidegger and Jaspers were soon close friends, united by their interest in thinkers such as Dilthey and their contempt for most university philosophy at the time.

Heidegger, with his call for a "return to the authentic origins of the spirit", was soon recognized as a teacher of amazing brilliance at Freiburg, where he interpreted, with mesmerizing, passionate intensity and startlingly original insight, great philosophers such as Plato, Descartes, Kant and Hegel. His courses on phenomenology, on Aristotle and on the human being in the world of everyday experience earned him the title of the "hidden king" of philosophy. He often used a method that, although popular today, was unheard of at the time. He would guide his students towards a deep understanding of the core of a philosopher's thinking by having them study just two or three carefully selected pages of the philosopher's work in a hermeneutic approach. Through this method, they often achieved a greater depth of understanding in a matter of months than others could gain during years of study (see Biemel 1976: 8).

Heidegger was so filled with intellectual passion that he could hypnotize his audience. Until Heidegger, people had been accustomed to opposing reason to passion, spirit to life, but he shocked his audiences by a fiery enthusiasm combined with incredible philosophical perception. "What he provided was the full investment of his energy and what brilliant energy it was. It was the energy of a revolutionary thinker … so filled with the passion of his thinking that he conveyed to his listeners a fascination not to be broken", recalled one student, Gadamer (1985: 19).

Another, Karl Löwith, later a significant thinker in his own right, wrote:

> We nicknamed Heidegger "the little magician from Messkirch" …
> This art of enchantment sometimes had the most disturbing effects
> in that it attracted more or less psychopathic personalities, and one
> female student committed suicide three years after such guessing
> games.   (1993a: 44–5)

In 1922, as a result of his insightful, creative interpretations of Aristotle, Heidegger was offered the position of Associate Professor of Philosophy at Marburg University. There he attracted students who travelled from the four corners of Europe to study with him. Although he had not as yet published any works, he quickly became known throughout Germany as a genius and radical thinker simply by the force of his teaching. Early in 1925 he began an intimate and very important relationship with a highly gifted eighteen-year-old Jewish philosophy student, Hannah Arendt. Many years later, writing to celebrate Heidegger's eightieth birthday, she recalled his impact:

> What was experienced was that thinking as pure activity – and
> this means impelled neither by the thirst for knowledge nor by the
> drive for cognition – can become a passion which not so much rules
> and oppresses all other capacities and gifts, as it orders them and
> prevails through them. We are so accustomed to the old opposition
> of reason versus passion that the idea of a *passionate* thinking,
> in which thinking and aliveness become one, takes us somewhat
> aback.   (Arendt 1995: 297)

In January 1926 the authorities in Berlin rejected the University of Marburg's proposal to grant Heidegger a full professorship, owing to insufficient literary accomplishments. However, later that year, at Husserl's sixty-seventh birthday party, Heidegger presented his work *Being and Time*, which he had dedicated to Husserl. Although it was far from complete, Husserl arranged for its publication on 8 April 1927.

Heidegger now gained international renown and a full professorship at Marburg University. In 1928 he was invited back to Freiburg to occupy the chair of philosophy formerly held by Husserl, now retired. Within a few years, *Being and Time* won recognition in many philosophical circles as an epoch-making work of twentieth-century European philosophy. It remains beyond question Heidegger's most famous and most influential work. The difficulties posed by its radical originality and highly obscure style make understanding its major claims extremely difficult, however, even for the philosophically trained reader.

In spite of this, the book was within a few years acclaimed as a deep and important work, not only in the German-speaking world but also in countries such as France, where phenomenology was already well known. It was a major influence on Sartre and the whole existentialist movement. Despite Heidegger's protests, he was classed, on the strength of this book, as the leading atheistic existentialist. However, it did not receive a similarly warm reception in the English-speaking world.

On the occasion of his inauguration as professor at Freiburg in 1929, Heidegger delivered one of his most famous lectures, "What is Metaphysics?" This powerful exploration of *angst* (anxiety) and its relation to Nothingness became a key text for existentialists, as well as the subject of great controversy. In this lecture Heidegger presents two theses that are diametrically opposed to Husserl's thinking: that philosophy must overthrow the dominion of logic and that the mood of anxiety is essential to true philosophical thinking. The following two statements in this lecture were largely responsible for Heidegger's long exclusion from the world of Anglo-American philosophy. The first, "Nothingness itself Nothings" ("What is Metaphysics?", in BW: 103) sounded to many anglophone philosophers like complete nonsense. The second hardly seemed to make more sense: "The idea of 'logic' itself disintegrates in the turbulence of a more original questioning" (*ibid.*: 105). Many philosophers at the time believed (and still do) that philosophy should express facts in an objective, logical, scientific manner; there should be no ambiguous propositions. Among English-speaking philosophers, Heidegger's work was for a long time not taken seriously, and he was categorized as simply an obscurantist follower of Husserl. This effective ostracism lasted many decades.

This lecture was a turning point in Heidegger's thought. By 1929 he began to realize that his philosophical approach was not working in the way he wished and thus he abandoned it for a significant change in direction, which became especially evident in 1936. The systematic metaphysics, his devotion to phenomenology and his ontology of his earlier years were left behind; his interest in Aristotle, the Scholastics and Kant waned, supplanted by his increased focus on Nietzsche's thought, and he began to indulge in a philosophical form of cultural criticism via essays such as "The Question Concerning Technology". Most importantly, *poetry* – in particular the work of poets such as Friedrich Hölderlin, Rainer Maria Rilke and Georg Trakl – displaced *logic* as the originary vehicle of our understanding of Being. This transformational period in Heidegger's thinking is often referred to as his "turn".

In 1930 Heidegger rejected the chair of philosophy at Berlin, Germany's largest university. He disliked not just the noise of big cities, but their social and cultural life and the cosmopolitan elegance of the German intellectual elite. Instead, he chose to live in the small mountain cottage that he had built in 1923 above the town of Todtnauberg in the Black Forest. Heidegger had no interest in a social life revolving round professorial dinner tables and similar gatherings, preferring his provincial existence in southern Germany with its small towns and often rugged landscape. Most of his writing was done in this remote environment, where he could take breaks from his work in physical activities such as chopping wood or cross-country skiing. He often wore traditional rural costume, including lederhosen, to signify his commitment to *Blut und Boden* (blood and soil). These peaceful, tranquil years, however, were not to last. Heidegger's next decision would dramatically alter the course of his life, causing irreparable damage to both his personal and professional reputations.

Heidegger and Nazism

The early 1930s saw the end of the Weimar Republic. The effects of the stock market crash on Wall Street in October 1929 were felt immediately in Germany, for German industry depended heavily on short-term American loans that began to be called in. Unemployment soared to three million in September 1930 and to six million by early 1932, or over 20 per cent of the workforce. The Republic, always fragile because it had been born in the aftermath of German defeat in 1918 and rocked by the great inflation of the early 1920s, now faced rising anti-democratic forces both on the extreme Left and on the Right. The National Socialist German Workers' Party, or Nazis, who had been insignificant in the later 1920s, saw the number of their deputies increase from 12 to 106 in elections in 1930. After further elections in July 1932 they became the largest party. Street clashes between Brownshirts, Nazi storm troopers and their communist opponents seemed to presage open civil war. Germany appeared to be at crisis point.

On 30 January 1933 the elderly President Hindenburg appointed Adolf Hitler chancellor of Germany. A month later, after the burning of the Reichstag building on 27 February 1933, Hitler persuaded the Reichstag to suspend the German Constitution and a permanent state of emergency was declared. Fundamental civil liberties such as privacy of mail and freedom of speech were cancelled. On 7 March Hitler arrested all the communist deputies who had just been elected to the Reichstag, and subsequently sent them to the concentration camps, the first of so many. An "Enabling Act" passed by the Reichstag on 24 March gave Hitler sole lawmaking powers and soon all parties other than the Nazis were abolished. The Nazi dictatorship had begun.

Many Germans greeted Hitler's resolute, brutal dismantling of the Weimar Republic, in the process called *Gleichshaltung* (coordination), with enthusiasm rather than dismay or passive acceptance. There was a widespread feeling of being liberated from a democracy that had ceased to function, a feeling that Heidegger fully shared. Despite being, with Wittgenstein, one of the two most renowned philosophers of the twentieth century, Heidegger as a man unquestionably had serious failures and flaws. That a philosopher of such stature could become an active supporter of such an evil and anti-intellectual regime remains one of the most controversial and hotly debated issues in all modern intellectual history.

On 5 April Nazi "cleansing laws" were passed to eject political opponents and "non-Aryans" from public employment. Jews, like communists, were now banned from all public office as well as from sports clubs and other institutions, and a national campaign was launched against Jewish businessmen, as well as Jewish academics, students, lawyers and doctors. The same month Heidegger was unanimously elected rector of Freiburg University, its chief administrative position. He started his office by enthusiastically promoting the policy of *Gleichshaltung*. For the sake of national unity, the traditional independence of the university was to be subordinated to the policies of the Hitler regime.

Up to the late 1920s Heidegger had shown little interest in politics, normally voting for small regional parties, but in the early 1930s he began to be drawn towards Nazism. On 1 May 1933 he officially joined the Nazi Party. In October 1933 he was re-inaugurated as one of the new non-elected "leader-rectors". He was now ending his lectures with "Heil Hitler" and in a radio broadcast that November he warmly supported German withdrawal from the League of Nations and its disarmament talks. In a plebiscite later that month, 95 per cent of German voters approved these actions, which suggests that Heidegger was going with the flow of German feeling, rather than guiding it as he had perhaps hoped. His direct influence on German politics was always almost nil.

Just six months later, in April 1934, Heidegger resigned the rectorship following apparent conflicts with the students, faculty and party officials. After his resignation, his public, pro-Nazi speeches and involvement in political affairs waned. He claimed later that he had become disillusioned with the Nazi Party after the Röhm putsch, when Hitler murdered Ernst Röhm, many Brownshirts and other potential opponents. But this "Night of the Long Knives" did not happen until 30 June 1934, so it cannot have caused his resignation. Possibly he had begun to realize that the Nazis neither needed nor heeded him.

Although Heidegger published very little in the 1930s, he continued to lecture, mostly on art. He presented *On the Origin of the Work of Art* in Freiburg in 1935, and travelled to Rome in 1936, where he commenced a series of lectures on the Romantic poet Hölderlin. In this same year he began his Nietzsche lectures, which continued over several years, a period when he came under the surveillance of the Gestapo. Supporters of Heidegger claim that these lectures were a covert attack on the political regime and were intended to undermine the Nazis' use of Nietzsche's thought in support of racist doctrines and practices. However, his criticism was so cryptic, and his depiction of Nietzsche – not that popular with many senior Nazis anyway – so unusual that few at the time noticed. In Rome, Heidegger, with a swastika badge prominent in his lapel, had again met Löwith – now in exile – and reaffirmed his belief that Hitler and Mussolini still represented the best bastions against the nihilism of modern life. Löwith was not impressed.

In 1938 Heidegger focused his attention on technology both in his Freiburg lecture *The Establishment of the Modern World-Picture by Metaphysics* and in a seminar on Ernst Jünger's essay *The Worker*. In his lectures at this time, which often referred to political events, he argued that the wilful construction of a world-empire intended to last for thousands of years demonstrates a preference for quantity over quality incompatible with the values of genuine creators such as the Greeks. This possible, if oblique, condemnation of Nazism by Heidegger was presented at the height of Hitler's power in the summer of 1941.

Heidegger faces the denazification commission

In October 1944, as allied forces closed in on the Third Reich, Heidegger was drafted into the German Home Guard in Freiburg to help dig anti-tank ditches. In December that year, after Freiburg was bombed, he fled to Messkirch. In 1945 the allies bombed Messkirch too and French forces occupied Freiburg. The French military government set up a "denazification commission" in cooperation with the university, to judge the members of the university. Heidegger first had to justify himself before this committee on 23 July 1945. The committee included several university professors, who were, with one exception, favourably predisposed towards Heidegger. However, the investigation concluded that Heidegger was not merely a Nazi sympathizer, but was guilty of political crimes, which included:

- enthusiastically transforming the university along the lines of the Nazi "leadership principle" or *Führerprinzip*;
- the incitement of students against non-Nazi professors;
- the denouncement of political undesirables to the Nazi authorities.

The commission's judgment in 1945 was relatively lenient. It concluded that, while at first Heidegger had actively supported the Nazi revolution, he had not been an active Nazi since 1934, after his resignation as rector of Freiburg, although he remained a party member up to 1945. They recommended that he be prematurely retired but not dismissed from office. This meant he could keep his right to teach but would lose all administrative powers.

The university senate objected to this excessively lenient ruling and the committee was instructed to re-examine Heidegger's case. At this point, Heidegger proposed that his former friend and colleague Jaspers be asked for an expert evaluation of his activities and character, which he hoped would exonerate him. It had the opposite effect. The following section of the letter written by Jaspers to the committee influenced their final decision:

> [I]t is absolutely necessary that those who helped place National Socialism in the saddle be called to account. Heidegger belongs among the few professors to have so acted ... Heidegger's manner of thinking, which to me seems in its essence unfree, dictatorial, and incapable of communication, would today in its pedagogical effects be disastrous ... To me the manner of thinking seems more important than the content of political judgments, the aggressive character of which can easily change directions. As long as in his case an authentic rebirth does not come to pass, one that would be evident in his work, such a teacher cannot in my opinion be placed before the youth of today, which, from a spiritual standpoint, is almost defenseless. The youth must first reach a point where they can think for themselves. (Jaspers 1993: 149)

On the strength of this assessment, on 19 January 1946 the senate proposed to the French military government that Heidegger be deprived of his teaching licence and removed from his post with a reduced pension. This proposal was duly adopted at the end of 1946 and was enforced until 1949.

Heidegger emerged from the denazification proceedings a broken man. In 1946, probably owing to the stress and humiliation caused by the interrogatory questioning by the commission, he suffered a nervous breakdown and spent three weeks in a sanatorium in Badenweiler.

During the denazification proceedings Heidegger did not express any sense of guilt. He claimed at the time – and again in 1966 in an interview with the weekly news magazine *Der Spiegel* – that he had been pressured into accepting the post of Nazi rector of Freiburg University, doing so only in order to prevent worse individuals taking the post. He strongly contested the interpretation of his inaugural speech as a political statement, asserting that it was simply a development of fundamental philosophical ideas originally expressed in *Being and Time*. He said that if at first he had believed in a new German dawn, it was not the one initiated by the Nazis. For a brief period he had committed himself to the Nazi revolution because he had believed it to be a metaphysical revolution. When it failed to deliver what it had promised, he rapidly recognized his error and often disagreed with the party and resisted its demands. He abandoned it in 1934 and pursued his philosophical work, uninfluenced by the party's approval or rejection. He denied all responsibility for the crimes that had been committed by National Socialism and felt it unfair that he should have to justify himself.

The post-war years

In spite of the sentence that had been imposed by the denazification committee, and the nervous breakdown that followed, Heidegger rapidly re-established his mental equilibrium, and his career in writing and lecturing soon recovered. He established his popularity among a new generation of students and also regained the cautious respect of the philosophical world.

In 1949 he was allowed to resume teaching. In 1950 his former lover Arendt visited him and his correspondence with her began again. So too did that with his former friend Jaspers, although this friendship ended when Jaspers, who with his Jewish wife had carried cyanide capsules throughout the war in case of arrest by the Gestapo, realized that Heidegger was *not* going to apologize for his actions in the Third Reich. In 1951–52 Heidegger delivered his first lectures at Freiburg University since 1944 (*What is Called*

Thinking?). His thinking now began to reach new audiences. In his later years he made frequent trips to France, where he met many artists, poets and thinkers, and his work rapidly became integral to the study of philosophy among French philosophers. Heidegger also turned his attention to Asian thought. His work had been known in Japan since the 1920s when Japanese philosophers first studied with him, and he spent the summer of 1946 translating the *Tao Te Ching* with a Chinese student. Heidegger's writings even attracted a modest following in the USA.

After his retirement in 1959, Heidegger left the academic world to spend most of his remaining life in his Freiburg home and his beloved mountain cottage, attempting to live in his Black Forest refuge in a way that embodied the values of his philosophy. After 1960, his publications and lecturing waned (his publications were now mostly revised versions of his lectures). During this period, he gave a couple of interviews – on German television and for the magazine *Der Spiegel* – and he made a few visits to Greece, but never remained away from his Black Forest origins for long. Heidegger worked consistently until 26 May 1976, when he died at the age of eighty-six, at his home in Freiburg.

In 1974 he had helped prepare a collected edition (*Gesamtausgabe*) of his works, which aimed to include his earlier publications as well as transcripts of all his lectures. He wanted all the thoughts he had ever expressed in his publications and lectures preserved for posterity. The first volume of this edition was published in 1975. To date, more than 100 volumes have been published.

CHAPTER TWO

The meaning of life:
the question of Being

Heidegger initiated a radical "thinking" – distinct from conventional forms of "philosophizing" – that cast doubt on the validity of the fundamental basis of Western philosophy. His approach questioned the authority of long-accepted notions of logic and truth by focusing its interrogation *not* on the *content* of existence, but on the "primary condition" that *enables* existence. Thus the most important and persistent view of Heidegger is as a pioneering thinker concerned first and foremost with investigating the significance of the primary condition for all life, which he called "Being":

> Parmenides, in the early age of thinking, says, *esti gar einai*, "for there is Being". The primal mystery for all thinking is concealed in this phrase ... because thinking should be directed only toward saying Being in its truth ... whether and how Being is must remain an open question for the careful attention of thinking. The *esti gar einai* of Parmenides is still unthought today ... When philosophy attends to its essence it does not make forward strides at all. It remains where it is in order constantly to think the Same. Progression, that is, progression forward from this place, is a mistake that follows thinking as the shadow that thinking itself casts.
> ("Letter on Humanism", in BW: 238)

The ontological "error" of Western philosophy

Philosophical speculation on the nature of Being is known as ontology. It began in fifth-century BCE Greece, when Presocratic thinkers such as Anaximander, Heraclitus and Parmenides became intrigued by the seemingly inexplicable fact of existence and introduced a new way of thinking about the world and the place of human beings in it. They were recognized in antiquity as the first philosophers and scientists of the Western tradition.

Heraclitus, for example, asserted that human rules for living must harmonize with divine law, which encompasses both the laws of men and the universal laws of the cosmos itself. He understood the cosmos as an intelligent, eternal (thus divine) system that intelligently orders and regulates itself: the *logos* – an objective law-like principle that embodies this order and governs the cosmos – is the account of this self-regulation that, like a language, can be *heard* and *understood* by those *attuned* to it (a viewpoint that would come to influence Heidegger's understanding of language).

Thus Heraclitus believed that divine nature, *not* human nature, has *right understanding*. Although he viewed experience derived from sense perceptions as important, he also regarded *thoughtful enquiry* as indispensable, since it is essential that one is able to perceive how the phenomena indicate the "larger order of things": "nature loves to hide itself" (Heraclitus fr. 123), so the evidence – the interplay of opposing states and forces, the unity of opposites and the roles of strife in human life as well as in the cosmos – must be carefully interpreted. Such thoughts would come to influence Heidegger's later writings on truth and the nature and function of "true" art.

So Heidegger respected, and was much inspired by, Presocratic thought, but observed that in Western philosophy since the time of Plato, and in science after Aristotle, hardly any attention was focused directly on the fundamental mystery of life: the fact that there actually *is* a world and a universe rather than Nothing. Consequently Heidegger saw the history of Western philosophy as rooted in a "forgetting of Being" that has resulted in a gradual disintegration of values, insatiable consumerism and technological domination of the earth. He thus took it as his mission in life to awaken a new sense of this unfathomable mystery that, whether attended to or not, looms like a gaping abyss beneath the comforting familiarity of the everyday world.

According to Heidegger, Plato and all philosophers who came after him made the grave mistake of adopting a "theoretical stance" for their interpretation of Being. This created an artificial but fundamental rift between the isolated subject or "mind" and an independently existing realm of objects, which has blinded most humans to the indivisibility and fundamental unity of Being. This gave rise to the "oblivion of Being" that persists today.

As a result, ontology has largely been preoccupied with "things" in existence and the facts connected with them, which Heidegger calls "ontic" knowledge: in other words, that which exists as a consequence of Being. This approach to ontology provides information about entities in the world as a whole, in terms of their most universal characteristics (measurements, similarities and differences, etc.) and their relations to other entities, and the question regarding the "Being" of entities has focused on "Being" only in the sense of what one can determine in general or universally about *all* entities, in other words, what they all have in common (BW: 126, 242, 432). For instance, Aristotle asserted that the Being of all entities can be understood with reference to *substances*. In modern times, science views the Being of all beings as varying forms of mass-energy in space–time, and according to Nietzsche's philosophy one can regard the Being of all entities as differing manifestations of the will to power.

But none of these ontological investigations of entities has any regard for, or interest in, the "primordial" fact of their Being: that which *determines* them as entities, that on the basis of which they are already understood (BT: 25–6). (Here, "determine" does not mean to create or cause, for Being does not produce entities, since only entities produce entities and Being is not an entity; instead, "determines" implies the sense "enables us to 'encounter' and 'understand'".) Heidegger observed the same fundamental flaw in *all* these approaches, which investigated the "Being of beings" without exploring what "Being" actually is: what it signifies or means in the first place. For, according to Heidegger, prior to answering any question about the "Being" of beings, one needs first to ask: what is the meaning of that which is referred to by the word "Being"? And the failure to do this means that these ontological approaches are conducting their investigations with insufficient understanding of that which is the fundamental precondition of their *entire* investigation. In other words, according to Heidegger there is no solid "grounding" or "basis" for any of their ontological conclusions.

Heidegger uses the word "meaning" in reference to "that in terms of which we understand something", and Heidegger's conception of *understanding* refers not merely to the comprehension of words, concepts and ideas, but also to the understanding of things or phenomena, which consists of a *knowing how* to interact with things. In other words, according to Heidegger's conception of understanding, to "understand" a railway underground system means knowing how to navigate it, knowing your way around it. And similarly, understanding a person means that you know how to be with them: how to relate to and communicate with them. In other words, what we are referring to here is *pre-theoretical* practical "ability" or "know-how".

The term "primordial", which Heidegger uses frequently, refers to that which is prior to everything and therefore cannot be derived from anything else. Thus Heidegger's *"question of the meaning of Being"* (BT: 40) is *the* primordial question because all other questions, including all ontologies of beings and their Being, and all forms of science, necessarily presuppose that there *is* Being in the first place, and it is *this* crucial truth of Being that is ignored.

15

> Every determination of the essence of man that already presup-
> poses an interpretation of beings without asking about the truth of
> Being, whether knowingly or not, is metaphysical ... Metaphysics
> does indeed represent beings in their Being, and so it thinks the
> Being of beings. But it does not think the difference of both. Meta-
> physics does not ask about the truth of Being itself. Nor does it
> therefore ask in what way the essence of man belongs to the truth
> of Being.   ("Letter on Humanism", in BW: 226)

Since metaphysics fails to ask about Being itself, it ignores what Heidegger views as being most distinctive and crucial about us: the fact that we actually have some understanding of what it means to *be*. We have a very real and tangible sense of Being that is an essential, fundamental feature of our exist-ing. Heidegger wants philosophers to recognize this unique destiny we have been given – of standing in the truth and understanding of Being – and to investigate Being, in all its aspects, in terms of this relation we have to Being.

Why did Western metaphysics forget Being? Why has it ignored the fun-damental difference between Being and beings? According to Heidegger, the answer can be traced back to the Greek word for "being": *ousia*. This word was ambiguous. The primary meaning was "being" in the infinitive sense of "to be", but it was also sometimes used to refer to "being" in the nominal sense of "substance", or "a Supreme Being". "Substance (*ousia*) is the enduring substratum (*hupokeimenon*) of something that underlies changes in its qualities, location and so on. The substance of something remains *constantly present* despite whatever else changes through time" (Davis 2010b: 7). Unfortunately, although the earliest Presocratic philoso-phers chose the former meaning, Plato and those after him chose the latter interpretations of this word: "supreme being" or "substance". This natur-ally led to a move away from radical "thinking on Being" towards searching for the meaning of Being in some ultimate principle or "divine agent" that brings everything else into existence.

For Plato, this took the form of what he termed the "Idea". Aristotle asserted that, although not all beings are substances, they can *all* be under-stood with reference to substances. Descartes proclaimed that the source of Being was rooted in *God* and the *thinking subject*, and Heidegger's teacher, Husserl, explained Being in terms of *pure awareness*. All these philosophers regarded their explanations of Being as ontologically fundamental.

However, Heidegger considers that all searches for an *origin* of Being – whether in some type of substance, or in a transcendental super-Being (God) – are an evasion of the fundamental question of Being because they commit the crucial error of confusing the investigation of the *Being* of beings (ontology) with the Greatest Being (theology). Such approaches fail to acknowledge the basic "ontological difference" between Being and beings: "The Being of entities 'is' not itself an entity" (BT: 26). Thus, according to Heidegger it is a fundamental error to investigate the question of Being by attempting to define "entities as entities by tracing them back in their origin to some other entities, as if Being had the character of some possible entity" (*ibid*.). For then we are making the mistake of reducing the relation between Being and beings to one of causality, with Being representing the "highest being or entity": the supreme entity (e.g. God) or "substance" that creates all other entities. Heidegger regards such paths as irrelevant to an investigation of the question of Being and calls them "onto-theologies".

Why is there something rather than Nothing?

In Heidegger's principal work, *Being and Time*, which is the subject of Chapter 3, the enquiry into the question of Being relies on the supposition that all entities manifest themselves as Being in certain ways, and it asks how this can be possible at all. That is, how is it possible for anything to manifest itself as Being in a certain way? The investigation is then conducted via an examination of our way of Being, since Heidegger reasons that in order to ask the question of Being we must already have a vague understanding of it. However, Heidegger also formulates his question of Being in other ways.

Sometimes he seems to be asking about the meaning of the verb "to be", but then it becomes the *prima facie* different question: what does being mean to us? These are as different as "What is the meaning of the verb 'to live'?" and "What is the meaning of life?" But then Heidegger, or for that matter Wittgenstein, could argue that one cannot attain an in-depth understanding of the verbs "to be" or "to live" without understanding the role that they play in our lives and discourse, and that leads into the questions "What is the meaning of being for us?" and "What is the meaning of life?"

The reader should take note that, although the differing formulations of the question of Being that are discussed in this chapter certainly do *not* amount to exactly the same question, it clear that Heidegger would have acknowledged a deep connection between them: they are all in play in his discussion of Being as "facets" of the one ultimate question "What is the meaning of Being?", a question he asked throughout his life over and over again.

Further, an initial exploration of this infinite question from different angles is far more thought-provoking, exciting and inspiring than it would be were one to focus the entire investigation on one single formulation of the question of Being. Also, ultimately, since there is only one question, understanding derived from any particular formulation simultaneously sheds light on all formulations. From the start, however, the reader needs to understand that the insights gleaned from this entire investigation can only be very provisional and incomplete, because, as Heidegger points out, there exists no possibility of finding any definitive or ultimate answers to this matter, since human speech cannot intelligibly explain the "isness" or meaning of Being: "the essence of Being is never conclusively sayable" (GA 65: 460).

One approach to the question of Being, taken originally by Heidegger in his *Introduction to Metaphysics* (but not in his major work *Being and Time*), is to ask, "Why is there something rather than Nothing?" Even a decade later he is still occupied with this same formulation of the question of Being, as is evidenced in his lectures on *Hölderlin's Hymne "Andenken"* during the Winter semester of 1941–42: "the wonder that a world is world-ing around us at all, that there are beings rather than Nothing" (GA 52: 64; Polt 1999: 1).

This question seems to reach beyond the power of human reason; no scientific investigation or theology is capable of providing the answer. And although Heidegger states, in *An Introduction to Metaphysics*, "this why-question does not seek causes for beings" (IM [Fried & Polt]: 3), it does not require too great a stretch of the imagination if we hear in Heidegger's question of Being, echoed in his phrase "the wonder that a world is world-ing around us at all, that there are beings rather than Nothing", the related question "What explains the Big Bang?", a question that, as we shall now see, leads only to an endless process of analytical reduction resulting either in an infinite regression or an arbitrary cessation at a "something" that remains unexplained.

For the Big Bang theory, if correct, does not answer why there *was* a Big Bang in the first place, rather than Nothing. One may believe God caused the Big Bang, but then why is there a God? Whatever we propose as the cause of everything is itself something that has an existence that requires explanation. For any "cause" presupposes Being, by being there as well. The current scientific approach to understanding reality seems inextricably caught in this trap: it is in some ways a contemporary revival of ancient natural philosophy's search for a fundamental "substance" as the source of all Being, but more scientifically conducted. Only this time, "subatomic particles" are believed to be the elemental substance of creation. Heidegger reveals that this analytical reduction merely shifts the mystery of life – that there is actually *something* rather than Nothing – to subatomic dimensions of existence and, in doing so, simultaneously ignores the important fact that, no matter how much scientific research advances, the mystery of the "something" will be preserved perpetually, at *every* level of reduction.

To distinguish this "something" that science will always be left with at the end of its reductions from the existence of this indefinable "Something" that always manifests its astounding presence in all aspects of our experience, Heidegger calls this mysterious "Something" "before-worldly" (*Vorweltlich*) (GA 56/57: 102). This mystifying "before-worldly" Something is the inexplicable miracle that anything exists at all and our amazement at this can be triggered by any experience whatsoever. Heidegger's choice of the term "before-worldly" is especially apt for describing the mood he is trying to convey, because it points to the primal feeling of wonder and astonishment that would arise in a sentient human who had just been born into the world.

Heidegger describes this primal experience of astonishment as "the index of the supreme potential of life, a fundamental phenomenon occurring at moments of especially intensive experiencing" (GA 56/57: 115; Safranski 1998: 105). Its rare occurrences invariably coincide with the realization that this experience of wonder and amazement is, *at all times* and *in all situations*, latently present. It remains concealed, either because we have adopted a detached, theoretical perspective that distances us from direct experience, or because we remain locked or immersed in our robot-like routines of living, experiencing only our conditioned responses, and thus we lose contact with the freshness of Being and cannot see life in its totality.

Our amazement "that something is there at all" inspires endless questions that have no answers, because all explanations remain trapped in a spiral of infinite regression since every single "why" stimulates, and is replaced by, yet another "why". Many philosophers argue that this implies that the question is meaningless, and yet the question still seems relevant to us at some level of our awareness, for as the cosmologist Stephen Hawking suggests, once science has described how everything works, we will still want to ask: "What is it that breathes fire into the equations and makes a universe for them to describe … Why does the universe go to all the bother of existing?" (Hawking 1988: 174).

The significance of unanswerable questions

"Every philosophy, as a human thing, intrinsically fails; and God needs no philosophy" (MFL: 76). However, philosophy also "conceals a richness that again and again demands a renewed awakening" (MFL: 156). So what is it that makes the question of the meaning of Being so important to

Heidegger? If it cannot actually be answered, then how can it possibly have any meaning at all?

For Heidegger, thinking is thoroughly and essentially questioning, a questioning not to be stilled or "solved" by any answer, a questioning that cannot calculate in advance the destination, nor even the direction in which it will be led. Thus it is precisely the non-answerable nature of this question that Heidegger finds so intriguing and meaningful. For he distinguishes between two sorts of questions. The first type (ontic questions), such as "How far away is the moon from the earth?", has terminal answers. Heidegger regards these as trivial, since the answer settles the question and renders it inert; there is nothing further to be gained from asking it again. The second type (ontological questions), which he views as "worthy of questioning", are unanswerable and therefore inexhaustible. Heidegger regarded the action of focusing on worthy questions as fundamental to deepening one's understanding of Being.

For him, the most worthy of such questions is the question of Being. Heidegger believed strongly that only when humans are able to feel in harmony with the paradoxical nature of this question will they find their way home. For this question is not meant to provide an answer as such, for "If the answer could be given it would consist in a transformation of thinking, not in a propositional statement about a matter at stake" ("The End of Philosophy and the Task of Thinking", in BW: 431).

Especially in his later thought, he often reiterated that one should avoid all attempts to subject Being to logical analysis and formal definition, for when we seek to articulate Being it is always as though we are reaching into the void. Instead he emphasized that the only legitimate tactic for investigating Being was questioning. The mind, fully absorbed in the activity of intense authentic questioning, gradually enters into a state of deep connection or oneness with that which is being questioned. Just as a guitar string will sympathetically resonate with a string of the same pitch that is vibrating on a guitar close by, perhaps the process of Heidegger's questioning allows the Being of the questioner to resonate sympathetically with the awesome and amazing phenomenon of Universal Being. In his final lecture series at Freiburg University (1955–56), he asserted that the mysterious revelation of Being is not to be explained rationally, but to be received with gratitude (PR).

So it would seem reasonable to conclude that Heidegger's "Why is there something rather than Nothing?" is not actually a question that is asking for an answer but, rather, an expression of sheer astonishment and wonder over the fact of existence. In asking this question, Heidegger wants to unsettle our normal understanding of life so that he can lead us into the unfamiliar and unknown territory that lies *within* the "familiar", thus surprising and inspiring us with the mystery that is hidden within the realm of ordinary everyday existence. For Heidegger claims that, in the mood of astonishment, the questioner is most receptive to hearing the "voice of Being": to becoming closely attuned to and aware of the nature of Being. As the poet Samuel Taylor Coleridge puts it, "in Wonder all Philosophy began" (1825: Aphorism IV).

We have become so accustomed to life that in our normal state of awareness we take everything for granted. But there are occasions when we may suddenly become aware of the miracle of existence. At these times questions such as "Why is there something, rather than Nothing?" may be as close as we can come to expressing the thoughts and feelings that accompany our profound realization. When Heidegger poses this question, he is revealing and expressing his awareness of the marvellous mystery of Being and he encourages us to ask the same question, so that we may experience this realization for ourselves.

Heidegger's great passion was asking questions, not providing answers, and the purpose of his enquiry was to re-instil the mystery of life that has been receding into oblivion through the passage of time. Even if one disagrees with many of the claims found in Heidegger's writings, his work is still worth reading, because the primary task of a philosopher is to alert us to what is worthy of questioning, and there is no doubt that this has been accomplished with regard to his emphasis on the question of the meaning of Being.

Heidegger's fundamental ontology

Heidegger's ontology in *Being and Time* was a revolution, because it established an entirely new way of thinking, radically different from all previous systems of ontological thinking. As mentioned earlier, the pre-Heideggerian approaches to ontology attempt to question Being "ontically". They study what kind of things exist and how to characterize them and thus ask questions such as: does God exist? Does freedom exist? Are body and mind separate or unified? How can we prove the existence of the outside world?

Although such questions may be highly significant, they fail to ask *directly* about Being itself: what "Being" actually *is*. Heidegger calls his approach a "fundamental ontology" because it focuses its investigation primarily and directly on this question of Being, by attempting to answer the most fundamental of all questions: what is the meaning of Being?

Another crucial difference in Heidegger's thinking is that, unlike earlier philosophers, he makes no attempt to isolate human beings from the world in which they live. Traditionally philosophers have distinguished the "knower" from the world it knows: the world is "out there" and the thinker's task is to deal with what is in the mind in relation to what is outside it. We are regarded as independently existing *thinking entities*, completely separate from the world; we are the subjects, and the world is our object. For example, according to Descartes, rather than being a fundamental part of the world in which we live, we are beings with mental states and experiences that can exist independently from the actual, concrete relations we have with the surrounding world.

Heidegger rejects this approach, pointing out that I cannot look at the world "objectively" because the world is not, and cannot possibly be, "outside" me, since I am – and always have been since birth – *in* the world existing as a *part of it*. I am inextricably linked to all other entities in a world-wide web of significance, and thus in philosophy it is not possible for me to exercise pure reason in isolation from concrete circumstance. Moreover, thought, like all human activities, is "historical" and thus it is also founded on my own particular heritage: "every metaphysical question can be asked only in such a way that the questioner as such is present together with the question, that is, is placed in the question" ("What is Metaphysics?", in BW: 93).

One could argue that Being is not a thing, or entity. If it is not an entity, it does not exist; and if it does not exist, it cannot be known; if it cannot be known, any enquiry about its meaning is at best poetic and at worst meaningless. Heidegger disagrees with this line of thinking because he is not striving to *know* Being, but to discover the *meaning* of Being as it expresses itself through mankind's *way* of Being. He further justifies the relevance of questioning the meaning of Being by pointing out the fact that most humans can, and actually do, wonder about the source and significance of the universe and their own life. The occasional feeling of the utter meaninglessness of life, which almost everyone has experienced, is itself proof that the meaning of Being is under question. So Heidegger's enquiry into the meaning of Being is already relevant and active in us; we intuitively recognize it as a genuine question, even though we might regard it as unanswerable. So Heidegger's question is neither pointless nor philosophically irrelevant.

Heidegger's vocabulary

One of the main objectives in Heidegger's philosophical style is to break the pattern of thinking that causes us to take Being for granted, and to make us question the meaning of Being: what it *means* to be. Like Husserl,

Heidegger felt the need to construct an approach distinct from any philosophical method used in the past: a new way of thinking about Being that attempted to describe "the things themselves" via "direct experience" – a tactic that does not rely on theories or preconceptions. However, in contrast to Husserl he felt that this called for a thorough rethinking of philosophical language.

For Heidegger, thinking is the *seeing* of what comes into view, and thus, potentially, it is in a profound sense a form of *experiencing*; as such, the traditional metaphysical distinction between thinking (conceived as reasoning) and experience is no longer applicable. Thus Heidegger speaks of the experience of thinking, thereby appropriating within thinking the "immediacy" that is present in mystical experience. To undergo an experience with something – be it a thing, a person or a god – means that this something befalls us, strikes us, comes over us, overwhelms and transforms us (OWL: 57). So what one undergoes on the path of Heidegger's approach to thinking is not mere "intellectual insight" but an experience, and, being an experience, it transforms us.

However, for this new approach to thinking Heidegger was convinced that a specialized linguistic style and vocabulary were essential. He considered language in general worn out from overuse, with its words emptied of meaning and incapable of addressing existence adequately. His intention, therefore, was to develop a vocabulary and style of expression that would attune the language of his philosophy to the nature of Being.

"Being" and "being"

To grasp Heidegger's thought, it is essential to begin with a clear understanding of two terms used throughout his writing: "being" (or beings), which is always written with a lower-case "b", and "Being", which is always capitalized. The distinction between these two terms forms the foundation of Heidegger's entire philosophy. This tradition of capitalizing the word "Being" became common in early translations of Heidegger's work, to make it easier for the English reader to differentiate between the two terms. To make this book more user-friendly, I have continued this practice, although the trend now is *not* to capitalize Being but instead to leave it to the context to make this differentiation clear.

A being (or "entity") refers to anything that has an existence of some sort: humans, animals, chairs, electric razors, stones, planets, atoms, molecules, chemical processes. It is any event or thing in existence. In contrast to this, Heidegger uses the word "Being" to refer to that which *determines* beings *as* beings: that on the basis of which all entities are already understood; the "primordial" condition that allows everything in the universe to come into existence. It is the shared factor of Being that inhabits all entities, which makes our own existence inseparable from everything else. In this sense, all "beings" truly are the same.

The original German term for Being is *das Sein*. This noun is derived from the infinitive of the verb *sein*, "to be". The literal translation therefore of the noun *das Sein* is "the to be". This should serve to remind the reader that whenever the term Being with a capital B is used it also includes the sense "to be". So a phrase such as "the question of the meaning of Being" also means "to question what it means *to be*". When reading Heidegger, "Being" should never be thought of as an abstract noun or entity, or regarded as referring to God, the universe or anything in it.

In spite of the difference in meaning of the two concepts "Being" and "being", each needs the other in order to make sense. Just as the notion of "night" is nonsense without the existence of "day", and vice versa, so *there can be no beings without Being and no Being without beings*.

To understand this relation better, one could compare Being with light and beings with vision; light is the necessary precondition for seeing things – without light, human vision would be impossible. Similarly, Being is the necessary precondition for beings to exist: without Being – without the basic fact of existence in the first place – no human (or any other entity) could exist, for Being is "that which determines entities as entities, that on the basis of which entities are already understood ... The Being of entities 'is' not itself an entity" (BT: 26). Also, light itself cannot be seen: only the objects that are visible as a result of the light. Similarly, Being cannot actually be seen: only the beings that exist as a consequence of Being. Heidegger then uses the adjective "ontological" to describe any information, statements, remarks or observations pertaining to Being. However, the major difficulty that is faced in ontology (the philosophy of Being) is that, since Being is not an entity or "thing", it does not have any measurable properties or characteristics. You cannot see, hear or taste it, so the process of thinking about it and understanding it is very different from the straightforward observation, measurement and classification that are used to comprehend beings. Heidegger calls this dissimilarity between Being and beings an "ontological difference" (BPP: 17, 319). Heidegger also sometimes distinguishes "Being" (*Sein*) from "What-being" (*Was-sein*), "That-being" (*Dass-sein*) and "How-being" (*Wie-sein*).

"What-being" says *what* something is, its constitution – it describes the essential features of an entity. Whenever "What-being" is used to refer to the "Being" of a particular entity it means its *essence* or *fundamental nature*. Enquiries into "What-being" are interested in what determines an entity as the particular type of entity that it is, what forms the basis of our everyday relations to it and our formal *ontic* investigations of the domain it inhabits, and what differentiates it from other *different* types of entities. However, "What-being" is *never* used in reference to the Being of Dasein *nor* to "Being" in general (Inwood, pers. comm.).

Note that Heidegger chooses to use the German word *Dasein* to refer to us and our way of Being, in place of the standard German terminology for "human beings". He does this for a variety of reasons, which are explained in detail at the beginning of Chapter 3.

"That-being" says *that* something is. When "That-being" is used in reference to the "Being" of a particular entity it means its *existence*, and thus ontological enquiries into "That-being" are occupied with discovering *that* which *grounds* an entity of a specific type as an *existent* being. However, sometimes Heidegger also uses "That-being" in reference to a being's *mode of Being* – thus equating it with "How-being". "That-being" is never used to refer to "Being" in general, nor to the Being or "existence" of Dasein. "That-being" is shared by everything that exists (Inwood, pers. comm.).

"How-being" refers to the type, manner or *mode of Being* of an entity. When we *ask about* the "How-being" of an entity we are interested in its *way of Being* or mode of being used (e.g. as a tool) rather than in its *properties*. Heidegger does not always distinguish between "How-being" and "That-being", regarding *both* as a being's *mode of Being*, in contrast to its "What-Being" or *constitution*, and this is because he tends to regard *possibility*, actuality and necessity as modes of Being (Ni: 461; Nii: 195–6). Thus if an entity is said to be "possible", rather than "actual", we are told about its That-being and its How-being simultaneously (Inwood, pers. comm.).

Heidegger also makes the seemingly paradoxical statement that "Dasein is ontically 'closest' to itself and ontologically farthest" (BT: 37). He is indicating here that, although Dasein is, in terms of physical distance and familiarity with itself, closer to itself than it is to any other entity, Dasein's capacity to understand its *own* Being is further from Dasein's reach than its capacity to comprehend the Being of other entities. This is because that which is closest, most familiar and ordinary is also that which is hardest to comprehend. Nietzsche encapsulates this effectively: "What is familiar is what we are used to; and what we are used to is most difficult to 'know'" (Nietzsche 1974: 301). Also, although Dasein's Being is *nearest* to Dasein, in the sense that it is the very basis of his life on this planet, simultaneously it is *furthest* from him, because it is not a being (or entity) to which he can relate directly: "Being is farther than all beings and is yet nearer to man than every being, be it a rock, a beast, a work of art, a machine, be it an angel or God. Being is the nearest. Yet the near remains the farthest from man" ("Letter on Humanism", in BW: 234).

Ourselves as the initial subject matter of the enquiry

Since "Being" is invisible – hidden in the beings or things that it brings into existence – it cannot reveal itself outside of the beings it inhabits. So Heidegger approaches the question of Being by investigating the Being of beings. He believes that, when any animate or inanimate entity is penetrated deeply by ontological thought, it has the potential to become what he calls a "clearing" through which Being reveals itself. To further illustrate the distinction between ontic and ontological investigation, we can look at how each would approach the examination of a piece of rock. An "ontic" science, such as geology, will study the material composition and history of the rock, whereas ontology will attempt to "think the Being of the rock"; it will try to understand that which enables us to encounter the rock as a rock and the way in which this manifests itself in the rock. In other words, ontology tries to experience and understand Being by immersing itself in the full "thereness" or "Beingness" of an entity. When this ontological thought achieves the required penetrative intensity, the being or entity then becomes a "clearing" or open space in which the true nature of Being will spontaneously reveal itself. Thus Heidegger asserts, "the Being of the entity is found only in the encounter" (HCT: 217) and *not* in some concealed dimension beyond our direct experience.

Although Being characterizes absolutely every entity, Heidegger concluded that we should begin by first investigating our own way of Being: the way in which Being expresses itself through *us*. Heidegger chooses us as the logical starting-point for his enquiry because he observed that we have a uniquely privileged relation to Being (BT: 33–5). Of all entities in existence, organic and inorganic, only humans can question and seek to understand Being. We alone ask "What is Being?", so our Being is very much an issue for us.

Also, the very fact that we raise the question in the first place clearly implies that we uniquely have some type of prior "understanding of Being" (BT: 33), however clouded it may be. For in order to ask *any* question, one needs some sort of understanding of the subject matter of the enquiry as well as a rough idea of where the answer might be found, for "every seeking gets guided beforehand by what is sought" (BT: 24). Heidegger describes our prior comprehension of Being as a "vague, average understanding of Being" (BT: 25). In other words, we understand Being, but not in a conceptually articulate manner. This "vague" understanding is similar to having a "sense of how something is" or "a feel for how to do something", but you cannot explain in words to someone else the exact nature of your understanding. Thus this type of understanding is more an ability to do something rather than an intellectual or cognitive comprehension. This *pre-conceptual* "sense" of Being is reflected in all our interactions with the surrounding world: we constantly notice things that do exist and things that do not and we have a general sense of the function or purpose of things that allows us immediately to notice when something is misused. Even human beings who have never questioned the meaning of existence are constantly using a tacit, rudimentary understanding of Being in all their activities, because living in the world requires us to interact with all sorts of entities in the environment, and this requires some understanding of our own Being as well as the Being of the entities that constitute our particular world (BT: 33–4). So, in this sense, we also function as a unifying link between the entities existing in the world.

Consequently, by choosing us as the starting-point for his investigation of Being, Heidegger is not excluding other beings, for any investigation of our Being will automatically and necessarily include an investigation of the world of entities we inhabit. Furthermore, unlike other entities that are encapsulated exclusively in a present moment and position, we are deeply rooted in a past heritage while simultaneously occupying the present and looking towards future possibilities. We define who we are in terms of all this. In contrast, other forms of life – animals and plants, for instance – are what they are. They are not required to determine their own existence or sense of identity.

Heidegger concludes from this line of reasoning that human beings are therefore "ontological" and that the vague understanding of Being we already possess will enable us to deepen our understanding of our own Being (as well as the Being of other entities) and that this, in turn, will allow us greater insight into the meaning of Being in general.

> Dasein is an entity which does not just occur amongst other entities. Rather it is ontically distinguished by the fact that, in its very being, that being is an *issue* for it. ... And this means further that there is some way in which Dasein understands itself in its being, and that to some degree it does so explicitly ... *Understanding of being is itself a definitive characteristic of Dasein's being.* Dasein is ontically distinctive in that it *is* ontological. (BT: 32)

Being and Time

In Heidegger's great work *Being and Time*, published in 1927, his lengthy attempts to satisfactorily answer the question of Being culminated in an admission of failure and the book was left unfinished. Heidegger concluded that Being is a continually evolving phenomenon that is intrinsically mysterious and self-concealing. He realized that the inherent limitations of human speech prevent us from intelligibly explaining the "isness" or meaning of Being, "the essence of Being is never conclusively sayable" (GA 65: 460), and thus we can only speak of it tautologically: "a being has its Being in Being, and Being persists as the Being of a being" (WCT: 221). His dissatisfaction with the limitations of language is visible in one of his essays on Being, "Zur Seinsfrage", in which he frequently crosses out the written word "*Sein*" (Being). Although obliged to use words when writing or speaking about Being, Heidegger seems to be emphasizing here that one must not confuse these verbal *representations* of Being with the actual *state* of Being. The word "Being" is not that to which it refers, as what it refers to is in a "wordless" dimension that has nothing whatsoever to do with any object or entity, concept or substance known to man, nor the whole subject–object relation, for it belongs to a dimension that precedes all knowledge. (The four points of the crossing out also point "to the four regions of the fourfold and their gathering at the place of the intersection" [QB: 83]. See Chapter 8 for explanation of Heidegger's somewhat esoteric conception of the "fourfold".)

Heidegger did acknowledge that such a thing as truth exists, and he viewed some interpretations of it, including his own, as better than others. He stated his opinion, however, that there is no final explanation. Perceptions of truth are only relevant to the time and context in which they arise, and he was very much against the idea that there existed ultimate, universal truths that are independent of time and place. In reference to this, Heidegger claimed "I have no philosophy at all" (HCT: 301–2), because for him philosophy was not something one has – like a theory or set of principles – but the untiring, passionate commitment to a question. He strongly believed that the primary objective of his work was not to provide answers to the question of Being, but to stimulate in us a keen awareness of the question. This potentially can make us receptive to experiencing the full force of its incredible mystery. Heidegger is not noted for offering convincing, reliable, final answers, but for his ceaseless questioning.

> Celebration … is self-restraint, is attentiveness, is questioning, is meditating, is awaiting, is the step over into the more wakeful glimpse of the wonder – the wonder that a world is worlding around us at all, that there are beings rather than Nothing, that things are and we ourselves are in their midst, that we ourselves are and yet barely know who we are, and barely know that we do not know all this.   (GA 52: 64; Polt 1999: 1)

The Nothing

In 1929, Heidegger started on a new approach in his search for the meaning of Being. On the occasion of his inauguration as professor at Freiburg, Heidegger delivered one of his most famous lectures, "What is Metaphysics?" In this lecture, he asks a question that is fundamental to his investigation of Being: "What is the Nothing?" ("What is Metaphysics?", in BW: 96). At the very end, in the very last line of this lecture, Heidegger asks what he terms "the basic question of metaphysics which the Nothing itself compels: Why are there beings at all, and why not rather Nothing?" (*ibid.*: 110). He later explains that in asking this question he means "Why is it that everywhere only beings have priority, that the Not of beings, 'this Nothing', i.e. Being in regard to its essence, is not rather considered?" (QB: 98).

From the point of view of logic, "What is the Nothing?" makes sense only if it is considered to be a question about how the grammatical process of negation works. But, according to Heidegger, "the Nothing" (or Nothingness) that he is talking about does not refer to the negation *not anything*; it is not the negation of Being – it is not merely a "nugatory" or "empty" nothing, the nothingness of nihilism; it is rather the "Nothing of Being (*Seyn*)". (Note the unusual spelling of *Seyn*, which Heidegger at times employed to differentiate it from *Sein*. Also, note that "The Nothing" is capitalized in German, since all nouns are capitalized, and I have kept the translation capitalized to emphasize the fact, as mentioned above, that what Heidegger is speaking about is not the negation *not anything*. "The Nothing … reveals itself as belonging to the Being of beings" ["What is Metaphysics?", in BW: 108].)

Parmenides and Spinoza asserted that, although distinctions appear completely positive, they also inherently involve negation, because whenever we identify something *as* a particular thing we are simultaneously asserting that it is *not* any other thing. Parmenides asserts that this is a *reductio ad absurdum* of the very possibility of all definitions since their requirement of negation illogically presupposes that Nothingness is real. Heidegger uses this argument in reverse by suggesting that, since distinctions are forms of negation that are *grounded* on the Nothing, then the Nothing obviously must "exist" in some sense.

The root meaning of the word "Nothingness" supports this view: *No-thing-ness* does indeed suggest a "presentness" or "thereness" (which is not defined or limited by any particular existence or object). Heidegger lends further support to his assertion, using science as an example. He suggests that the goal of science is to investigate "solely beings, and beyond that – Nothing" (*ibid.*: 95). But, according to Heidegger, in the act of eliminating the "Nothing" from its investigations, science is simultaneously acknowledging it and using it: "Science wants to know nothing of the Nothing. But even so it is certain that when science tries to express its proper essence it calls upon the Nothing for help. It has recourse to what it rejects" (*ibid.*: 96). In other words, just as asking the question of Being requires a pre-ontological understanding of Being, similarly, in wishing "to know nothing of the Nothing", science is revealing at the same time that it possesses *some* understanding of the Nothing that it rejects, since we can use a word to refer to something only if we have some understanding of "the something" to which we are referring.

Heidegger now offers three obstacles that question the validity of asking his question "What is the Nothing?" (*ibid.*). The first suggests that the wording of the question not only clearly implies that the "Nothing" is a being (when we know for certain that it is not) but it also obliges impossible answers – that the Nothing is "this" or "that" – and thus both the question and answers are "inherently absurd" (*ibid.*: 97). The second objection states that, according to the "ground rule of all thinking", consciousness is always and necessarily consciousness *of* something and thus to think of the Nothing would seem to be impossible since it is incompatible with the essential nature of thinking, which is always essentially *about* some*thing*. The final obstacle is concerned with the fact that the definition of the Nothing is "the negation of the totality of beings" (*ibid.*), but in order to negate the "totality" of beings we first need to grasp beings *as a whole*, which is an undertaking that is far beyond the capacity of our limited, finite intellects.

Heidegger now points out that these obstacles are only valid "assuming that in this question 'logic' is of supreme importance, that the intellect is the means, and thought the way, to concieve the Nothing" (*ibid.*). In other words, although these three objections show that reason cannot grasp the Nothing, this only invalidates Heidegger's enquiry if we assume, as the vast majority of philosophers have done throughout the history of philosophy, that reason is our *sole* means of investigating existence – that our access to reality is exclusively cognitive – for since it is clear that we cannot think our way to an understanding of the Nothing, if rational analysis is the only option available for philosophical enquiry, then Heidegger's endeavour becomes futile.

However, Heidegger offers a strong case for doubting this conclusion since, as mentioned previously, the fact that one can actually talk about the Nothing or even reject it demonstrates that we already must have some understanding of it: "If the Nothing itself is to be questioned as we have been questioning it, then it must be given beforehand. We must be able to encounter it" (*ibid.*: 98). It should be noted that Heidegger by no means rejects logic or rationality: "'logic' and the 'logical' are simply not *the* ways to define thinking without further ado, as if nothing else were possible" (IM: 127). But he emphasizes that there are other legitimate modes of experiencing and understanding beings and Being that have been fundamentally ignored or discredited throughout the history of philosophy, as subjective distortions that merely obscure our understanding of reality. Traditionally, philosophers have regarded emotion and reason as separate and distinct faculties, and have endeavoured to prevent the former from contaminating the latter since, throughout the centuries, philosophy has relied exclusively on reason. Heidegger, however, regards our understanding of the world as arising from a holistic fusion of both these aspects of our mode of Being.

Thus, although Nothingness cannot be thought or grasped by human reason, Heidegger nevertheless asserts that, far from being "nothing at all", it is a dynamic, creative force that constitutes the "meaning of Being". For just as no sound can exist without silence, no-"thing" can exist without Nothing: without the empty space that enables it to be. Perhaps the closest one can come to defining the Nothing is to say that "Nothing" or "space" is the "appearance" of the Unmanifested as an externalized phenomenon in a sense-perceived world. However, the paradoxical nature of this statement, and the fact that "Nothing" has no physical existence, means that it cannot ever become an object of knowledge. "To exist" means literally "to stand out". "Nothing" – space – cannot be understood because it does not stand out. However, in spite of the fact that in itself it has no "existence", it is the factor that allows everything else "to be". The same applies to "silence", which does not "exist" but which allows sound "to be".

Perhaps, in this sense, one could view silence as more important than sound, and space, or "Nothing", as more important than the objects or forms that exist in it. For example, if one considers a room with objects in it and then asks the question "What is the essence of this room?", the answer is not the furniture and other objects that are *in* the room but are *not* the room; nor can one say that it is the walls, ceiling, floor and so on, as these factors merely define the boundaries of the room. Rather, it is the empty space or "Nothingness" of the room that is the essence, for without this there would be no room. Thus, in this sense, what is *not* there – "Nothing" – is more important than what *is* there.

Heidegger claims that the "Nothing" is constantly in the background of our existence, but in our "everydayness" we tend to lose ourselves in beings and fail to attend to that which lets them be: to the empty horizon of the world, the background of Nothing against which every being presents itself as *not* nothing, that is, as something. For every physical entity has emerged out of Nothing, is surrounded by Nothing and eventually will return to Nothing. Moreover, physicists have discovered that the apparent solidity of matter is merely an illusion, since inside every physical body there is far more "Nothing" than "something". So-called "solid matter" – even our physical body – is nearly 100 per cent empty space, owing to the vast distances between the atoms in comparison to their size. Furthermore, even the insides of atoms consist mostly of empty space or "Nothing". Thus matter is not really solid at all. This fact was expressed more than 2500 years ago by Buddhists, who regarded form as emptiness and emptiness as form (Tenzin Gyatso 2005: 125–7). Thus the very essence of all things is emptiness or "Nothingness" and yet everybody pays attention to "things" while ignoring their essence: the space or Nothingness *in* them and *surrounding* them.

However, certain conditions can change this: the mood of deep anxiety (*Angst*) and despair, which afflicts numerous people, at times for no apparent reason, is often caused by a sudden perception of the Nothing (that may or may not have occurred at a conscious level of awareness): "Anxiety reveals the Nothing" ("What is Metaphysics?", in BW: 101). This creates a sense of emptiness and insignificance. All beings appear to be threatened by the Nothing, which makes everything seem non-sense.

Heidegger believes that during moments of deep anxiety we can also sometimes become acutely aware of the Nothing in such a way that it opens our understanding to the true nature of Being, for "with the fundamental mood of anxiety we have arrived at that occurrence in human existence in which the Nothing is revealed and from which it must be interrogated" (*ibid.*).

Heidegger also asserts that Being is finite, and is surrounded by the Nothing, and he considered Being and the Nothing to be mutually dependent and indivisible, like two sides of a coin. Thus "Nothing" and "Being" are equiprimordial, and therefore, "to think *that* Nothing that is equiprimordially the same as Being" (QB: 101). This makes good sense if one considers the following: if there were nothing but silence, it would not exist for you because you would not know what it was. Silence only comes into being when sound appears. Similarly, if there were only Nothing – or space – without any objects in space, it would not exist for you. For instance, if you existed as pure consciousness in an infinite space or Nothingness that contained no stars nor any other entities, this Nothingness or space would cease to be infinitely vast since it would not be there at all because at least two points of reference are needed for space and distance to come into being; without this there can be no speed nor any movement in any direction. The Nothing exists only in the presence of Being or beings: the Unmanifested depends on the manifested. In other words, Nothing (space) and Being arise simultaneously. Nothing could *be* without space, and yet space is Nothing. Thus before the Big Bang there was not a vast empty space or Nothingness waiting to be filled. Since there were no things, there could not be space/Nothing. There was only the One: the Unmanifested. The Big Bang was the event in which Nothing and Being/beings appeared simultaneously; Nothing/space enabled Being/beings.

The close connection between Being and Nothing is also evidenced by the fact that they share an important intrinsic attribute: they are not "beings". "The Nothing is neither an object nor any being at all" ("What is Metaphysics?", in BW: 104). Being (like Nothing) is not a thing – if it were, it would instead be a "being" (rather than Being) – so in this sense one can conclude that Being is *no-thing*. Humans participate in both Being, by existing, and the Nothing, by ceasing to exist. Only the two possibilities of Being and Nothing are constant. Heidegger felt that the world we live in, and the entities it contains, can only be understood in the light of this "existence" and "non-existence" of Being and Nothing, for "Nothing 'belongs' for us to 'Being'" (IM: 85). And it is exactly because Being and Nothing essentially belong together that any attempt to clarify the *meaning of Being* must also concern itself with the *meaning of Nothing*.

Heidegger regards the Nothing as the creative womb from which Being emerges: "From the Nothing all beings as beings come to be" ("What is Metaphysics?", in BW: 108). Just as great works of art at times emerge from artists who have been through great suffering, the Nothing, which Dasein perceives in anxiety, has the potential to expand awareness into an illuminated perception of existence: "Only in the Nothing of Dasein do beings as a whole, in accord with their most proper possibility – that is, in a finite way – come to themselves" (*ibid.*). Acknowledging the Nothing can stimulate intense awareness of the dramatic contrast between beings and the Nothing.

The background threat, anxiety or sense of the insignificance of everything cleanses our vision and allows us to see that there *is* a great difference between something (beings) and Nothing: "In the clear night of the Nothing of anxiety the original openness of beings as such arises: that they are beings – and not Nothing ... Without the original revelation of the Nothing, there is no selfhood and no freedom" (*ibid.*: 103). Awareness of this Nothingness restores in Dasein the feeling of primal astonishment in the face of Being, and simultaneously generates an awareness of the fact that at the heart of Being is generative Nothingness: "This (true) Nothing ... is nothing nugatory. It belongs to presencing (Being). Being and Nothing are not given beside one another. Each uses itself on behalf of the other in a relationship whose essential richness we have hardly begun to ponder" (QB: 97).

So Heidegger's understanding of "Nothing" bears no relation to "nihilism", which is frequently how it has been understood since Nietzsche. On the contrary, it aims to help overcome nihilism, for Heidegger states as early as 1935 what nihilism essentially means for him: "to concern oneself only with beings in forgetfulness of Being" (IM: 203). He describes the "getting over" of nihilism as requiring a pressing of "the *inquiry* into Being expressly to the border of Nothing and to incorporate it (Nothing) into the question of Being" (*ibid.*).

He further clarified this matter in a letter to a Japanese colleague, Kojima, which dealt with the misunderstandings to which his major idea of "Nothing" has been subject: "The Nothing that is talked about there refers to that which in relation to what-is is never any kind of being, and 'is' thus Nothing, but which nevertheless determines what-is as such and is thus called Being" ("Briefwechsel mit einem japanischen Kollegen" [1963]).

Heidegger's response to nihilism

The world-historical context in which Heidegger raises the question of Being is one that he has described as "the darkening of the world, the flight of the gods, the devastation of the earth, the transformation of men into a mass, the hatred and suspicion of everything creative" (IM: 31). This state of the world to which he refers is rooted in the emergence of a condition called "nihilism". Nihilism is a word generally used in reference to the rejection of all moral and religious values as well as all forms of tradition and authority. It is one of the key concepts in Nietzsche's philosophy, and his ideas on the subject influenced Heidegger's own understanding of the topic. A fundamental motive behind Heidegger's questioning of Being is his wish to overcome this condition of nihilism, which he believed to be the most destructive force on this planet.

Nietzsche believed that modern man is becoming increasingly aware of the fact that the ethical and intellectual foundations of Western civilization are fundamentally flawed and about to collapse. As a consequence, people are getting more and more disillusioned with religion, metaphysical thinking and traditional cultural values. This alarmed him, for he saw on the horizon an impending crisis threatening the future of humanity. He warned that eventually all traditional religious and philosophical interpretations of reality would completely collapse and be abandoned. He saw this crisis in terms of "the death of God" and the "advent of nihilism" that would follow: a nihilism that would shake Western civilization to its core.

Nietzsche's term "the death of God" covers all forms of the "God hypothesis", with all metaphysical or scientific substitutes for it and all absolute or universal truths. For Nietzsche, all these are merely "lies and fictions". Among his chief objections to religion, in particular Judaeo-Christianity, was that it devalues *this* life and *this* world in favour of a purported life to come. Nietzsche considers this a terrible "crime against life": "If one shifts the centre of gravity out of life into the Beyond – into Nothingness – life is deprived of its centre of gravity. The great lie of personal immortality destroys all rationality, all instinctive naturalness – all that is salutary" (Niv: 223–4)

When people come to realize that "God is dead" – that the Christian, or Jewish, or any other personal God has lost power over humanity and the universe – this "collapse of cosmological values" will produce a "devaluation of the highest values". There will then seem to be no purpose or significance to the universe, no sense of any unity that gives life meaning: no eternal truths or values, no "truth". Nietzsche saw this as setting the stage for the advent of nihilism, for an epidemic of despair that could have catastrophic consequences for the future of humanity.

Heidegger saw the validity of Nietzsche's fears already clearly reflected in a modern world that no longer solicits the high level of shared social interests and commitment that it used to: God(s), thinkers, poets, heroes, even politicians and the clergy have lost their authority and are no longer respected. As a result, people tend to retreat into private experiences and so feel ever more lonely and isolated.

To counter this, Nietzsche strove to show that "God or bust" – that is, faith or despair – is a dangerous false dichotomy. He also emphasized the merely provisional character of all knowing: there exists no "absolute knowledge" that transcends all perspectives and thus ultimately no conception of truth or knowledge of ourselves and our world that is absolute and certain. Deeply concerned with the question of what kinds of value in life will remain or become available to us after the death of God, he embarked on a radical "revaluation of all values". When he wrote *Thus spoke Zarathustra* he proclaimed a vision of superabundant human life and possibility, which offered value and meaning to overcome nihilistic thinking and its corresponding pessimism. Nietzsche, unlike Heidegger, saw in the "death of God" potential liberation for humankind, for he predicted a new cultural era he called "positive nihilism", in which "free spirits", famously his *Übermensch* (superman, or superior human), would create their own values.

Nietzsche was attempting to overcome nihilism with new values, which – since heaven no longer exists – had to be derived from mortal beings. Nietzsche, argued Heidegger, simply created a new metaphysics, which understands all living things as ruled by a fundamental force or biological instinct that Nietzsche called "the will to power". This is power for its own sake with no external goal, but which itself becomes the "highest value", treating and sustaining all values. Nietzsche suggested that life is to be comprehended and justified solely in terms of this fundamental "characteristic" or "force". "For Nietzsche, will to power is the utimate *factum* to which we come" (Niv: 73).

With "will to power" the only fundamental value, and humans no longer led by any gods, transcendent ideals or values, the *Übermensch* (superman, superior human) embodies the highest expression of this power or life force. The *Übermensch* is to transcend ordinary humanity of the present as much as humans have transcended apes. The *Übermensch* would be capable of a self-overcoming, independence and creativity that would elevate him above the level of ordinary men. Nietzsche hoped that he would bring about an enriched, creative, cultural life that would eventually transform civilization into a "higher humanity". Thus he saw, as the highest value for mankind, the attainment of a way of life in which the will to power – raised to its highest level of intensity and qualitative expression – would creatively enhance and transform existence. The "enhancement of life" and creativity became the guiding ideas behind his revaluation of values. According to Heidegger, however, the goal of such power is the mere "aimlessness of man's unconditional mastery over the earth. The man of this mastery is the super-man" (Niv: 82).

Heidegger asserts that Nietzsche's approach *strengthens* nihilism, instead of overcoming it, for in Nietzsche's way of thinking, "man is made the unconditional centre and the unique measure of beings as a whole" (Niv: 83), and thus Nietzsche intensifies Descartes' man-centred metaphysics, and also strengthens the grip of modern technology (Niv: 129ff.). Further, the belief that we create value through willed acts of valuing feeds nihilism by ignoring the deep meaningfulness we find all around us.

Further, Heidegger claims that any belief that suggests that nihilism is the consequence of lost values and that the solution to it lies in reviving these lost values or choosing new ones is merely another sign of nihilism. For he suggests that our current loss of meaning is the inevitable outcome of our having had values in the first place: that treating our deepest concerns *as* values is the essence of nihilism.

Plato understood values as embodying and attracting us to what is good for us, independently of our personal interests and desires. With the Age of Enlightenment in the eighteenth century, the apparent triumph of rationalism, values came to be viewed as objective matters of personal choice that had no claim on us until we chose to adopt them. According to Heidegger, this belief that we can choose, from a variety of values, which ones we wish to incorporate in our life to give it significance results in the modern view first espoused by Nietzsche, especially in *Thus Spoke Zarathustra*, that *we* create our own values in life and it is this that gives our life its value or significance.

But Heidegger points out that once we become aware that we are creating our own values we realize that we can also "uncreate" them, and this realization eventually leads to the total undermining of their authority over us. So, instead of giving meaning to our lives, thinking of what matters to us in terms of values inevitably leads us to the mistaken belief of nihilism: that ultimately our existence has no intrinsic meaning whatsoever.

Heidegger concludes that if we believe that we need only create our own individual meaning, then we shall overlook the fact that it is our shared everyday social skills, cultural practices and concerns that provide the conditions required to make sense of the world and give it significance. Consequently, we shall never discover anything that elicits our total, sustained commitment. For, as Heidegger points out, "No one dies for mere values" (QCT: 142). However, according to Heidegger, our cultural practices embody a non-articulated, implicit or intuitive understanding of *Being* and what truly matters: of what it really means to be a human being.

This intuitive understanding can guide our lives and make the humans and beings around us intelligible without any need for concepts, beliefs, values or critical reflection. Indeed, to subject our cultural practices to any form of critical questioning and objective analysis undermines their beneficial influence and causes us to create instead our own objective or personal values. To deal with this problem of nihilism, we must realize first that viewing the problem of nihilism as arising from a loss or lack of values merely perpetuates the problem. Only then will we be in a position to discover a cure for this condition. According to Heidegger, Nietzsche cannot recognize this fact because he is unwittingly trapped in a nihilistic mode of thinking, and is thus incapable of understanding the essential nature of nihilism, which, according to Heidegger, is the neglect of Being by metaphysics that (paradoxically) is the consequence and cause of the "withdrawal" and "failure to appear" of Being itself. Therefore, according to Heidegger, the problem of nihilism can only be dealt with by paying attention to Being itself. Nietzsche, however, recognizes only "beings" and the "Being" of beings and exacerbates this error by reducing "Being" to a mere "value": a "power tool" in service of the "will to power" as it seeks its own continual expansion.

In addition, Heidegger asserts that, in view of the fact that man is essentially the "abode that Being prepares for itself" (Niv: 223–4), Being is not under man's control, and since (according to Heidegger) the roots of nihilism reach *into* the truth and "question" of Being, nihilism also cannot be overcome by man, as Nietzsche proposes, since it is an inextricable part of the destiny of Being and, as such, it is beyond man's control. However, although we cannot force the coming of Being, we are, according to Heidegger, able to prepare ourselves for its arrival.

We can prepare ourselves for the overcoming of nihilism and the arrival of Being by recognizing the true nature of Being itself while simultaneously acknowledging and experiencing the existence of nihilism, which is an inevitable occurrence in the destiny of Being. But "the most essential and difficult thing in this overcoming is the *knowledge* of nihilism" (GA 65: 140–41), for the existence and continuation and dangers of nihilism depend on the concealment of its true nature, which it skilfully hides behind various superficial guises.

If, as nihilism suggests, human existence is totally insignificant, there is also no point in questioning existence in order to find principles for understanding it. In showing that it *is* worthwhile to ask about the meaning of Being, Heidegger has taken an effective first step towards the overcoming of nihilism, for he is demonstrating not only that we exist, but that our life *is* meaningful.

CHAPTER THREE

The central ideas in *Being and Time*

Being and Time was Heidegger's first major publication. It was originally published in 1927 in Husserl's *Jahrbuch für phänomenologie und phänomenologische Forschung* and appeared simultaneously in a separate printing. A carefully constructed, tightly woven masterwork, it was originally intended as a preliminary text for a much larger project that was never completed. (*Being and Time* remained unfinished because Heidegger was in a hurry to get it published in order to obtain a full professorship, first at Marburg in 1927 and then Freiburg in 1928, and then in subsequent years his attention shifted during the change he called *die Kehre* [the turn].)

In *Being and Time*, Heidegger's investigation of the meaning of Being is carried out via an analysis of human existence. Heidegger does not separate the study of Being from the study of humanity because he believes that we cannot have one without the other, for, according to Heidegger, true thinking can take place only within the total relation of Being and man's nature. So *Being and Time* is simultaneously an analysis of our way of Being *and* an enquiry into the meaning of Being. Heidegger's approach to philosophical interpretation is based on his premise that when we philosophize we are attempting to reach a clearer understanding of something that is already vaguely familiar to us. So when he asks the question of Being he does so on the basis that we already understand Being *in general*, for it is this that allows us to raise questions about it. Thus his objective is to reach a more lucid understanding of Being. His method has a "spiral" structure, in that he begins with a preliminary, general understanding and analysis of existence, which leads to insights that result in a revision and deepening of this previous analysis, which in turn leads to further insights and so on (BT: 193–5). In this manner he continually reinterprets the facets of our existence on increasingly deeper levels that provide a more profound understanding of our own Being – the truth of who we are – thus getting closer to an understanding of the meaning of Being as a whole.

Dasein: ourselves as the starting-point

This journey begins with Heidegger's most prominent new term: "Dasein". In English books on his work, this word is usually left untranslated. Prior to Heidegger, philosophers such as Kant in the eighteenth century and Husserl much later began using this purely German word, which parallels the English word "existence", instead of the previously used Latin-derived *Existenz*. For these philosophers, the term could be used to refer to the existence of *any* entity, animate or inanimate. Heidegger's use of the word, however, carries quite different connotations. He uses the term Dasein to refer exclusively to us and our way of Being, in place of the standard German terminology for human beings. The word has no plural so it can refer to a single human being as well as all human beings.

Heidegger chose to use this innovative expression Dasein for several reasons. To begin with, he felt that the words we use no longer adequately express their original sense. They have become "worn out" from overuse, so we miss their deeper significance. In using Dasein, however, he awakens our awareness and inspires us to look at ourselves with fresh eyes. He hoped this would encourage us to think about who we are in a revolutionary manner, uninfluenced by the traditional opinions of religion, philosophy, psychology and anthropology. Heidegger specifically selected the term Dasein because he felt that it best encapsulated, emphasized and expressed the fact that we are unique beings, qualitatively very different from all other entities, because the essence of who we are is contained in our way of Being, and thus cannot be grasped via a description of our ontic characteristics because Dasein's Being has no "fixed" nature that exists independently of its way of Being.

> The essence of Dasein lies in its existence. Accordingly those characteristics which can be exhibited in this entity are not "properties" present-at-hand of some entity which "looks" so and so and is itself present-at-hand; they are in each case possible ways for it to be, and no more than that … So when we designate this entity with the term "Dasein", we are expressing not its "what" (as if it were a table, house, or tree) but its Being. (BT: 67)

This distinct and special way of Being is reflected in the linguistic structure of the term Dasein. To begin with, this noun is also the infinitive form of a verb (to exist), which suggests one of the distinguishing features Heidegger attributes to humanity; namely, that we are more like an activity or process than any sort of thing. However, the characteristic in our way of Being that most differentiates us from other beings is reflected in

Heidegger's emphasis on the root meaning of the word "Dasein", which is "there being", or "being there" from *da* (there) and *Sein* (being). His use of "there" in this context refers to the world and the unique way we can inhabit it, with a capacity for understanding Being (our own Being as well as the Being of other beings) not found in any other entities.

It is vital to remember when reading Heidegger that, in both his early and later writings, his primary interest is in *Being*. His preoccupation with Dasein is due to the fact that it is the *only* entity in existence with an understanding of Being, and, more importantly, Dasein and Being are interdependent. Dasein needs to understand Being in order to *be* Dasein, and Being is not revealed except in relation to Dasein (BT: 269–70).

Once again, Heidegger makes use of the linguistic structure of the word "Dasein" to emphasize his point. He claims that the "there" of "Being there" is in fact us, and that we are there on behalf of Being – "man occurs essentially in such a way that he is the 'there', that is, the clearing of Being" ("Letter on Humanism", in BW: 229) – that we are, in a sense, the guardians of Being, for if Dasein did not exist at all then there would be no self-consciousness on the part of beings and no such thing as Being, for according to Heidegger we are the "clearing" or "open space" that Being needs to be able to express itself. Without Dasein, the world as we know it would cease to exist; other entities would continue to exist, but there would be no one to relate to them *as* entities, so their *Being* would have no meaning at all and, in this sense, would therefore not exist. "Being 'is' only in the understanding of that entity to whose Being belongs such a thing as understanding of Being" (BT: 228). Later, Da-sein sometimes means not "being-there", but "there where Being dwells", when it arrives: "This Where as the There of the abode belongs to Being itself, 'is' Being itself and is thus called Da-sein" (Nii: 358; Niv: 218).

Thus Dasein is the site at which Being can manifest itself as the light of man's understanding; it is the human being's selfhood. However, it is perfectly possible to live one's entire life without assuming this selfhood, to remain absorbed in the undifferentiated mass of beings. Mankind's selfhood, Dasein, is thus at a point at which beings as a whole are illuminated – become visible to themselves – in the light of Being. Thus Dasein is the finite site or clearing in which beings are understood in their Being and the site at which Being can *be*; Being is thus founded upon Dasein. The Being of other beings and thus Being as such is disclosed because how Dasein is in the world always already transcends (steps beyond) its own particular being.

Here it seems that Heidegger agrees with Husserl and Kant that our experience of "reality" is fundamentally determined by what we contribute to it. However, whereas Kant and Husserl view the essence of man as "pure consciousness", Heidegger regards Dasein's essence as defined by its *various possible ways of Being*; we are concrete, existing human beings, not pure consciousness.

In later writings, Heidegger asserts that Being does *not* depend on our understanding of it; it existed in some way even prior to Dasein's arrival on earth. Instead, Being creates man as its abode.

Heidegger now regards Dasein's "forgetfulness of Being" as engendered by Being itself: by its "abandonment" (*Seinverlassenheit*) of beings (GA 65: 111). There exists here a paradox of circular thinking: Being would *not* be absent if Dasein did not forget it, but Being is either present or it can withdraw itself, creating varying degrees of absence (although not complete absence) and it is this absence that is responsible for Dasein's forgetfulness of Being (GA 65: 293). In *Being and Time*, humanity's forgetfulness of Being is regarded as primarily affecting philosophy and having little effect on everyday existence. But later, since metaphysics is seen to be the dominant underlying influence over human existence, Dasein's forgetfulness of Being is viewed as the ground of nihilism that underlies technology and the overall sickness of modern life.

In 1943 and 1949 (but not in *Being and Time*), Heidegger concludes that no beings whatsoever could exist if there were a complete absence of Being, a "blank nothing". But he clearly implies that beings can still exist in the absence of Being, where Being has merely "withdrawn" or "failed to reveal itself" (GA 65: 115). He also asserts (in 1943) that, even if no entities at all existed, Being would still exist in some way, but he adds (in 1949) that, under such circumstances, Being would not "essence": that Being would be in a state of (latent) "absence" (*Verlassenheit*) or "withdrawal".

However, in 1969 Heidegger once again asserts: "The fundamental thought of my thinking is precisely that Being, or the manifestation of Being, *needs* human beings and that, vice versa, human beings are only human beings if they are standing in the manifestation of Being" (Wisser 1990: 82).

The *a priori* structure of Dasein

Heidegger uses the word "existence" (*Existenz*) not in the traditional sense of referring to the fact that an entity "exists", but in a narrow, unusual sense to indicate Dasein's *unique* "essence", which is fundamentally different from the "essence" or "nature" of all other entities. So he applies the term *only* to Dasein: *"The essence of Dasein lies in its existence"* (BT: 67). By "existence" Heidegger means Dasein's "mode of Being" (and never the fact that Dasein *is* – "exists"). Further, Heidegger wants us to understand that

Dasein's *essence* is *rooted* in its mode of Being. For Dasein's self is not any sort of thing or entity, or unchanging centre of our Being that remains the same throughout our lives. Rather, it is a *way of existing* (BT: 152–3). Thus, faced with the task of investigating the Being of Dasein in a manner that does justice to its character as existence, Heidegger suggests that we must examine that which is "ontically closest" to us (BT: 69), which is everydayness: "the How in which Dasein 'lives from day to day', whether in all its conduct or only in certain conduct prescribed by being-with-one-another" (BT: 422). Since it is so close to us, it is invariably overlooked, for "Dasein is ontically 'closest' to itself and ontologically farthest" (BT: 37).

To understand the nature of everydayness in the correct manner, Heidegger emphasizes that we must realize that in everyday existence we are engaged actors, and thus it would be an error to think that we can view ourselves as if we were essentially detached observers of the world.

A fundamental claim in *Being in Time* is that Dasein has an "*a priori*" awareness of its own Being and of the Being of other entities in its world. *A priori* comes from the Latin for "what comes before, earlier"; the *a priori* is "the earlier" (GA 20: 99). So in our dealings with the world, "'we always conduct our activities in an understanding of Being" (BT: 25). In other words, we possess a pre-reflective, rudimentary understanding of our own nature and that of the entities surrounding us, which allows us to make sense of our world.

Heidegger explains this understanding in terms of various *a priori* "existentials" (*Existenzialen*), which are Dasein's fundamental characteristics. The term "existential" (*existenzial*) can also be used as an adjective that refers to the "ontological structure of existence", to existentials and their interrelations, as well as to the philosopher's understanding of it. For example, the fact that "existence" consists of "being-in-the-world" is an existential matter, and so is the philosophical understanding of it. Further, Heidegger also coined another adjective, "existentiell" (*existenziell*), which pertains to the spectrum of possibilities available to Dasein, its understanding of them and the choice it makes (or evades) from among them. The particular choices Dasein makes (or avoids making) are "existentiell" matters. The distinction between "existential" and "existentiell" parallels the distinction between "ontological" and "ontical" (see Inwood [2000b]: 61–2] for complete discussion). "Existence" and its derivatives are rarely used by Heidegger in his later writings after *Being and Time*.

Each existential refers to a specific *a priori* mode of Dasein's way of Being and understanding. Heidegger analyses all these existentials, which together constitute Dasein's complete *a priori* way of understanding and being-in-the-world, and this forms the basis of Dasein's capacity to question and investigate the meaning of Being.

Thus Heidegger points out that, since ontology is the investigation of our understanding of Being and we have an *a priori* or pre-ontological understanding of Being, then the role of the philosopher is to interpret this pre-ontological understanding and make it explicit in an ontological theory. Thus ontology for Heidegger is "interpretive" or "hermeneutic" and because our pre-ontological understanding is embedded in our pre-reflective mode of being-in-the-world, ontology is therefore the endeavour to express our *practical* understanding of Being in a conceptually articulate form.

The world

Heidegger's conception of Dasein describes its Being as a "being-there" in which "there" refers to the world. The "world" in Heidegger's usage of the word is not a physical space but a context of meaning: a domain of possibilities that is inhabited by Dasein's *active* understanding, which manifests as Dasein's knowing *what* to do and *why* it makes sense to do it. Heidegger's usage of "world" in this sense of possibilities refers to the entire circumstances or context that influence a particular Dasein's total existence, "that 'wherein' a factical Dasein as such can be said to 'live'" (BT: 93) (what Husserl terms the "life-world"). This includes its country of residence, the particular culture and environment, education, family, friends, career and pastimes and so on. For instance, a British lawyer's "world" will have a structure articulated in terms of all the different modes of organizing life in terms of work objectives, social roles, personal interests and leisure activities that are available to him as an Englishman, who is a lawyer, a father and so on.

Another Dasein, for example, might inhabit primarily a "business world" or sporting, academic or entertainment world. Each world gives us different potentialities-for-being: a different set of possibilities for determining who one is and how one can live. Thus the world in which a particular Dasein is involved will structure its mode of living, and determine the purpose and significance of its actions and reactions to life events. For instance, a surgeon unconnected with the business world may be quite unworried by a stock market crash, whereas a Dasein who is a stockbroker will be devastated. So any particular Dasein will be defined by its involvement in a particular world or worlds.

Western philosophers, such as Descartes, have traditionally tried to observe "objectively" and understand humanity by "lifting" people out of their world in order to isolate an independent "essence" or "pure aware-ness". Heidegger considers this approach completely erroneous, futile and misleading, for Dasein and the *space of possibilities* (the world) it inhabits are not things that can be measured or described objectively since Dasein is inextricably enmeshed or rooted *in the world* and its fundamental experience of the world is one of familiarity. Thus we do not normally experience a sense of detachment from the surrounding world, but rather we feel at home and connected with a world we already understand and in which we are immersed. Indeed our sense of identity – embodied in the way we live, rather than how we think or talk about our lives – arises *from* our world and cannot be disentangled from it. To stress this point Heidegger sometimes hyphenates *Dasein* so that the literal translation of *Da-sein* as "there-being", in which "there" refers to the world, now becomes "world-being".

Dasein's being-in-the-world

The first *a priori existential* that Heidegger describes, therefore, is Dasein's "being-in-the-world". What Heidegger means by "being-in" is our *a priori* capacity to understand, relate to, care about and concern ourselves with the things in the world around us. In other words, Dasein is fundamentally *familiar with the world* and this familiarity is a constant, pervasive background feature of Dasein's experience, although Dasein is not normally consciously aware of it. Heidegger's use of hyphens emphasizes his view of the world and Dasein as an indivisible unity. Dasein, however, blinded by the apparent banality of the world, tends to be unaware of the crucial significance of being-in-the-world. But in the same way that a tree cannot be truly appreciated or understood when it has been uprooted, so Heidegger emphatically asserts that Dasein cannot be comprehended in isolation from the world it inhabits for being-in-the-world is Dasein's basic state or constitution. Dasein is fused with the world. It is not possible to separate Dasein from the world because the world is Dasein's most "vital organ", the fundamental source of Dasein's existence.

Dasein's ordinary, everyday existence

Although there may be vast differences between the various "worlds" a Dasein might inhabit, there is a basic underlying infrastructure, or Being, that they all share (Heidegger calls this the "worldhood" of the world): the context of means–ends relations that orient and guide our daily interactions, thus encompassing the totality of all our practical functional relations with everything in our world. Heidegger believes that, to understand the infra-structure of *worldhood*, and thus better understand ourselves, we need to analyse our way of living in the ordinary, everyday reality of the immediate world around us.

Heidegger describes how the world is first experienced and made meaningful to us, not by scientific knowledge, not by knowing particular facts, but by pre-scientific experiences derived from our practical involvement or relations to the things (entities) around us, which we employ for a useful purpose to accomplish our goals. He emphasizes that the practical world is primordial, as it is the one we inhabit prior to any philosophizing, abstract thinking or scientific investigation, and it is where we spend most of our time. Indeed, he argues that science proceeds on the basis of our pre-ontological assumptions about the Being of the domain of research that is investigated and that "all positive investigation is guided by this understanding" (BT: 30). In other words, ontological reflection lays the foundations for empirical science since "Ontological inquiry is indeed more primordial, as over against the ontical inquiry of the positive sciences" (BT: 31). Further, he asserts that scientific revolutions take place when pre-ontological assumptions change. Indeed Heidegger states that ontological research:

> must run ahead of the positive sciences, and it *can* ... it leaps ahead, as it were, into some area of Being, discloses it for the first time in the constitution of its Being, and, after thus arriving at the structures within it, makes these available to the positive sciences as transparent assigments for their inquiry. (BT: 30–31)

So, for Heidegger, to possess factual knowledge about something does not denote understanding, since it is only when we interact with things that we can truly comprehend them. Indeed, the ability to see what to do with things is essential to understanding the world one inhabits. "Detached" or "objective" thinking about things is derived from the practical world, not vice versa, and this detachment from entities artificially disables our contact with the practical world, causing us to lose our deep sense of the nature of things.

According to Heidegger, we possess an *a priori* understanding of our being-in-the-world that allows us a prior sense of the practical potential of the things in our environment. Our awareness of the world and its entities is then increased via our practical involvement in, or relation with, all the entities around us. Heidegger uses the term "circumspection" (BT: 98) to describe the kind of involved (rather than detached or objective) "looking around" that has a practical motive. This circumspective looking around takes place in, and is guided by, the demands of practical interests or activities. Circumspection recognizes how the things we use in our daily existence relate to one another. It should be noted here that, although Heidegger begins his investigation of Dasein's existence in the world by observing and examining the way Dasein *uses* things for practical purposes, he is not trying to imply that the essence of man ultimately can be reduced to various productive manipulations of useful entities.

Heidegger chooses to begin his investigation of the world by examining the totality of our practical functional relations simply because this is the way in which the world is first experienced by us, and made meaningful to us, and the practical world is also the one we inhabit prior to any form of existential questioning.

Ready-to-hand and present-at-hand

Heidegger's analysis reveals that the entities we encounter in everyday life do not all have the same way of Being. To emphasize this, he describes their Being as either "ready-to-hand" or "present-at-hand". These two terms, which normally are applied only in reference to non-human entities, do *not* refer to two set classes of things but rather to two different ways in which things can be encountered. For it is the *way* we relate to a particular entity – in a practical way or theoretical way – that determines which classification is applicable. Things that are regarded by Dasein as having a useful function for human purposes are called "equipment" (BT: 97) or *ready-to-hand* entities (BT: 98). Relating to entities as ready-to-hand is Dasein's fundamental way of being-in-the-world; Heidegger calls these relations of "concern". All of nature – the wind, water, trees and especially the sun – can be experienced by us as ready-to-hand.

> The sun, whose light and warmth are in everyday use, has its own places – sunrise, midday, sunset, midnight ... Here we have something which is ready-to-hand ... The house has its sunny side and its shady side; the way it is divided up into "rooms" is orientated towards these. (BT: 137)

In contrast to this, "present-at-hand" is Heidegger's description of the Being of entities for which we have no use or interest; alternatively, their significance to us may be merely one of detached, objective interest. Science treats entities as present-at-hand when it observes and studies their physical properties. Also, the same object – depending on the way we relate to it – can be present-at-hand or ready-to-hand. For example, natural entities, such as rocks, that have a completely neutral resting state are generally experienced as present-at-hand, but for a stonemason who makes use of them they are definitely ready-to-hand. A botanist who does pull-ups from the bough of a tree on his day off is treating it as ready-to-hand – a tool for exercise – rather than as something that is present-at-hand, which is the way in which he would normally relate to the tree when at work.

Manufactured products or raw materials that serve human purposes are usually experienced as ready-to-hand, but a piece of equipment (a ready-to-hand entity) that is broken, rendered useless or in the hands of someone who does not know what it is for, is experienced as present-at-hand.

To take an example, a screwdriver is experienced as ready-to-hand by a car mechanic who is occupied repairing a car, but for a rainforest tribesman the same screwdriver might be seen as being present-at-hand (unless he views it as a weapon). If, however, the screwdriver is broken, and therefore useless, the mechanic will then experience it as "unready-to-hand" (BT: 103), Heidegger's term for the present-at-hand condition of equipment that is broken or rendered unusable.

Similarly, in the case of a carpenter working on wood with a hammer and nails, all three items will be experienced as ready-to-hand. If, however, he runs out of nails, or misplaces his hammer, and consequently can no longer use the remaining tools and materials, he might now regard them as present-at-hand (unready-to-hand). Conversely, someone may come across an apparently neutral, useless object that later turns out to be useful to them. Although initially perceiving the thing as present-at-hand, they will now experience it as ready-to-hand.

In his later writings, Heidegger speaks about a third way of relating to entities that are part of the natural phenomenon of nature, which is to "understand" them as manifestations of the power of nature.

Heidegger's "equipment totality"

When Dasein relates to a ready-to-hand item, it understands the item as fundamentally existing within a network of other entities. This network reveals where things belong and how they fit into our lives. In other words, the world is a context of *references* (BT: 121). Our understanding of this is *a priori* and generally subliminal (although, in a very conscious Dasein, this awareness may be frequent). An example of this entity network is evident in the simple act of writing: I pick up a pen in order to write a letter. The paper I use exists in order to be written on, the envelope "in order to" contain the letter, the stamp to pay for it, the postbox to receive it in order for the postman to deliver it. This "in order to" indicates the chain of connection between entities in Dasein's environment. Thus one tool is ontologically impossible; a tool is always part of an implicit network of inter-referential equipment in Dasein's place of work. A hammer exists within the network of other related tools, raw materials, the job it is used for, its end result or product and so on. This collection of instruments and materials related to a ready-to-hand item Heidegger calls "equipment totality" (BT: 97–8).

Heidegger refers to the ongoing purposes and projects that describe the relations between our activities and goals – the structures of "worldhood" – as "towards which", "in order to" and "for the sake of", and these structures of the worldhood of the world are *a priori* in the sense that they are universal (they belong to *all* the worlds that Dasein potentially could inhabit) and indispensable not only to the functioning of our *practical* everyday world (our practical engagement with the things that surround us) but also to the procedures that are intrinsic to the theoretical domains of science, logic and mathematics. The medical researcher is occupied *with* his microscope *in* the act of observing *in order to* determine the effects of a particular antibiotic on a specific type of bacteria *for the sake of* finding an effective cure for a life-threatening illness. Thus the everyday world, both practical *and* theoretical, is always already characterized by a large network of relations between everything that is in any way, however remotely or indirectly, related to Dasein's purposes or goals.

We do not typically pay much attention to the things we use, or to their place in the "referential totality" (their existence in a network). Practical things around us serve their instrumental function invisibly, for in our everyday activity our concern is not with the implements themselves, for our focus is on our activity and/or its objective, and *not* on the equipment that helps us to accomplish it. Heidegger calls this invisibility of equipment *inconspicuousness* (BT: 106) and indicates that this withdrawal of attention from the things we use characterizes most everyday actions, which thus are performed, for the most part, in auto-pilot mode. It is only when something goes wrong that the relational context that conditions and makes all such activity possible comes to light. Thus, when something we use malfunctions, breaks down or goes missing, we suddenly become aware of the network of relations in which its functioning was embedded. For instance, when a doorknob comes off in my hand I might suddenly notice how it belongs to the latch of the door leading to the hallway that I need to walk down to get into my office to collect a book for a lecture; the world of practical activity is thus very clearly revealed to me.

So Dasein's involvement with ready-to-hand equipment lights up the surrounding character of the worldhood of our world as being a unified web of significance, which is often of practical significance. In contrast, the detached "objective" present-at-hand experience of things is relevant and essential in areas such as science, where theories are a necessity, but it is only a very specialized, highly restricted way of seeing things that is fundamentally derived from our being-in-the-world: in other words, from our direct experience of the things around us.

Heidegger emphasizes that, when we view life principally as a collection of independently existing animate and inanimate entities, or if we treat things generally as present-at-hand, we are limiting ourselves to a very narrowed perception of Being. We are disregarding our fundamental unity with the world, the interconnectedness of everything around us and our practical and personal concerns, which constitute our primary way of Being in the world. This attitude allows humans to be treated as ciphers in statistics as though they are mere present-at-hand "scientific objects" or, alternatively, as ready-to-hand "tools" for business or political purposes.

Space, time and distance

Heidegger also pays close attention to the role that space, time and distance play with regard to our experience of the practical significance of the entities around us. He is not interested in the formally measured, objective, scientific understanding of these features, but instead focuses on how we *experience* them, which is influenced by the nature of our concern and the mood we are in. Thus phrases such as "a stone's throw", "a long haul" and so on are more descriptive of space as it is *actually* experienced, prior to its representation in terms of quantifiable distance, even if they are impossibly vague and useless from the perspective of the latter. The dimensions of space in terms of our experience are measured in terms of accessibility and interest. Things are near when they are accessible and available for use when needed, and they are far away when they are inaccessible or unavailable for use, even if they happen to be very close to us in terms of objective, physical measurements. Similarly, things are near to us when our interests or needs make it necessary for us to use them and they are far away from us when they play no role in our current activities (BT: 135–6, 140–42). In addition, that which is objectively extremely near to us, such as the reading glasses we are wearing, the shirt on our back or the pavement under our feet, is usually too close to be noticeable to us; these things are thus "further away" than entities that are physically more distant, such as an approaching friend (BT: 142). So Dasein needs to distance itself from beings to a certain extent in order to engage with them as beings (GA 65: 482).

This concept and experience of space leads to some strange, but very normal, phenomena. For instance, a caller on the telephone may be experienced as being nearer to us than someone in the same room if our concern and attention are with the caller and not with the person in the room. So practical concern, understanding and states of mind can make space stretch or contract. In addition, Dasein often experiences the objects it uses in its environment as significant in terms of their existence in all three dimensions of time: the past, the possible futures and the present moment. For example, the existence of a bicycle I ride may be significant to me in terms of its past, seen in paintwork scratches from minor accidents. It signifies all the possible future rides I will have on it, and, as I ride it, I enjoy my freedom in the present moment. (For a complete discussion of time, see Chapter 6, "Dasein's primordial temporality".)

Being-with-others

Up to now, Heidegger has described Dasein's existence in the everyday world as characterized by a purposeful use of things in the environment, which exist in an extended network that defines their connection with one another and their role in our lives. He now asks "*Who* it is that Dasein is in its everydayness?" (BT: 149). He is not interested in answering this question via self-conscious introspection, which invariably leads to conceptions of "Self" as some kind of independently existing or transcendental "thing". For Heidegger, Dasein is not any sort of "thing", and introspection is not Dasein's fundamental or normal way of Being, so the conclusions I reach via this approach usually lead to false assumptions about who I normally am.

Heidegger suggests that I should investigate who I was *before* I began to reflect, while I was still absorbed with my life in the everyday world. According to Heidegger, this leads to the realization that in my being-in-the-world I always, and essentially, experience things in relation to other people (BT: 153–4). As long as I exist, I am always involved with others in some way, for it is ontologically impossible for me to exist as Dasein without depending on some shared, communal norms. All my material possessions depend on others, and virtually everything I do requires others, whether it is at work, during holidays or leisure activities, or in medical matters. My world is essentially a public or social world. Even when there are no other people around – for example, on a deserted station platform, or when working in isolation – others are conspicuous by their absence, and they are there via the man-made things around me.

Heidegger calls this communal dimension of Dasein's being-in-the-world "being-with", and he asserts that this is a fundamental feature of Dasein's Being: the world of Dasein is a "with-world". Heidegger regards "being-with" as an *a priori* existential that enables Dasein to relate to others. In other words, "being-with" is the *a priori* dimension of the self, which provides us with the potential to understand and relate to others in all possible ways. So Dasein always has the capacity to relate to others, and this is why its Being is a being-with. So even if I have been deprived of all human contact since earliest childhood, because I live on a deserted island with no man-made products, I would still be a "being-with" because it is my *a priori* inheritance from mankind; thus even being completely alone is a mode of being-with (BT: 156–7).

Dasein's thrownness

We are "thrown" (*geworfen*) into the world, according to Heidegger. The random forces of chance or destiny determine our country and place of birth, race, religion, culture and the family and environment surrounding us: our world. Aside from knowing the facts of our conception and birth, ultimately – from the larger, more universal perspective – we have no idea whatsoever where we came from, or why we are here. We did not choose any of the aspects of our existence and yet they fundamentally influence our current situation and all our future possibilities for Being. Heidegger calls this event of being thrust into an involuntary existence our "thrownness" (BT: 173–4), and the "burden" we carry as a result is termed our "facticity" (BT: 174).

Our facticity is the sum total of our current situation, combined with what this enables us to become in terms of our own future possibilities; in other words, every morning when I awaken, and at every moment of my existence, I am faced with the responsibility of choosing what I can be on the basis of what I have been and what I am.

Thrownness is a central feature of Dasein, and is not a completed fact that is over and done with, like one's family tree. The momentum of Dasein's "throw" never diminishes; Dasein remains permanently in the state of being thrown, and this influences and shapes his entire existence. I am *thrown* out of the past and into the present while projecting from within my thrownness towards the future. The term "projection" refers to Dasein's efforts to fulfil its own possibilities. I can never get behind or break free from my thrownness (BT: 329–30). To emphasize this, Heidegger uses the peculiar double adverb that appears throughout

Being and Time: "always already". He points out that I am always a *Being-already-in-the-world*.

Our possibilities are determined by the chance event of our thrownness, which is responsible for where we always already are, and who we always already are. In other words, my thrownness means that I have a past I always carry with me that must serve as a foundation for my present existence, and which defines and limits my future possibilities. My projections for the future are always thrown, and even my creative achievements are thrown, because the choices I make, and all I create, must be made on the basis of what I already am at the moment, which is influenced by my past: the continuing momentum of my thrownness. So I can never create myself anew, as I have to work with what I have been and what I am now in order to become what I want to be in the future. Consequently there is a continual struggle between the drive to actualize my potentials and the influences or restraints of my thrownness.

The fact of my thrownness shows that, in the final analysis, I can never say I have really chosen my current situation. Ultimately everything I am and do has been made possible by the "already given" situation into which I was thrown.

Inauthenticity: the "They-self"

According to Heidegger, each Dasein is unique, and experiences its Being in two ways: "authentically" or "inauthentically". Heidegger claims that most of the time Dasein lives inauthentically because Dasein forgets its uniqueness owing to its complete involvement in the everyday world of current preoccupations. This inauthentic mode of living is marked by a lack of self-awareness, which stems from our absorption in the ways of living that *others* provide us. The "They-self" is Heidegger's term for the inauthentic mode of the self. He explains it by pointing out that Dasein's primordial state of being-with (the social context of its world) includes a fundamental and necessary feature of our Being, called the "They". This refers to the full range of social and cultural customs, expectations and interpretations of life offered by the particular world that Dasein inhabits. As the They-self, Dasein simply accepts the "way of the They", allowing it to structure and guide its mode of existence.

> We take pleasure as *They* take pleasure; we read, see, and judge about literature and art as *They* see and judge; likewise we shrink back from the "great mass" as *They* shrink back … Everyone is

the other, and no one is himself. The *"They"*, which supplies the answer to the *"who"* of everyday Dasein, is the *"nobody"* to whom every Dasein has already surrendered itself in being-among-one-another.   (BT: 164–6)

From birth, Dasein lives as the They-self, and so its understanding, behaviour and basic mode of survival are shaped by the ready-made explanations, evaluations and standards of the They of the particular society and period in time into which it is *thrown*. It makes Dasein's existence meaningful and comprehensible. So our way of living and self-understanding is rooted in, and complies with, the anonymous public "They": we behave, speak and value as "one" speaks, behaves and values. In the world of the They, there is a levelling off of distinctions and a levelling down of possibilities (BT: 165); at school, children who are "different" are rejected until they learn to conform to the They-world of their peers. So the They restricts "the possible options of choice to what lies within the range of the familiar, the attainable, the respectable – that which is fitting and proper" (BT: 239). In following the way of the They, one tends to go with the flow, "satisfying the easily handled rules and public norms of the 'They', thereby being disburdened of all 'responsibility' for ourselves" (BT: 334).

The They instils in us the sense we have of ourselves and the world around us. It even subliminally influences the physical distance we maintain in social situations (BT: 164): the space dictated by the They of one culture can differ greatly from that of another culture, potentially causing problems.

One can see the influence of the They everywhere, even in Dasein's clothes and hairstyle. Each Dasein adopts an appearance that essentially conforms to the They of their particular world. The businessman adopts a style in keeping with the "business They", and Dasein in each of the uniformed services (police, military, etc.) have a They that determines their style.

Members of the rebellious world of counter-culture who think they are escaping the influence of the They by "doing their *own* thing", with rebellious hairstyles, body-piercing, tattooing and "cool" clothes, are deluding themselves, for the They can make us think we are authentic, original individuals even when we are still under its influence: "we shrink back from the 'great mass' as *They* shrink back" (BT: 164). Such nonconformists are merely conforming to the They of the counter-culture world. Indeed, these types are often rigid conformists within their chosen subculture.

Various events, however, especially an episode of intense anxiety, can potentially trigger an awakening from the They-self. For instance, traumatic life experiences such as the death of someone loved or the discovery that one has an incurable disease can dramatically alter one's perspective on life, leading to a complete rejection of the values and expectations of the They.

But it also requires great existential courage to maintain such freedom from the power of the They because the moment you deviate from its path, it will continually try to re-establish its control via numerous pressures: financial commitments ("The mortgage needs to be paid off"), legal commitments (job contracts), emotional or social pressures ("How can she leave her whole family?"), feelings of guilt ("How can I leave him after twenty years of marriage?"). Indeed, the worst critic, and close ally, of the They is frequently oneself: "One belongs to the others oneself and enhances their power" (BT: 164). So to go against the expectations of the They frequently involves being socially rejected and invariably is emotionally very painful. Lacking the strength of character to stand up to such social pressures – to remain steadfast to who you are and the way you want to live – is described by Heidegger as follows: "by thus disburdening it of its Being, the 'They' accommodates Dasein if Dasein has any tendency to take things easily and make them easy" (BT: 165).

Heidegger's description of the They, as well as his later account of death, was influenced by Tolstoy's *The Death of Ivan Ilyich*:

> Ivan's carefully redecorated house seems quite exceptional to him, but in fact contains "all the things people of a certain class have in order to resemble other people of that class"; when Ivan's family discuss Sarah Bernhardt's acting, it is "the sort of conversation that is always repeated and always the same".   (Inwood 2005: 373)

Inauthenticity: falling

Heidegger uses the term "falling" to describe Dasein's mode of living as the They-self in the everyday world and he asserts that falling is a universally human condition:

> Dasein is proximally and for the most part alongside the "world" of its concern. This "absorption in …" has mostly the character of Being-lost in the publicness of the "They". Dasein has, in the first instance, always already fallen away from itself as an authentic ability to be its Self, and has fallen into the "world". "Fallenness" into the "world" means an absorption in Being-with-one-another, in so far as the latter is guided by idle talk, curiosity, and ambiguity.
> (BT: 220)

Falling, according to Heidegger, characterizes Dasein's general mode of everyday being-in-the-world in which Dasein lives mostly, or even entirely, inauthentically, as a They-self, absorbed in its everyday dealings with the world, which it understands and relates to in a superficial manner that conforms to the normal way that others generally think, speak and act: "we do not say what we see, but rather the reverse, we see what *one says* about the matter" (HCT: 56).

Heidegger thus asserts that, in the state of falling, talk becomes inauthentic speech, which is manifested in idle chatter (BT: 213–14) in the form of gossip about trivia: restless, empty talk that echoes no real truth. The counterpart of this in writing is scribbling: popular writing that is absorbing, distracting and "disburdening", typical of newspapers and popular fiction.

Our inauthentic understanding of the world and our general attitude towards life are characterized by idle curiosity and indifference. We feel the need to keep up to date and well informed regarding what we believe to be happening in the world around us. But instead of a genuine interest in deeply understanding ourselves and the world, we display merely a superficial, short-lived "curiosity" (BT: 214–17) for the latest news and most recent fashions and entertainment that reflect the interests of the They. Thus, rather than making a genuine effort to investigate for ourselves issues that particularly concern us, we instead become involved with general matters about which everybody can offer opinions, and we lose interest in, and become indifferent to, the distinctions between suspicion and proof or personal viewpoints and truth.

A common example of falling is finding ourselves in a store in front of a rack filled with magazines and newspapers covering every possible subject. We pick up one publication after another, browsing through articles on health and fitness or celebrity gossip, and skimming the latest computer magazines or newspapers to get up to date on the most recent developments. Everything seems fascinating, and our attention becomes absorbed in one article after another, but only very superficially and briefly, before switching to the next topic. Suddenly, as if coming out of a trance, we jolt back into our bodies and carry on with our lives again. But we are left with the uncomfortable feeling that what we indulged in was a complete waste of valuable time. Casually browsing the internet is a common modern example of this same pattern, but perhaps the worst time-wasting example of falling is seen in the continual, mindless shifting from one station to another in television "channel-surfing".

In falling, one drifts along with the fads and trends of the crowd, oblivious that one's own being is an issue. Caught up in the mindless busy-ness, lulled by feeling that everyone else is doing the same, Dasein becomes blind to all its possibilities, and tranquillizes itself with that which is merely "actual". In its simplest form, *falling is the non-awareness of what it means to be.*

Despite the condemnatory tone of his description, Heidegger claims that he is not making any personal moral judgements regarding falling (BT: 211, 220), for he considers it to be an automatic and direct consequence of our thrownness (BT: 223) and therefore a basic and permanent tendency of the human predicament. "Dasein has, in the first instance, fallen away from itself as an authentic potentiality for Being its Self, and has fallen into the 'world'" (BT: 220), and this fall is an anxiety-driven "*fleeing* of Dasein in the face of itself – of itself as an authentic potentiality-for-Being-its-Self" (BT: 229). Thus falling reveals an essential ontological structure of Dasein itself. Indeed, since Dasein's Being essentially involves being-with, it is ontologically impossible to exist as Dasein without some dependence on shared, communal standards. So from the very beginning, Dasein exists in the state of falling, completely in the inauthentic world of the They, and "In no case is a Dasein, untouched and unseduced by this way in which things have been interpreted" (BT: 213), and thus we can never simply extricate ourselves from the "They" of our community (BT: 213, 224, 345, 435).

Dasein, in its falling, spends most of the time absorbed by the practical matters of daily survival. It views the past merely in terms of a series of no-longer-actual events (forgetting) rather than authentically, as still significant possibilities (repetition). Its awareness of the future is restricted to actual not-yet events (waiting) rather than possible projections of one's ability-to-be (anticipation). Instead, it attends to its present concerns involved in everyday business. Dasein's "authentic ability to be itself" is thus evaded and buried beneath its current preoccupations and shallow interests of its dead past and future desires. It pays no attention to its thrownness and therefore lacks an overall perspective of its life from birth to death. Consequently, its self-concept is defined fundamentally by its current situation in life rather than in terms of its future possibilities.

However, in rare moments, Heidegger offers a more balanced perspective of Dasein's average everydayness, which is less disparaging and more plausible (see Dreyfus 1991: 27). Sometimes he asserts that "average everydayness" is "undifferentiated" (GA 21: 229–30). Thus Heidegger seems to be implying (although the text is ambivalent on this issue) that average everydayness can be regarded as neutral (unowned) and, as such, authentic (owned) and inauthentic (disowned) can be considered to be *existentiell modifications* of average everydayness:

> At the outset of our analysis it is particularly important that Dasein should not be interpreted with the differentiated character of some definite way of existing, but that it should be uncovered in the

undifferentiated character which it has proximally and for the most part. This undifferentiated character of Dasein's everydayness is *not nothing*, but a positive phenomenal characteristic of this entity. Out of this kind of Being – and back into it again – is all existing, such as it is. We call this everyday undifferentiated character of Dasein *averageness*.   (BT: 69)

Heidegger never clearly elaborates this concept and invariably he presents Dasein's average everydayness as a mode of inauthentic (dis-owned) existence. However, we could hypothesize or argue (see Blattner 2009: 130) that in most Dasein, average everydayness is, in fact, mostly undifferentiated or unowned, because they have not yet deeply experienced the anxiety that arises in the face of death and thus have *not* been confronted with the choice of owning or disowning their lives. If, however, the choice does arise, most Dasein respond by disowning their life, which Heidegger calls "fleeing in the face of death". They escape their anxiety by immersing themselves again in everyday life but the only way they can do this, now that they have been made aware of the existential choices facing them, is to ignore or bury their awareness of this challenge and in so doing they are disowning the possibility of an authentic mode of Being, and their everydayness can now accurately be described as an inauthentic mode of Being.

Heidegger's proposition that everydayness – even for authentic Dasein – is fundamentally an inauthentic mode of Being can be questioned yet again in the following example, which seems clearly to suggest that this does not necessarily have to be the case.

Authentic Dasein that has resolutely chosen to be engaged in its current everyday activities may be acting in a manner that is, fundamentally speaking, independent from the They, in the sense that its choices and actions are, essentially, no longer prescribed by the They. The They merely influences Dasein's interpretation of the tools it is using to carry out the everyday actions, but not the actions themselves. For example, Dasein accepts that the typewriter is for writing the reports it has resolutely chosen to make, and the bus is the mode of transport that has been resolutely chosen for getting to work.

So in this particular example of everydayness, Dasein is in fact resolutely doing its own thing, not what the They dictates – a fundamental description of authentic behaviour – and thus its everyday actions do not accurately fit the characteristics of inauthenticity. Nevertheless, neither can this Dasein's actions be accurately described as authentic, since its absorption in its everyday activities, no matter how resolutely chosen, still entails seeing things as the They interpret them and not in its own way. This "in-between" state is yet another example of a mode of average everydayness that perhaps can best be described as "undifferentiated" rather than "inauthentic".

However, according to Heidegger, everydayness is invariably character-ized by a state of fallenness and inauthenticity to such an extent that "it determines Dasein even when it has not chosen the 'They' as its 'hero' ... Existence can, indeed, master the everyday in the moment of vision, and of course often only 'for the moment', but it can never extinguish it" (BT: 422). In other words, the inauthentic state of everydayness rules *all* Dasein. Authentic Dasein can briefly transcend it in the authentic "moment of vision", but it can never escape it or "extinguish it".

When we live inauthentically, our general way of living is based on a means–ends perspective, in which all our actions are *in order to get some-thing*. So we might swim fifty lengths per day to get healthy. We might live for weeks on a diet we dislike to get thin. We might accept dinner invita-tions to make contacts. In addition, we constantly check our performance against public criteria, because we worry about what others think of us and fear that we shall not meet standards of success set by the They of our particular "world". In this means–ends approach to life, our moment-by-moment existence becomes unimportant as we are like the proverbial donkey chasing the carrot at the end of the stick, unconcerned with the quality of the route we are taking.

Heidegger explains that the inauthentic condition of Dasein's Being serves a necessary function in everyday life. The acceptance of our pre-established ways of existence allows us to interpret our daily circumstances and deal with practical concerns: "The self must forget itself if, lost in the world of equipment, it is to be able 'actually' to go to work and manipulate something" (BT: 405). If everyone constantly challenged this "given" basis for existence – our conventional ways of thinking and living – we would have no solid foundation for interpreting life around us and society would come to a halt. We would all find ourselves on the edge of what Heidegger calls "the abyss of meaninglessness" (BT: 194).

So when Heidegger uses the term "inauthenticity", he is definitely not suggesting that it is less real than authenticity. He emphasizes that Dasein's inauthentic existence characterized by falling and the They-self has nothing to do with wrong choices or moral failings, but is part of the structure of normal everyday existence in the world. He also asserts that the process of becoming deeply aware of our inauthentic modes of Being (for instance, in the experience of profound anxiety) highlights the structure of authenticity. In other words, if Dasein successfully achieves an authentic understanding and approach to existence, this will have arisen and evolved from Dasein's superficial everyday attitudes and judgements, and not from outside it (BT: 213, 224).

Moods

Although Heidegger uses the unusual word *Befindlichkeit* (meaning roughly "how one finds oneself", or "how one is doing") to express the concept of mood, the more usual German word for mood is *Stimmung*. This word also means the tuning of a musical instrument, suggesting a metaphorical relation between moods and musical instruments: the same events that we might joke about when we are in a good mood are likely to upset us when we are in a bad mood, and, paralleling this, an uplifting phrase of music played in a major key is likely to sound melancholy in a minor key. Thus Heidegger views "being in a mood" as being "tuned to" life in a certain way and this influences the nature of our understanding at any given moment: moods can enhance or reduce our clarity of perception. Owing to the hardships of existence, most moods are evasive and tend to conceal reality; for example, depressed irritability probably "veils" the environment more than it discloses it (BT: 175).

It is also possible to be caught up in an entirely inappropriate mood that absorbs our awareness to such an extent that we completely miss what is going on around us. For instance, if I am elated, I may not notice feelings of anger in a crowded room, an error of judgement that could potentially place me in danger. Or my mood of angry depression may reduce my awareness of the possibilities of my current situation (BT: 175) so that I simply complain about my circumstances rather than taking appropriate action. Heidegger thus suggests that Dasein needs to achieve some level of control over its moods (BT: 178), so that its attunement to its overall situation – its "Being in the world as a whole" – is compatible with its current circumstances.

Moods, often ignored by philosophy, are a primordial part of Dasein's essential character and way of Being, for Dasein is never moodless. Moods reveal the world and one's place in it, and they enable one to respond to other beings in the world. Thus if I am not in a mood I will not be "affected" or moved by anything – nothing will "matter" to me (BT: 176) – since it is via my moods that I become aware of the world or beings as a whole and in this open realm I can encounter other humans and entities. Even apparently moodless states, such as indifference, are themselves a mood. And the dispassionate activity of "objective" scientific investigation is also characterized by a mood, perhaps one of fascination or wonder (BT: 177). Similarly, the condition of seemingly "moodless", detached, meditative contemplation or observation, in which everything is "flattened out" to a uniform realm of purposeless objects, is also a type of mood: according to Heidegger, a *"tranquil* dwelling on" (BT: 177).

So we are always attuned in some way to things in general – to our overall situation, our *"Being-in-the-world as a whole"* (BT: 176) – permanently in some kind of mood, which in turn influences our feelings and behaviour and our general outlook on the world, for mood "has always already disclosed being-in-the-world as a whole, making it first possible to direct oneself towards something in particular" (BT: 176).

Love or profound joy can render life full of significance, beauty and magic, and we feel motivated, so in spite of the fact that people often think "love is blind", Heidegger asserts that "love really gives us sight" (HCT: 296) and he mentions the delight we derive from the existence of someone we love ("What is Metaphysics?", in BW: 99). Such moods can potentially remind us of the significance of Being.

Julian Young suggests that the enlightening mood of *cosmic gratitude* is evident in Heidegger's later texts when he interprets the mature verse of the poet Hölderlin. According to Heidegger, in Hölderlin's poetry the disclosure of the world as a "holy place" points to a fundamental mood of "gratitude" or "thankfulness" (GA 52: 197), which, if properly understood, will also be experienced by the reader. Thus Young speculates that "To experience one's world as a holy place is, as a matter of conceptual necessity, to inhabit the mood of *cosmic gratitude*, to 'give thanks' for the 'gift' of such a world and for one's own existence in it". And to be in this mood "of cosmic gratitude, is to experience the world as a whole, as full of the presence of, in Hölderlin's words, the 'wonderfully all-present' [GA 4: 52], as sparkling with the 'divine radiance' [PLT: 91] ... It is, in other words, to experience the world as a holy place" (Young 2001: 105–6).

Heidegger, however, focuses his discussion primarily on disclosive moods in which the burdensome character of Dasein is revealed. In particular, he emphasizes the mood of "boredom". Not boredom in the sense of finding something specific boring – such as a boring person, documentary, journey and so on, which Heidegger would label "ontic" boredom – but profound, existential boredom: "Profound boredom, drifting here and there in the abysses of our existence like a muffling fog, removes all things and human beings and oneself along with them into a remarkable indifference. This boredom reveals beings as a whole" ("What is Metaphysics?", in BW: 99).

In this mood, the pleasures of life that we normally might enjoy suddenly seem utterly uninteresting and uninviting, and their presence seems almost oppressive; the television with its numerous channels no longer offers a single worthwhile programme; our magazines and books no longer attract our curiosity; and there is no desire whatsoever to reach for the telephone and call someone, because there is nothing we want to say and no one we wish to talk to. Thus boredom discloses the world and beings as a whole, in the sense that the totality of *what-is* contains nothing whatsoever that attracts our interest any longer because we are now totally indifferent to ourselves and everything surrounding us.

But it is anxiety that he regards as being the most revealing of all. This mood enables us, potentially, to realize that the essence of who we are is beyond our control, for anxiety fills us with dread as we sense in our deepest Being the threat of infinite Nothingness: the inevitability of our own death. This alienates us from our everyday world, causing existence to appear senseless, ambition futile and all achievements insignificant. Heidegger asserts that intense moods such as anxiety and existential boredom can reveal fundamental truths of existence, for they can disclose with intensity the bare nature of existence as it is, without the "trappings" of job, house or personal social life. They are therefore potentially a vital source of insight into the nature of our Being in the world.

In contrast, ordinary everyday moods rarely provide fundamental insights, as they usually entail an avoidance of authentic perception. He describes our most common everyday mood as a somewhat pallid, evenly balanced "lack of mood" that contains traces of irritation and boredom. Everyday activity is often an escape from that mood; we refuse to look at the "burdensome character of Dasein", which the mood potentially can reveal to us, because, according to Heidegger, Dasein for the most part evades the truth of Being that is disclosed in the mood.

Dasein's moods arise out of its *past*, and so moods are ways in which we experience and disclose our *thrownness*, "at first and mostly in the mode of evasive turning away" (BT: 175). This is reflected in everyday statements such as "I got out of bed on the wrong side this morning", which refers to the past: to the fact that I find I have been *thrown* into the world in a particular way that has put me in an overall bad mood. My getting out of bed on the wrong side is not the *dead* past, for it lives on with me as a "heavy weight" in my present situation (BT: 173).

Heidegger emphasizes several important differences between moods and emotions. First, since moods are involved with, and reveal, "being-in-the-world as a whole", he regards them as existentially far more important than emotions, since these disclose only specific things and do nothing to reveal our authentic self.

Fear reveals something particular, such as a guard dog, as a potential threat. I am bored *with a book*, angry with *someone* or about *something* or over a *certain* situation. In contrast to this, I can be in a generally angry mood without being angry about anything in particular (although while in this state I might also become emotionally angry).

Emotions are "triggered" by something that happens, whereas, although it is possible to drive oneself *into* a mood, the essential characteristic of moods is that they come and go as they please, sometimes creeping up on us slowly and unobtrusively and sometimes striking like lightning, without warning. Heidegger also points out that *emotions* are founded on *moods*, which are – as previously mentioned – a primordial mode of Dasein's way of Being.

Moods differ from emotions in another important way. I can sometimes control emotions. For instance, if I become alarmed as I enter a bar with a threatening atmosphere, I can escape it by leaving. In contrast, the mood of dread that results from the awareness of the inevitability of my own death or, alternatively, the profound existential boredom that is not caused by any specific thing that I can avoid are conditions *not* under my control. It is, however, possible to *invoke* moods. Some music has the power to produce in the listener intense moods of sadness, elation or even dread. The music accompanying films takes advantage of this to disclose the underlying mood of the storyline: excitement, contentment or ordinary everydayness.

The sense we have of beings as a whole, provided by our moods, determines the nature of our relations with entities and the world around us. Most importantly, Heidegger asserts that there is a basic philosophical mood that is a prerequisite for true understanding (see "Anxiety", below). In the absence of this mood, ideas that previously have been deeply grasped are now experienced as a tiresome jumble of "word-husks" and "forced" concepts: "All essential thinking requires its thoughts and propositions to be dug out like ore, each time anew, from the basic mood. If the mood fails, then everything is a forced clatter of concepts and word-husks" (GA 65: 21).

In Heidegger's later thought, he asserts that the *dominant* "basic mood" of mankind varies historically. For example, at the time of the "first beginning" of the Presocratics, the basic mood was "astonishment" (see GA 65: 14, 22). In modern times, there is a tendency to let all moods be public and communal, which disguises the "growing void" (GA 65: 123). Nevertheless, "anxiety before Being is as great today as ever" (GA 65: 139). Later Heidegger speaks of a "basic mood" as one that "carries us away to the limits of beings and puts us in touch with the gods"; unites us with "the earth and our native habitat"; "opens up beings as a whole ... as the unity of a world"; "hands our Dasein over to being, to undertake, shape and sustain it" (GA 39: 223; Inwood 2000b: 132–3).

Virtues

Virtues, like moods, cannot be chosen, but they can be cultivated and thus they are experientially passive. They can attune us to aspects of ourselves and others that otherwise might be overlooked, so a person who possesses the virtue of kindness or generosity will immediately notice, in social situations, instances where acting kindly or generously to another is called for;

a virtuous person *experiences* the world differently from one lacking in virtues. Sometimes virtues can be "atmospheric". For instance, the presence of someone with a strong "stoical" character can create an atmosphere where one's physical aches and pains might suddenly seem insignificant or trivial.

Understanding

In the philosophical realm, as well as in the everyday world, Dasein's behaviour is constantly guided by some level of understanding of itself and its situation, for it always already possesses a preliminary, rudimentary understanding of anything that it asks about or interprets. This prior understanding inspires, directs and enables Dasein to question existence and make interpretations of the world.

Thus Heidegger asserts that all understanding is circular, in the sense that any interpretation that is to contribute to understanding must already have understood what is to be interpreted. So all interpretations are based on a prior *context of intelligibility*: "Interpretation is grounded existentially in understanding; the latter does not arise from the former" (BT: 188). Consequently, interpretation does not enable the discovery of *new* facts about ourselves but is fundamentally the unfolding of our unspoken, but experienced, self-understanding. Thus the "meaning" or significance of a situation, occasion, text or some aspect of our mode of Being is essentially the articulation, clarification and open disclosure of what we already see or understand.

So Dasein possesses a primordial or prior understanding of its everyday world, the things in it and how it fits into this world; this includes the capacity to recognize tools or equipment for what they are. This pre-conceptual sense, or comprehension, of existence is a part of Dasein's being-in-the-world. According to Heidegger, however, the most important function of understanding is to project or see things in terms of their future possibilities. To understand myself and thus find meaning in myself is to be aware of my own possibilities and to realize that I not only *have* possibilities, but also *am* my possibilities, for my Being includes my "can be" (*Seinkönnen*) (BT: 183): my "potentiality-for-Being". In other words, I am not just what I am; I am also who I am not yet (BT: 185–6). "The Dasein which I myself am in each instance is defined in its Being by my being able to say of it, *I am, that is, I can*" (HCT: 298).

In being aware of my own possibilities I realize I have a choice between authentic choices, in which my *own* Being is significant, and inauthentic choices, in which the Being of the *They-self* is significant, and as I project possibilities for myself (whether they are authentic or not) I am simultaneously disclosing other entities in terms of their own possibilities (BT: 184).

So Dasein's authentic understanding essentially consists of the awareness of its own range of available possibilities, which are the already "given" concrete possibilities of the worldly situation into which it has been *thrown*. This understanding involves a holistic projection of a context in which particular possibilities become intelligible. So, according to Heidegger's understanding, what we *are* is the concrete given possibilities of our thrownness, and these possibilities, which constitute what we always already are, and who we always already are, are what we should develop and thus become. To become what one is, however, requires interpretation. Interpretation is the concrete working-through of the possibilities projected by understanding, for in the process of interpretation "the understanding appropriates understandingly that which is understood by it. In interpretation, understanding does not become something different. It becomes itself" (BT: 188).

Interpretation: the "as-structure"

Understanding is fundamentally global, whereas interpretation is local. In other words, I understand my office, town – the world around me – as a global network of significance and involvement. However, when I interpret an entity I see it simultaneously *as* something that is used *for* a certain purpose, "*as* a door, *as* a house" (BT: 190), *as* a tray used for serving meals. My interpretation of entities makes clear their relations to other entities in the environment and to the possibilities in terms of which I understand that environment.

Heidegger emphasizes that we do not interpret what things are by initially perceiving them as present-at-hand items and then deducing their identity and function from their characteristics. Instead, our interpretation is instant because our prior understanding of the totality of the world surrounding us automatically discloses the nature and purpose of the entities within it. All interpretation is based on this pre-existing understanding of the possibilities associated with the things around us: "interpretation is never a presuppositionless apprehending of something presented to us" (BT: 191–2). Heidegger describes the process of interpretation in an important lecture that he devoted entirely to understanding the precise *experience* of the lectern at which he was standing and lecturing:

[E]ntering the lecture room I see the lectern … What do I see: brown surfaces intersecting at right angles? No … I see the lectern at a single stroke, as it were; ... I see the lectern in an orientation, in a lighting, against a background ... but the significant aspect is the primary experience, which presents itself to me directly, without any mental detour via a grasping of things. Living in an environment, it means to me everywhere and always, it is all of this world, it is worlding.   (GA 56/57: 71–3; Safranski 1998: 94–5)

Heidegger's innovative "it is worlding" is used in an attempt to convey something for which no single expression exists, because what is being described normally goes unrecognized, first, because it is too close to us, and second, because our habitual conditioned patterns of response tend to block out such experiences from conscious awareness. "Worlding" is a word Heidegger uses to refer to the *dynamic presence* of the world. Our primal experience and interpretation of the significance of ourselves and our surrounding environment is always as a living totality, and not in terms of individual characteristics or entities in isolation, and the "activity" contained in the term "worlding" expresses the energetic aliveness – the *presencing* of an environment that is a *process* in constant flux: nothing in existence is static; humans and all entities are "processes"; even rocks are in a constant state of transformation. The term "worlding" suggests that each environment in which we find ourselves simultaneously embraces, encapsulates and signifies our entire world of experience. The experience of the lectern and the lecture room, therefore, assembles our entire existence in time and space – "it is worlding". It calls forth the totality of our being-in-the-world: our mood; the clothes we put on; the journey by car to the lecture hall; the motivations for being a student, which are rooted in family and social influences, our culture and country of birth, our physical and intellectual characteristics. In other words, every situation we are in comprises and reflects our *a priori* understanding of being in the world, our thrownness, facticity, the sense we have of our future in terms of our knowledge of the possibilities available to us: the totality of our Being. This explains why a single item, even from the past – perhaps just the fleeting memory of a toy robot we owned – can dredge up a *whole world* of associated memories and emotions; the toy robot "is worlding". Thomas Sheehan suggests that "the world worlds" means "the meaning-giving context gives meaning" (Sheehan 2010: 100).

So in "interpretation", we immediately see things *as* something. When we see a motorcycle, we do not see a shape and some colours and hear some noises, and then infer that we are seeing a motorcycle. Instead, we first see a motorcycle, and only then we may possibly abstract its properties. Similarly, Heidegger points out that, when we see a row of trees or a flock of wild ducks, the fact that we see them *as* a row or a flock "is not based upon a prior act of counting. It is an intuitive unity which gives the whole simply. It is figural" (HCT: 66). The same process of interpretation takes place during listening:

> We never really first perceive a throng of sensations, e.g., tones and noises ... Much closer to us than all sensations are the things themselves. We hear the door shut in the house and never hear acoustical sensations or even mere sounds. In order to hear a bare sound we have to listen away from things, divert our ear from them, i.e., listen abstractly.   (OWA: 26)

In other words, our intuitive perceptions of things always involve a certain structuring of experience that is embedded in the nature of human experience itself.

When we understand the purpose or usability of an item, we are interpreting or explaining its "as-structure", which means that we are seeing its practical significance in terms of the possibilities it opens up for us; Heidegger called this an interpretation of the "in order to" function. The kettle exists *in order to* boil the water; the heater exists *in order to* keep me warm. The interpretation of this as-structure is based on our primordial *ready-to-hand* relation with our everyday environment, where we experience entities as being in a contextual web of significant relations or involvements with other entities.

Interpretation: the "fore-structure"

A prior awareness of something's place within this web is a prerequisite to interpreting its as-structure. This background, "global" understanding is what Heidegger calls the "fore-structure" of understanding. Heidegger divides this fore-structure into three separate parts, although all are simultaneously active during any given act of interpretation. He emphasizes that interpretation is always guided by this fore-structure:

> [I]nterpretation is grounded in *something we have in advance – in a fore-having*. As the appropriation of understanding, the interpretation operates in Being towards a totality of involvements which is already understood ... *something we have in advance ... a foresight ... something we grasp in advance ... a fore-conception.* (BT: 191)

This fore-structure is in play during interpretations at every level.

- "Fore-having" is the general understanding of the entity to be interpreted and of the complete context in which it is involved. The fore-having of a mechanic will be his global understanding of everything in his workshop, whereas the fore-having of a psychologist would be his broad understanding of human nature.
- "Fore-sight" sets its sights on what is to be interpreted (or a specific feature of it). The mechanic will focus his attention on an engine, or a specific mechanical fault in it, whereas the psychologist might construct a personality profile of an individual or focus on one specific behavioural dysfunction.
- "Fore-conception" refers to our capacity to interpret things, which is dependent on our prior familiarity with that which is to be interpreted. In other words, although I may see something as a tool, I will be unable to see it as a "monkey wrench" if I have no concept of a "monkey wrench". Contrary to what many would like to think, even modern natural science is founded upon a distinctive set of presuppositions, rather than presuppositionless, "objective" observations (BT: 413–14), for *all* knowledge and *all* experience are influenced by some form of pre-judgement.

Meaning

"Meaning" is what one arrives at when "understanding" becomes aware of the *as-structure* of entities. To comprehend the meaning of something is to understand its function while simultaneously seeing its significant purposive relations with other entities. According to Heidegger, Dasein possesses an *a priori* understanding of its being-in-the-world, which provides it with a sense of the practical potential of the things in its environment. Because of this, Dasein experiences its own existence as part of a network of meaningful relations to other beings; thus it is able to understand its own Being and its own possibilities in relation to its being-in-the-world as part of a significant whole. Consequently, Dasein's world is a sphere of meaning, a multifaceted web of options and possibilities. It is precisely because of this fact – that beings and Being already mean something to Dasein – that it is inspired and able to question deeply the meaning of Being. Since the sphere or context of meaning essentially derives from Dasein's ability to project possibilities, one can say that meaning "is an existential of Dasein" (BT: 193).

Heidegger points out that "meaning", in terms of logic as a theory of propositional truth, is *not* of primary importance for Dasein's comprehension of its world or for philosophy. For logic deals only with "theoretical propositions", which Heidegger views as merely the *surface phenomena* of meaning. Furthermore, theoretical propositions would be meaningless if it were not for our *a priori* comprehension of existence that first discloses to us, and gives meaning to our surrounding world and the entities within it. He emphasizes that this latter sense of meaning is primordial, as it is the one we inhabit prior to any form of philosophizing or scientific investigation. "Detached" or "objective" thinking about things is derived from this prior sense of understanding our world and not vice versa, and the theoretical detachment from entities that arises from the use of logic artificially disables our contact with this deeper sense of the true nature of things and the meaning of Being.

Anxiety

[T]he state-of-mind which can hold open the utter and constant threat to itself arising from Dasein's ownmost individualized Being, is anxiety.   (BT: 310)

Heidegger's analysis of anxiety highlights a fact that is of crucial importance to his enquiry into the meaning of Being; namely, that the ontological structure of reality becomes far more apparent to us in "breakdown situations". We have already observed this phenomenon in his analysis of ready-to-hand "equipment"; typically, we do *not* encounter the things we use in terms of their ontologically constitutive elements, since they serve their instrumental function "inconspicuously". It is only when something we are using malfunctions, breaks down or goes missing that we suddenly become aware of it and the network of relations in which its functioning was embedded. This same pattern of "invisibility" or inconspicuousness also applies to our social existence, where the people we meet are normally experienced as strangers, friends or family rather than in terms of their submission to, and reinforcement of, the influence of the They. Similarly, our self-understanding largely ignores the fact that we are fundamentally responsible for choosing who we are. Anxiety represents the "breakdown" in humans equivalent to malfunctioning or broken equipment, and similarly, it sheds light on the fundamental ontological features of our being-in-the-world.

Thus in *Being and Time* the experience of anxiety (*Angst*) is considered a potentially "enlightening" event: the royal road to authenticity that can motivate Dasein to re-evaluate its existence and see its possibilities. Anxiety is the revelation of Dasein's basic groundlessness and meaninglessness, for it comprises a total collapse of the entire structure of meaning in which one lives. Thus it calls into question Dasein's familiar identity and world, and impels it to ask about the meaning of Being, the meaning of its *own* Being: to answer the inner call of Conscience (see Chapter 4), summoning it to recognize the unique wholeness of its Being, especially its *Being within the time-horizon of its own death.*

Heidegger regards anxiety as a kind of ontological queasiness that arises when Dasein senses (consciously or subliminally) the inherent precariousness of its existence. Although in some ways this feeling resembles fear, Heidegger emphasizes that it has nothing to do with our instinctive (or conditioned) fear of *something specific*, which we perceive as a real, immediate danger or future threat.

Fear opens up a world of potentially genuine threats in the environment; my fear "has already disclosed the world as a realm from which such a thing as the fearsome can approach" (BT: 181). "Fear is Angst (anxiety) that is fallen on the 'world', inauthentic and concealed from itself as Angst" (BT: 234). In contrast, anxiety is usually an extremely vague feeling, defined by a seemingly bottomless, sometimes suffocating, apprehensiveness both incomprehensible and inexplicable:

> That in the face of which one has anxiety is characterised by the fact that what threatens is *nowhere*. Anxiety "does not know" what that in the face of which it is anxious is. … That which threatens cannot bring itself close from a definite direction within what is close by; it is already "there", and yet nowhere; it is so close that it is oppressive and stifles one's breath, and yet it is nowhere.
>
> (BT: 231)

According to Heidegger, anxiety is a "mood", not an emotion. In *Being and Time,* he emphasizes that, although it is not possible to know all beings, we can, nevertheless, *feel* or sense the totality of beings in a "mood" ("What is Metaphysics?", in BW: 99). Thus anxiety (*Angst*, also sometimes translated as "dread"), unlike an emotion, is not about any *particular* being (BT: 231); rather, it is about *beings as a whole* and about my being-in-the-world as a whole (BT: 233). Consequently, when I am in its grip, it influences my entire outlook on existence and determines the nature of my overall involvement with the world and my responses to entities in general.

Heidegger describes two ways of experiencing anxiety. The usual experience is an uneasy, indistinct, constant background feeling that is literally about nothing and in another sense it is about a not-yet-discovered latent something, because the mood is not yet intense enough to be truly revealing. From our everyday perspective, it may surface occasionally merely as a moment of meaningless confusion, perhaps a mild "panic attack". Our normal response to this type of anxiety is an escape into familiar everyday activities that block it out; the inauthenticity of "falling" becomes very tempting (BT: 221).

The other, far less frequent, form of anxiety is characterized by an intense and overwhelming sensation that disrupts our normal sense of existence. Whenever this deeply illuminating mood collides with our superficial everyday experience of the world (characterized by "falling"), the effect is always extremely jarring, for this mood reveals the naked truth of ourselves and the world, stripped of all our familiar ways of perceiving things. Heidegger sees this experience as absolutely essential to the philosopher, since the detachment it provides from worldly concerns, personal prejudices and other conditioned ways of seeing things is essential to true thinking. In stripping away the significance normally attributed to things, we are able to see things *as they are* in their naked beingness, rather than in terms of their particular usefulness or lack of usefulness. This elimination of all the familiar use-meanings connected with things, which Heidegger calls nihilation, "discloses these beings in their full but heretofore concealed strangeness as what is radically other – with respect to the Nothing. In the clear night of the Nothing of anxiety the original openness of beings as such arises: that they are beings – and not Nothing" ("What is Metaphysics?", in BW: 103). In this state of consciousness, seeing something just as a "being" means perceiving a chair, for instance, *not* as a thing one sits on to do one's writing, nor as an expensive antique or as something made from material that once was a tree, nor even as a chair, but it means that one perceives the chair just as something that *is*. In other words, once the usual significance of things is eliminated, we are able to experience simply the "being-there" of "naked" beings. Van Gogh's vibrant painting of the chair seems to express this very state of consciousness.

Also, since "each one of us is what he pursues and cares for. In everyday terms, we understand ourselves and our existence by way of the activities we pursue and the things we take care of" (BPP: 159), when anxiety strips the world of its significance, this usual sense of self is simultaneously eroded because I no longer care about my projects, and the roles in life that used to determine my identity and my actions no longer feel as though they *belong* to me: "Anxiety thus takes away from Dasein the possibility of understanding itself, as it falls, in terms of the 'world' and the way things have been publicly interpreted" (BT: 232). And in the absence of these identity-defining daily activities and goals, I "slip away" from myself ("What is Metaphysics?", in BW 101). And "in the altogether unsettling experience of this hovering where there is nothing to hold on to, pure Dasein is all that is still there" (*ibid.*).

71

Unable to immerse myself in the everyday activities of the world, I am able to notice that I am *open to the world* and that, in this openness, the world *manifests itself to me*. This suspension of content when "our concernful awaiting finds nothing in terms of which it might be able to understand itself" (BT: 393) is the state of consciousness that allows me to become *aware of my awareness*, for when beings and the activities of everyday life no longer have any hold on my consciousness, I then come face to face with my "naked self" in its "Being", and thus become aware of my openness or awareness, which is *always already there*, but which I normally ignore. According to Heidegger, the most appropriate mode of being "aware of awareness" is when we are in the state of "wonder", as this enables us to perceive our openness, or ability to be aware, as an extra-ordinary mystery.

However, we spend most of our lives trying to keep anxiety at bay. According to Heidegger, our unreflective absorption in the They-self – our identification with the commotion of our practical daily concerns and inauthentic life roles (jobs, family, education, entertainment) – is a mode of "evasion" or "fleeing" this anxiety. There are understandable motives for this denial, for anxiety reveals to us the disturbing nature of facing up to our human condition. Human awareness, existence or reality always entails a collision between actuality and possibility, between what is and what is not (but that could be) and everything arising in reality also contains its antithesis as a possibility. Therefore, at every moment of our existence, confronted with an unknown future, and unrestricted freedom of choice between all the possibilities facing us, we stand on a precipice and before us lies a gaping abyss of uncertainty and utter insecurity. The resulting anxiety that arises if we face up to this fact is unsurprising.

When a person in a state of deep anxiety realizes that they have this possibility of freedom, they simultaneously understand that they are already free. For freedom only remains as a potential, or possibility, while a person is unaware of its existence; but in the exact same instant that a person recognizes this possibility of their own freedom, the possibility is transformed into a fact. And since this transformation is instant, what a person in the grip of anxiety recognizes is not the possibility, but the fact, of their own freedom (in other words, personal freedom is always already present; what is not always present is our *awareness* of it). This profound realization is characterized by an ambivalent mixture of desire for personal freedom and, simultaneously, a fear of the potential consequences of making choices.

In this state of awareness we realize that our moment-by-moment existence is not characterized by "Being", but is a constant process of "becoming" that is influenced by our choices in life, for Dasein "is always only that which it has chosen itself to be" (BPP: 278). In other words, in this state of consciousness we realize that the "answer" to the question "Who am I?" is unanswerable, for our "sense of self" is the "non-self" of mere "being-possible". This conscious awareness that we are not a definable, fixed entity, but simply a continuously changing, uncertain process that could end at any moment can shatter the illusions created by the habitual thoughts, feelings, attitudes and material values that we derive from anonymous public interpretations of existence. So the "breakdown experience" of anxiety is a collapse in the living of our everyday life, rather than a portal to the truth of who we really are, for in order to have *any* identity, our existence must be embedded within a social context, but in the mood of anxiety we no longer feel part of *any* social context since we find ourselves:

> [F]ace to face with the "Nothing" of the possible impossibility of existence ... anticipation reveals to Dasein its lostness in the They-self, and brings it face to face with the possibility of being itself, primarily unsupported by concernful solicitude, but of being itself, rather, in an impassioned *freedom towards death* – a freedom which has been released from the Illusions of the "They", and which is factical, certain of itself, and anxious.
>
> (BT: 310–11, emphasis altered)

The fact that the "They-world" cannot protect us against death makes us realize that we cannot rely on it for our life. Thus the tie between Dasein and its They-world is broken: "anxiety ... takes away from Dasein the possibility of understanding itself, as it falls, in terms of the world and the way things have been publicly interpreted" (BT: 232).

So it would seem that we pay a very high price for our freedom, which we discover only as a result of being cut off from our relations to others and from our normal self-understanding, while confronting our utterly lonely death. And there exists no self-understanding whatsoever, of oneself or the world, that is immune to the powerfully corrosive effects of such anxiety.

In "They-dominated" everydayness, Dasein feels at home in the world, but when anxiety disrupts Dasein's familiarity with things, *being-in*-the-world enters the existential mode of the *not-at-home*-in-the-world. Everything is now stripped of its significance, and life is drained of its meaning. There no longer seems to be any valid reason for doing whatever I am doing and thus I lose interest in the world since it has nothing to offer me; consequently I derive no pleasure from everyday life and lose all motivation to continue with my existence for I no longer feel "at home" in my world. I feel unsettled, alienated and homeless:

In anxiety one feels *"uncanny"* ... As Dasein falls, anxiety brings it back from its absorption in the "world". Everyday familiarity collapses ... Dasein has been individualized, but individualized as being-in-the-world. Being-in enters into the existential "mode" of the "not-at-home". (BT: 233)

We feel alienated not only from the "things" around us, but also from other humans, from our family, friends and colleagues: "The 'world' can offer nothing more, and neither can the Dasein-with of others" (BT: 232).

Heidegger asserts that this sense of homelessness and alienation is more primordial than our normal feeling of familiarity with the world: "the 'not-at-home' must be conceived as the more primordial phenomenon" (BT: 234). It is more primordial than the everyday sense of "feeling at home" in the world, because the latter is built on an *illusion* of security, whereas the "homelessness" of anxiety is rooted in the *reality* of human mortality: the utter insecurity and unpredictability of human existence. Homelessness is thus the basic condition of mankind and, according to Heidegger, it impels us to seek a home: "Falling flight *into* the at-home of publicness is a flight *from* the not-at-home, that is the not-being-at-home (*Unheimlichkeit*) that lies in Dasein as thrown being-in-the-world, delivered over to itself in its being" (*ibid.*).

Heidegger regards this "homelessness of historical man within beings as a whole" (Nii: 394–5/Niv: 248) as the fundamental motivating force behind all mankind's endeavours. It impels man on to "the conquest of the planet Earth and the venture into cosmic space":

Homeless man lets himself be driven – by the success of his enterprise and of his organization of ever greater masses of his own kind – into flight from his own essence, in order to represent this flight as his homecoming to the true humanity of homo humanus and to take charge of it himself. (Nii: 395/Niv: 248)

According to Heidegger's interpretation, Sophocles too alleged that mankind's accomplishments are driven by the feeling of homelessness (*Unheimlichkeit*) (IM: 123ff.), and Heidegger, quoting Novalis, states that philosophy also is inspired by homelessness (GA 39: 7) and "what Novalis calls *homesickness* is the *basic mood of philosophizing*" (FCM: 120). For this sense of not-feeling-at-home-in-the-world, triggered by anxiety, reveals Dasein in its unity and detaches the philosopher from worldly concerns and prejudices, which is essential to genuine philosophical thinking.

When the homelessness of anxiety strips the world of all pre-assigned significance, the world becomes decentred, and includes the remote as well as the nearby – beings as a whole; thus the world is prepared for "true thinking". Thus philosophers must attempt to enter the state of mind of homelessness (*Unheimlichkeit*) because the "liberation of the Dasein in man" depends on this (FCM: 490). In his later thought, Heidegger asserts that the decision to commit one's life to philosophy is not a *choice* made by individual Dasein; rather, it is *Being*, which firmly grips the philosopher and compels him to do its bidding (Niii: 215).

Anxiety can arise suddenly in any situation. For instance, I might be busy at work, or weeding the garden, or travelling home on the train, when suddenly as if from nowhere I am overwhelmed by the suffocating feeling that everything is meaningless and pointless. I may start to wonder "What am I doing here?" or "Why do I bother with all this?" The feeling of security I get from my normal everyday existence, personal relationships and friendships is destroyed in an instant. Life suddenly appears utterly senseless; ambition seems futile and all achievements and all things in existence seem irrelevant and insignificant (BT: 231) as I am confronted with my own mortality and realize that my life is continuously and precariously balancing on the edge of infinite Nothingness. Although it can and often does arise without any warning, the conscious act of contemplating one's mortality can easily trigger this overwhelming sense of insignificance (see HCT: 291). Why, at the age of fifty-three, should I tolerate all the stress and effort involved in writing this extremely complex book on philosophy when I will probably be dead within the next thirty years and forgotten soon after? In the shadow of such thoughts the activities of everyday life seem utterly insignificant because we realize that all our projects are grounded on Nothing.

It is not the experience of dying that is dreaded in the mood of anxiety, but our *being-able-not-to-be*: the fact that our finite form becomes *nothing*. "The 'Nothing' with which anxiety brings us face to face, unveils the nullity by which Dasein, in its very *basis*, is defined; and this basis itself is as thrownness into death" (BT: 356). This strange feeling that one's awareness will be completely and permanently terminated – that one day one will truly cease to be – cannot be compared to any other form of human experience, for all other experiences exist in the continuum of time. Heidegger asserts that only Dasein can experience the mood of genuine anxiety, for animals cannot question their instinctive understanding of the world they inhabit; thus they are more firmly attached to their "home" than humans ever can be. Indeed, he asserts that "World-impoverished" animals have pains, but no moods (GA 39: 82) (a statement that many poodle-owners might strongly dispute).

Anxiety thus can be summarized as a deep crisis of meaning because it makes one feel utterly alienated from everything that seemed worthwhile.

This mood makes existence seem inhospitable; the normally familiar things around me seem strange and unwelcoming. And yet, according to Heidegger, because anxiety challenges and undermines my normal interpretations of existence, it can enable me to experience life at a much deeper, more intense level. If I submit resolutely to what is revealed by anxiety, by accepting the truth of my own mortal Nothingness, I can begin living authentically, accepting and assuming responsibility for my life and my death. Heidegger claimed that this acceptance is essential to human freedom, for it allows us to see the possibility of our freedom mirrored in the realm of possibilities that reveals itself to us when the influence of the They-world is undermined.

Anxiety constantly reminds me that my life is "thrownness toward death". I can now deeply sense the *temporal* nature of my life: that I am a finite being, responsible for making something of my life in the light of my inevitable death. No longer feeling at home in the world, I am forced to focus on my *own* Being, which individualizes me and reveals to me my own possibilities and the fact that my being-in-the-world is rooted in a fundamental attitude of caring about my existence on all levels. I am now confronted with the choice between an authentic or inauthentic approach to existence and I understand in my very bones that my life is my own and that it is always up to me to make something of myself.

So anxiety makes me realize that I can no longer base my sense of who I am on the things that I deal with day to day. It therefore reveals to me the task of choosing who I am, since my social status, career and belongings can no longer define the purpose of my existence. Consequently, I need to decide my purpose and direction by choosing consciously from among the various possible modes of existence available to me (BT: 232, 393). I may now experience a crisis in my life that inspires me to make a radical change of course in my existence.

Alternatively, I might decide that what I am doing at the moment is in fact what I really most want to be doing, but now it has become an "authentic" choice. (However, I could also *escape* – a common response to anxiety – and turn my back on this disturbing experience so that I can get back to my old existence.)

Even if the They-self effectively uses escape strategies to avoid anxiety, there are certain situations familiar to most of us in which anxiety and the freedom it discloses *cannot* be ignored. The majority of people standing at the verge of a tall cliff or roof edge of a tall building and looking over the edge have experienced a perfectly normal instinctive fear of falling. But this is sometimes accompanied by the terrifying impulse to throw oneself intentionally off the edge; this strange feeling simultaneously draws us towards, and repels us from, the edge. What we are experiencing is the dread or anxiety of our complete freedom to choose even such an unpleasant possibility. Not everyone has looked downwards from a high place, but almost everyone has periodically experienced the same sensation of dread in some form or another. Sometimes, and quite commonly, it can express itself in a pathological way: driving along a narrow road, late at night in the pouring rain, furious at an oncoming car's blinding headlights, the thought may dart through one's mind, "*I could* steer right into him". This "*I could*" – my freedom – triggers in me an immense feeling of dread. I am horrified by the immense fragility of my own existence and my unrestricted freedom of choice, which includes my freedom to choose even the most terrifying of options. There is absolutely *nothing* to stop me from driving my car head-on into the other vehicle: nothing but *myself*, my freedom of choice.

It should now be clear that, rather than being something that needs to be cured or avoided, Heidegger clearly views *existential* anxiety (as against *pathological* anxiety, caused by emotional imbalance) as being a valuable part of the human predicament. Similar to the situation whereby great works of art can emerge from an artist's suffering, the overwhelming pain of anxiety potentially can expand our awareness into an authentic, illuminated perception of existence. Escaping our anxiety through the numerous routes offered to us by the They-world is truly a pyrrhic victory, since the path to authenticity is *essentially* "paved with dread".

Care: the primordial condition of Dasein

"I care therefore I am": although Heidegger did not actually say this, it expresses very appropriately the level of importance he attaches to Dasein's most fundamental feature, the most basic characteristic of the human condition (see also Chapter 6, "Heidegger's temporality of care", below). Dasein's Being *is* care, in the sense that it is "care" that makes human existence meaningful and makes a person's life really matter to them, and it is "care" that ultimately directs us to the mystery of Being itself. Thus *what* we care about – our life commitments – determines our direction in life, and the amount of energy we put into our caring defines the intensity with which we live.

Heidegger asserts that *all* the features that constitute Dasein's being-in-the-world in its average everydayness – fallenness (its absorption in the They-world), being-with (its social context), thrownness (its living past), moods and understanding – are "equiprimordial" and inseparable from one another. In other words, no single feature is a derived or secondary addition (BT: 225–6; GA 21: 226). Also, all features are simultaneously present in Dasein's way of Being; no feature can exist without all the others also being present. But Heidegger points out that, since Dasein's fundamental state is care, all these features have their roots in, and are unified by, this primordial condition (BT: 237, 293). In other words, care embodies Dasein as a whole: it is the "constellation" in which Dasein exists, the basic feature in us that underlies and constitutes *all* our experiences and involvements in the world, thus providing us with a sense of existence as an integrated "organic" whole. It is care that potentially provides a cohesive, unifying structure to Dasein's life that is necessary for an authentic, autonomous existence (BT: 365ff.), for during special moments of insight provided by the call of Conscience (see Chapter 4), Dasein as care silently calls out to Dasein as the fallen They-self, alerting this inauthentic mode of Dasein to the indebtedness and responsibility that are part of care itself (BT: 322).

On a purely intuitive level it is easy to accept Heidegger's understanding of care, for there is an undercurrent of care in everything I do: in my interests, responsibilities, passions and disappointments, and especially when I am deeply introspective. In contrast, when a person no longer seems to care at all about their existence during moods of extreme depression, even the will to continue living may disappear.

Care: authentic and inauthentic solicitude and "concern"

> Dasein's basic mode of Being is that in its Being its very Being is at issue. This basic mode of Being is conceived as care (*Sorge*), and this care as Dasein's basic mode of Being is just as originally concern (*Besorgen*), if Dasein is essentially Being-in-the-world, and in the same way this basic mode of Dasein's Being is solicitude (*Fursorge*), so far as Dasein is Being-with-one-another.   (GA 21: 225)

Heidegger explains that our manner of caring varies, depending on the situation facing us. Our basic mode of *caring* is characterized by an attitude of worry or anxiety arising out of apprehension concerning our *own* Being and our *own* future possibilities. Towards other people (being-with-one-another), however, care takes the form of solicitude: taking care of, or providing for, the welfare of those in need of help (BT: 158). There are three modes of solicitude: the default mode is "indifference", simply passing others by. In this mode of indifference, the being-there of others is simply ignored or neglected. The other two modes are "inauthentic solicitude" and "authentic solicitude".

Heidegger describes inauthentic solicitude as the type of concern that "leaps in" for the other but is characterized by a form of domination (BT: 158) because the manner of helping reduces others to dependency. In "leaping in", we encourage the other to give up their struggle and we take over that which is their responsibility. Thus, although we appear to be helping them, in fact we are enslaving them by making them dependent on us. Heidegger asserts that this mode of helping another fails to recognize the other person's existential project and thus one is treating them like a "thing" or a "what".

In contrast to this, authentic solicitude assists others in a manner that helps them to take responsibility for their own life, to stand on their own two feet and take care of themselves (GA 21: 223; BT: 159). Heidegger describes this as a "leaping ahead" of the other in a way that frees the other to face their Being, thereby clearing the path for them to assume the burden of their own existence. Instead of taking over another's task for them, one enables them to do it on their own. In so doing, one is acknowledging the other's unique existential project.

During the practical activities of our job and daily life, in our use of machines, computers, tools or any other objects employed to achieve our aims, care becomes *concern* (*Besorgen*), in the sense of "attending to" or "taking care of" the way we handle things that are ready-to-hand ("equipment") and its focus is fundamentally on the present (BT: 83–4, 237). Heidegger explains that when he uses the term "care" this simultaneously includes the meanings *concern* and *solicitude*; in other words, "care" refers to "concerned-solicitous care", which means "that in this concern and solicitude the caring being is itself at issue" (GA 21: 225). He points out that, even when Dasein is neglectful of others, or unconcerned or uncaring in his actions, "care" is *still* active, but in a "deficient mode" (BT: 83).

However, the aspect of Dasein's way of being-in-the-world that it most *cares* about is the fact that it is *alive*. When Dasein faces, during the identity crisis of deep anxiety, the inescapable fact that it may die at any time, it begins to *care* about its way of living in a far more intense and profound way. Care makes Dasein a unified, autonomous self (BT: 366ff.). It now enters an authentic mode of existence, where what it *cares* about most of all is the fact that it is a being-towards-death: "as regards its ontological possibility, dying is grounded in care" (BT: 296). "As care Dasein *is* the 'Between' (birth and death)" (BT: 427).

Although in *Being and Time* "care" appears to apply specifically to Dasein's way of Being, later on Heidegger asserts that care is "solely 'for the sake of beyng', not the beyng of man, but the beyng of beings as a whole" (GA 65: 16). Mankind's role, on the basis of "Dasein-care", is now: (i) the seeker of Beyng (event); (ii) the true preserver of the truth of being; (iii) the guardian of the quiet of the passing of the last god (GA 65: 294; cf. 240). So Being has become central and Heidegger's mode of thinking more historical and visionary, for man is now required to: (i) found a "world" or culture; (ii) preserve this world; and (iii) oversee its decline with dignity.

CHAPTER FOUR

Conscience, guilt and authenticity

A central Heideggerian claim is that conscience and guilt are fundamentally important human existentials because they reveal our authentic self-hood and the basis of freedom. The voice of conscience calls us to focus directly on our authentic self.

Conscience

Heidegger ignores traditional ethical or religious views of conscience and guilt, and instead offers a fundamental, existential interpretation that sheds further light on our way of Being. He emphasizes that not everyone has a "conscience" (lower-case "c"), in terms of our conventional understanding of the word, but everyone has a "Conscience" (capital "C") in the more fundamental, existential sense. This fundamental Conscience – unlike conscience in the traditional sense – does *not* have an inner voice that judges, commands, forbids, condemns or excuses actions on moral grounds. Heidegger regards the moral judgements of traditional conscience as relatively superficial (BT: 328–9, 332, 334), and his "existential" Conscience is stripped bare of all such ethical content. He claims that only when we respond to the special moments of insight offered by our Conscience can we develop the authentic understanding necessary for a genuine "conscience" (in the traditional sense). Like "traditional" conscience, Heidegger's fundamental Conscience also involves a division of Dasein into a caller and a called, and his enquiry is rooted in how this "call" of Conscience focuses on and highlights the conflict between Dasein's two contrasting ways of Being:

- The They-self in which Dasein is absorbed in the present, preoccupied with the worldly concerns of everyday reality, where the choices it makes, the way it thinks and all of its behaviour is under the influence of the They; and

- the "homeless" self, which has been thrown naked into a bare, meaningless world – the source of Conscience.

Under the influence of the "homeless" self, Dasein experiences a sense of anxiety or dread, which arises from the awareness that it has been *thrown* naked into a seemingly insignificant existence that is constantly haunted by the spectre of death. Thus it has lost any comforting feeling of belonging with the crowd and feels instead like "a stranger in a strange world". Homeless Dasein's anxiety, however, usually causes it to "flee" from itself to live within the tranquillized familiarity of "everydayness" that comforts us, by perpetually distracting us from the significance of our mortality and by reassuringly providing us with the sense that we are "all in this together". But "homeless" Dasein also functions as our primordial, ontological Conscience, which silently calls out to the They-self: "The call of conscience has the character of an *appeal* to Dasein by calling it to its ownmost potentiality-for-being-its-Self; and this is done by way of *summoning* it to its ownmost Being-guilty" (BT: 314). "The call reaches Dasein in this everyday-averagely concernful always-already-understanding-itself" (BT: 317), and it summons this "fallen" inauthentic self to turn away from the influence and restricted possibilities of the They and to contemplate instead its *own* possibilities and, from among these, to make its own resolute choices in life, in the light of its own mortality, for death gives Dasein a "freedom which has been released from the illusions of the 'They'" (BT: 311). However, before Dasein can *make* resolute choices, it has to choose to do so, and it is to this initial choice (which *frees* Dasein from the They to make resolute choices) that Conscience is calling Dasein.

Since Dasein's existence in the They-world is a "fleeing of Dasein in the face of itself – of itself as an authentic potentiality-for-being-its-Self" (BT: 229), it always has a residual awareness, if only subliminally, of what it is fleeing from. So it is never *completely* and irreversibly lost in the They. It is the They-self's background awareness of its potential for authenticity that motivates the primordial Conscience to call out, and which allows the They-self potentially to respond. The requirement for "hearing" the call of Conscience is that one must *want* to have a Conscience and one must *listen in silence*, since, if we are to perceive the call to authentic existence, we must be quiet enough to hear it (BT: 318, 342–3). What we then hear is the *ontological disclosure* of the possibility of authentic Being. To understand the call of Conscience is to perceive that one is not-at-home in the world and this realization is disclosed by the mood of anxiety. Thus "wanting to have a conscience" also indicates "a readiness for the mood of anxiety" (BT: 342).

The call of Conscience appeals to fallen Dasein to become an individualized authentic self by summoning Dasein to face up to its own *primordial* guilt (BT: 314). If Dasein were *not* guilty, this Conscience would be of no significance. According to Heidegger, Conscience may call out to us at *any* moment, but not everyone responds to this call and no one responds all the time. Often when our Conscience reminds us of our potential for authenticity we prefer to turn away from this awareness to escape the responsibility of authentic Being. Yet the call of Conscience is always hovering at the periphery of our awareness, destined to return on other occasions when perhaps we shall choose to respond to its appeal.

Guilt

Generally speaking, when individuals feel guilty they become aware of themselves as beings who can be held responsible; that is, they *are* guilty. At this point, they can try to escape or deny feelings of guilt by blaming it on external causes. Alternatively, they may choose to admit their guilt and thus also their responsibility. According to Heidegger, if Dasein decides to *avoid* the significance of its existential guilt, it is simultaneously avoiding awareness of its authentic self and, in doing so, it becomes an inauthentic self: a non-self. By admitting its existential guilt and responsibility, Dasein demonstrates that it wants to have a conscience and that it wants to own up to its guilt if it *is* guilty, and this willingness to do so is the basis for authenticity. Conversely, to deny one's guilt – one's existential, primordial guilt – is to ignore the call of Conscience, and this is the basis of inauthenticity.

The "guilt" Heidegger is interested in has nothing to do with our normal understanding and use of the word, which is connected with ethics and morals that assert we are guilty, either of doing something that we should not have done, or of not doing something that we should have done. In this ordinary sense, I can *become* guilty only in the sense that by breaching a moral requirement I incur guilt. Instead, Heidegger is referring to an ontological guilt, which is an intrinsic part of my Being as Dasein. This guilt is prior to, and the foundation of, ethics and morals, which presuppose or emerge from an understanding of this guilt rather than the other way round: "This essential being-guilty ... the existential condition for the possibility ... for morality in general and for the possible forms which this may take factically. Primordial 'Being-guilty' cannot be defined by morality, since morality already presupposes it" (BT: 332). It is also distinct from the theological concept of original sin, but, like the latter, it is "primordial".

Heidegger's "authentic", ontological guilt refers to a non-specific, unconditional, existential guilt that is a primordial part of our essential way of Being as "care": "entities whose Being is care … *are* guilty in the very basis of their Being" (BT: 332). This "primordial existential meaning" (BT: 326) of my guilt can be deduced "from the fact that this 'guilty' turns up as a predicate for the 'I am'" (*ibid.*). If the "guilty" is to be taken as the predicate of the mere "I am", it is due to the fact that my very existence is found to make me guilty; otherwise I would be proclaimed guilty "*of something*". But the call of Conscience informs me that I am guilty in the very basis of my Being. Thus the very fact of my existence automatically makes me guilty. Hubert Dreyfus summarizes this:

> Existential guilt reveals not inauthentic Dasein's moral lapses, or its essential failure to choose; it reveals an essentially unsatisfactory structure definitive of even authentic Dasein. Even if Dasein has done nothing wrong there is something wrong with Dasein – its Being is not under its own power. (1991: 306)

So Heidegger asserts that every Dasein is *always essentially guilty*, but Dasein, when in the mode of the They-self, flees from and lives in forgetfulness or denial of this essential guilt. In the authentic mode of Being, however, Dasein realizes its guilt and bases its actions on a full awareness of it.

According to Heidegger, Dasein's guilt is "Being-the-basis of a nullity" (BT: 329). In other words, Dasein is existentially guilty because its very Being is built on "*not*-ness", in that, as Dasein, my guilt is inherent in the structure of "care", which embraces both past and future dimensions of my Being. I am guilty of having a *past* based on "not-ness" owing to my thrownness, thus "Dasein is not itself the basis of its Being" (BT: 330); in other words, ultimately I have *no possibilities that are truly my own*. For this past has to serve as the basis for my existence, but I cannot control it (BT: 329–30), since I am *not* responsible for my entry into the world, nor the circumstances into which I was born. I cannot change what I have been until now. What I become will always, in some way, be based on my past. I also bear existential guilt because on the basis of my past I have to choose possibilities for my *future*, but I have no rules and no intrinsic nature to guide me, as in essence I consist of pure, naked, "homeless" possibility that is "rooted" in the void of "not-ness": the Nothingness of my *finitude*, "The 'Nothing' with which anxiety brings us face to face, unveils the nullity by which Dasein, in its very *basis*, is defined; and this basis itself is as thrownness into death" (BT: 356).

In addition I choose possibilities for my future that are *not* other possibilities (BT: 331). I am fundamentally responsible for the choices I make that determine who I am. Each time I choose one possibility I also choose to *ignore* other possibilities, so I am always actualizing one possible self at the expense of many others, perhaps equally worthwhile. Our guilty indebtedness to these other possible selves is thus a fundamental structural feature of existence. It reveals my ontological *finitude*: the fact that I can never be all that I could be.

Authentic choices will often be swimming against the current of expectations from the They. All choices I make have unforeseen consequences for which I am nonetheless ultimately responsible. Most importantly, when I choose my fundamental way of Being for my whole life, I cannot justify this particular choice rather than another equally relevant choice. In other words, choosing or preferring one particular way of life entails the rejection of all the other equally valid available choices.

In everyday existence Dasein is absorbed in the demands of the They-self and the only guilt it understands is that which arises from its failure to follow rules and satisfy public norms (BT: 334). Only authentic Dasein realizes its essential guilt and acts in full awareness of it. So when Conscience calls us, it is asking us to acknowledge and take responsibility for this essential, ontological guilt and to make our actions our *own*. By doing this we can exist authentically. Dasein's guilt is uniquely its own, because Dasein is free to accept or reject its possibilities. Like facing death, this acceptance of guilt requires confronting the truth of our own fragile existence, acknowledging the guilt that our existence is "as an entity which has to be as it is and as it can be" (BT: 321).

Authenticity

Heidegger describes two fundamentally different ways of Being in which Dasein can understand and live its life: *authentically* and *inauthentically* (BT: 312). The authentic way allows for a far deeper experience of the significance of existence. Heidegger's discussion of these two modes is central to his enquiry into Dasein's way of being-in-the-world. These terms allow him to differentiate between the ways in which the meaning of our existence is revealed to us, or concealed from us. His aim is not to preach morals but to help provide insights that shed light on the question of Being.

Authenticity refers to a mode of existence in which I become aware of my *own* self and *own* possibilities, and "choose to choose" my *own* way of life: to *be* myself (BT: 313–14). In direct contrast to this, when I am inauthentic, I am not aware of my own self or my own possibilities , so instead of taking responsibility for my own life, I live in the way that others think I should because the They has "disburdened" me of my responsibility to my own self.

This distinction is applicable to every possible way in which I exist. For example, if I think "authentically", I can learn something truthful about the meaning of my existence, but not if I think "inauthentically". Heidegger makes it clear, however, that becoming an authentic being is *not* a return to an "original self" that I *used* to be, since the inauthentic They-self has been my identity from the beginning. Instead, the process involves a struggle to win my freedom from the all-pervasive domination of the They-self, and what is left will be my authentic self, experienced perhaps for the first time.

So to be authentic is to be true to my own self, to be my own person, to "do my own thing", regardless of the opinion of the They. But Heidegger points out that even *"Authentic Being-one's-Self is ... an existentiell modification of the 'they' – of the 'they' as an essential existentiale"* (BT: 167). So the They is a basic structure of Dasein's Being because it belongs to Dasein's ontological constitution. For *all* human possibilities, as well as the language used to conceptualize these possibilities, are derived from the They. Indeed, even the most authentically original musical composition, painting or personal choice for one's existence is still, in some way, rooted in and dependent on the particular variety of possibilities opened up to us by our heritage and culture.

Thus Dasein's existence is always inseparable from the wider context of the public world it inhabits and shares with others. Living authentically is not an escape from our world (BT: 318, 344); instead it is an involvement that arises from a deeper, more authentic understanding of life, which enables and inspires us to make clear-sighted, determined choices from among the possibilities made available to us by our culture. Hence Heidegger asserts that authenticity:

> is so far from extricating itself from the way of interpreting Dasein which has come down to us (from the "They"), that in each case it is in terms of this interpretation, against it, and yet again for it, that any possibility one has chosen is seized upon in one's resolution. (BT: 435)

However, the most fundamental characteristic of authenticity is the awareness of one's own possibilities in the light of the finite nature of existence: mortality. Thus authentic Dasein is snatched "back from the endless multiplicity of possibilities which offer themselves as closest to one" (BT: 435), and instead focuses on a range of possibilities, "which are determined by the *end* and so are understood as *finite*" (BT: 308).

This authentic outlook can arise out of the mood of anxiety, which can help me to recognize the unique wholeness of my Being. In this mood a deep awareness of my own mortality leads me to the realization that I am at all times a being-towards-death. I now understand that I (and not the They) am responsible for my own death, which means ultimately that I also must be responsible for my own life. I now *care* authentically about my existence. Heidegger emphasizes that this authentic life is not about detachment, changing the content of my world or breaking contact with others to form new relationships (BT: 344). My authentic choices may, or may not, result in an alteration of the actual content of my life, for the only pertinent matter here becomes the fact that I am now exercising freedom of choice. Whatever I choose to do with my life – even if this is exactly what I have been doing up until now – is my own free choice uninfluenced by the expectations of others. So the *form* of my life (living as a being-towards-death rather than as the They-self) is changed, while the actual content – my particular world and life – in a sense becomes irrelevant.

However, Heidegger repeatedly affirms that there is no way to live permanently in authenticity, since we have to take the everyday world and our daily routines for granted for them to run smoothly. Further, since my personal interpretations of life are *always* filtered through the They, my understanding of existence can never be created completely anew. But although I shall remain under the influence of the They in certain ways – especially in daily practical concerns – and limited by, and dependent on, the range of available possibilities offered by my world, I nevertheless have freedom *within* this context to make my own choices, as I no longer take the familiar expectations of the They as "the only game in town".

Dreyfus offers the following interesting observation:

> [O]ne can think of the transformation from inauthentic to authentic existence as a gestalt switch. Fleeing is inauthentic Dasein's response to its sense of its unsettled way of being. Its double nullity, experienced as something terribly wrong with it, shows up as a constant threat to its security – a threat that it cannot face. But this same nullity and the anxiety that reveals it could equally well reveal Dasein and its world as an exciting manifestation of Dasein's finitude. Death and guilt would then show up not as a threat or as something wrong with Dasein, but simply as revelations of the essential structure of Dasein's way of being. If Dasein accepted its nullity, the same structure that seemed to threaten all its secure projects and its very identity would be seen to be challenging and liberating. Anxiety then would not be paralyzing like fear but would make Dasein clear-sighted and fearless.   (1991: 317)

Heidegger calls this transformation "resoluteness" (BT: 318), which he regards as the fundamental mindset, and essential and key feature, of authenticity, and he asserts that we become resolute when we own up to our ontological guilt. The resolute person *knows* they are guilty, and they *want* to have a Conscience. In other words, when Dasein truly understands the nature of its Conscience and its guilt, it becomes resolute. The accusation of guilt understood in this "primordial ontological meaning" is addressed to Dasein in so far as it fails to respond to the task of shaping its life within a thrownness that it can and never will master and control. Heidegger asserts that, when you assume this authentic responsibility for your entire life, choosing to live as a being-towards-death, exhibiting care towards your world, that you can "become what you are" (BT: 186; cf. IM: 101). He associates resoluteness as an "opening up" of oneself to the truth of one's *own being-in-the-world*. Resoluteness is "the *specifically* undertaken self-opening of Dasein *for* the open" (DT: 81). Being resolute is not characterized by calculation in the form of weighing alternatives in order to make a specific choice. Nor does it require speculating in advance what action (if any) will be taken in a given situation. "Resoluteness brings the self right into its current concernful being-amidst what is available, and pushes it into solicitous being with others" (BT: 344). Thus, resolute Dasein, being totally immersed in the moment, can see clearly the range of authentic possibilities available to it, and simultaneously there is an understanding of what action, if any, is required by the circumstances (facticity) of that situation:

> On what is it to resolve? *Only* the resolution itself can give the answer ... *The resolution is precisely the disclosive projection and determination of what is factically possible at the time* ... Resoluteness "exists" only as a resolution which understandingly projects itself. (BT: 345)

Being resolute, I now take over my life circumstances with a decisive dedication to what I experience as being the demands of my life situation, and my attitude towards the future is that of "anticipation" or "forward directedness". My existence is now focused by authentic future-directedness that is rooted in a constant sense of my mortality. This inspires me to view my past – and to assume responsibility for my past – as a latent resource of possibilities that can be accessed and brought to realization through my present actions to accomplish my future objectives. This narrative-like continuity of authentic existence is a fundamental key to achieving a sense of personal identity, which Heidegger describes as a "constancy of the self", which is characterized by a "steadfastness" and "steadiness" that can span the entirety of one's life. This is the only sort of constancy we can achieve (BT: 369), since, according to Heidegger, we do not possess an underlying, enduring soul or self because this would entail a present-at-hand essence in

Dasein's Being, when in fact the essence of Dasein's Being lies in its mode of existence. The tendency to believe in an unchanging thing-like self arises from our state of "falling", which causes us to treat ourselves as if we had the same sort of Being as the entities we encounter in our world (BT: 368).

Heidegger does not discuss whether or not resolute actions can be wrong. There are no rules by which we can decide for ourselves or for others what has to be done. There are no objectively correct answers to life's basic problems and there are no objective criteria that he offers for determining the rightness or wrongness of a course of action. Heidegger provides no such guidelines, because he asserts that this "would deny to existence nothing less than the very *possibility of taking action*" (BT: 340), since rules and regulations, in his opinion, have no authority for "a free existing". We can look instead at "the repeatable possibilities of existence" (BT: 443) and perhaps find inspiration from the lives of heroes or role models, past and present. But the attempt to search for, or advocate, some particular mode or possibility of existence as *the* universal purpose of existence is, Heidegger asserts, "*the* misunderstanding of human existence in general" (MFL: 185).

Ultimately, the best one can do, while engaged in resolute action, is to maintain a clear perspective of the totality of one's whole life and heritage and the certainty of one's death. And there is no remedy for the fact that our resolute actions, which seem to be appropriate now, may turn out to have negative consequences.

Further, for Heidegger, resoluteness is *not* morally superior to irresoluteness, and resolute individuals do not necessarily behave in a benevolent manner to others. Mahatma Gandhi was resolute, but so was Joseph Stalin. Also, although authenticity requires resoluteness, this does not mean that a resolute person will be authentic. The "virtue" of resoluteness as a way of Being is that it enables one potentially to become aware of one's own possibilities and wholeness. However, Heidegger points out that even resolute Dasein needs to guard against a constant tendency to drift back into irresoluteness (BT: 345).

Indeed, Heidegger claims that most of us are irresolute most of the time. When irresolute Dasein has a job to do, it concentrates on that without questioning whether what it is doing is a fitting way to spend one's life. Lost in the They-self, it ignores the range of its future possibilities, because it is completely absorbed in the present or the immediate past and future and thus it forgets itself as an autonomous entity and interprets itself instead in terms of its current preoccupations: "One is what one does ... One is a shoemaker, a tailor, a teacher, a banker" (GA 20: 336).

In contrast, if Dasein is resolute it surveys and takes into account its entire life by traversing the totality of its past, present and future, which enhances resolute Dasein's perception of its available possibilities.

Heidegger explains that resolute Dasein, in a moment of vision, "makes the situation authentically present". This moment of vision, which *is* "authentic presence", embraces both the future and the past, thereby providing the coherence, continuity and *"constancy* of the self" that gives Dasein "time *for* what the situation demands", enabling it to understand what is genuinely at stake (BT: 463). Heidegger explains that authentic Dasein "runs ahead" into the future to experience the impact of the inevitability of its own death and then "backwards" beyond its birth to assess its own individual and historical past. So it knows that its normal everyday existence, into which it has been thrown, is only one possible set of circumstances among many, for its life is rooted in the larger drama of our shared cultural history, and its possibilities therefore arise not only from its personal past, but also from the "wellsprings" of a "heritage" from previous generations. Authentic Dasein thus relates to the future in terms of the possibilities it makes available, and *anticipates* the future by going towards it. By contrast, inauthentic Dasein relates to the future merely by waiting to see the success or failure of the current activity or situation: the possible future outcome of events and affairs of everyday projects. In other words, it *waits* for the future to come towards it.

To sum up, the authentic perspective provided by my death-awareness snatches me out of the grip of the They-self, and frees me from all such comfortable but shallow inauthentic possibilities, thereby significantly expanding the horizon of possibilities available to me, because in escaping the limited options for existence offered by the They, I can see clearly now the potentials of my *own* unique situation and thus resolutely choose to follow my *own* path. My authentic understanding is characterized by a lucid self-awareness of my cultural, historical and social being-in-the-world, so I am fully aware of, and accept, that I am subject to the following fundamental limitations:

- the life I create is founded on my "facticity" – who I already am (the entirety of my current circumstances, personality and potentials, etc., which in turn determine my future possibilities);
- any life I choose simultaneously excludes numerous other possible lives I could have chosen; and
- death is my constant companion and may terminate my existence at any moment.

My existence has now become *individualized* because all my actions arise from a full recognition of these basic limitations. I no longer blame anyone else for what happens since I have taken full responsibility for my life, and my stance towards the future is one of clear-sighted anticipation based on a total commitment to the fundamental direction I have *freely* embarked on. This way of living lends a sense of cohesiveness and integrity to my existence, and my reactions to positive and negative occurrences tend to be toned down because both are seen in the light of the ever-present possibility of my own permanent extinction. This helps me maintain emotional equilibrium in tragedy, and keeps my feet on the ground when faced with seemingly "good" news.

In all areas, winning and losing now matter much less to me, so if I am obliged to change direction, leaving behind a path I currently enjoy, I accept this with equanimity, and clearly see the unique possibilities that are available to me in the new circumstances in which I find myself. I recognize the fragility of long-term commitments, and thus remain flexible and open to change. Dasein:

> simply cannot *become rigid* as regards the Situation, but must understand that the resolution, in accordance with its own meaning as a disclosure, must be *held open* and free for the current factical possibility. The certainty of the resolution signifies that one *holds oneself free for* the possibility of *taking it back*. (BT: 355)

Knowing, therefore, that circumstances may force me to alter my decisions and change direction, I keep renewing my commitments; Dasein "resolves to keep repeating itself" (*ibid.*). But since I no longer invest my sense of identity in, nor attribute ultimate significance to, *any* project, I can be fully engaged with something and yet effortlessly and painlessly cease the activity when it is no longer appropriate. "Resoluteness is freedom to give up some definite resolution, and to give it up in accordance with the demands of some possible Situation or other. The steadiness of existence is not interrupted thereby but confirmed" (BT: 443). Realizing that all projects ultimately are equally meaningless and meaningful makes it easy to accept whatever unique possibilities for action arise from my changing circumstances.

In his later writings Heidegger's conception of authenticity undergoes some significant alterations. He tends now to use a language of receptivity in which he urges us to cease imposing our will on beings. Instead, he stresses that we need to begin listening to and obeying the voice of Being. He now emphasizes a much less "voluntary", "will-full", subjectivist dimension to the essential precondition of authenticity than he does in *Being and Time*; it is closer to the *literal* meaning of resoluteness, *Entschlossenheit*, in the sense of "being unlocked", of "being open". Authenticity is now conceived of as *Gelassenheit*, which in Heidegger's usage is perhaps best translated as "releasement": a releasement from will. The root of the word

"*Gelassenheit*" is *lassen*, "letting", "allowing", and it is a conception that becomes more and more central in Heidegger's later works. In everyday German the word suggests a state in which one is free from strong and turbulent emotions, for it conveys a sense of "calm composure"; a *gelassener Typ* can be translated as "a laid-back or cool character". For Heidegger, *Gelassenheit* refers to, and encapsulates, the proper attitude and fundamental attunement that we should have towards beings and Being (DT: 58–90).

Heidegger adopted the term from Meister Eckhart, the fourteenth-century German mystic and theologian. This term, which was of key importance to Eckhart and later mystics and theologians, was used to describe the state of divine peace stemming from a complete absence of self-will combined with total detachment from the world, arising from a deep experience of "letting go" and "letting be", the result in Christian terms being total submission to the "Will of God". Heidegger's understanding of this state of consciousness, however, excludes all such theological connotations (DT: 62).

Heidegger uses the term *Gelassenheit* to describe a state of consciousness that closely resembles the Taoist condition of *wu wei*, which refers to the state of awareness in which one has "released" or let go of all "conscious willing" in favour of a "let it be" attitude that is open and attuned to nature and the "voice" of Being.

For Heidegger, the "releasement" of *Gelassenheit* is neither active *nor* passive, for it has nothing to do with consciously "willing" anything and it is certainly not merely a passive "doing nothing". Heidegger explains, "Releasement lies – if we may use the word lie – beyond the distinction between activity and passivity … because releasement does *not* belong to the domain of the will" (DT: 61).

Instead, Heidegger characterizes *Gelassenheit* as a kind of waiting (DT: 62). This "waiting" is qualitatively very different from the usual kind of human waiting, in that it has no concrete objective; in other words, Heidegger is not speaking of the type of waiting that has an object of any sort, the state of "waiting *for*", which expects or hopes for something in particular to arrive or happen in the future. Instead, he is referring to a waiting, without any expectation, for the "openness" that Heidegger now calls the "regioning" (DT: 66, 74), which is equivalent – in Heidegger's sense of the word – to "truth" (DT: 83–4).

So *Gelassenheit* is a totally alert "openness" that is free from all expectations, and yet this state cannot be described as a *passive* waiting because the awareness is intensely and fully alert, entirely immersed in the moment, in a state of wide-open, non-excluding presence that is utterly receptive to the "regioning" of truth. There exists no possible explanation regarding what one is doing or should do to achieve Heidegger's state of *Gelassenheit*, for it is a state of Being in which one has ceased doing all the things one constantly does.

For Heidegger, the human will is the most insidious constituent of metaphysics since it cannot just "let beings be", and this ultimately leads to the "will to will", or technology. *Gelassenheit*, in "letting a world world" (GA 65: 391), can serve to provide a potential remedy or counter-force to *Gestell*, the essence of technology. "Perhaps a higher acting", he writes, "is concealed in releasement than is found in all the actions within the world and in the machinations of all mankind" (DT: 61).

But how is one to achieve this state of "releasement", which is free from willing, when, as Heidegger points out, most forms of *negating* or "refusing" willing are simply other forms or variations of the "will" (GA 77: 76–8)? In answer to this, Heidegger offers the following explanation of "non-willing":

> Non-willing still signifies, on the one hand, a willing, in that a No prevails in it, even if it is in the sense of a No that directs itself at willing itself and renounces it. Non-willing in this sense means: to will-fully renounce willing. And then, on the other hand, the expression non-willing also means: that which does not at all pertain to will.　　(GA 77: 106; Davis 2010c: 176; see DT: 59)

Heidegger suggests that this "willing non-willing" results only in a preliminary stage of *Gelassenheit*, characterized by "being-released" (*Los-Gelassenheit*) from the will, but this is *not* its most proper sense because the state of "non-willing" is rooted in a "negation of willing" (GA 77: 121). However, this initial stage acts as a catalyst that naturally releases us into the authentic or fully realized state of *Gelassenheit*, defined by a non-willing that "remains absolutely outside any kind of will" (DT: 59).

Thus the question of what we are "doing" in *Gelassenheit* if we are, as Heidegger claims, not in fact "willing" anything and yet simultaneously *not* in a state of passive inactivity, leads Heidegger to describe *Gelassenheit* as a release of oneself from thinking in the sense of re-presentation, and so a "relinquishing" of the "willing of a horizon". This type of relinquishing is a "letting-go" that is free from all conscious willing, but the actual moment of releasing oneself to belonging to that which "regions" – the openness of the truth of Being – requires what might be described as a subliminal trace of "willing". This trace, however, dissolves during the process of releasing oneself, and in the state of complete releasement is utterly extinguished (DT: 79–80).

Those familiar with the practice of meditation should intuitively understand what Heidegger is trying to convey here: "trying" to meditate tends to have the opposite effect. Similarly, a person cannot *will* "not to will", which is why the state of "letting-go" and the state of "enlightenment" cannot be reached simply by *trying* or consciously *willing* it. And yet such conditions do not arrive *automatically*, without any help from us whatsoever. Inevitably, there is always at least a subliminal trace of "willing" that acts to catalyse the initial stage in the process of release that leads to states such as meditative enlightenment or Heidegger's condition of *Gelassenheit*; but, as mentioned earlier, this "willing" is "dissolved" in the process.

So, according to Heidegger, Dasein's freedom lies in being attuned to Being and the presence of beings in this state of *Gelassenheit*, which simply "lets Beings be" (BT: 117, 405; "On the Essence of Truth", in BW: 125). Letting beings be means "allowing beings to be", which means allowing "presencing": *allowing-presence*. This allowing of presence is the "presence of allowing": *Gelassenheit*. "Freedom, understood as letting beings be, is the fulfilment and consummation of the essence of truth in the sense of the disclosure of beings" (*ibid.*: 127).

Also, in Heidegger's understanding and usage of the expression, *letting beings be* is an option available only to Dasein; other entities, such as inanimate objects and animals, can let things be only in the sense of leaving them alone, unaltered, unaffected. What Heidegger means is that only human beings can allow other beings to show themselves as they really are in their intrinsic Beingness. For example, I can let a river *be*. In other words, I can let the true nature of the river reveal itself to me by attuning myself to the myriad of sounds and movement of the river's water: its swirling, rippling, splashing and flowing. According to Heidegger, "to let be is to engage oneself with beings" (*ibid.*: 125–7), which means being attentively involved with other entities in a manner that allows their Being to be disclosed to me. If I want the river to reveal to me its Being, its true nature, I cannot just gaze at it with passive indifference; I have to care sufficiently about it for it to make a real difference to me, so that I truly become aware of it in my own deepest Being.

CHAPTER FIVE

Being-towards-death

At the end of his life, in the moments prior to fulfilling his sentence of death by poison, Socrates contemplates, in deep serenity, the relation of truth and death: "The one aim of those who practice philosophy in the proper manner is to practice for dying and death" (Plato, *Phd.* 64a). Imagine a scenario where *you* are lying on your death-bed, reviewing your entire life. How would you evaluate your current existence? If you could travel back in time to this present moment, with your "death-bed" perspective, would you make any major changes to the way you currently live? Questions such as this, if contemplated deeply enough, potentially can catalyse a dramatic shift in consciousness, for when we have a truly deep awareness of our own mortality, our petty worries and strivings tend to fall away as naturally as leaves from autumn trees.

In Heidegger's view, it is the encounter with death that most profoundly highlights the question of Being. "Only humanity 'has' the distinction of standing and facing death, because the human being is earnest about Being (*Seyn*): death is the supreme testimony to Being (*Seyn*)" (GA 65: 230). "Death opens up the question of Being" (GA 65: 284). Thus Heidegger's detailed examination of human mortality was motivated by the question: what can death tell us about the fundamental meaning of Being?

Death was a central theme of Heidegger's thought throughout his entire philosophical career. The immense popularity of *Being and Time* owed much to his emphasis that "preparedness for death" is a fundamental key to authentic existence – that the disclosure of authentic Being only occurs when Dasein confronts its own finitude by resolutely accepting that it is always, and inescapably, on a journey towards its own death. In his later writings, inspired by the poetry of Hölderlin (see Chapter 8), Heidegger views "death" – in the sense of the *mortality* of humans – as one of the pillars of his poetic vision of Being: the unified interplay of the "fourfold" of earth, sky, gods and mortals (PLT: 179). Further, in a lecture in 1961, when

Heidegger asked rhetorically *where* we should go to reflect most effectively on the mystery of our origin, his answer was, to the graveyard, "God's acre". His unusually direct approach to the subject of death, as compared to most other philosophers, did not imply any romantic morbidity on Heidegger's part but rather his constantly reawakened awareness of his own mortality.

The semantics of death

When Heidegger discusses death he is not referring to our "demise", the state of being dead when all our body functions have come to a permanent end (BT: 291). Instead he asserts:

> Let the term "dying" stand for that *way of being* in which Dasein *is towards* its death ... when Dasein dies – and even when it dies authentically – it does not have to do so with an Experience of its factical demising, or in such an Experience.   (BT: 291)

> Dying is not an event; it is a phenomenon to be understood existentially.   (BT: 284)

So what matters to Heidegger is not one's physical death, but the attitude one has towards one's mortality.

So when reading his analyses on the subject of death it is helpful to think of the term "mortality" instead of "death", since the former, unlike the latter, is not a one-off occurrence, but an intrinsic and continual condition of human existence: "Dasein is dying ... constantly, as long as it has not yet come to its demise" (BT: 303). Indeed, in some of his later writings (see "Building Dwelling Thinking" and "The Thing" in *Poetry Language and Thought*) Heidegger chooses to call us "mortals". Thus Dasein's possibilities are always overshadowed and limited by "the possibility of no-longer-being-able-to-be-there ... *as the possibility of the impossibility of any existence at all*" (BT: 294, 307) and this is what Heidegger means by "death".

Why Heidegger's animals do not die

Heidegger thus describes Dasein as a "being-towards-death": "Factical Dasein exists as born; and, as born, it is already dying, in the sense of Being towards death" (BT: 426). He further asserts that only humans can "die" in the fullest sense, through consciously choosing to face up to the fact of their own mortality. But Heidegger also adds:

> Dasein too "has" its death, of the kind appropriate to anything that lives; and it has it not in ontical isolation, but as codetermined by its primordial kind of Being. In so far as this is the case, Dasein too can end without authentically dying, though on the other hand, *qua* Dasein, it does not simply perish. We designate this intermediate phenomenon as its "*demise*". (BT: 291)

In contrast, Heidegger clearly implies that animals and plants only "perish":

> *Dasein*'s going-out-of-the-world in the sense of dying must be distinguished from the going-out-of-the-world of that which merely has life. In our terminology the ending of anything that is alive, is denoted as "perishing". We can see the difference only if the kind of ending which Dasein can have is distinguished from the end of a life. (BT: 284)

Before proceeding further with an analysis of death as it pertains to Dasein, we shall briefly look at *why* Heidegger holds the belief that animals only "perish", since although this question is hardly mentioned in introductions to Heidegger, it seems especially relevant in today's philosophical climate, given Tom Regan's observation that in the past twenty-five years, "Oxbridge-style analytic moral philosophers ... have written more on 'the animal question' than philosophers of whatever stripe had written in the previous two thousand" (1999: xi–xiii). There is insufficient space here to do justice to this subject, thus my intention is only to bring it to the reader's attention so that those interested can investigate the matter further. For secondary literature containing a variety of excellent readings on Heidegger's main treatment of this topic in *The Fundamental Concepts of Metaphysics*, see Franck (1991), Haar (1993), Glendinning (1998), McNeill (1999), Agamben (2004) and Calarco (2004).

To understand Heidegger's reasoning behind his claim that animals only perish, we need to compare his *ontology* of animals with the ontology of Dasein, for he does not reveal any significant *ontical* distinctions between humans and animals; instead, he shows through ontological analysis that it is in the mode of Being that we can see a crucial difference. That he makes this dramatic distinction is unsurprising given the following observations. First, from Derrida: "the distinction between the animal and man has nowhere been more radical nor more rigorous than in Heidegger" (1991:

105). Similarly, Giorgio Agamben describes Heidegger as "the philosopher of the twentieth century who more than any other strove to separate man from the living being" (2004: 39).

Indeed, whenever Heidegger discusses the ontology of animals they are invariably portrayed as lacking or deficient, as compared with humans: they are world-poor, without history, without language; they do not dwell nor do they have hands; they do not die – only perish; and so on. Stuart Elden suggests that most of these claims by Heidegger are grounded on the most fundamental of all distinctions: that man is a *zoon logon ekhon*, or *animal having speech*. Elden emphasizes that "In Heidegger's analysis this is not the *animal rationale* of metaphysical thought, but the living being that has and is held by *logos*, speech ... Rendering *logos* as speech, instead of reason, *ratio*, is a crucial argument in Heidegger's overall project" (2006: 273–4).

Heidegger analyses the differences between humanity and animality in several key texts – *The Fundamental Concepts of Metaphysics* (1929–30), the *Parmenides* lectures course (1942–43), the "Letter on 'Humanism'" (1946) and "What are Poets For?" (1946) – and he also discusses the matter, some three decades after *Being and Time*, in "The Essence of Language". However, investigations of Heidegger's thinking on animals have focused mainly on material from *The Fundamental Concepts of Metaphysics*. Here, Heidegger defines the world-poor nature of the animal in the following way:

> It is not simply a question of a *qualitative otherness* of the animal world as compared with the human world, and especially not a question of quantitative distinctions in range, depth, and breadth – not a question of whether or how the animal takes what is given to it in a different way, but rather of whether the animal can apprehend something *as* something, something *as* a being, at all.
>
> (FCM: 383–4)

He suggests that if it is *incapable* of apprehending something *as* something, then "the animal is separated from the human being by an *Abgrund*" (FCM: 384), the "abyss of the ontico-ontological difference" (Beistegui 2003: 114).

Heidegger asserts that animals do not relate to the presence of entities as either "ready-to-hand" or "present-to-hand", so a lizard sunbathing on the rock, although aware of the rock, does not understand the rock *as* a rock, and the bee that is guided in its flight by light is not aware of the light that impinges on it *as* light (FCM: 198). Nor do animals understand "space" *as* space. Note the following dialogue between Heidegger and a participant in one of the seminars he ran at Zollikon for the psychoanalyst Medard Boss:

MH: Again, it is a different relationship toward space [*Raumverh-altnis*]. The animal does not speak. The human being is a *zoon logon ekhon*. The animal does not experience space *as* space.

SP: What does this "as" mean?

MH: The animal is acquainted with the ditch it jumps over as a simple matter of fact [*Sachverhalt*], but not as a concept [*Begriff*]. (Zollikon: 16)

Thus animals do not comprehend or understand their environment *as* an environment because they lack the conceptual capacity to comprehend what they encounter as having any objective existence. Thus they are "world-poor" but only, of course, in relation to humans (Beistegui 2003: 106). Indeed, Heidegger explicitly notes that "animal being is not a deprivation of world" (FCM: 270–71): he acknowledges, for instance, the falcon's great eyesight and the dog's sense of smell (FCM: 286).

Heidegger claims that, since animals *cannot grasp concepts*, they are not able to understand the Being of beings, the question of Being *as* Being. (The phrase "Being *as* Being" comes from Aristotle, *Metaph*. 1031a22. For Heidegger's most sustained discussion, see FCM: 416ff.)

Most importantly, he regards this incapacity as being linked to language, both in the restrictive sense of "verbal articulation" and, more importantly, in the broader sense of "indication". The animal is thus very different from the human, who is the *zoon logon ekhon*, because although animals and humans have various obvious characteristics in common, there is one crucial distinction that sets them apart: whereas humans have *logos* (speech), animals have only *phone* (voice or sound). Thus, although animals can distinguish between, and vocally express, sensory experiences such as pleasure and pain, and they have instinctive discernment that allows them to differentiate between environmental factors such as safety and danger, in contrast, human speech enables a much more evolved faculty of judgement that is able to signify, for instance, the distinction between that which is just or unjust, good or bad, and so on, and it is these two crucial factors of speech and specialized judgement that separate human Being from animal Being (GA 18: 45–9). So Heidegger asserts that the human is the judgement-making animal (GA 87: 53), whereas the animal is fundamentally *zoon alogon* (GA 33: 124): *without* the *logos*.

Furthermore, Heidegger claims that, because they are without the *logos*, animals do not see into the "open" (GA 54: 230–31), they lack an understanding of Being (GA 34: 236), and they are never in the "clearing of Being" (GA 9: 326; GA 39: 75). Consequently human existence as Dasein is strictly demarcated from the mode of animal existence, and perhaps the most crucial of all these distinctions for Heidegger is that animals perish or expire; they do not die, because their demise is not the same as that of humans (BT: 284–5, 290–91; see also FCM: 388; GA 7: 180; GA 10: 203). For Dasein is unique among all entities in that it alone possesses the possibility of gaining access to the experience of death as such: of being capable of properly dying, of having a proper death.

Therefore, unlike humans, animals are not mortals (GA 7: 180), for "Mortals are they who can experience death *as* death. Animals cannot do so. But animals cannot speak either. The essential relation between death and language flashes up before us, but remains still unthought" (OWL: 107–8). Animals can thus be characterized as *entities*, within the fourfold of gods, mortals, earth and sky, such as the examples of "heron and roe deer, horse and bull" (GA 7: 184; Elden 2006: 280).

Thus speech, according to Heidegger, is a fundamental determination of Dasein's being-in-the-world, and since speech is lacking in animals it is this distinction that separates our mode of Being from the animals' way of being-in-the-world (GA 18: 17–18, 49). Additionally, this is the reason why animals do not dwell or abide; nor do they look, but rather they peer, glare, gawk or gape – because there is not "a self-disclosure of being", nothing is disclosed to it (GA 54: 158–9; see FCM: 319–20). "Plants and animals *are* as well, but for them Being is not existence, Dasein, but life ... Humans *are* as well, but we call their Being as historical existence, Dasein" (GA 38: 135; Elden 2006: 276). Heidegger contrasts this "historical existence" with that of the animal, via his discussion of Nietzsche's suggestion, in the second of his "Untimely Meditations", that the animal is distinguished from the human because the animal forgets, or does not remember, that they live without time and history, that they are the *ahistorical* animal (see GA 46: 15–17, 20, 31). For, according to Heidegger, although animals are *affected* by their past, they have only a *Vergangenheit*: a past that is dead and gone. They do not possess a *Gewesenheit*, a living past (BT: 374) that they can "go back to", a past that lives on in their present, informing them of their future possibilities.

As Beistegui clarifies: "All other beings *are*, naturally, but they do not *exist*. Why? Because they do not have this irreducible connection to the world, the openness to the world *as* world that defines the human being" (Beistegui 2003: 15). Thus, unlike animals, humans in their *way of being* understand that their Being is an issue and so the possibility of gaining access to an experience of death as such is an experience that Heidegger argues is open to Dasein's mode of Being alone. Animals, although mortal, are not *mortals* because they are not *conscious* of the fact. Mark Wrathall thus asserts: "We are distinguished from animals and other living creatures by the fact that we *experience* ourselves *as* mortal. The experience of death (mortality) is, then, an essential distinguishing mark of what it is to be human" (2005: 62).

Theodore Schatzki notes that Heidegger's understanding of animal life is "closely tied to the biology of his day", in that he sees that "animal exist-ence is a series of blind, non-conceptually mediated, instinctual reactions activated by an animal's meeting up with certain entities in its environment" (1992: 83). In this light it is unsurprising that, for Heidegger, animal life pales in comparison with the existence of human Dasein. Schatzi further asserts: "it is true that, on a contemporary view of animal life, creatures such as dogs and baboons do share certain components of Dasein's way of being, for instance, conceptually mediated apprehension of the environ-ment" (*ibid.*). From Heidegger's standpoint, however, the animal *cannot* be Dasein if it does not exhibit in its Being *all* of Dasein's way of Being.

Having presented various viewpoints offered by Heidegger in support of his proposition that only Dasein can die, it would seem appropriate now to conclude this discussion by pointing out that Heidegger's distinctions between the human and the animal are considered by some (including the author) to be problematic and open to question, for, as Derrida states, "the Heideggerian discourse on the animal is violent and awkward, at times contradictory" (1991: 111). For example, Derrida points out that, in *An Introduction to Metaphysics*, Heidegger writes that the animal has neither world nor environment (Derrida 1989: 47). However, these comments contradict the three "theses" about world that Heidegger presented several years earlier in *The Fundamental Concepts of Metaphysics* (Derrida 1992: 291; 1995: 277); namely that (i) the stone is without world, (ii) the animal is poor in world and (iii) man is world-forming. Derrida asserts that if, for Heidegger, the animal is *poor* in world then clearly it has *some* world; ani-mals' lack is not a "pure Nothingness" so they are *not* "world-less" (Derrida 1989: 49). More significantly, in the following quote Derrida questions Heidegger's entire position:

> Against, or without, Heidegger, one could point to a thousand signs that show that animals also die. Although the innumerable struc-tural differences that separate one "species" from another should make us vigilant about any discourse on animality or bestiality in general, one can say that animals have a very significant relation to death, to murder and to war (hence to borders), to mourning and to hospitality, and so forth, even if they have neither a relation to death nor to the "name" of death as such, nor, by the same token, to the other as such, to the purity as such of the alterity of the other as such. But neither does man, that is precisely the point! ... Who will guarantee that the name, that the ability to name death (like that of naming the other, and it is the same) does not partici-pate as much in the dissimulation of the "as such" of death as in

its revelation, and that language is not precisely the origin of the nontruth of death, and of the other?   (Derrida 1993: 75–6)

For Derrida, what is crucial is that if Dasein is neither an animal nor present-at-hand or ready-to-hand – since *possibility* is what most properly defines Dasein's Being – then Dasein's most proper possibility as impossibility, proper possibility as the *negation* of Dasein's proper possibility – this "as" – makes death Dasein's *least proper* possibility (*ibid.*: 71). Derrida points to the following as important:

> The *als* (*as,* considered as) keeps in reserve the most unthinkable but it is not yet the *als solche* (as such): we will have to ask ourselves how a most proper possibility as impossibility can still speak as such without immediately disappearing, without the "as such" already sinking beforehand and without its essential disappearance making *Dasein* lose everything that distinguished it – both from other forms of entities and even from the living animal in general, from the beast. And without its properly dying being, originarily contaminated and parasited by the perishing and the demising.
>
> (*Ibid.*)

This question posed by Derrida is of exceptional importance, because if we were able to render uncertain the claim that "Dasein has access to the 'as such' of death" (if Dasein has access to its most proper possibility only as mediated by the "as" of impossibility), then simultaneously we would be rendering uncertain the separation between human existence and animal life: "the stakes naturally – I'm not hiding this – are so radical that what is at issue is the 'ontological difference', the 'Question' of Being, the whole structure of Heidegger's discourse" (Derrida 2006: 219; Lawlor 2007: 51). Given this final observation from Derrida, it would seem that this whole topic warrants further consideration by scholars of Heidegger's thought.

Mortality: the fundamental basis of care

Heidegger's analysis of Dasein's relation to death begins with a reminder that since "care is the basic state of Dasein" (BT: 293), which underlies *all* Dasein's experiences, it must also be deeply enmeshed with Dasein's mortality. This is intuitively obvious: a fundamental reason why my life matters to me so much is that I am aware that it can, and will, be snatched away from me by the power of death. In fact, "care" is Dasein's fundamental condition only because Dasein senses its own mortality.

> I can die at any moment ... *I myself am this constant and utmost possibility of myself,* namely, to be no more. Care, which is essentially care about the being of Dasein, at its innermost is nothing but this being-ahead-of-itself in the uttermost possibility of its own can-be. (HCT: 313)

Conversely, if Dasein's basic state were not care, it would not be fundamentally affected by the constant possibility of its death, for "*As regards its ontological possibility, dying is grounded in care*" (BT: 296). Thus care and the sense of one's mortality are "equiprimordial". Since care is the basic condition of Dasein that continuously underlies all its experiences, then, clearly, Dasein's exposure to the threat of death must be equally constant and all-pervasive since care is the basic condition only because of Dasein's sense of mortality.

The "afterlife" issue

Although Heidegger saw the "question of death" as an essential part of any philosophical examination of life, he is not interested in "ontically" analysing factual claims about human mortality in terms of Dasein's ageing process. He also offers no comments on how one thinks, or should think, in the last moments just prior to death (where conditions are often not geared to reflection). He is concerned only with an "ontological" analysis of human mortality as it sheds light on Dasein's way of Being.

One reason for the avoidance of any discussion of the actual or specific event of death itself is that Heidegger realized that the *event* of death is something we cannot experience. He shared the same attitude towards the event of death as the philosopher Epicurus, one of the chief proponents of materialism in antiquity: "when we exist death is not present, and when death is present we do not exist" (Long & Sedley 1987: 150). (Wrathall [2005: 66–8] offers an interesting critique of Epicurus' dismissal of death by contrasting it with Heidegger's view of death as a *possibility*.)

With regard to the question as to whether or not there is an afterlife, Heidegger remains uncommitted, but does not deny the possibility:

> If "death" is defined as the "end" of Dasein – that is to say, of Being-in-the-world – this does not imply any ontical decision whether

> "after death" still another Being is possible, either higher or lower, or whether Dasein "lives on" or even "outlasts" itself and is "immortal".
>
> (BT: 291–2)

In making this statement he is perhaps suggesting that his account of death is compatible with both believing and not believing in an afterlife or personal immortality.

However, he argues that, prior to any appropriate discussion of an afterlife, one first needs to provide a noncommittal explanation of Dasein's death (mortality): "As long as I have not asked about Dasein in its structure and as long as I have not defined death in what it is, I cannot even rightly ask what could come after Dasein in connection with its death" (HCT: 314). He makes one final comment in *Being and Time* on this issue: "Whether such a question is a possible *theoretical* question at all will not be decided here. The this-worldly ontological Interpretation of death takes precedence over any ontical other-worldly speculation" (BT: 292).

If Heidegger did in fact believe in an afterlife, perhaps he avoids debates in this area because they enter the realm of theology, a field of enquiry that he regarded as inappropriate to proper philosophical thinking. His apparent openness towards the afterlife issue, however, could also have been motivated merely by a desire to attract universal interest in his analysis of death, for his account of Dasein does not readily allow for a belief in immortality, since, according to Heidegger, Dasein cannot be understood separately from the world it inhabits. Dasein's Being is fundamentally a "being-in-the-world". The "world", like a vital organ, is an *essential* source of its existence. So if Dasein dies, how can it still survive as Dasein, since it is no longer "in-the-world" because its "world" has come to an end? It cannot, unless one argues that, after death, Dasein *still* exists in our world as a "*spirit-being*-in-the-world", or leaves this world to enter a different world as a "being-in-the-*spirit-world*".

Death as a possibility

> Beings cannot, however, throw off the questionable thing about them that whatever they are and how they are – they also could *not* be. This possibility is not something we … merely add in thought, but the Being itself announces this possibility, announces itself as the Being in the possibility.
>
> (IM: 29)

Heidegger asserts that viewing death primarily as an actuality is inauthentic. Instead, he conceives of death as one of the possible ways of being.

This seems strange and illogical, for "death and life cannot exist simultaneously". But since I may die at any time, death is a possibility that hangs over everything I do: "*it is possible at any moment*" (BT: 302), a constant possibility of my Being (albeit finally a certain one) that limits all my possibilities. Indeed, as each year of my life passes by, this fact becomes steadily more obvious to me as I observe the range of possibilities open to me relentlessly narrowing, and in certain moments I realize in every cell of my Being that eventually they will converge on the limit of one single possibility and then vanish altogether.

However, in reference to Heidegger's assertion that death is "possible at any moment", Michael Inwood asks why Heidegger neglects mentioning the equally significant factor of probability, "when it is as important for the management of my life as possibility". Inwood clarifies further:

> Though it is *possible* that I shall die at, or before, 10 o'clock this evening, it is very *unlikely* ... I would not sign a contract (to write a book) ... if I did not think it fairly likely that I would live to complete it ... it is hard to see how a reasonable ordering of one's life could dispense with some estimate of one's life expectancy ... I cannot manage my life prudently if I have no idea whether I shall live for one minute or 500 years.   (Inwood 2000a: 74–6)

Heidegger's "facts of life" and death

For Heidegger it is death that potentially gives everything in my life ultimate value; the sum total of my existence can best be defined as what will be subtracted from the world by my death. Death will sever all my relationships with others and complete the story of my life because, unlike any other possibility, it is the one possibility that strips me of all my other possibilities, so I will have no possibilities left. This is what Heidegger means in his understanding of death "*as the possibility of the impossibility of any existence at all*". For "Death, as possibility, gives Dasein nothing to be 'actualized', nothing which Dasein, as actual, could itself *be*" (BT: 307).

But as long as I am alive, I am inhabited by what Heidegger calls "a constant lack of totality ... As long as Dasein *is* an entity it has never reached its 'wholeness'" (BT: 279–80). In other words, I live amid a continual overhang of unfinished business: my not-yet-realized possibilities for Being. Each choice I make has the potential to reshape and redefine my identity and the meaning of my existence. So a complete perspective on my life, the significance of my *whole* existence, can be achieved only when all my possibilities – my potential choices – are extinguished. But Heidegger points out that, since this only happens when my life is over, I will not be around to reflect on it (BT: 280). So it appears that it will always be either too early or too late for me to comprehend the complete picture of my existence. However, Heidegger suggests that this dilemma arises only if we conceive of Dasein as something that is "present-at-hand" and its death merely as a not-yet-present-at-hand event (BT: 280). But this is clearly an erroneous way of approaching this whole question, since "Dasein's 'Essence' lies in *existence*" (BT: 365). "Dying is not an event; it is a phenomenon to be understood existentially … indeed death signifies a peculiar possibility-of-Being in which the very Being of one's own Dasein is an issue" (BT: 284).

According to Heidegger, the true importance of the realization that it is possible *not-to-be* is that it focuses our attention on the possibility of being-*able*-to-be. It establishes my life as uniquely mine, because my rendezvous with death is the only possibility in my life that I cannot avoid; my death belongs exclusively to me as my "ownmost" possibility (BT: 294). No one can *do* my death for me or participate in my personal experience of it, and no one can take it away from me (BT: 284). Of course, no one else can have an operation for me, experience old age on my behalf (like the painting of Dorian Gray) or take a bath for me, but all such situations differ profoundly from death because they are avoidable; my presence or absence is my choice. I can avoid bathing, refuse surgery and even elude old age if I commit suicide when I am still young. But there is no chance that I can escape my rendezvous with the Grim Reaper. Thus what is of fundamental importance to Heidegger is the fact that Dasein is *individualized* by death:

> Death does not just "belong" to one's own Dasein in an undiffer-
> entiated way; death *lays claim* to it as an *individual* Dasein. The
> non-relational character of death, as understood in anticipation,
> individualizes Dasein down to itself. This individualizing is a way in
> which the "there" is disclosed for existence. It makes manifest that
> all Being-with Others, will fail us when our ownmost potentiality-
> for-Being is the issue. Dasein can be *authentically itself* only if it
> makes this possible for itself of its own accord.   (BT: 308)

Such facts are obscured by Dasein's fallenness; in a futile attempt to achieve ontological security, it tries to hide from death via an absorption in numerous evasive strategies in the everyday *They-world*, thus losing the valuable benefits that could be derived from facing up to the fact of death. Awareness of mortality arises from introspection, but the fascinating, constantly evolving world of technology, with its MP3 players, mobile phones, emails and internet browsing, shapes a consciousness that is entirely "outwardly directed", providing perhaps the ultimate evasion of mortality: "the self-assertion of technological objectification is the constant negation of death" (PLT: 125). Furthermore, reminders of death in Western society are carefully tucked out of sight. The aged are concealed in homes, the terminally ill in hospices and the corpses in crematoria, and often death is simply regarded "as a mishap which is constantly occurring" (BT: 296), treated as a potentially *avoidable* event – such as a needless accident or perhaps deficient medical care – rather than an intrinsic feature of life. Indeed, many people in Western culture have never even seen a dead body.

The inauthentic mood that discloses death is fear, which focuses on the specific event of death and flees from what it sees. Death is experienced as a remote possibility in the distant future that for the moment happens only to others; this is probably the most subtle, common and widespread evasion of death because, although we acknowledge that one day we shall die, we do not really feel or believe that it could happen at any moment. So whenever I think about death, while simultaneously feeling "One day I will die, but certainly not today", I confer on myself a type of immortality, because death will happen only to a "future-me", who barely seems related to the "present-me". Thus, although inauthentic Dasein may readily acknowledge the *fact* of death, with clichéd comments such as "Life is short, you know we don't live forever", the literally true implication, and stinging significance of this fact, is excluded from Dasein's "feeling-awareness", for "Dying is levelled off to an occurrence which reaches Dasein, to be sure, but belongs to no one in particular. Dying ... is perverted into an event of public occurrence which the 'They' encounters" (BT: 297). Thus Dasein is deprived of a sense of the totality of its own life by the "chattering" They-self, which does not allow it to look death in the face through the courage of anxiety.

Consequently, although death is obviously still a possibility for inauthentic Dasein, it is not present to this Dasein *as* a possibility and thus it does not significantly influence the way Dasein experiences things or conducts its life. A possibility that is present to Dasein *as* a possibility will always influence Dasein's perception and behaviour in matters related to that possibility. For example, if Dasein is walking down a dark street late at night in a dangerous part of town, the possibility of being mugged will be present to Dasein *as* a possibility and this will influence the manner of walking and the response to approaching individuals. When death is continually present to Dasein as a possibility – the most significant of all possibilities – it fundamentally alters Dasein's entire perception of life – any choices made are now authentic rather than mere expressions of conditioned responses embedded in and influenced by social and cultural norms.

Heidegger warns, however, against a "death-awareness" that is characterized by a morbid obsessive thinking on death, since this is unlikely to lead to a lifestyle based on an authentic being-towards-death. Furthermore, he makes it quite clear in *Being and Time* and his later writings that he considers suicide to be an inauthentic or inappropriate response to the possibility of death. Concerning the act of "bringing about one's demise", he asserts, "if this were done, Dasein would deprive itself of the very ground for an existing Being-towards-death" (BT: 305; see also GA 20: 439). Since death is the essential portal to authenticity, it seems clear that Heidegger certainly does not regard the fact of one's mortality or inescapable death as an affirmation of nihilism or the senselessness of existing and thus does not consider that living in its shadow should make one sombre and morose. Indeed, he asserts that running ahead to death opens us up to Being: "death is the highest and uttermost testimony of beyng" (GA 65: 284) and alongside the anxiety that brings us face to face with our mortality "there goes an unshakeable joy in this possibility" (BT: 358).

Heidegger calls the "authentic" attitude towards death *Vorlaufen*, which literally means "running forwards" or "to run on ahead" (BT: 306); the English translation is "anticipation". This is different from "expecting" death, which is imagining its realization; in authentically anticipating death, I relate to my death not as an actuality or event but as a possibility and I am *holding open* its possibility (BT: 306). So, according to Heidegger, there are two forms of death. One form is the actual fact: the event of death, which belongs to all human beings. The other is the existential response or relation to this fact, and amounts to the process of individuation called Dasein. Each of us can and *should* die twice – once as a human being and once as an individualized Dasein – because when I experience myself always as this "being-towards-death", thus realizing that my death is my "ownmost possibility" and an impending certainty that is "possible at any moment" (BT: 303), I am provided with a vantage point from where I am able to grasp my situation as a whole and understand its significance: that my life is a permanent incompleteness, without solid ground, that will come to an end (BT: 294–5).

I now understand that everything on which my life is based is utterly fragile and transitory because I can die in any moment and all of it will just disappear. Thus I am "snatched back from the endless multiplicity of possibilities which offer themselves as closest to one" (BT: 435), and am now able to appropriate my past as a resource of possibilities that can be brought to realization through action in the present, and I focus on those possibilities that "are determined by the *end* and so are understood as *finite*" (BT: 308).

I have become resolute. My actions arise out of a decisive dedication to accomplishments and a way of living that are definitive of my existence as a whole. My actions are no longer simply a means to an end – for example, eating healthy food to avoid getting sick; now the reason I choose to eat well is not merely to achieve the extrinsic end of escaping illness, but because it is an integral part of my resolute commitment to a generally healthy lifestyle. Thus my actions tend to have a cohesive, cumulative significance instead of being just a series of different calculative strategies that are independent of any overall unifying force. (Chapter 4 dealt with this important topic in detail.)

Note that Heidegger's authentic death perspective does *not* refer to the simple acceptance of death as sometimes seen in "primitive" societies, because in this context the apparent acceptance of death frequently is not due to an authentic attitude towards death, but is derived from the individual's sense of identification with the "larger body" of the group that never seems to die. This identification thus provides a sense of continuity to life that reduces the ego's fear of extinction. Nor is Heidegger's understanding and acceptance of death based on any belief in the immortality of the soul, which allows an individual to escape the fear of death through identifying with a transcendental immortal Self. Rather, authentic death-awareness is rooted in anxiety. Authentic Dasein is not fearful of death, nor does it worry about the actual event of death; instead, it suffers from an anxiety that brings it face to face with the inevitability of its own death (BT: 295, 310–11). In the light of this awareness it realizes and accepts that its possibilities are limited by death and bases its choices in life on this understanding. For a detailed discussion of anxiety see Chapter 3.

Near-death experiences of any sort do not guarantee this state of awareness, as what is required is an ontological understanding of the matter: the continual anticipation of *"the possibility of the impossibility of any existence at all"* (BT: 307). Anticipation (*Vorlaufen*) "shatters all one's tenaciousness to whatever existence one has reached" (BT: 308); in the light of the indefinite yet constant threat of death, everyday relations and attachments cease to offer any security and thus lose their dominating influence. "When Dasein stands before itself in this way, all its relations to any other Dasein have been undone. This ownmost non-relational possibility is at the same time the uttermost one" (BT: 294). This gives death "the possibility of acquiring *power* over Dasein's *existence*" (BT: 357).

Dasein now realizes in each moment of its existence that it is powerless to escape the possibility of dying *right now this very instant*, and it is freed from the pressures of having to live as others expect it to live. "This certainty, that 'I myself am in that I will die', is the *basic certainty of Dasein itself* ... The moribundus *first* gives the sum its sense ... Only in dying can I to some extent say absolutely, 'I am'" (HCT: 316–18). Thus the Cartesian *cogito sum* is replaced by what Heidegger views as the ultimate "primordial certainty": *moribundus sum*. For this is the one truth that cannot be doubted, no matter how much I struggle to conceal it from myself.

In practical existence, this death-awareness allows Dasein to see through the network of equipmental relations to the ultimate "for-the-sake-of" that gives all things their meaning: the empty horizon of "world" and death. This "liberates him *from* possibilities which 'count for nothing', and lets him become free *for* those which are authentic" (BT: 395). Dasein now experiences *moments of vision* that are deeper and broader than the present "now", for with one eye on Nothing, an ear open to the voice of stillness and one foot always already in the grave, authentic Dasein opens and surrenders to the power and guiding wisdom of Being.

Death confirms and reveals the sobering truth that the essence and meaning of human life is grounded in time; all the possibilities of my life are defined by, dependent on and only make sense in the light of my eventual death. My days are numbered. Although "time" itself may be infinite, my time on earth is running out each second, like sand falling through an hourglass. Hence people who are "generous with their time" are perhaps demonstrating – whether they are aware of it or not – the greatest form of generosity known to humankind. Heidegger himself died on the morning of 26 May 1976, at the age of eighty-six. His final utterance was "Thanks" (Petzet 1993: 224).

In *Being and Time*, Dasein's "anticipation" of death (its authentic awareness of mortality) relates only indirectly to the question of Being, for its essential importance is that it is regarded as the fundamental means for all Dasein to achieve authentic individuality. Later, however, Heidegger regards this same state of consciousness and the authenticity it entails as having more to do with Dasein's relation to Being itself than to Dasein's own individual life.

Young suggests, however, that in *Being and Time* even the description of the resolute approach to life characterized by authentic being-towards-death is a life "lived *in spite of* and in the face of homelessness, not its overcoming" (Young 2001: 131). He suggests that "in spite of *setting out* to overcome 'forgetfulness of Being', *Being and Time* is … a work in which Heidegger has not yet liberated himself from metaphysics" (*ibid.*: 132). Indeed, Heidegger himself states that the work is one in which "metaphysics … is still dominant" (P: 256).

Thus Young asserts that *Being and Time* is a "work of 'heroic nihilism'" (2001: 132). It is heroic because it advocates "living in the truth" about death, nihilistic because the "truth" it discovers is that beyond the intelligible world of beings is the absolute Nothing, "the abyss" (BT: 194).

Transcending metaphysical death to dwell in the world

According to Heidegger, because humanity is trapped within the metaphysical understanding of Being that has given rise to the mindset "enframing" (*Gestell*), mankind ignores Being to focus only on *things* in existence. Thus we have a restricted understanding of ourselves and all entities as "resources" for exploitation, and "The result is that Being remains forever shrouded in oblivion, its deeper and richer meaning neglected and forgotten" ("The Question Concerning Technology", in BW: 333).

Since enframing is always the source of our worldview, we remain permanently closed off from all other ways of Being, and thus we remain cut off from our own Being, the Being of other entities, and the mystery and sacredness of Being and "beings". Imprisoned within this metaphysical outlook, the world of beings appears to be the totality of what there is. Beyond beings there is "Nothing" – an absolute, "empty" (ID: 28; PLT: 151), "privative-negative" (GA 15: 363), "abysmal" (BT: 194; PLT: 92), "nihilistic" (OWL: 19) and annihilating Nothing – no other "side" to our world of beings who are "suspended" in "a complete emptiness" (OM: 86). Efforts to avoid the terror that arises in the face of this seemingly total annihilation leads to a constant state of anxiety, usually modulated by evasion into continual uneasiness, and as such the world becomes a threatening place and one never really feels at home in it.

According to Heidegger:

> This homelessness is specifically evoked from the destiny of Being in the form of metaphysics. ("Letter on Humanism", in BW: 243)

> Homelessness ... consists in the abandonment of Being by beings. Homelessness is the symptom of oblivion of Being. Because of it the truth of Being remains unthought. (*Ibid.*: 242)

And the reason for this feeling of homelessness is that "dwelling is not experienced as man's Being; dwelling is never thought of as the basic character of human being" ("Building Dwelling Thinking", in BW: 350). Thus Heidegger believes we are "homeless" because we have lost our sense of "dwelling" in the world.

But what exactly does Heidegger mean by this and why, as he suggests, is this homelessness a consequence of metaphysics? We shall answer these questions, but first a brief clarification of his usage of the term "dwelling" will help to explain why he asserts "Dwelling is the manner in which mortals are on the earth" (*ibid.*) and yet also claims that modern man is "homeless". Heidegger utilizes two senses of dwelling: "dwelling", which is the human "essence", which is essential dwelling – the fundamental and continual possession of all human beings; and "existential dwelling", which describes the state of consciousness in which Dasein has achieved an authentic understanding of its essential dwelling and lives according to that understanding (see Young 2002: 73–4).

In Heidegger's later thinking, his alternative to the metaphysical experience of existence derives from his in-depth interpretation of the significance of this term "dwelling", and he concludes that dwelling is the "essence" of who we are. The German for "I am" is *ich bin – bin* stems from the Old High German and Old English *"buan"*, which means "to dwell" ("Building Dwelling Thinking", in BW: 349). Since "It is language that tells us about the essence of a thing, provided that we respect language's own essence" (*ibid.*: 348), Heidegger thus claims that the original and true meaning of "I am" is "I dwell", and thus he concludes that "To be a human being ... means to dwell ... man *is* insofar as he *dwells"*, but the word *"buan" "also* means at the same time to cherish and protect, to preserve and care for" (*ibid.*: 349); thus Heidegger asserts: "the basic character of dwelling is safeguarding" (*ibid.*: 352).

Heidegger claims that the human "essence" is to be in the world as in a dwelling place; thus "to dwell" means the way humans *are* on this earth. The original meaning of *"buan"* (*bauen*) is *wohnen*, which means to reside, to dwell at peace, to be content; it is related to words that signify to feel at home in a place. It is also connected to the German word for "delight", *Wonne*.

> In what does the essence of dwelling consist? ... to be at peace, to be brought to peace, to remain in peace ... preserved from harm and danger ... taken care of ... to care-for. The caring-for itself consists not only in the fact that we do no harm to that which is cared-for. Real caring-for is something *positive* and happens when we leave something beforehand in its nature, when we gather something back into its nature, when we "free" it in the real sense of the word into a preserve of peace ... *The fundamental character of dwelling is this caring-for.*   ("Building Dwelling Thinking", in BW: 350–51)

Heidegger also suggests that dwelling lies in being attuned to Being, and the presence of beings, in a manner that simply "lets Beings be" (BT: 117, 405; "On the Essence of Truth", in BW: 125). Letting beings be means "allowing beings to be", which means allowing "presencing". This allowing of presence is simultaneously the "presence of allowing": releasement from the human will (*Gelassenheit*).

Thus for Heidegger there are two main aspects to dwelling: to dwell is to be cared-for and protected from harm in the dwelling place and also to care for and protect from harm the things of the dwelling place. So "to dwell" is to feel fundamentally safe in the world, ontologically secure, and since the ultimate threat to our security is death – understood as permanent extinction or Nothingness – then dwelling implies that we feel safe, even in the face of death. Rather than fearing mortality it is accepted with equanimity (*Gelassenheit*):

> Mortals dwell in that they initiate their own essential being – their being capable of death as death – into the use and practice of this capacity, so that there may be a good death. To initiate mortals into the essence of death in no way means to make death, as the empty Nothing, the goal. Nor does it mean to darken dwelling by blindly staring toward the end.
>
> ("Building Dwelling Thinking", in BW: 352–3)

So the "good death" arises from "dwelling" in the world, which is founded on authentic being-towards-death that derives from the understanding that death as the end of life is not merely an "empty Nothing". But how do we reach this ideal state of dwelling?

Heidegger asserts that, since the metaphysical conception of existence is the *cause* of human anxiety in the face of death, we can overcome this anxiety by freeing ourselves from the grip of this metaphysical outlook. He suggests that to achieve this objective we need to understand that (and here he borrows from Rilke) "death is the *side of life* that is averted from us, unilluminated by us", that "death and the realm of the dead belong to the whole of beings as its other side", and that "within the widest orbit of the sphere of beings there are regions and places which, being averted from us, seem to be something negative, but are nothing of the kind if we think all things as being within the widest orbit of beings" (PLT: 124–5).

Thus Heidegger claims that the other side of the world of beings is not an abysmal "annihilating Nothing", but rather the dark or hidden side of the "globe of all Beings as a whole" (PLT: 124), and although it is unknown and incomprehensible to us it is still "positive" (*ibid.*). In other words, one needs to realize that as the "shrine of the Nothing … death harbours within itself" not the abyss of annihilation, but rather "the mystery of Being itself" (PLT: 178–9).

But even if we understand that death is *not* merely an "annihilating abyss of Nothingness", but that it is the "Nothing of the mystery of Being itself" (PLT: 178), and that there *is* something beyond the presence of beings – "something completely and utterly Other than beings" but undoubtedly "something" (GA 15: 363) (and thus the "Other" of beings is not an "absolute" but only a "relative" Nothingness) – why should this free us from anxiety in the face of death?

The implication is that this "Other" exists *beyond* the extinction of beings, and that, in the state of equanimity characterized by "dwelling", Dasein experiences itself, in some sense, *as* this "Other". Heidegger hints at this when he distinguishes between the "self" and the "ego" in his analysis of Hölderlin (see GA 4: 102, 129; GA 39: 86–8). Since identity is determined by "that with which you identify", and what you identify with is what you "care about", then if Dasein succeeds in severing its identification with the "mortal ego", and instead, for some reason, identifies with something that it experiences as being its "authentic or deeper self" – a self that is *untouched* by death – then Dasein would cease caring about the death of its mortal self (the physical body and the ego), it would no longer feel any need to "evade" death, and thus it might experience complete equanimity in the face of death.

The "enframed", metaphysical understanding of life locks us within an ego-centred perception of reality, where satisfying the demands of the ego becomes the keynote of existence. In this state of awareness, "Being" is ignored and only "beings" exist; thus death represents that which annihilates everything that matters: one's entire sense of self. But when we escape this egocentric prison, we set free the possibility of a new sense of self – a self that may arise simultaneously with our freedom from metaphysics, "bestowed" upon us by the grace of Being – for, as Heidegger states, "Being is still waiting for the time when it will become thought-provoking to man … Metaphysics closes itself to the essential fact that man essentially occurs only in his essence, where he is *claimed* by Being" ("Letter on Humanism", in BW: 227). Thus perhaps this new sense of self is one that *cannot* be annihilated by death because its roots lie in an identification with the oneness of eternal Being. This sentiment is possibly expressed by Heidegger when he quotes from Hölderlin: "the peace of all peace … the goal of all our striving, whether we understand it or not … unification of ourselves with nature, with the One infinite totality" (GA 52: 176; Young 2002: 71).

So, according to Heidegger, equanimity in the face of death arises when Dasein is released from its egocentric, metaphysical understanding of existence and is unified with the infinite totality of Being itself. Most importantly, in this unification with Being there arises an ecstatic "belonging to the essential in all beings" (GA 52: 65) that enables him to "guard the truth of Being, in order that beings might appear in the light of Being as the beings they are" ("Letter on Humanism", in BW: 234). Thus for Dasein, dwelling as an ordinary mortal "being-in-the-world" requires simultaneously dwelling *beyond* the world (in the sense that Dasein identifies its essential Self with the totality of Being). So Dasein now understands that the Nothing of death is not an absolute or ontological Nothing, for it is Nothing only in the sense of being beyond all available criterion of intelligibility; death, as "the shrine of the Nothing" is "the presencing" of "the mystery of Being itself" (PLT: 178).

It should now be clear that in Heidegger's later thought he views the fundamental importance of Dasein's authentic relation to death in terms of its indispensable function in the disclosure of Being, and thus "Dasein is authentic if it belongs to the truth of Being in such a way that priority over beings is granted to Being" (GA 49: 66; Inwood pers. comm.). Since Heidegger at this stage is far more concerned with Being than with the welfare of individual Dasein, authenticity is no longer a mode of existence that he regards as necessary for everyone. He emphasizes now that only philosophers, and those who are contributing to the preparation of a "new beginning", need to attain this authentic relation to death (since "true thinking" on Being requires detachment from "everydayness" and the influence of the They):

> [N]ot everyone need perform this Being towards death and assume the Self of Dasein in this authenticity; this performance is necessary only in connection with the task of laying the ground for the question about Being, a task which is of course not confined to philosophy. The performance of Being towards death is a duty only for the thinkers of the other beginning, but every essential man among the future creators can know of it.　　　(GA 65: 285)

CHAPTER SIX

Dasein's primordial temporality

> Our treatment of the question of the meaning of Being must enable
> us to show that *the central problematic of all ontology is rooted in
> the phenomenon of time, if rightly seen and rightly explained,* and
> we must show *how* this is the case. (BT: 40)

From Heidegger's analysis of human existence it soon becomes clear that,
in order to develop a deeper understanding of Being, to answer the question "What does it mean *to be*?", we must go beyond Dasein's various
modes of existence to the ultimate reference point by which these modes
have meaning. In *Being and Time*, the central issue of the entire work (as
its title suggests) is to show that, for a human being, for Dasein, "to be"
is always "to be temporal", since temporality makes up the primordial
meaning of Dasein's Being. Thus our provisional aim is the interpretation
of *time* as the possible horizon for any understanding whatever of Being.
"Time must be brought to light – and genuinely conceived – as the horizon
for all understanding of Being and for any way of interpreting it ... *and in
terms of temporality as the Being of Dasein, which understands Being*" (BT:
39). For if Dasein's sense of *what it means to be* is indeed temporal, this
suggests that the appropriate horizon or context for understanding Being
must be time; in other words, it is Dasein's temporality that makes Being
accessible to us.

Heidegger thus proposed that Being could be explored and understood
only in relation to, or in terms of, time. It should be emphasized that his
primary concern is not with "time", as denoted by a noun, which gives
the impression that time is some kind of substance such as "clock-time",
but with "time" in the sense of Dasein's *temporal way of Being*. Thus
Heidegger uses the term "temporality" specifically in reference to Dasein's
mode of existing: to the way Dasein experiences and lives *as*, *through*, and
in time.

There are two main notions of temporality: "authentic (primordial) temporality", which is exemplified by resolute Dasein; and "inauthentic temporality", the temporality of everyday and/or fallen Dasein. There is also "world-time" – the natural movement of time defined by the rising and setting of the sun – which is the same for everyone, and which is used for the practical ready-to-hand tasks of everyday survival. Finally, there is "ordinary time" or "now-time", inauthentically understood as a continuous sequence of "nows".

From the start, Heidegger's analysis of time differs significantly from most Western concepts of time, since the question Heidegger is actually asking is "What does it mean *to be* in time?", rather than "What *is* time?"

Previous philosophies of time

Plato encapsulated the essence of time as "a moving image of eternity". Aristotle's cosmic view of time viewed it as the time of the natural world, which can be determined from planetary motions and natural changes and which is characterized by "the number of movements in respect of the before and after", that is, a sequence of homogeneous present-at-hand "nows" that continue onwards uninterrupted. Broadly following Aristotle, Augustine describes the essence of time as "a present of things past, a memory, a present of things present, sight, and a present of things future, expectation". The Christian theological conception was that time, organized by God, is finite and *eschatological*: it eventually comes to an end. Descartes and later Enlightenment thinkers maintained the subjective view that time is something understood in the mind of a rational observer.

However, by the late nineteenth century this modern "Cartesian" conception of time came under criticism. The French philosopher Henri Bergson, in his *Time and Free Will* (1889), points out that there is a clear distinction between scientific knowledge of ourselves and the way we actually *experience* ourselves, a viewpoint shared by Heidegger. Bergson points out that, because science is concerned with measurement, it treats time spatially, as though it were a set of separate, quantifiable geometric units, similar to the spaces – hours, minutes and seconds – found on the face of clocks, or similar to a calendar grid that is divided into days, months and years. Also, since science is interested primarily in causes and effects, it deals in *linear time*, in terms of before and after, earlier and later: in other words, A before B before C and so on. So time is seen as a "timeline", made up of a uniform sequence of "nows" in which each moment is conceived of as an independent, actually existing point along the line of duration. We exist in the present moment, but are continually moving on to the next moment, leaving behind us an infinite line of past moments, and ahead of us there stretches an infinity of future moments. On this understanding of time the not-yet-now becomes the now and the now becomes the no-longer-now in a beginning-less, endless and irreversible sequence.

Indeed, in our "common-sense" understanding of time *itself* we do in fact usually represent it as a line, and clocks are used as a means of keeping track of our progress along this line as we journey towards the future. But strangely, when one starts thinking more closely about time in this way, it suddenly seems to have no objective reality at all and one begins to wonder if it is entirely an artificial construct: a subjective projection of the mind. For if we exist only in the present moment, which disappears the instant it arrives, it would appear that time amounts to nothing at all and yet we do seem to experience the passing of time. But Heidegger asserts that questions of this nature only arise if we think of time as a "timeline" (which is merely a superficial phenomenon), instead of understanding time in terms of Dasein's *temporality*, which is *primordial time* (BT: 457). As we shall see later, Heidegger diagnoses the "timeline conception" as the product of inauthentic falling. Heidegger also points out that, although time is *not* fundamentally a succession of "nows", this is exactly how philosophers have always attempted to understand it (BT: 472–80).

Bergson observes that humans generally do *not* experience time in this scientific manner. Instead, he notes that our experience is that of existing within a continuous "flow" that involves past, present and future. This flow is resistant to objective measurement because the experience of time as "flow" is unique to each individual. Thus we may be convinced that an excruciating dental procedure took at least five minutes of clock-time when in fact it lasted only sixty seconds, while someone with an extremely high pain threshold might not experience this strong distortion of time. Conversely, an enthralling three-hour film might be experienced as lasting only half that time. These sorts of experiences do not mean that time is merely a subjective phenomenon in the sense of being illusory, for we really do live temporally, but this temporality does not exist apart from us as a physical property of the universe, since the universe is temporal only because we are temporal and not the other way round. So time is not a substance nor a *property* of beings (such as size or shape or colour) but a *way of Being*: it is existential rather than categorical.

Also, in the flow of time, an experience in time turns into a past experience, becoming something qualitatively different as a memory. And future experiences – that which is not yet – also exist in a different way, as imaginations or projections. Time in a traffic jam can seem significantly longer when we are already late for an important appointment, because our future projections or anticipations of negative consequences coexist with our present experience, distorting our perception. So we see that the human experience of time is generally *not* linear.

Husserl took Bergson's work a stage further by asking how time "appeared" in awareness. For instance, how is it that we experience a musical melody as something whole, that is, complete from start to finish – even when we hear it for the first time – when in reality we encounter the melody in time, as a succession of separate notes? Husserl suggests that the melody is knowable only through the simultaneous operation of three acts of awareness: retention, in which notes that are no longer sounding have to be retained in memory; attention, in which a "primal impression" of each note, as it sounds, must be gained; and protention, in which the auditor must "listen ahead" and construct expectations of what might or might not follow. Crucially, these three acts have to occur together. Our awareness of time is thus a gathered-togetherness – a *simultaneous* occurrence – of past, present and future in retention, attention and protention, and this clearly does not fit into the linear theory of time, as A before B before C. Heidegger mentions that Mozart had stated that while composing he could often look over an entire piece of music in his mind at one glance, hearing it all together in his imagination, not serially. In other words, Mozart was "thinking" a non-linear gathering of time not measurable in clock-time.

Heidegger's temporality of care

Influenced by the ideas of Bergson and Husserl, Heidegger thus proposed in 1927 that Dasein's Being is in time and that the ontological meaning of Being is time. His assertion becomes clearer when one examines the ontological nature of the self, which can be carried out only via an analysis of Dasein's being-in-the-world. Heidegger's investigation reveals that, although Dasein is an entity, its "self" is not an *entity*: "being-a-self is ... only in its process of realization" (MFL: 139), which is an unfolding happening, the "movement" of a life course "stretched out between birth and death" (BT: 427). This self is structured within the phenomenon of *caring*: it is an "I who cares" (see Chapter 3, "Care", above). So care is the basic state of Dasein (BT: 237) that underlies *all* Dasein's experiences. "Care" is Dasein's fundamental condition, because Dasein senses its own mortality, either "authentically" or "inauthentically". In other words, my life matters to me so much only because I know that it will be snatched away from me by death (see Chapter 4). In its most developed form, "resoluteness", the key feature of authenticity, requires a lucid and continual anticipation of

119

death, and it is this "anticipatory resoluteness" – the *authentic* form of caring – that Heidegger uses to illuminate Dasein's temporality, which he claims is the "ultimate" basis for understanding Dasein (BT: 351).

Since Heidegger has ascertained that Dasein's Being is *care*, and that authentic existence as care is characterized by "anticipatory resoluteness", he can now demonstrate that the fundamental meaning of Dasein's Being, and the ontological ground of human authentic existence as care, must be temporality: *"Temporality reveals itself as the meaning of authentic care"* (BT: 374). He achieves this by showing that the ontological meaning of care *is* temporality, because the existence of the structure of care and "anticipatory resoluteness" is made possible only because there is a future, not because there will be a future. In other words, the future is not merely an abstract not-yet-now, because through my anticipation it has become a way of existing fundamental to authentic existence; my deepest sense of meaning is derived from my future. Heidegger demonstrates this by revealing how Dasein's "care" embraces its past, present and, most importantly, future; Dasein's Being simultaneously occupies all three phases of time (BT: 237). Thus "In temporality, the constitutive totality of care has a possible *basis* for its unity" (BT: 427).

In its *thrownness*, being-already-in-the-world (BT: 236), Dasein is dealing with its facticity, received from the past. Thrownness and facticity are disclosed by moods, anxiety being the primary one for authentic Dasein, and fear for inauthentic Dasein. Inauthentic Dasein's absorption in everyday life is characterized by a forgetting of its thrownness – it lives without questioning, or explicitly choosing, its current mode of existence. In contrast, authentic Dasein recalls the significance of its past and understands it in terms of the current possibilities it provides, which it can resolutely choose or *"repeat"* (in the sense of retrieve, in order to use) in the present.

In its *projection*, being-ahead-of-itself (BT: 236), Dasein focuses on defining itself in the present, through an awareness of its future possibilities. Future means "the coming in which Dasein, in its ownmost potentiality-for-Being, comes towards itself" (BT: 373). For inauthentic Dasein, the future is purely a matter of awaiting the results of its efforts at work or in other activities, or, alternatively, it is characterized simply by a generalized waiting to see what will happen. Authentic Dasein, however, anticipates its mortality and remembers that its life is its own responsibility and not in the hands of the They. In this light, and with an awareness of the possibilities provided by thrownness, it now makes resolute choices for the future during an authentic moment of vision.

The third element of care, being-alongside entities encountered in the world, primarily concerns the *present* as "making present" (BT: 374): the process of letting oneself be encountered by surrounding entities by allowing them to unconceal themselves to us. This "making present" happens within a world already temporally "opened up" by the past and future, because our past and future give rise to our present circumstances. Further, Heidegger shows that our practical everyday living in the present as "making present" involves Dasein's temporality in yet another way. When *using* a hammer I "make it present" through my deep absorption with it in the present to the exclusion of past and future. Nevertheless, in this everyday absorption in the immediate present I still have some sense of my immediate past for I "retain" or have a "non-explicit, muted awareness" of other tools and matters related to my work (BT: 389). Also, similarly, I "await" – I have a "muted" or non-explicit expectation of the immediate future (BT: 386–7) – my hammer functioning and the nails being there when I reach for them and so on. Thus my awareness of the present is grounded in the ecstatical unity of making-present, which awaits and retains:

> Even if concern remains restricted to the urgency of everyday needs, it is never a pure making present, but arises from a retention which awaits; on the basis of such a retention, or as such a "basis", Dasein exists in a world. Thus in a certain manner, factically exist-ent Dasein always knows its way about, even in a "world" which is alien. (BT: 407)

All Dasein are required to engage in "making present" in order to effi-ciently carry out everyday tasks, for such activities flow more smoothly and effectively when we take them for granted rather than questioning them. For instance, Dasein master craftsmen and master athletes usually achieve their highest potential while "making present" in a state of utter absorption in the immediate present, apparently oblivious of past and future.

Heidegger claims that "making present" is the *inauthentic present of inauthentic temporality*, a fact that is certainly obvious in the case of inau-thentic Dasein, since it has not resolutely chosen its mode of existence and thus its "making present" is still under the influence of *the way of the They*.

However, *resolute* Dasein's "making present" is embedded in and inspired by an authentic understanding of its own temporality that is grounded in a prior resolute decision made in the authentic present, which Heidegger calls *der Augenblick*, "the moment (of vision)", a moment of resolute decision where Dasein seizes the authentic possibilities presented by its "situation" (BT: 388). Moreover, just as absorption in everyday tasks "retains" a "muted" awareness of the immediate past that is relevant to the present, it would not be unreasonable to speculate that, even when authen-tic Dasein is utterly absorbed in its daily activities, it nevertheless "retains" a subliminal or "muted" awareness of the fact that its current actions have been resolutely chosen. Perhaps, therefore, authentic Dasein's "making present" could be more accurately construed as neutral or undifferentiated temporality. ("Undifferentiated" is a term sometimes, although rarely, mentioned by Heidegger [BT: 69] in reference to the fact that "average everydayness" can potentially be seen as neither authentic nor inauthentic [BT: 78]. See also Chapter 3, "Falling", above.)

The main thing to remember is that both irresolute and resolute Dasein have a "making present", but only resolute Dasein has experiences of an *authentic present*, characterized by the *moment of vision*. This "moment of vision" is thus of exceptional significance to Heidegger, for it is an expression of resolute Dasein's sharpened sense, and authentic understanding, of the "moment", the pulsing heartbeat of time. In Heidegger's understanding, the "moment" is not simply the passing of time through a moment-point of the present, not a mere occurrence, something that is automatically "given" to Dasein; rather, it has to be discovered because our normal inauthentic relation to time conceals the moment. In other words, the moment of vision is an achievement derived from Dasein's authenticity: a manifestation of Dasein's return to itself from dispersal in fallenness – "The moment of vision is nothing other than the look of resolute disclosedness in which the full situation of an action opens itself and keeps itself open" (FCM: 149). To acknowledge and face up to the moment – which compels one to decision – is what Heidegger regards as a "fundamental possibility of Dasein's existence proper" (FCM: 149).

The ecstatic unity of time

Heidegger uses the term "ecstatic" – in Greek literally "standing outside itself" – to describe Dasein's temporality. For the essence of temporality, which is also the essence of Dasein, is its expansion or *stepping outside itself* into the unity of the "ecstasies" of future, present and past, each of which expands into the others (BT: 377). The moments of Dasein's authentic temporality stand outside themselves, linked to each other by countless pathways of memory and anticipation that reach into both past and future. Like a compass needle drawn to the North Pole, each moment of authentic Dasein's existence is "magnetized" by an awareness of its finitude. The unified self of authentic, resolute Dasein is rooted in its ability to traverse its whole life by running ahead to its future, which holds the promise of death, and coming back from this future to its past (which extends to its birth and perhaps beyond to its ancestral heritage), from where it returns to the present, where, in the "moment of vision", it resolutely makes choices for its life from among the possibilities uncovered and made available to it by its past and future.

So Dasein's past is not merely the dead and gone past – that is, the past that has been and is now left behind – for Dasein's temporal past is alive in the immediate present since it is responsible for Dasein's present circumstances and it combines with Dasein's current situation and actions to create and limit its future possibilities, thus shaping Dasein's future by determining the possibilities available to it in the present. Heidegger emphasizes this fact by coining a different German word for the past, using the perfect participle of *sein*, "to be" – *gewesen*, "(having) been": (die) *Gewesenheit*, "(having) beenness, living past" (BT: 374). The usual word, *Vergangenheit*, implies a past that is dead and gone, for it is derived from the verb *vergehen*, which means "to pass, go by, die, literally go away".

In contrast to this, *Gewesenheit* emphasizes the fact that the past is significant in a *present* sense. In German, the past tense of the verb *sein*, "to be", uses a form of this same verb as the auxiliary; thus *ich bin gewesen* translates literally as "I *am* been" (although the usual translation is "I *have* been"). This idea that the past can be very much alive in the present moment is also evidenced in English in expressions such as "the past *is* meaningful". Heidegger exploits this sense in explaining his usage of *Gewesenheit*: "As long as Dasein factically exists, it is never past (*vergangen*), but it is always already *been* (*gewesen*) in the sense of 'I *am*-having-been' ('ich *bin*-gewesen')" (BT: 376). Although entities such as plants, rocks and animals are affected by their past, they have only a *Vergangenheit*; they do not possess a *Gewesenheit* that they can "go back to" – a past that lives on in their present, and which informs them of their future possibilities.

Heidegger also emphasizes that the future, especially for authentic Dasein, is not a mere "not yet", since Dasein's *temporal future* exists in the present in the form of Dasein's potential future choices, which in turn influence Dasein's present actions.

The *ordering* of these three ecstasies of time is prior to and independent of any temporal chronology (BT: 375–6). Thus the ecstatic future is not "later" than the ecstatic present, for at any moment of my life I am vulnerable to the power of death, thus my vulnerability is always an *actual*, living issue for me. Nor is my future later than my past, because my past, as "thrownness", is currently shaping and giving meaning to my present and future experiences. Further, my present is always enmeshed with and influenced by my future possibilities and my living past. In other words, the present moment simultaneously comprises the past and future, and in this sense it goes beyond, or "transcends", the *merely present*. So we can never occupy exclusively, or merely, a "punctual" here and now moment, because in our understanding, and in our mode of Being in the world, we always already exist in three temporal dimensions at once (BT: 370ff.). Temporality is thus the transcendental condition for experiencing a universe of meaningful entities, so our sense of the meaning of Being is rooted in the temporal structure that underlies our understanding of everything in existence.

Unlike traditional theories of time, which usually view the present as the only meaningful locus of reality and existence, Heidegger claims that the future is by far the most important dimension of temporality for authentic Dasein – "The primary phenomenon of original and authentic temporality is the future" (BT: 377) – and also, in a modified sense, for inauthentic Dasein, since its time is most frequently used for "achieving" objectives that concern the future more than the past or present: "Anticipation (*Vorlaufen*) makes Dasein *authentically* futural, but anticipation itself is only possible because Dasein, simply in virtue of Being, always comes towards itself, is, that is, futural in its very Being" (BT: 373). In Dasein's mode of Being it is always "ahead of itself", "beyond itself" (BT: 235–6); it has always "projected itself on definite possibilities of its existence" (BT: 363). "As long as it is, Dasein understands itself – it always has and always will – in terms of possibilities" (BT: 185). "The Dasein which I myself am in each instance is defined in its Being by my being able to say of it, *I am, that is, I can*" (HCT: 298).

Further, the choices I make for my future determine who I am now and, paradoxically, the future can also be the *source* of my past. This assertion seems nonsense in terms of our normal understanding of time as a timeline. However, in light of Dasein's *way of existing*, it does make sense because the significance of my past is derived from, and thus depends on, the nature of my future projections. "The actuality of what has been resides in its possibility. The possibility becomes in each case manifest as the answer to a living question that sets before itself a futural present in the sense of 'what can we do?'" (MFL: 72).

For instance, a person from a very underprivileged background who becomes a successful businessman will interpret his past as a life of deprivation from which he has emerged. But to a novelist, this same past might be appropriated and interpreted as a rich source of writing material for future publications. Although the events of my past obviously cannot be altered, what my past means to me – how I experience and interpret it now – is strongly influenced by the conception I have of myself in terms of my future possibilities.

"The character of 'having been' arises from the future, and in such a way that the future which 'has been' (or better, 'which is in the process of having been') releases from itself the Present" (BT: 374). For life is a continual process of taking over – in the present – what we have been in the past in order to use this as a basis for what we become in the future: "we are what we were, and we will be what we receive and appropriate from what we were, and here the most important factor will be *how* we do so" (PS: 158).

So it should be clear that, in both authentic and inauthentic existence, all three ecstasies are always at work together (BT: 401), but in the inauthentic way of living, the past and future are subordinated to the present, whereas in the existence of authentic Dasein, the present moment is enriched with a fresher and deeper significance, provided by the past and, most especially, by the future.

So the unity of Dasein is founded on *care*, whose unity in turn is founded on temporality. This is manifested at all times by Dasein being ahead of itself already in the world (Dasein's disposition or attitude – the way it finds itself already disposed towards things) alongside entities encountered within the world (BT: 237). So the past, present and future are "alive" in every moment of human existence and constitute all our current actions. "Dasein *itself* ... is *time*" (HCT: 197). This is why Heidegger states that our existence and lived experience of time is *always already* three-dimensional: an "ecstatic" unity of time. This suggests that time itself is also three-dimensional – the past, present and future are unified – for Dasein's way of Being reveals that these elements of time are fused together and thus cannot be divided. We can never avoid living in a present that is rooted in a past and faced with a future. Thus Heidegger would perhaps consider that we are deluding ourselves if we think that certain meditation practices, which absorb our awareness into a state of presence, can extricate us from the web of time that is a fundamental part of our Being.

If we attempt to refute this viewpoint by asserting that the past is simply "dead and gone", and therefore irrelevant to my "here and now" (a popular New Age perspective on life), then the promise I made yesterday surely would not matter because "yesterday is no more". We know instantly, however, that this is not the case. Nor is it relevant to argue that it is only memory that is important here, for memory is simply the means of transporting the past into the present.

Intuitively, it seems impossible for me to reflect on what, or who, I am at this moment without taking into account what I have done in the past and my direction in life, which lies in the future. Although these observations may seem obvious, they further confirm, at an intuitive and common-sense level of understanding, this essential point made by Heidegger: the past, present and future are, without any doubt, an inextricable and fundamentally significant part of our way of Being.

Dasein's ecstatic temporality is thus very different from the way all other entities relate to time. Inanimate entities such as rocks and living entities such as plants clearly do not reflect on time, and in reference to animal Being, Heidegger asserts that the world of animals is impoverished, since animals are trapped in an instinctive "ring" (FCM: 255), a predetermined, unalterable set of possibilities for obtaining food, mating and so on. Also, since they cannot make free choices outside their instinctive patterns, they cannot question the *meaning* of their environment nor determine their present on the basis of their past and their choices for the future.

The temporality of Dasein's transcendence

Heidegger asserts that "Every disclosure of Being ... is *transcendental* knowledge" (BT: 62). His use of this term is intended to communicate his understanding of Being as that which lies "*beyond*" all entities (BT: 22, 62). This crucial distinction between Being and beings underlines the emphasis of his search, which is for *ontological* knowledge of *Being*, and aptly called "transcendental knowledge". He also sometimes describes time as "the transcendental horizon for the question of Being" (BT: 63), and Dasein's being-in-the-world as "transcendence" (BT: 415). With regard to Dasein's mode of Being, his use of the word "transcendence" refers to the state or locus by which, or from which, Dasein can reflect on the totality of human experience.

Heidegger asserts that Dasein's freedom entails being-in-a-world of entities, and thus, to retain its freedom, Dasein is required to transcend all present-at-hand and ready-to-hand entities by keeping them in the world at a critical distance, where it is able to view all entities as possibilities rather than as sheer actualities. This is what enables and inspires Dasein to ask about the source of all creation: to ask "Why is there anything at all rather than Nothing?" Without this ability Dasein would be incapable of providing the account of entities that is given in *Being and Time*, because Dasein's potential for transcendence is the fundamental basis for philosophy.

Aside from Dasein, the existence of all other entities, living and inanimate, is fully determined by their immediate surroundings. Dasein, in contrast, transcends all entities because it has the freedom and space to live beyond the control of its immediate environment and beyond the control of any particular entity. Its transcendence allows it to choose its "being-with", and to let other entities be as they are, without influencing them; it is only because of this fact that it can truly *encounter the significance* of other beings.

According to Heidegger, Dasein's capacity for transcendence is rooted in its relation to the Nothing:

> In the clear night of the Nothing of anxiety the original openness of beings as such arises: that they are beings – and not Nothing ...

> Only on the ground of the original revelation of the Nothing can human existence approach and penetrate beings ... Da-sein means: being held out into the Nothing. Holding itself out into the Nothing, Dasein is in each case already beyond beings as a whole. This being beyond beings we call "transcendence". If in the ground of its essence Dasein were not transcending, which now means, if it were not in advance holding itself out into the Nothing, then it could never be related to beings or even to itself.
>
> ("What is Metaphysics?", in BW: 103)

Not even God can transcend entities by choosing his "being-with", and thus he is unable to encounter entities in the way that Dasein can, because as God is the infinite *creator* of all things, God's "being-with" is inextricably linked to *all* the entities in his creation; therefore he cannot, as Dasein can, "let entities be", independent of his influence, and in his "infiniteness" he also cannot interact with finite entities as a *finite* being (unless, unlike Heidegger, one believes in God incarnated as Jesus Christ).

Most importantly, Dasein transcends entities by treating them primarily as possibilities rather than as actualities. For example, Dasein's past is significant not in terms of what it has been but rather for the possibilities it provides for Dasein's present and future existence. Similarly, for Dasein, a particular tool is not merely actual but, rather, it is something that Dasein has the potential to use for a purpose that transcends the tool and its actual use of it.

Dasein's transcendence would not be possible if it were not for its ecstatic temporality. For each of Dasein's future, past and present ecstasies corresponds to and is defined by a worldly counterpart: an aspect of purposive human activity that serves as a *horizonal schema*, a temporal framework that grounds the significance of Dasein's being-in-the-world by making it possible for Dasein to understand its worldly experiences, to understand Being and encounter beings (BT: 416). Thus, according to Heidegger, the following three horizonal schemata provide our general understanding of Being in all its variations (BPP: 307):

1. *For-the-sake-of-itself* (BT: 416) – the schema of the ecstasis of the future. This schema opens up the "horizon of possibility in general, within which a definite possibility can be expected" (MFL: 208). Dasein's current actions and the equipment it is using are *for the sake of* fulfilling a future possibility: Dasein's aim in life.
2. *What has been* (BT: 416) – the schema for the ecstasis of the past. This is the sheer fact that Dasein is "thrown"; its life circumstances, moods and states of mind, which provide the "backdrop" for its

being-in-the-world and all its projects, are not of its own making, and on the basis of this, Dasein has to construct a life for itself.

3. *Praesens* – a Latin term designating the schema for the ecstasis of the present (BPP: 305). This is the schema that makes it possible for us to understand the Being of ready-to-hand entities. The "equipment" Dasein is currently handling is used in order to accomplish a particular purpose in the *present* (BPP: 306) (the means by which Dasein realizes its aims). Thus, for a Dasein using a hammer, the meaning or significance of the hammer lies in the fact that it is being used in-order-to drive in the nails.

Dasein's temporality: the primordial source of time

In the final chapter of *Being and Time*, Heidegger sets out to demonstrate that "time" is "temporal", and for this reason he now focuses closely on the difference in meaning between the two terms, for important ontological reasons, since the seeming obviousness of the fact that "time is temporal" is deceptive.

As Heidegger uses the terms, "time" refers to the world, objects within the world and also the relation between subject-knower and object-known. "Temporality" refers specifically and exclusively to Dasein's mode of existence. Moreover, since Dasein *is* temporal it "creates" time. Thus, according to Heidegger, it is only in reference to Dasein's authentic temporality that a proper ontological view of time is possible, since Dasein's prior sense of its ecstatic temporality is the *basis* of time, rather than vice versa, thus Dasein's temporality is *"primordial time"* (BT: 457).

Heidegger begins his investigation by focusing on the question "What is the relationship between Dasein's temporality and that which we call time?" Although Dasein's experience of time, in its fundamental everyday interaction with the world in which it plans and carries out its daily activities and, with circumspective concern, makes use of the equipmental ready-to-hand structure of the practical world, is, in Heidegger's view, "inauthentic", it is nevertheless more intricate than a simple timeline, for it involves the actions of "awaiting", "retaining" and "acting" or "making present".

When Dasein is being-in-the-world in the existential mode of "awaiting", it is oblivious of its existential possibilities, for it simply "awaits" the results of its actions, and its temporal outlook is characterized by the temporal term "then". For instance, a phone call that I am expecting is a not-yet "then", when the phone will actually be ringing.

In the existential mode of "retaining", Dasein has forgotten about the "thrownness" of its past and, instead, "retains" merely a subliminal awareness of the tools it might need, and other past matters such as clients, that are directly related to its current actions. Its temporal perspective is represented by the phrase "on that former occasion" or "ago", for instance "one month ago".

When Dasein's existential mode of being-in-the-world is "acting", it is absorbed in its current situation, where it is concerned only with "making present" the things it is dealing with, via a mindfulness of its current actions. Its perspective is represented by the temporal term "now"; I am aware of my action (e.g. of making a cup of tea) as something that is taking place *now*-at-this-moment. In the "making present" of my everyday life, "making present has a peculiar importance" (BT: 459), for my future and past are significant to me only in so far as they are relevant to my current practical involvements.

Thus, from these existential modes of awaiting, retaining and making present, one derives the primordial time references "then", "ago" (i.e. on that former occasion) and "now". These different temporal features belong to the fundamental way in which Dasein relates to its worldly activities and to entities in the world in the mode of ready-to-hand. Heidegger calls the structure of this existential its *datability*: time is datable by events. "Now", "(a not-yet) then" and "on that former occasion" are worldly events that can be "dated" by reference to specific things or events: "on that former occasion *when* you fell over"; "then, when the post arrives"; "now that you have finished eating". In other words, Heidegger demonstrates that my "time" has a *content* or *datability* that relates to my practical activities of everyday existence.

Thus I do not only keep track of what I am doing in terms of clock-time but more importantly time is *significant*; it is time *to do* a particular something. So I relate to time in terms of its significance, what it means to me in terms of my engagements: time for an important lunch appointment; time to go to work; the right or wrong time to ask for a rise in salary (BT: 461–2). So my sense of time is inextricably linked to the *meaning* it has for my daily survival in a goal-directed world. Heidegger calls this understanding of time "world-time", for it allows us to "meaningfully structure" and organize our future plans, *in-the-world* of everyday activities.

By showing that the basic temporal concepts of "then", "ago" and "now" are derived from the ways in which we exist in the world in terms of the existential modes of awaiting, retaining and acting, Heidegger has also demonstrated that *Dasein's temporality* is the *basis* of time, and *not* vice versa. For it is only because I *can* await, retain and act that I am able to understand the elements of datability: now, then and ago. Thus chronological time arises out of Dasein's inauthentic temporality – "'Time' as ordinarily understood ... arises from inauthentic temporality" (BT: 374) – for inauthentic temporality relates to the chronological time of a "dead past", which happened *earlier* than the circumstances of the present facing me *now* or which I am about to deal with in the near *future*.

"Waiting" is the inauthentic mode of relating to the future (BT: 387), for it is a waiting for something in the future that has not yet happened. "On that former occasion" or "ago" mirrors Dasein's inauthentic relation to its past, since it refers to a "dead" past that happened earlier. "Now" in terms of "now at this moment" is Dasein's fallenness or absorption in the inauthentic present that only occupies "today". Heidegger also points out the fact that world-time "spans" or extends itself. It is most frequently experienced in terms of a duration of time, rather than as a durationless instant in time: "I have had headaches ever since the accident last year" (a past experience, that is extending itself into the present and probable future); "He will continue sleeping until his alarm rings" (a present occurrence that is simultaneously extending into the past and future).

In the present moment, too, our awareness and action are usually experienced as a duration of time, of indeterminate length, rather than as a mere "instant". It is an "extending now" that varies in length depending on the situation and the agent's future-oriented purpose: "'now' – *during* the concert or *throughout* the intermission, *while* one is eating, *during* the evening, *during* summer" (BT: 409). This "extending time", determined by its datability, is the natural way that inauthentic and authentic Dasein experience worldly events because most human activities and most occurrences in the world take time. Events in the world are rarely experienced as instantaneous.

World-time is also public. This is shown by the fact that we can all refer to the same period in time by "now" or "then" even if we date it by completely different events. A particular *then* in the past may be dated by me "When I graduated from college" and dated by you as "When I won the marathon". Alternatively, two people may date a time by an event common to both of them. Appointments are also often arranged according to public time: "We will meet *then*, when the pub opens".

The ordinary understanding of time

When man first walked the earth, world-time – the "right time" and the "wrong time" for the events of dealing with daily survival in the world – was solely defined, governed and dated by the movements of the "primeval clock": the rising and setting of the sun (BT: 465–6). We used such events to determine or *measure* how early or late it is in order to plan, coordinate and carry out the activities of our everyday life, while always keeping the present as our main reference point: "*now* is time to finish my work day and return home". Thus in measuring time, world-time is the same for all Dasein, and it is primarily concerned with the present. The most natural and fundamental public measurement of world-time – the day – arose in terms of this dating of events.

As time measurement evolved, and we became less dependent on sunlight for our daily activities, our need to keep track of what we are doing now led to our use of clocks, which in turn led to an alteration in our concept of time, resulting in our common, ordinary understanding of time. This common-sense understanding of time is symbolized by the clock, and thus when we try to *think* of time we usually represent it as a line and regard our wristwatch, clocks, calendars and so on as allowing us to keep track of our constant movements as we move forwards along this line, accompanied by everything else in the universe, in the direction of the future.

There are numerous puzzles and paradoxes associated with attempts to understand time, ranging from those triggered by Einstein's theory of relativity to those arising from questions such as: how can the past and future *be* when the past is *no longer* and the future is *not yet*, and, without these, how can there be a time such as the present, since the "present" requires the existence of a past and a future?

Husserl, for instance, was troubled by the fact that sensory perception takes place only in the present: we can feel, see, hear, smell and touch only what exists *now* – or what exists in the *immediate past*, if we take into account the speed of light or sound. How is it possible to be *conscious* in the present of the past or future? According to Heidegger, these enigmas arise only because our attempts to understand the nature of time focus on time as *linear*, instead of focusing on Dasein's temporality, which is "*primordial time*" (BT: 457).

Our faulty perception of time began when we uncoupled world-time from the web of its intricate involvements with the world and began thinking of time in the way clocks *measure* time (BT: 470). Clocks are "present-at-hand" *things*. So the importance of the present was accentuated, its true nature misunderstood, and the significance of our "living" future and past was forgotten or ignored. Our relation to time, measured in terms of the numerous separate time divisions on a clock, creates an impression of now in our thinking mind, as an independent "thing" or "substance" that exists as a fleeting instant, rather than as an extended now, which is our actual experience of the "now" in the more primordial world-time. Deprived of its datability and worldly significance, ecstatic temporality gets "levelled off" (BT: 422). Time is no longer an experience, unique to each individual, but instead it belongs to everybody – and that means to nobody.

Consequently, according to Heidegger, the present is commonly – and erroneously – viewed as one of a "sequence of pure 'nows'" (BT: 462) that are independent, actually existing points, along a timeline. Thus, similar to movements of the hands on a clock that measure the seconds, minutes and hours ticking by, we understand our existence as a journey along an infinite timeline of passing seconds, minutes, hours and days in which we occupy only one moment, the present, which is continually moving on to the next present moment in an infinite succession of "nows": what Heidegger calls *now-time* – the objective, infinite, homogenous time of the natural sciences (BT: 474).

So we no longer understand time in terms of how we actually experience it in our temporal way of dealing with practical everyday life, because our "thinking mind" ignores this direct experience of time in favour of its erroneous "clock-time" *conception*, and thus our existence seems to be merely the sum of fleeting, independently existing "now-moments", which arrive in succession and disappear. Thus we sense our self as made up of self-sufficient "now-points": a series of "experiences", as separate from each other as the individual frames of a filmstrip, which are "present" only for a brief moment. Since in essence we are temporal Beings, the adoption of this false *conception* of time has divorced us from the richness of everyday being-in-the-world and it has prevented us from experiencing our authentic self that is rooted in primordial authentic temporality.

To sum up: our "inauthentic" understanding of existence, or *all* Dasein's inauthenticity, can be traced back to our erroneous understanding of time as a sequence of "nows" or instants, time conceived apart from Dasein's activities and purposes, time as conceived by Aristotle and Hegel (BT: 420ff.).

The more our life and awareness become dominated by this clock-time understanding of existence, the more inauthentic our relation with reality. In this mode of understanding time, waiting alone at an isolated bus stop can be an excruciating boredom, marked only by the movements of the clock, and, during periods of stress, this clock-time understanding can totally dominate our awareness: "*Now* it is 5 o'clock, and I have an important appointment at 6 o'clock. *Now* the train is keeping me waiting and I am *now* going to be late – time is going by so slowly *now* – where is the damned train *now*? It is taking so long that I am *now* already late. *Now* I will have to get a taxi … thank goodness I am nearly there *now*…". In states of mind such as this, we are not *wholly* oblivious of the past and future, since the past is sensed as a "retaining" of when one left and how much time one was kept waiting, and the future is sensed through "awaiting" the train to "get here now", and as a fear of being late. However, these two ecstasies of time are submerged by the immediate present, the overwhelming presence of an oppressive sequence of seemingly endless nows.

However, clock-time, in itself, is not the problem as long as we only view time measurement in terms of its ready-to-hand usefulness and do not allow it to shape our understanding of our own temporality. For example, at 8:05 my train leaves; this measured time serves a necessary purpose for Dasein's day-to-day existence. The ecstatic character of primordial or "authentic" temporality had to be "levelled off" into world-time and "now-time" in order for the world, and the items that are ready-to-hand and present-at-hand within it, to become accessible to us in everydayness and in science (BT: 474–5). Living in "now-time" is the price research scientists have to pay to do their job, but, according to Heidegger, if a scientist's dedication to his career is the result of a resolute choice to exist scientifically, then in this case "science has its source in authentic existence" (BT: 415).

Therefore, although world-time and ordinary time are not "authentic temporality", Heidegger does not suggest discarding them because this would undermine resolute Dasein's ability to handle practical ready-to-hand activities and those activities that require a detached, theoretical understanding of *present-at-hand* entities. We can again see that the "diagnosis" of Dasein's authenticity or inauthenticity in relation to world-time (and also, now-time) depends on whether or not Dasein's immersion in world-time, or now-time, is based on a resolute choice rooted in an authentic understanding of its own temporality.

Problems arise only if I start believing in the *actual existence* of measured time: that there really *is* a particular moment that is 8:05 that precedes another moment called 8:06, for this produces an inauthentic understanding of myself and time, for now I have lost sight of the *temporal basis* of this measured time and I am in danger of attributing metaphysical characteristics to this measured "public time".

Heidegger regards this ordinary understanding of time as being a manifestation of our inauthentic state of "fallenness". This view of time is inauthentic, according to Heidegger, for three main reasons. (i) It lacks datability – the *moments* of ordinary time are not existential, thus they provide no temporal understanding of agos, thens and nows, which form the basis of our ready-to-hand relation to the world. (ii) It lacks significance; significance requires a participation in the as-structure of the world that is based on our primordial *ready-to-hand* relation with our everyday environment, where we experience entities as being in a contextual web of significant involvements with other entities. Measured moments cannot participate in this. (iii) Heidegger's greatest objection is that ordinary time is viewed as a seemingly endless chain of now-points. Time viewed in this way causes Dasein to conceive of time in such a way that it has no meaning, and in this sense no end. Thus ordinary time is treated as if it were infinite. As long as this understanding of time continues, Dasein is prevented from truly grasping its own finitude: that it is a self that is able-not-to-be. For it is Dasein's temporality that forms the basis of Dasein's existential understanding of itself as *finite*, whereas in the infinite "now" Dasein lives as the They-self, and "The 'They' never dies because it *cannot* die ... To the very end 'it always has more time'" (BT: 477).

Heidegger asserts that speculations of infinite time are meaningless, because even if infinite time or infinite entities existed they would not be available to us in any way. Dasein is *finite* – it dies – so the conception of infinity clearly must be irrelevant to all human activity. We are radically temporal beings and only our finite temporality is meaningful to us; thus everything has to be *understood* by us on the basis of this fact and the failure to truly understand in each moment the *finitude* of time is the fundamental basis of all inauthenticity. Moreover, *time and temporality are not autonomous entities*, so although "time", in our understanding of it, existed long before man and continues after we die (BT: 477), it can have no significance independent of human existence; time and temporality *are* only in so far as human beings exist.

Obviously, the conception of linear time is essential to everyday life and it is invaluable in contexts such as palaeontology, where it allows us accurately to place the origin of dinosaurs prior to humankind. However, it is crucial that we realize that time itself is neither subjective nor objective (BT: 471–2), for it is *prior* to both since it is the primordial source of our existence as Dasein, and it discloses to us all other entities.

It is because Heidegger views Dasein's temporality as more "primordial" than linear time that he asserts that "in the order of possible interpretation" we first need to understand Dasein's temporality as this is the essential basis and requirement for comprehending the significance of time as it relates to other entities in the universe (BT: 479). For instance, entities are disclosed as present-at-hand *only* when we modify our everyday temporality by adopting a theoretical attitude. So even though present-at-hand entities exist independently of humans, the classification and significance of "presence-at-hand" can be understood only in relation to our own temporality.

Further, as Heidegger points out, "Being (not entities) is dependent upon the understanding of Being" (BT: 255); thus, the *Being* of an entity can have meaning or disclose itself only *to someone* because, of all beings, only Dasein has an understanding of Being, so without Dasein there would be no one to whom the entities can make a difference.

Further, since our ability to grasp the significance of entities, whose relation to time is different from our own, depends on our own temporality, we obviously cannot reach an understanding of our own temporality via an understanding of how present-at-hand entities relate to time. This offers further support to Heidegger's claim that Dasein's authentic temporality is more "primordial" than a timeline.

Temporality and historicality

Heidegger's fundamental question regarding time "is not whether beings are in time or not. It is rather whether the Being of beings gets understood by reference to time" (MFL: 144). His enquiry leads him to investigate temporality in terms of Dasein's fate, destiny and heritage to see if time, in this richer, historical sense, forms the basis of our understanding of Being.

In his discussion of history, Heidegger is not primarily concerned with history in the ordinary sense, as the systematic, scientific study and narration of past kings and queens, political movements, wars and so on; rather, he is interested in the fundamentally *historical* nature of human existence, which he calls *Geschichlichkeit*. (This word from *Being and Time* is translated by John Macquarrie and Edward Robinson as "historicality", although in Joan Stambaugh's translation it is called *historicity*.) Historicality is used exclusively in reference to Dasein's unique mode of being-in-the-world as a historical being. The word used by Heidegger to refer to the scientific study of the past is *Historie*, translated as "histriology" in the Macquarrie and Robinson translation.

Descartes despised history, because it lacks the certainty of the sciences such as mathematics and physics. Husserl was not interested in history, nor even in the history of philosophical ideas, which he saw as irrelevant since he believed philosophy to be founded on intuitively evident truths that can, in principle, be discovered at any time. Heidegger disagreed with such ideas, asserting that truth could not be discerned without taking into account historical context, since the situation in which we disclose truths – our present circumstances – is immersed in historical heritage and thus truth is always relative to the historical period and cultural context in which it arises: "Because Dasein is historical in its own existence, possibilities of access and modes of interpretation of beings are themselves diverse, varying in different historical circumstances" (BPP: 22). Further, Heidegger emphasizes that even science is in the grip of historizing (BT: 444). The fact that Heidegger points out "universal" structures common to all Dasein – such as *care* – is not in conflict with his claim of the "historical relativity of truth" since this claim refers to his *way of interpreting* such structures: it is *his understanding* of truth that is *historically situated*.

Heidegger was impressed and influenced by the German philosopher and historian Dilthey, especially his attempts to isolate the *a priori* conditions that enable us to study history, and Heidegger's vision of the historical character of our existence, which contains some of his most intense descriptions of authentic existence, is clearly indebted to Dilthey. Heidegger also shared Oswald Spengler's (1880–1936) concern over the problem of historical relativism: the fact that ideas are always relative to a specific culture and thus have no universal validity.

However, in Heidegger's opinion all previous philosophers of history had made a fundamental error in their approach by ignoring the inextricable intertwining of the past with the present. In their study of history (historiology) they divide historical events into separate and extinct "epochs", reducing history to a mere chronicle of an inert past that is over and done with. Thus Dasein's uniqueness is dissolved within the dead past of a previous culture that is treated as quite different from our own.

Heidegger, in contrast, believes that the study of history should be first and foremost the investigation of Dasein's "living historical past" in the form of *past Dasein's world of possibilities* that are significant, in terms of the possibilities they open up and make available to us in our world now, as present and future possibilities.

For, according to Heidegger, an authentic approach to history (as historicality) struggles to keep past existences open to the future as the "quiet force of the possible" (BT: 445–6). The authentically historical historian is concerned not only with what past Dasein actually *did* choose and *could* have chosen to do, but also with any of past Dasein's possibilities that are available to us now as current possibilities for our existence today (BT: 446–7).

Thus the "historical past is not determined by its position in what has been", nor by any and every event that happens to result from it, but by "possibilities of its future … what is future as possible" (GA 31: 213), and thus the historian's disclosure grows out of the future (BT: 447). In other words, the future is not only of primary importance in Dasein's temporality, but it is also definitive of history: "History as a happening is an acting and being acted upon which, passing through the present, is determined from out of the future and takes over the past" (IM: 44).

Heidegger believes that the study of history (as historicality) requires the projection or anticipation of "monumental" possibilities concerning the conclusions of historical development, for this is the essential basis for developing our sense of where history as a whole is headed and for selecting those past events that should be "reverently preserved" as a historical record of our culture's achievements and as historically relevant to our account of the significance of history (BT: 447–8).

A sense of the difference between the "living historical past" of historicality and the past of histriology that is truly "dead and gone" can be illustrated by the following simple example. Antiques in a museum, such as pieces of household equipment, belong to a *time that is past* and yet they are still ready-to-hand in the "present". The equipment's past is "alive" in the present because its possibilities for use in the past can also be present and future possibilities. It also belongs to "history" (histriology) as the "dead past" because the "world" within which the equipment belonged to a network of equipment and was encountered as ready-to-hand by a concernful Dasein who was in-the-world – that *actual* "world" – exists no longer.

Heidegger asserts that it is only because of Dasein's historicality, which is rooted in Dasein's temporality, that we have any interest at all in past events and an ability to study them scientifically in a way that is meaningful to us, for the past is still with us, serving as our heritage. Thus there would be no such thing as history, in any sense of the word, if Dasein were not historical, since Dasein's historicality provides an *a priori* understanding, or sense of history, that *discloses* the historical past, and in doing so provides the basis for histriology (BT: 427). For Dasein's "Temporality temporalizes world-time, within the horizon of which 'history' can 'appear' as historizing within time" (BT: 436). Thus, from the existential viewpoint, claims of objectivity in the case of history as "histriology" are false, since the scientific study of the past cannot ignore the fact that the historian's existence is itself *historical*.

Of all entities, only Dasein is "historical" in Heidegger's use of the word. A rock or a dog has a past that influences its present circumstances. But Dasein "*is* its past" (BT: 41) and Dasein is not merely its "very own" past, but also the past of the community to which it belongs, before as well as after its own birth, and thus its existence is inextricably linked with the existence of *past Dasein*. It understands itself and its own possibilities in terms of interpretations of existence inherited from its immediate and distant past (BT: 41).

Fate

Dasein's historicality depends on the structure of its "historizing". This term refers to the unique and peculiar way in which Dasein's being-in-the-world stretches itself between its birth and its death (BT: 425, 427). Dasein's *historizing* is not something that happens automatically. Historizing occurs when Dasein runs ahead to its own death, returns to its own birth, or beyond, and rebounds into the *authentic present* to resolutely choose and adhere to one of its possibilities in a "moment of vision".

We can see that this description of Dasein's "historicality" also describes the nature of Dasein's authentic, ecstatic temporality. This is because the interpretation of historicality is just a more concrete working out of temporality (BT: 434). Thus, because of our historizing, our lives form "stories" or dramas that unfold from the time of our birth up until our death. Heidegger calls the resolutely chosen possibility to which Dasein steadfastly commits itself "Dasein's fate".

Heidegger does not use the term fate in the ancient Greek sense of "predetermination beyond our control", but our freedom to choose our fate is necessarily limited because it must be derived from our own heritage in the face of the constant possibility of death, which can happen at any time (BT: 436). Thus Dasein's self-chosen fate is rooted in an act of authentic resoluteness "in which Dasein *hands* itself *down* to itself, free for death, in a possibility which it has inherited and yet has chosen" (BT: 435). Irresolute Dasein, who flows with the way of the They, may have "bad luck" but it cannot have fate, or suffer at the hands of fate, and thus it is not authentically historical. Only a Dasein who has *chosen* his fate can suffer the hardships of fate in the external sense.

Destiny

For Heidegger, "destiny" is different from fate in the sense that it is something that is *shared* – it is the *destiny of an entire community* – and thus it is not something that individual Dasein can have on their own. Destiny arises, or "becomes free", only when the fates of individual Dasein are unified through social interaction in a common world with a shared history: the historizing of each individual Dasein then becomes a "co-historizing" that determines or creates this single shared destiny. Under such circumstances each individual Dasein has a destiny, which is simultaneously the shared destiny of the entire community (BT: 436).

The authentic historicality of heritage

Although authentic awareness of death frees Dasein from the grip of the They to develop the authenticity of resolve, it does not inform Dasein of *all* the possibilities available to it for determining its fate. Heidegger claims that to be fully authentic the possibilities Dasein projects for its future have to be drawn from its past in terms of its *heritage* (BT: 435). This heritage, which Dasein shares with others, provides Dasein with many possible self-interpretations accumulated over thousands of years. For it is impossible to invent a *brand new* life project completely on my own, since ultimately my source for all possible projects is rooted in some way or another in my shared heritage. Unless my heritage is embraced in a resolute manner through a knowledge of and commitment to the significance of my historical roots, then authentic historicality is impossible.

In other words, according to Heidegger, authentic existence always "repeats" (in the sense of "retrieves") some inherited possibility (BT: 437). So Heidegger views the past as a stockpile of possibilities for living authentically: "everything 'good' is a heritage, and the character of 'goodness' lies in making authentic existence possible" (BT: 435). Heroes are obviously "good", which is why Heidegger asserts that, from its heritage, Dasein can now "choose its hero" in order to identify what is worthy of being retrieved from the past (BT: 437) as a model or point of reference to guide its own life. Dasein is free to choose any number of historical "role models" of any type from among great philosophers, musicians, painters, saints and so on: indeed anyone, even perhaps someone "humble" and unknown, who inspires Dasein's admiration:

> *Repeating is* ... going back into the possibilities of the Dasein that has-been-there ... (who) is not disclosed in order to be actualized over again ... Arising, as it does, from a resolute projection of oneself, repetition ... does not abandon itself to that which is past, nor does it aim at progress. In the moment of vision authentic existence is indifferent to both these alternatives.   (BT: 437–8)

Inauthentic Dasein does not repeat in this way; its hero is the They (BT: 423).

Authentic Dasein's "repetition" or "retrieval" of possibilities made available to it by its heritage does not imply mere imitation. An authentic person is no "copycat", since Heidegger's concept of repetition refers to the act of appropriating freely and creatively a way of living derived from one's heritage (BT: 437). "Hero figures" or significant events from Dasein's heritage simply serve to inspire and suggest possibilities that are *currently* available to Dasein: possibilities that then can be questioned, interpreted and adapted to Dasein's own circumstances and potentials. The outcome of this can be construed as Dasein's "fate".

Most commonly, however, people adopt roles from their immediate past rather than from long before their birth, and *inauthentically* historical

Dasein remains dispersed or absorbed in its present undertakings, and any interest it has for the past will be merely "histriological". According to Heidegger, it is because of the inauthentic state of "falling" that we normally view history merely as a sequence of facts or events, as "one damn thing after another", rather than understanding history in terms of our heritage, fate and destiny.

More importantly, Heidegger emphasizes that *Dasein's temporality* can truly be understood only in terms of its *fate, destiny and heritage*, which hold the key to understanding the nature of Being itself. He stresses that we need to "win back our roots in history", to take "a creative view of our tradition" and to "repeat the beginning ... in order to transform it into a new beginning" (IM: 38–9). Heidegger suggests that a "dialogue" or "conversation" with the thinkers of the "first beginning", the Greeks, is an essential preparation for the "other beginning" (GA 65: 6, 169, 187, 432), for "Being itself is inherently eschatological", and thus "we must someday anticipate the former dawn in the dawn to come" (EGT: 18). So the question of Being opens the "happening" of human existence to "yet unquestioned possibilities, futures, and at the same time binds it back to its past beginning, so sharpening it and giving it weight in the present" (IM: 44).

At the end of *Being and Time*, having conducted a lengthy and highly detailed investigation of his original proposition that Being – our sense of what it means to be – has to be grasped *in terms of time*, and having enlightened us in so many ways regarding Dasein's mode of being-in-the-world, Heidegger writes at the end of the book, "Does *time* itself manifest itself as the horizon of *Being*?" (BT: 488). It would appear from this, that after his time-consuming analysis of Dasein's temporality, perhaps Heidegger still has some doubt as to whether the appropriate horizon for understanding Being *is* indeed *time*.

CHAPTER SEVEN

The "truth of *alētheia*" and language

Philosophy is the search for truth. Heidegger claimed that essentially there are two main approaches to truth. The traditional one, which has existed at least since Plato, claims that the truth can be defined in terms of specific criteria for assessing true or false propositions. In contrast, Heidegger investigates the meaning or essence of truth that exists independently of, and prior to, any criteria. "Truth", in his sense of the word, is no mere presentation of static facts, but the experience of a process of disclosure that is alive and *happening in each moment*. For Heidegger such "truth" is the essential foundation of all knowledge.

Traditional concepts of truth

In *Being and Time*, at the beginning of his discussion of truth as "disclosure", Heidegger comments that in philosophy, the questions of Being and truth have always been associated (BT: 256), but whereas originally their relation was characterized in terms of "disclosure", this insight was eclipsed by the *logical conception of truth*, first formulated by Aristotle via his philosophical account that expresses a basic intuition about truth: "to say of what is that it is not, or of what is not that it is, is false, while to say of what is that it is, and of what is not that it is not, is true" (*Metaph.* Γ 1001b25). The "correspondence theory" (BT: 266–8), which is the traditional and standard conception of truth used today, interprets and expresses Aristotle's basic intuition in terms of a relation of correspondence between mind and world (e.g. between facts and reality). For a belief or statement to be *true*, it needs to correspond to – to be verified or "proved" by – the "facts". Propositions are correct or true only if they factually "match" the object or situation they refer to: "The true, whether it be a matter or a proposition, is what accords, the accordant" ("On the Essence of Truth", in BW: 117). A proposition is either true or it is not. There are no degrees or gradations of truth or untruth. In all such systems, truth is something that occurs only within the perimeter of specific "rules" or "conditions" that are used for its assessment and, meanwhile, according to Heidegger, the question of what truth actually *is*, or what it *means*, is completely ignored. For as William Large points out, in reference to this conception of truth as "agreement":

> [T]he more we think about agreement, the more puzzling it seems. Although the existence of the statement is obvious enough and the object it is supposed to agree with, what is it that allows them to agree with one another? Is it something in the statement, or in the object itself? But if they are two different kinds of beings (nobody thinks that a statement is the same as a thing), what allows them to agree at all?
>
> (Large 2010: 64)

Heidegger noted that such views of truth place man "at the centre of the universe" in terms of controlling all definitions of truth/falseness and right/wrong. He regarded this attitude as being responsible for our technologically obsessed outlook that regards the planet as a vast resource that is exploitable, exclusively for our benefit. So it is of central importance to Heidegger to loosen the assumptions and prejudices of this traditional perception of truth so that Dasein understands that truth cannot be understood merely via the assimilation of knowledge derived from "true" propositions. This futile attempt to know life via theories offers "truths" that provide a severely narrowed perspective on reality. "True sentences" are merely true sentences, but the primary ground of truth is in *actual existence*, which resides in the living process of life itself, as it is unfolding. Moreover, how can truths that are based on the correspondence between our thoughts (the content of our consciousness) and the outside world be regarded as "objective" truths when they are rooted in our *subjective* impressions?

However, instead of simply dismissing it, Heidegger sets out to unpack the hidden ontology of the correspondence theory of truth, to uncover its basis, "to lay bare the ontological foundations of that conception", so that "the primordial phenomenon of truth becomes visible", thus enabling him to demonstrate "the way in which the traditional conception of truth has been *derived* from this *phenomenon*" (BT: 257). Thus he will come to show that the traditional account of truth presupposes this primordial truth, which establishes what kind of "facts" there *are* to which statements or beliefs may, or may not, correspond.

Heidegger's approach, therefore, is not a theory, but an analysis of truth; he investigates what actually happens in situations where truth occurs. This is radically different from any earlier philosophers' approaches. Truth is no longer the relation between a subject-knower and the object-known; instead it is something that is occurring, as the *meaning* of an event is revealed to us. The obvious advantage of such an approach is that, unlike the traditional systems of truth, it makes it possible to investigate the meaning of Being itself, rather than merely the entities that arise out of Being.

Heidegger's truth of *alētheia*

Heidegger's understanding of truth was influenced by his readings of Presocratic texts. He regarded the Presocratic era as the dawn of Western civilization, a "first beginning", in which the Greeks brought to light the ontological difference between Being and entities by asking the question "What is the Being of entities?" Being, according to these early Greeks, is "*appearance* as a definite mode of emerging self-manifestation" in which things emerge from concealment into "*truth* in the sense of unconcealment" (IM: 109).

Heidegger claimed that "propositional truths" are derived from this more primordial and far deeper truth, which he called "*alētheia*", ancient Greek for "truth", which etymologically means "unconcealment" (BT: 261). He asserted that propositional truths can deal only with surface phenomena of meaning, since such truths must always already be grounded on a prior understanding of Being and beings: a more fundamental "truth as unconcealment" that is central to our existence. So Heidegger (like the early Greeks) did not see truth as an agreement between a thought or statement and its object, nor as any type of theoretical attitude, such as a judgement, belief or representation, but instead he viewed fundamental truth as an uncovering, revealing or unveiling of something, as "what shows itself – *entities in the 'how' of their uncoveredness*" (BT: 262).

So Heidegger believed that for us to really know or experience any entity (including ourselves), it first has to be revealed to us, or unconcealed to us. He regarded such disclosure as the essence of truth from which all other theories and uses of truth are derived. The traditional view of truth is, in comparison, shallow and limited because all the "components" of this truth (the statements or judgements, the objects they refer to and the "statement-maker") are themselves "entities" that first have to be recognized as such, prior to any "matching up".

To clarify this, Heidegger describes in his later works a hierarchy of three levels of truth. (i) *Propositional truth* is the lowest of these three truths, and dependent on the other two. He illustrates this via the statement "the

143

picture is askew on the wall". Confirmation of the truth of this proposition is possible only because of (ii) *ontic truth* (factual information), which reveals that the picture is obviously hanging crookedly. Heidegger sees ontic truth as the first stage of unconcealment. However, the picture can reveal itself to us as hanging askew only because of (iii) *ontological truth* (the highest sense of truth) in which the event of our existence is revealed, or unconcealed. In other words, Dasein first needs *to exist* and have an *a priori* understanding of its being-in-the-world, in order for the crookedness of the picture to matter and be noticed. So *alētheia* – truth as unconcealment – is clearly also a prerequisite for the application of the "correspondence theory" of truth and all other truths. Heidegger therefore regarded *alētheia* as fundamental truth.

However, entities also need some *place* where their unconcealment can occur. In *Being and Time* that place was Dasein. Entities were "disclosed" (revealed) to Dasein via direct, primarily practical, experience. The Being or "hammer-ness" of a hammer was disclosed while Dasein was using it for its intended purpose; an event such as rain "revealed itself" in the presence of Dasein's passive, but interested, awareness of it.

For Heidegger, then, truth occurs each time the *meaning* of an event is revealed to us, and Dasein is a being that always remains receptive to experiencing the truth of other beings. Heidegger regards Dasein's receptiveness as an "open space" of intelligibility, a "region" in which entities can manifest themselves. He often refers to this open region as "a clearing" (*Lichtung*), and says that Dasein itself *is* this "clearing".

The German word *Lichtung* can also be used in reference to a "forest clearing". It was probably inspired by Heidegger's regular treks through the Black Forest and is especially appropriate for what he is trying to communicate. Often, when walking through thick forest with restricted visibility, one can encounter an open space, a "clearing", where the sparsity or complete absence of trees allows the sunlight to stream in and light up in clear visibility all that lies within the clearing, but always encircling this open space is the dense, dark surrounding forest: an image reflecting the unconcealment/concealment of Heidegger's understanding of truth as *alētheia* (clarified below).

Further, the word *Lichtung* implies the *adjective* "light" (*licht*), which Heidegger interprets not as "light" in terms of brightness, since "light never first creates the clearing. Rather light presupposes it" ("The End of Philosophy and the Task of Thinking", in BW: 442), but "light" in the sense of making "light, free and open, e.g., to make the forest free of trees at one place. The free space thus originating is the clearing" (*ibid.*: 441). This sense of lightening or thinning out the trees implies the involvement of human beings (i.e. Dasein), which appropriately reflects Heidegger's fundamental assertion that Dasein is a "clearing" in the midst of reality, in which beings are disclosed in the "clearing" of Dasein's understanding of Being and beings; we are the "there" (*Da*) where entities are revealed in the sense that only through *our* understanding can they be thought about and seen as they truly are.

According to Heidegger, although we *are* this "clearing" of Being, we almost never notice this fact, because the "clearing" withdraws or conceals itself in the very act of unconcealing beings. Thus Heidegger frequently asserts that "unconcealment is concealed in favour of the unconcealed". He means that we pay attention to the entities that are revealed and their mode of being rather than to the fact that they are present to us – that they are and that we can encounter them – and thus the phenomenon of unconcealment itself, that is the "clearing" of Being, is completely overlooked since we "keep to what is present without considering presencing" (EGT: 99). In other words, the disclosure or revelation of *beings* distracts our attention from the realization of the incredible and simple fact *that they are revealed to us* and thus in our focus on beings we overlook Being.

However, this tendency in Dasein to pay attention to "beings" rather than "Being" is well adapted to the needs of ordinary survival. For we would tend to cope far less efficiently with the demands of everyday living if we continuously focused on our "openness" or "awareness" rather than on our interaction with the surrounding world, because the open clearing of *alētheia* must, in a sense, be overlooked for effective daily functioning (see EGT: 100, 122). However, when we do explicitly attend to the clearing itself, we do not just experience unconcealed beings but also are simultaneously aware of the fact that there *are* beings and that we are aware of them. Heidegger calls this "awareness of our awareness" *standing in the clearing*.

According to Heidegger, truth is therefore a *characteristic* of Dasein and *dependent* on Dasein. This conclusion led to his statement that truth exists only so long as Dasein exists – there is no truth without Dasein:

> There is truth only in so far as Dasein is and so long as Dasein is. Entities are uncovered only *when* Dasein *is*; and only as long as Dasein *is*, are they disclosed. Newton's laws, the principles of contradiction, any truth whatever – these are true only as long as Dasein *is*. Before there was any Dasein, there was no truth; nor will there be any after Dasein is no more ... Before Newton's laws were discovered, they were not "true"; ... Through Newton the laws became true; and with them, entities became accessible in themselves to Dasein. Once entities have been uncovered, they show themselves precisely as entities which beforehand already were. Such uncovering is the kind of being which belongs to "truth".
>
> (BT: 269–70)

Heidegger does *not* mean that Dasein determines what truth is. However, since truth is defined as unconcealment and since entities need the "open clearing" of Dasein in order to reveal (disclose) themselves, then, logically, truth can exist only as part of Dasein's mode of existence, which provides this clearing for disclosure. Dasein is therefore an entity "in truth". This same pattern of reasoning can also be seen in traditional theories of truth; without propositions there would be no truth, and since *we* make the propositions, how could there be truth without us?

Heidegger adds that, because of Dasein's fallenness, it always contains closed-off or unexpressed "hidden" possibilities; thus Dasein is always, in part, "hidden" or concealed (GA 65: 362). This is why Heidegger describes Dasein as being simultaneously in "truth" *and* "untruth" (BT: 263, 264): "Truth is un-truth, insofar as there belongs to it the reservoir of the not-yet-uncovered, the un-uncovered, in the sense of concealment" (PLT: 60).

In terms of conventional thinking, in which things are either true or false, this idea of the coexistence of truth and untruth seems absurd. Understood in Heidegger's sense, however, the statement makes perfect sense. Truth is constantly in the process of uncovering what is still concealed in it, and this activity never ends, which is why in Dasein's case and in all other situations, "truth is always simultaneously in untruth". This whole discussion crystallizes in Heidegger's claim that an understanding of Dasein's way of Being is the fundamental foundation of truth; the disclosure of Dasein via its own relentless enquiry to reveal itself as it exists is what truth *means*.

In his later writings, however, Heidegger saw the vastness of *Being* itself, rather than Dasein, as the "clearing": "In the midst of beings as a whole there is an open place. There is a clearing. This clearing is, thought from the side of beings, more 'being' than beings ... The luminous middle itself encircles like Nothing ... all that is" (PLT: 53). He describes this place as an open region or field of relatedness where entities manifest themselves and interact in varying ways, and although humans are not in power here, they are still of fundamental importance. Heidegger speaks of this open region as the place that illuminates the presence of entities – where Dasein experiences the unconcealment or "truth' of an entity's presence or Being.

Heidegger points out, however, that in order to understand the most fundamental events of Being we should realize that this clearing is not a clearly definable place, but rather an infinitely complex area of possibilities. In it, all beings cannot be disclosed simultaneously; they may or may not appear.

The concept of *alētheia* contains at the same time both unconcealment and concealment. Paradoxically, it is unconcealment that produces this concealment; thus truth is always essentially a "mystery" (P: 148ff.) since

Being is always beings *together with* their "other side", the *lighted* side of the "globe of Being" together with its dark side. Ordinarily, however, we are oblivious of this mystery of truth, believing that we dwell exclusively in "the immediately surrounding circle of beings" that are "familiar, reliable, ordinary" (PLT: 54). Thus we forget the true *depth* of Being: the fact that our realm of beings is just one disclosure of a reality that contains within itself an infinite number of other possible realms of beings. Trapped within this impoverished experience – which finds philosophical expression in the belief that truth is fully encapsulated by the correspondence theory – we are now as ignorant as the young child, who understands the moon only as a flat illuminated disk because he is completely unaware of its dark side: the concealment that belongs to its unconcealment.

This idea of truth as simultaneous concealment and unconcealment can be grasped easily if one thinks about how a radio functions: tuning in to one wavelength automatically blocks out all other wavelengths, but these other channels, nevertheless, remain as unheard possibilities. Similarly, when an entity is revealed in one particular way, this simultaneously conceals all the remaining possible ways of its Being. Thinking about truth in this way opens up a very flexible view of truth in which something can express *degrees* of unconcealment, like a landscape seen in the half-light of dawn. The clarity of truth, in this sense, often emerges only gradually, similar to discovering meaning in true works of art whose deeper significance is not immediately apparent.

So there is great ambiguity in this "clearing" that Heidegger describes, every unconcealment automatically resulting in concealment. But, for Heidegger, this *is* the truth of Being: an endless cycle of the unveiling-veiling of entities in existence. He hints at the nature of this process via his choice of the Greek word *alētheia*, which contains the word *lethe*, meaning *forgetfulness*.

In *Being and Time* Heidegger discusses how truth can be seen in the disclosure of the "meaning" of ordinary everyday events and things. In his later works he adds that "the essence of truth is the truth of essence" ("On the Essence of Truth", in BW: 137). Here he is offering the additional insight that truth as the unconcealment or disclosure of what it means to be can be found only via the uncovering of "essences". Heidegger's term "essence" has nothing to do with the traditional idea of essence as a single, covering definition; instead, this concept refers to "that which makes something what it is", in other words *Being*. So the "truth of essence" means the truth of the meaning of Being, which is also the intrinsic "meaning" of any entity. Thus Heidegger asserts that the question of truth emerges from the question of Being: "The question of the essence of truth arises from the question of the truth of essence" (*ibid.*). To sum up, to understand the meaning of essence is to understand the meaning of Being, which is the essence of truth.

Das Ereignis: the primordial source of truth

In *Being and Time* Heidegger sets out to explore how the manifestation of *meaningfulness* in the world depends on the reciprocal *a priori* relation between Dasein and Being; each needs the other for meaningfulness to occur. He attempts to investigate this relation via a "transcendental-horizonal" framework, where Dasein is understood as projectively holding open the "arena" of the meaning-giving process. When Heidegger describes Dasein's mode of being-in-the-world as "transcendence" (BT: 415), he is pointing out that Dasein is always "more than" or "beyond" its particular circumstances or "life form" because the basis of Dasein's transcendence is its temporality, which embraces the threefold unity of past/present/future, and as such Dasein is able to reflect on the totality of human experience and to relate to itself and to all entities in terms of possibilities rather than as actualities.

The world is "transcendent" in the sense that it is a non-entity, "beyond" all entities, that provides a meaning-full context of references (BT: 121) via an entity-network that discloses the interconnectedness of everything: where things belong, and how they relate to our lives as ready-to-hand or present-at-hand. The world's transcendence is also enabled-by and founded-upon its temporality, which accommodates the essentially temporal references of any ongoing practical activities in which "things" are used in a manner determined by the projected completion of a particular task. It is Dasein's transcendence in this transcendent world that allows it to choose its "being-with", and to let other entities be as they are. According to *Being and Time*, it is only because of Dasein's transcendent mode of "being-in-the-transcendent-world" that it can truly encounter the significance of other beings and provide the account of entities that is given in *Being and Time,* because Dasein's potential for transcendence is the fundamental basis for philosophy.

In the "turn" of Heidegger's thinking it has often been claimed that there is a change in focus from *Dasein* to *Being*, especially since he talks of "abandoning subjectivity", and Division Three of *Being and Time* was intended to shift the emphasis of his investigation from the Being of Dasein to the *meaning of Being* as such. But *Being and Time* makes it clear that the manifestation of meaningfulness in the world depends on the *a priori* relation between Dasein and Being and each needs the other for meaningfulness to occur. Therefore, because the relation between Dasein and Being is recip-rocal, Heidegger is obliged both in his earlier and later writings to main-tain the focus of his thinking on both Dasein and Being, since they are interdependent.

However, what does change is that, following the publication of the first two divisions of Part One of *Being and Time*, he abandons the "transcendental-horizonal approach", and avoids the term "transcendence" for two reasons. First, this Kantian notion implies that Dasein has a certain priority over Being, in the sense that it suggests that Dasein's temporal structure determines what "Being" potentially could mean. Thus, in his later thinking Heidegger empha-sizes instead that *Being has power over us*: that we do not create it or influence it, but respond to it. Second, this Kantian expression could potentially give the impression that we can formulate a single, fundamental and ultimate con-cept of Being and demonstrate its necessity, whereas Heidegger views Being as historical, in continual flux and taking many forms.

So in the mid-1930s, having concluded that transcendental think-ing cannot be applied to Division Three of Part One of *Being and Time*, Heidegger instead adopts what he terms a *seingeschictlich* approach in the attempt to question Being from within Being itself. According to Shee-han, this term has the sense of *Es gibt Sein*, which Sheehan translates as "Meaning-giving is *a priori* operative wherever there is human being":

> [This] means that the ... (the "sending" or "giving" of meaning) is the same as the meaning-giving bond of man–meaning. The presupposition of the *seingeschictlich* approach is that meaning is always-already given with human being itself rather than through some projective activity ... Moreover, the emphasis now is less on man projectively *holding open* the world and more on man's *being required* to hold open the world. On this *seingeschictlich* basis the later Heidegger could bring the work of BT I.3 to fruition outside the limitations of transcendental method ...
>
> [T]he outcome of the analysis: an understanding and acceptance of the fact that all meaning derives from the finite meaning-giving source, which soon will be called *Ereignis*, the *a priori* "appropria-tion" of man for sustaining meaning-giving.
>
> (Sheehan 2010: 90–91)

Ascertaining exactly what Heidegger means each time he uses the term "*Ereignis*" has been a source of frustration both for students and for advanced interpreters of his thought. Perhaps this explains why many intro-ductions to Heidegger do not even mention the term, in spite of it being at the very core of his thinking on Being. The complexity of interpreting this concept is utterly unsurprising; after all, what could be more difficult than trying to reach a satisfying understanding of an aspect of a philosopher's thinking that the philosopher himself constantly struggled with? And the fact that Heidegger did experience significant difficulties with his interpretations of *Ereignis* is mirrored in his continually changing and developing explanations that begin from his first mention of the term and continue throughout the entirety of this thinking until finally he acknowledges that a true understanding of *Ereignis* cannot be encapsulated by thought. And yet this still does not deter him from continuing his attempts.

That Heidegger, and all his interpreters, should encounter such insurmountable difficulties in the thinking of this concept is also no great mystery, given the fact that Heidegger chose to use this term in reference to that which is an intrinsic and thus inseparable aspect of Being itself; and as we know, in an analytical sense, all attempts to verbalize or explain Being are ultimately futile.

It may at this point appear to some readers that there is no valid reason for discussing this matter if satisfying explanations can never be reached. Also, the question might arise as to why Heidegger nevertheless persisted with this endeavour. Perhaps the following somewhat unconventional answer to this latter question also provides justification for our continued efforts to think and discuss this term.

It seems that Heidegger realized that the attempt to think the unthinkable is one of the most worthwhile endeavours of all philosophical thought. But why should this be so? Perhaps the answer lies in that which was already discovered thousands of years previously by masters of Zen, who gave their students unsolvable riddles called *koans*. These masters discovered from their own experience, and through observation of transformations in consciousness occurring in some students, that if our efforts to think the unthinkable are continued with deep intensity to their final conclusion, what may and sometimes does arise is a state of Being liberated from the confines of thought, and in that moment the illusory separation between the Being of the individual and the great mystery of Being is transcended. Thus, for Heidegger, in thinking the unthinkable mystery of *Ereignis*, one is opening oneself to the possibility of an "*Ereignis*-experience": awareness that is unified with the wonder and mystery of Being, that arises as a gift from Being itself (an event that religious thinkers might describe as "grace").

Since I am attempting to present one of the most complex issues of Heidegger's thought in a very limited space, the discussion offered cannot be in depth, but should serve to give those interested a solid basis for further investigation of this important matter. Also, in order to facilitate a more coherent overall sense of what Heidegger is trying to communicate, the various interpretations are not always presented in chronological order.

Heidegger's question "How does meaning occur at all?" is asking about the meaning-giving source of the meaning of things, so it is referring to the *a priori* process that gives rise to the significance of anything that is meaningful to us. And the very fact that things are meaningful at all is, for Heidegger, "the wonder of all wonders: that things *make sense*" (P: 234). Indeed he considers meaningfulness to be the most basic structure of the things we encounter. In *Being and Time*, he understood this source-of-meaning in terms of Dasein's meaning-giving *a priori* existential, which he called "being-in-the-world".

Later, however, his investigation underwent a considerable change that arose as he developed his conception of the term "*Ereignis*", which is the ordinary German word for an event or happening. This word first appeared as a main concept in a lecture course from 1919, where it was presented as signifying an event that happens to Dasein, not an event as an "objective occurrence" where Dasein is merely a detached subject or observer, but rather an event that is a "lived experience" in which Dasein is immersed, involved and experiencing "anew" (as *Ereignis*) whatever it encounters (see GA 56/57: 75). So it could apply to being caught in a storm, the act of renovating, the arrival of a friend and so on.

However, in Heidegger's post-1938 writings, *Ereignis* becomes fundamental to his thinking on Being, following the publication of *Contributions to Philosophy*; *Ereignis* is presented as the central message of this highly important text. In this particular work he claims that "*das Seyn west als das Ereignis*", which is translated as "Being essentially unfolds as appropriation". He uses the old German spelling "*Seyn*" for "Being" to hint at the mysterious quality of Being concealed behind our conventional perception of Being. Also, the *sound* (although not "etymology") of the word "*Ereignis*" when spoken out loud resonates with the sound made by the adjective "*eigen*" (own), and Heidegger wants to suggest through this audible similarity a connection in meaning with words such as "*geeignet*" (appropriate), "*eigentlich*" (authentic) and "*Eigenschaft*" (property), So for Heidegger, "*Ereignis*" means "appropriation" ("event of appropriation" or "propriative event"), and he uses it to refer to the event in which *Being is given to us*. However, Heidegger also explains that the "it" (the event of *Ereignis*) that *gives* Being, is Being itself (OT: 45); thus *Ereignis* is not meant to be regarded as the source of Being. So Heidegger wants us to understand that *Ereignis* (appropriation) is neither a cause nor an entity: it is not some*thing* that gives us Being; rather, it is the very *event of giving* (see Polt 1999: 146).

Ereignis is crucial to Being in the sense that appropriation (*Ereignis*) is Being's own way of happening, its way of giving itself to us: of imparting to us a sense of the meaningfulness of Being and "beings", via its illuminating presence. This seemingly strange conception of Being in terms of *Ereignis*, which is an "event of giving" that contains no distinction or separation between the giver, the giving and the given (since Being is, all at once, the giver, the act of giving and that which is given) might be easier for some readers to grasp if one thinks of the phrase "it is raining". This too can be seen as an "event of giving" where the raining is simultaneously the giver, the giving (the act of raining) and the given (as the rain that falls to the ground).

The term "appropriation" also points to the fact that our involvement in this "event" is essential for the significance of the truth of Being and beings to arise (EGT: 367–8) since, according to Heidegger, the world is only disclosed to us when we are fully engaged participants in it. So the disclosure of Being needs Dasein as the site of its occurrence and Dasein is appropriated by this disclosure. Heidegger regarded Dasein's nature as fundamentally hermeneutical – always requiring meaning and always making meaning possible (GA 21: 151) – and he understood the human condition as being inextricably fused with the *a priori* givenness of disclosure, since meaning requires *Dasein* as its grounding "where". In other words, Dasein is the *site* ("clearing" or "open space") of the occurrence of Being, so without Dasein there is no *Sein* (Being). Equally, without *Sein* there is no Dasein. Thus Dasein must be appropriated for, or thrown into, maintaining the *a priori* process of giving-meaning. And being appropriated as such, Dasein is required to projectively hold open this giving-of-meaning (GA 65: 261).

Heidegger also frequently uses *Ereignis* in reference to the "initial revelation of Being" as the "supreme event", which constitutes the *Anfang*, "the beginning" or *essencing* of Being: the initial disclosure of Being in the Presocratic era that shed light on the ontological difference between Being and beings and first let human beings have meaningful access to the Being of entities (GA 65: 3). In this usage of *Ereignis*, Heidegger is referring to the occurrence in which mankind was first appropriated by Being, the result being a complete transformation of man's essence from "rational animal" to "Da-sein": the "there" of Being, that is, the site of Being's revelation or disclosure. In other words, this supreme event of Being makes man into the "property" of Being; man is now *owned* by Being.

In his lecture "On Time and Being" in 1962, Heidegger also uses the term "*Ereignis*" to refer to the "happening" or "sending" of the events of appropriation out of which the historical epochs of the Western world arise (OT: 19). Indeed, he views the entire history of Being as having been determined by various *Ereignis* – usually equated with epochs of Western thought – that send the different modes of Being or "presencing" that have shaped Western history into its Greek, Roman, medieval, modern and technological epochs. But Heidegger views all these epochs as belonging to metaphysics, which itself can be regarded as one large epoch in relation to which Heidegger "thinks" the possibility of *Ereignis* as "the other beginning in history". Each epoch is a "propriative event", an *Ereignis*, into which Dasein is thrown, and in which Being is "thrown" or given to Dasein as a particular mode of understanding Being and all entities. Heidegger referred to the *a priori* givenness of *Ereignis* in its various epochal forms as "the dispensations" of disclosure. Every time such an event happens it ushers in a new epoch by letting beings appear in a profoundly new way. According to Heidegger, these epochal understandings of Being furnish us with a coherent sense of how things are, thus providing us with whatever meaningfulness we find in this life. For instance, he refers to nihilism as a long-drawn-out *Ereignis* in which truth about beings as a whole gradually changes, moving towards a conclusion determined by nihilism (Niv: 4–5), in which the technological understanding of existence thrives; beings as a whole are revealed as exploitable and manipulable objects. Since these various understandings of Being are "sent" or "given" to us by Being itself, as the inexplicable event of *Ereignis*, this means that, ultimately, they are beyond our control.

So, according to Heidegger, we cannot escape "inheriting" a meaning of Being and because the disclosure of meaning is always already operative everywhere in the human world – and Dasein is a being that always remains receptive to experiencing the truth of other beings – all entities are, in principle, open to human appropriation. That is, everything is continuously accessible to Dasein, except for the fact that everything is continuously accessible. Further, as Dasein, we are guardians of the particular meaning of Being that we have inherited and our purpose is to keep it alive and open, in order to allow it to continue unfolding.

Heidegger also claims that the *Ereignis* of Being belongs to us and we belong to it, in the sense that we are appropriated by it and it is what determines us as Dasein rather than any other entity; furthermore, it is the event that *shapes the destiny* of our particular community. And similarly, we as Dasein can appropriate the event of Being by allowing it to come alive to us via our questioning of its meaning, which stops us taking it for granted. Each time humans appropriate Being *en masse*, through great philosophical, artistic, political or spiritual acts of creativity, previous interpretations of existence are abandoned and a fresh meaning of Being is established that gives birth to a new historical era by laying the foundations for a brand new culture. In this sense the event (*Ereignis*) of Being creates a new dwelling place for Dasein and a new mode of dwelling in which Being reveals itself again with a vibrant new intensity. So, for instance, when the *Ereignis* of the Greek meaning of Being happened, it created the ancient Greek mode of understanding the *meaningfulness* of beings and *significance* of Being, and this new understanding founded the civilization of ancient Greece.

For Heidegger, who throughout his career claimed to be the thinker of "one thought only" (expressed in numerous variations), this "event" of Being is the "thing itself" that philosophy has to interrogate since it is the ultimate *a priori*, and yet it is also ultimately unfathomable because one cannot possibly get behind the *a priori* inexplicable givenness of the relation between man and Being in order to discover *das Ereignis*: the origin of the essencing of Being that brings disclosive comportment and disclosible entities together into the openness of disclosure, thereby giving Dasein access to the being of entities. Nor can one "get behind" the *a priori* inexplicable finitude that is the essence of human existence. Thus Heidegger asserts that regarding the originating source of this disclosive correlation – the "how-and-why-it-comes-about" – all one can finally say is that "disclosure just happens to happen", since we cannot answer this question without already presuming the fact of disclosure and thereby moving in a circle. Therefore, all one can conclude is that this disclosure is an *a priori* givenness on the basis of which entities become accessible:

> Wherever man ... gives himself over to ... shaping and working ... he finds himself everywhere already brought into the unconcealed. The unconcealment of the unconcealed has already propriated whenever it calls man forth into the modes of revealing allotted to him. When man, in his way, from within unconcealment reveals that which presences, he merely responds to the call of unconcealment, even when he contradicts it.
>
> ("The Question Concerning Technology", in BW: 324)

Enteignis

According to Heidegger's conception of truth as *alētheia*, truth is essentially an unconcealment, and as such "every revealing simultaneously includes a concealing" and it is the unconcealment that produces this concealment. This fact of truth permeates every facet of Being. So there belongs to all truth closed-off or unexpressed "hidden" possibilities: a "reservoir of the not-yet-uncovered ... in the sense of concealment" (PLT: 60). Thus when Dasein is tuned in to one mode of understanding "beings" and "Being", all other possible modes of understanding are simultaneously blocked out, although always remaining as possibilities. Each time this happens there is a danger that we might forget the fact that the current mode of understanding is just one disclosure of a reality that contains within itself an infinite number of other possible realms of understanding Being and beings, and in so doing we forget the true depth of Being.

So it should come as no surprise to learn that, according to Heidegger, "Being" manifests itself not only as *Ereignis*, the appropriative "given event" of the disclosure of the meaningfulness of Being and "beings", but it also can, and does, manifest itself as a withdrawal from or abandonment of beings and, simultaneously, as the concealment of itself as the source of all modes of understanding (an event that has led to mankind's obliviousness of Being). In other words, *Ereignis* as the event of "appropriation" includes its own "*expropriation*", which Heidegger calls "*Enteignis*".

In *Contributions to Philosophy* Heidegger asserts that in our current epoch, Being does not yet occur as the appropriating event of *Ereignis*, but rather as the expropriative concealing/withdrawing of *Enteignis* (GA 65: 107ff.): "In this Epoch 'beings' are ... expropriated by Being" (GA 65: 120). This situation exists because, according to Heidegger, the metaphysical understanding of Being that has prevailed in the West from the time of Plato and Aristotle onwards has been conducted within the paradigm of *Gestell*, "enframing": the utilitarian, restricted understanding of ourselves and all entities in existence simply in terms of *resources* that are to be made more accessible for the pursuit of our objectives. Thus things are forced to fulfil a specific purpose: "disclosed" only in terms of their particular type of usefulness.

Operating from within this enframed perspective, each epoch in the history of Being has expressed its own particular mode of taking Being for granted, as something that is already given as the Being or presence of beings. And as each epoch attempts to define the nature or "substance" of this "Being" or "presence" of beings, Being itself is concealed and forgotten and, as such, it has remained largely unthought within each of these epochs. Importantly, the truth of this withdrawal of Being is increasingly covered over or hidden by each epoch via each different mode of (mis)understanding the significance of Being merely in terms of the presence or "Being of beings". This has resulted in what Heidegger terms a "withdrawal and oblivion of Being", which has continued – via its different manifestations – throughout the epochal sendings, on a trajectory towards ever-increasing oblivion: "what is appropriate shows itself in the belonging together of the epochs. The epochs overlap each other in their sequence so that the original sending of Being as presence is more and more covered over in different ways" (OT: 9).

Heidegger emphasizes, however, that this withdrawal of Being is part of the destiny of the sending of Being, because it stems from the "enframed" destined disclosure of Being, which is a manifestation of one of the potential modes of disclosure of Being available to mankind: "Enframing, as a challenging-forth into ordering, sends into a way of revealing. Enframing is an ordaining of destining, as is every way of revealing" ("The Question Concerning Technology", in BW: 330). Moreover, he claims that eventually this withdrawal will result in the collapse of every possible logic of history, leading to the ending of philosophy via the collapse of metaphysics. This will happen because ever since the beginning of the history of philosophy (which for Heidegger means "metaphysics"), philosophy has progressively exhausted its attempts to say what Being *is*, but only in terms of it being the ground or Being of beings, and this has caused Being itself to drift deeper into oblivion.

Thus the history of metaphysics discloses a destiny in which mankind's oblivion of Being has steadily increased until, in our current epoch, the ultimate epoch of metaphysics, the withdrawal and oblivion of Being has reached its maximum via our scientific and technological disclosure of Being (which is the logical, and unavoidable consequence and final outcome of the enframed metaphysical disclosure of Being), where all beings, including the entirety of nature, have been reduced to nothing more than exploitable resources for technological manipulation. This scientific perception of existence, which regards itself as the *ultimate* approach to understanding, offering all answers now or in the future, seems to absorb the entirety of Dasein's awareness, thus concealing Being more effectively than any of the previous epochal understandings of Being, where Dasein still potentially could experience *some* "meaningfulness" as arising from a source other than ourselves.

Thus, according to Heidegger, we are now, more than ever before in the history of Being, uniquely positioned to experience *en masse* the full impact of this groundless withdrawal of Being. And when this happens – and Heidegger believes it will do so in this epoch – it will mean potentially the ending of metaphysics and, in turn, the arrival of a new *Ereignis*: a historical occurrence that is the moment that would mark the other beginning of history where beings are no longer abandoned by Being and the truth of Being reigns as the appropriating event. But this *Ereignis* can happen only when we are liberated from our enframed mindset, because:

> as a destining, it [enframing] banishes man into the kind of revealing that is an ordering. Where this ordering holds sway, it drives out every other possibility of revealing. Above all, enframing conceals that revealing which, in the sense of *poiesis*, lets what presences come forth into appearance.
>
> ("The Question Concerning Technology", in BW: 332)

So enframing banishes from our awareness all other potential modes of understanding beings and Being, and in particular it conceals that essentially important mode of disclosure *poiesis*, which allows the meaningfulness of beings – beings as they really are – to emerge in their "radiant presence": a disclosure of Being and beings that Heidegger hopes will be *Ereignis* as "the other beginning in history". Until we are freed from this restricted perception, Being will continue to remain shrouded in oblivion, because we shall be blind and unreceptive to all other potentially benevolent modes of the disclosure of Being.

According to Heidegger, to overcome our forgetfulness of Being (*Seinverlassenheit*) we must first become fully aware of its existence as the basic happening of our history and realize its dangers: "We look into the danger and see the growth of the saving power" (*ibid.*: 338). But it is not Heidegger's intention to overcome the forgetfulness of Being via the recovery of something forgotten; "the previous non-thinking is not a neglect, but is to be thought of as something that follows from the self-concealing of Being" (OT: 29–30). Instead, he wants us to think from *within* the oblivion of Being about the oblivion of Being in order to expose the full extent of this oblivion, which he hopes will result in a destructuring of our enframed, technological mode of understanding, so that we, as Dasein, can become a receptive *site* ("clearing" or "open space") in preparation for the possibility of a historical transformation arising from the "propriative event" of *Ereignis*: "Only the dismantling of the coverings – this means the destructuring – offers to thinking a provisional glimpse into what then reveals itself as the destiny of Being" (OT: 9).

But Heidegger makes it clear that all such efforts are merely provisional, preliminary preparations, since we cannot produce or found this new beginning (OT: 60) because we still operate from within, and interpret through, the metaphysical mode of understanding Being; so all our attempts to hasten the arrival of *Ereignis* will still be an expression of our "enframed" perspective. But to prepare the "ground" for the event of appropriation he asserts that it is crucial for us to deepen our awareness of the "distress" or "neediness" (*Notlosigkeit*) resulting from this "oblivion of Being", for if we experience this in its most acute, intense manifestations, then forgetfulness of Being itself will disclose Being to us (GA 65: 410ff.). For this to occur, we need first to experience the shocking realization that beings have been abandoned by Being and that we no longer understand the importance of the question of Being – that we have forgotten Being – and that, as a result, our lives are utterly dominated by our current enframed, technological understanding.

What thinking can then realize, attuned by our shock, is that our epoch is defined fundamentally by a withdrawal or "refusal" of Being (GA 65:

107ff.). So the first stage of our deepening awareness of the truth of Being is our encounter with the withdrawal or "expropriation" of Being as *Enteignis*, rather than with the illuminating presence of the "propriative event" *Ereignis*, and our shock realization of the plight arising from this abandonment of beings by Being discloses itself as a groundless "abyssal opening". Heidegger claims that in order to enable the possibility of "the other" *Ereignis* – by providing a "clearing" (*Da-sein*) for this "presencing" of Being as such – it is essential that we sustain our awareness of this abyssal truth that has been disclosed by our understanding of *Enteignis*.

Using rather esoteric and mystical poetical language that is inspired by his readings of the poet Hölderlin, Heidegger also comes to see the "withdrawal of Being" of *Enteignis* in terms of Hölderlin's "flight of the gods", and he claims that for *Ereignis* to occur, such that a new beginning of history is founded, the gods are required – more specifically, what Heidegger calls "the passing of the last 'god'" is required – since this would mark the grounding of the other beginning of history, which will occur simultaneously with the *sheltering* of truth in beings. In this grounding of the truth of "beyng" in being-there, beyng and beings are transformed into their simultaneity (GA 65: 14). (For a discussion of this, as well as Heidegger's highly esoteric analysis of *Ereignis* in terms of the "mirror-play of the fourfold", see Vallega-Neu [2010: 146–9].)

The *Ereignis/Enteignis* "cycle of Being"

In *On Time and Being*, written some twenty years after *Contributions to Philosophy (From Enowning)*, Heidegger refers to *Enteignis* in a positive sense; now it is seen as serving an *essential function*. "Expropriation (*Enteignis*) belongs to Appropriation as such. By this expropriation, appropriation does not abandon itself – rather, it preserves what is proper to it" (OT: 22–3). So Heidegger now understands the "concealment" of *Enteignis* as being an integral part of the primordial truth of Being as concealment/unconcealment, and thus, as such, the concealment/withdrawal of *Enteignis* "belongs to" *Ereignis*. So *Enteignis* and *Ereignis* are mutually dependent and indivisible, like two sides of a coin. This sense of the indivisible oneness of these two facets of Being is perfectly encapsulated in the following observation on *alētheia*:

> Concealment deprives *aletheia* of disclosure yet … concealment preserves what is most proper to *aletheia* as its own … the nonessence remains always in its own way essential to the essence and

158

never becomes unessential in the sense of irrelevant … "non-" of the primordial nonessence of truth, as untruth, points to the still unexperienced domain of the truth of Being (not merely of beings).   ("On the Essence of Truth", in BW: 130–31)

So, according to Heidegger, *Enteignis* functions as a primordial "reservoir", belonging to *Ereignis*, that contains all the not-yet-disclosed potential modes for understanding beings and Being: possibilities of epochal beginnings that are "preserved" *by their concealment*. Consequently, *Ereignis* (as the other beginning of history, in which beings would shelter the truth of Being instead of being expropriated by it) must neccessarily arise from *Enteignis*, which is the essential "provider" of *all* "appropriative events". Moreover, if and when this *Ereignis* "happens", although beings will no longer be "expropriated" by Being – and thus *Enteignis* and the enframed scientific and technological disclosure of Being will no longer reign over mankind – *Enteignis* itself will, of course, still remain, since it is inseparable from *Ereignis*, because it is the other half of the "totality of Being" – the unilluminated, concealed side of the "globe of Being" that is averted from us.

Keeping this in mind, there seems to be no reason for regarding the concealing/withdrawal of *Enteignis* as something "negative" – as a "yawning abyssal opening"; instead, one can understand it as being the dark or hidden side of the totality of Being that contains all the unexpressed, concealed potential, or possibilities, of the mystery of Being itself. And similar to the idea that *psychological* "wholeness" requires an acceptance of the "shadow self" or dark, concealed side of the personality, one could reasonably speculate that the sustenance of Dasein's illumination, in terms of the meaningfulness of "beings" and "Being" that is "given" to it in the propriative event of *Ereignis*, depends on Dasein's continued awareness and acceptance of *Enteignis* as part of the natural *Ereignis/Enteignis* "cycle of Being".

An understanding of this unity of the *Ereignis/Enteignis* cycle can help us to realize that the present withdrawal of Being, with all its consequences, is simply an inevitable part of the "cycle of Being" and, as such, it is as natural as the day/night cycle. And just as "night" turns into "day", so our current "withdrawal of Being" will inevitably become "appropriation". In other words, *Enteignis* always contains within itself the possibility of *Ereignis* and vice versa (perhaps it was an awareness of this that inspired Heidegger to say in his 1962 seminar "On Time and Being" that he regards "enframing" as a "preliminary form" of *Ereignis*; OT: 53).

Seen in this light, Heidegger's belief that our "enframed" disclosure of Being bears within itself the seed that can lead to the flowering of the event of appropriation no longer seems so strange; in fact it seems rather obvious. And this realization should be more than sufficient to neutralize any nihilistic perceptions of existence, which can now be replaced by "utterly rational hope". So, as with all cycles, whenever one side reaches its peak, it naturally begins to transform into the opposite part of the cycle, just as grain that reaches its full height in summer will produce seeds and die back in winter in an endless cycle. Perhaps Heidegger has this cyclical pattern in mind when he asserts that we should *prepare* ourselves now for the coming of the next *Ereignis* because the withdrawal and oblivion of Being has reached its ultimate level, which will lead to the total collapse of the metaphysical understanding of Being and open the way for a new beginning in history: another way of saying that the *Enteignis* part of the cycle has reached its "peak", and thus the *Ereignis* part of the cycle will soon hold sway. One should realize, therefore, that although it may be possible to influence the longevity of an *Ereignis* cycle – perhaps via various forms of meditative awareness – eventually, in accordance with the nature of cycles, transition is inevitable: "to the appropriation of being there always belongs an inevitable expropriation, an erasure in the granting of being" (Warnek 2010: 160).

Heidegger also asserts that in our present epoch, although *Ereignis* as "the other beginning in history" cannot yet be experienced as such (since *Enteignis* presently reigns), its possibility can already be sensed if one is "attuned" to Being in the right way, for this intuitive anticipation emerges from *Ereignis* itself: "Man has a presentiment of Being … because Being appropriates him to itself" (GA 65: 245). This "presentiment" potentially can arise when thinking experiences, in a state of deep shock, the full impact of our present oblivion of Being and the abandonment of beings by Being (and all its consequences). Presentiment can also arise via meditation on what Heidegger regards as the first *Ereignis*: the beginning in ancient Greece, when the truth of Being *first* arose and the concealed dimension of Being withdrew behind that which came to presence in this propriative event; with time, Being gradually withdrew, and then, no longer an experience of the *presencing* of beings, it became an empty concept, was *forgotten* and beings were *abandoned* (Vallega-Neu 2010: 145).

Heidegger also claims that there are some leading-edge thinkers and poets who, well ahead of their time, have already been "appropriated" by *Ereignis*, in spite of the fact that it *has not yet* become the epochal event of appropriation and disclosure that will provide "the other beginning of history" that Heidegger awaits. These few individuals who hear, and respond to, the faint echo of Being that calls to them from the depths of its oblivion *no longer* live amid a forgetfulness of Being because, instead, they now deeply experience the withdrawal of Being, which has led to its oblivion. They also realize that the cause of this withdrawal is the "enframed" disclosure of beings, which has now reached its maximum expression via the scientific, technological mode of understanding. Thus the creative expression of these poets and thinkers is refreshingly liberated from this restricted perception of reality, and because their work arises from a preliminary presentiment of the "coming *Ereignis*", they are open to the "*Ereignis-experience*" and thus, potentially, according to Heidegger, they can help to pave the way for the "happening" of this epochal event. But what exactly is this *Ereignis*-experience?

Hölderlin's disclosure of the world as a holy place is considered by Heidegger to be indicative of a fundamental mood of "gratitude" or "thankfulness" in his verse (GA 52: 197). Young speculates that "To experience one's world as a holy place is ... to inhabit the mood of cosmic gratitude", which is: "to experience the world as a whole as full of the presence of, in Hölderlin words the 'wonderfully all-present' [GA 4: 52], as sparkling with the 'divine radiance' [PLT: 91]. It is, in other words, to experience the world as a holy place" (Young 2001: 105–6).

In *Contributions*, Heidegger suggests that when we are aware of being appropriated by *Ereignis*, this is an *Ereignis* "experience" (GA 65: 70). He adds that when the "lighting-concealing" that is truth is "experienced as *Ereignis*", it happens as "transport and enchantment" (GA 65: 70). In "As When on Holiday" he uses identical words to describe the poet's experience of the presence of the "wonderfully all-present" (GA 4: 54; Young 2001: 107). Young speculates that:

> to share in the poet's "epiphany" ... his ecstatic experience of the holiness of the world (in other words the festive mood that celebrates "the wonder that around us a world worlds, that there is something rather than nothing, that there are things and we ourselves are in their midst" [GA 52: 64]) *is* the *Ereignis* experience. Properly experienced, the *Ereignis is*, as Heidegger puts it, "the *Ereignis* of the holy" [GA 4: 76–7].   (2001: 107)

Young suggests that "Since the experiencing of the holiness of world ... and the *Grundstimmung* [mood] of cosmic 'gratitude' are the same, it follows that the *Ereignis*-experience and the world-disclosing mood of cosmic gratitude are one and the same" (*ibid.*).

Heidegger's efforts to understand and articulate *Ereignis*, influenced by his readings of Hölderlin and various other thinkers ahead of their time (such as the poets Rilke and Trakl), are evidence of his own attempt to tune in to, and to speak from, this preliminary and potentially transitional presentiment of *Ereignis* as "the other beginning".

Richard Polt suggests that in some of his later writings it seems as if Heidegger no longer thinks of *Ereignis* as the time when time begins.

Although in *Contributions* he often thinks of *Ereignis* as the "initial revelation of Being", as an inceptive happening (GA 65: 57, 183, 247), there are several essays written after the war that emphasize that it is not a happening at all (OWL: 127). Heidegger also insists that "time itself is nothing temporal" (OT: 14) and that since *Ereignis* is "something which is not temporal" we should not misconstrue it as an event within time (OT: 20, 47; see Polt 2010: 79). Thus Polt concludes that "The usual sense of the word *Ereignis* (event) seems to have disappeared: *Ereignis* is no longer a historical inception from which truth and being erupt, but appears to be a timeless ground" (2010: 79).

Heidegger's concept of language

Although Heidegger asserts that in language "there occurs the revelation of Beings" (GA 39: 61; Pattison 2000: 174), there is also, paradoxically, a phrase from his favourite poet, Hölderlin, in which language is described as "the most dangerous of goods" (HEP: 293). He makes this latter statement in reference to the fact that language separates humans from the linguistically silent life of nature. For language stands apart from, and transcends, nature, and as language users we are also partly separated from the rest of nature and thus from Being. Moreover, a silent world is simply what it is, but a world experienced through, or represented by, language is radically unstable since the dimension of language is highly ambiguous and thus open to multiple and often conflicting interpretations. Language "first creates and alone holds open the possibility of any kind of threat to Being" (GA 39: 62; Pattison 2000: 174). "Because man *is* in language he creates this danger and brings the destruction it threatens" (GA 39: 62; Pattison 2000: 17).

Heidegger suggests that this danger potentially may manifest in one of two forms. The first is that we might mistakenly conclude that our capacity to name is creation – the reason why beings are as they are: *logos* as reason. In Heidegger's commentary on Hölderlin he terms this as being the temptation to blasphemy, to a presumption of our own god-likeness that will inevitably lead to our downfall. Alternatively, there is the danger that language may lose touch with what it names and degenerate into the superficiality of idle talk (GA 39: 63–6), which will in turn shape and define a world in which all our relationships are drained of any original, authentic relation to Being.

Thus Heidegger closely investigates the influence that language has on our understanding of Being, and connects his explorations on the subject to his thoughts on his notion of "appropriation" (*Ereignis*), for he viewed language as a fundamental medium in which Being "appropriates" us, takes hold of us and allows us and all other entities to be as we are: "Language is the house of Being because, as the saying, it is propriation's mode" ("The Way to Language", in BW: 424). A common reaction to this somewhat puzzling statement, that "Language is the house of Being", might be something like: what exactly is implied by this poetical or metaphorical use of *house*? This type of question arises for two fundamental reasons. (i) We have been conditioned to view language primarily as a *representational* tool for communicating information as precisely as possible. We expect words to point unambiguously at what they represent. When this happens in normal modes of efficient communication, individual words tend to become completely inconspicuous. (ii) We automatically presume that our daily language is the norm from which poetic language is derived. So we assume that poetry is an aesthetically pleasing art form that arises from the application of certain techniques – such as rhyme or metaphor – to ordinary everyday language. Consequently, we immediately classify the remark "language is the house of Being" as a poetical or metaphorical statement since we know that language is not literally a house.

Heidegger realized that truth and language are always linked to cultural contexts and historically evolving interpretations. For example, among the ancients of the Middle East, if you described a person's appearance as including a long flowing beard, those listening would understand and assume that this was someone of wisdom and power. Indeed, in certain ancient Egyptian monuments, even reigning queens and boy rulers such as Tutankhamen were shown with beards to emphasize their authority. In many modern cultures today, however, if someone were due to meet another person they knew nothing about and were informed that this individual had a long beard, they would be more likely to view this with suspicion, or in some other derogatory way, than as a sign of authority or wisdom.

So we inherit and are constrained by the linguistic structures of intelligibility that allow us to think and experience only in terms of our epoch's particular understanding of Being: "language speaks after the manner of the given mode in which propriation reveals itself as such" ("The Way to Language", in BW: 420). The great poets and thinkers are exceptions to this rule since they are able to reach beyond the specific understanding of Being they live in. Heidegger thus realized the various drawbacks and limitations of attempting to lock a language into fixed structures of interpretation in order to create a tool for unambiguously representing beings and communicating information. For if we manage successfully to lock every sign, word and sentence of a language into unambiguous, precise interpretations, the language will no longer be able to respond creatively to new experiences and the revealing power of language will be lost. It will have become a "dead" language, for its very "being" – its "living creative essence" – will no longer exist.

Heidegger discusses this phenomenon of dead languages in a lecture from 1925, taking Latin as his example:

> [A]s "dead" this language is no longer subject to changes in meaning ... whereas in any "living" language contexts of meaning change with changes in the interpretation of historical Dasein at the time ... A language has its genuine Being only as long as new correlations of meaning and so – although not necessarily – new words and phrases accrue to it from understanding.   (HCT: 271)

For Heidegger, poetry more than anything else has the greatest potential to express the "genuine Being" of language. Far from viewing poetry as merely derived from everyday language, he regards it as more fundamental than ordinary prose because it is "the elementary emergence into words, the becoming-uncovered, of existence as Being-in-the-world" (BPP: 171–2). Thus Heidegger views poetry not just as an aesthetically pleasing art form, but as a powerful force that potentially can disclose our world and transmute our existence. In contrast to this, everyday "idle talk", or "chatter", is merely a dull reflection of the creative meanings that can be achieved in poetry: "slogans and catchphrases are indices of chatter, a mode of being of Dasein in the 'They'" (GA 20: 375), and even good, original words are prone to being degraded by chatter. According to Heidegger, language is the vehicle for philosophical thought; the objective of such thinking is to let language itself speak, and the essence of language – language's own primordial speaking – is heard in poetic diction.

This standpoint challenges the standard way we normally distinguish between metaphorical and literal uses of language. It strongly suggests that our usual assumption that "poetry is derived from everyday language" is not necessarily true. If we consider instead the reverse – that normal daily language is in fact derived from poetic language – then the words we use in daily communication do not necessarily have perfectly clear, literal meanings; their meanings are simply taken for granted and only appear to be obvious. Indeed, Heidegger regards everyday language as, in fact, poetry that has lost its disclosive power: "Everyday language is a forgotten and therefore used-up poem, from which there hardly resounds a call any longer" (PLT: 208).

So when Heidegger states that "Language is the house of Being" he is in many senses *not* speaking metaphorically but literally, for in Heidegger's understanding Being really does "dwell" in language as its abode. He clarifies this viewpoint by explaining that thinking accomplishes the relation of

Being to the essence of Dasein, but does not cause it, since this relation it brings to Being is, in fact, given to "thinking" *by* Being, because in the act of thinking, Being "penetrates" and thus inhabits language, and this is one important way in which language becomes the "house of Being": the house in which human beings *also* dwell. Thinkers and poetizers are the guardians of this house, for the manifestation of Being is accomplished in so far as they, in their saying, bring this manifestation to and preserve it in language ("Letter on Humanism", in BW: 217). The following description concerning how we relate to language further supports the validity of this assertion.

The "sound" of the wind in the trees, or the "sensation" of a scarf round my neck, steps forth out of the undifferentiated background of my awareness to capture my attention the instant someone mentions them to me. Thus Heidegger defines language as a "pointing, reaching out to every region of presencing, letting what is present in each case appear in such regions" ("The Way to Language", in BW: 411). But first, things must show themselves to us before we can talk about them: a speeding car presents itself to me *as* "dangerous", so I warn my taxi driver. So speech is also a response to how the world *"lets itself be told"* (*ibid.*), how it presents itself to me: "every spoken word is already a response" (*ibid.*: 418). So the world must disclose itself in an intelligible and sayable form for me to be able to speak about it.

Thus, according to Heidegger, the intelligibility of the world – its "Being" – and the language we use to express it are inextricably linked: language *points*, thus initially opening up and articulating the world, "letting what is present in each case appear" (*ibid.*: 411). So we see only what has been singled out and named. "Only where the word for the thing has been found is the thing a thing. Only thus *is* it" (OWL: 62). But this "pointing" is simultaneously a response to the world *letting itself be shown* via things that call attention to themselves in terms of their significance, and thus "to point" is also to "reiterate the saying we have heard" ("The Way to Language", in BW: 411).

So language discloses Being and Being tells language what to say, and in this sense, language and Being are "equiprimordial" and Heidegger asserts that the "happening" of their presencing to each other is an *Ereignis*: "The saying is the mode in which propriation speaks … For the saying that propriates brings what comes to presence out of its propriety to a kind of radiance; it lauds what comes to presence; that is it allows it in its own essential unfolding" (*ibid.*: 424). Thus, in the disclosure of Being as *Ereignis*, we are drawn by "Being" into the "clearing" of Being, which opens all our senses to the presence of beings, enabling us to think and talk about them, and, simultaneously, beings are drawn into the clearing of Being, which allows them to appear to us.

Language, by naming beings for the first time, first brings beings to word and to appearance. Only this naming nominates beings *to* their Being *from out of* their Being. Such saying is a projecting of clearing, in which announcement is made of what it is that beings come into the open *as*.

("The Origin of the Work of Art", in BW: 198)

Lee Braver elegantly summarizes this simultaneous "presencing" of language and Being *and* beings:

Propriation is nothing beyond the presence of speakable beings around us ... the appearance to each other of beings and speech as an event ... propriation bestows upon us a meaningful clearing in which an articulated world appears and appeals to us to articulate it. Since our essence is to be the beings to whom beings appear and who speak of these beings, propriation is what allows us to become who we are. (2009: 112–14)

We human beings, in order to be who we are, remain within the essence of language to which we have been granted entry.

("The Way to Language", in BW: 423)

Thus *true* poetry as the ultimate expression of the primordial, disclosive language of Being is, for Heidegger, not merely "language" that uses "poetic techniques" such as alliteration, metre, rhyme or metaphor, but a mode of expressing language that recaptures the illuminating power latent in commonplace words, in such a way that we see and experience the world as if for the first time (*Ereignis*). Indeed, it is clear from Heidegger's later writings that he considers our most authentic relation to language is as a vital source of poetic disclosure (see Chapter 10 for a detailed discussion of poetry).

The emptiness of everyday language

Heidegger observed that words in general had become impotent: worn out and emptied of meaning from overuse and thus unfit for "thinking Being" in depth. For instance, look at how the word "love" is used today: "I love beer"; "I love football"; "See you later, love". Add to this the appearance of the word "love" on thousands of shirts, greeting cards and commercials, and it comes as no surprise to learn that the word has now been sucked dry of its original meaning and intensity. According to Heidegger, this was not always the case. There was a time when the word "love" was first used, when no difference existed between the word and the intense emotion it was expressing; each time the word was spoken there existed simultaneously the real experience of love. For Heidegger, a fundamental key to understanding ourselves lies in recognizing and reliving the initial moments of existence when "Being first spoke" to us through fundamentally important words such as "peace", "love", "truth" and "compassion". When this happens, someone who says "I love you" will truly experience the original significance of these words, and their behaviour will reflect their experience.

The language of Being

Dissatisfied with the current state of language, Heidegger constructed a new vocabulary and style of expression attuned specifically to Being. He developed a unique and complex way of expressing ideas that involved the usage of obsolete words, personal spellings (such as the archaic spelling *Seyn* ["Being"] instead of *Sein*), multiple resonances, brand new words and strange verbal constructions. He created dozens of hyphenated compound words that in their original German end with the word *-sein*, meaning "-being", and he introduced the word Dasein to refer to *us*. This attachment of the German word for "being" throughout his writing continually brings the reader back to Heidegger's primary question: the *meaning* of Being.

He felt that this new way of expressing philosophical concepts would regenerate the language, stimulate a fresh, new perspective on existence and make us think radically about who we are. The increased effort required to comprehend his unusual style also tends to result in a far deeper understanding of its content. However, it is important to remember that his terminology, although unusual and often complex, is easier to grasp in its original language than when translated into English. This is because Heidegger plays with etymological family relations that exist only in German. Indeed, although he praised translations of his work *Being and Time*, he considered efforts to translate his later writings largely a waste of time, as their meaning was so totally dependent on and exclusive to German and its linguistic past. Some of Heidegger's writing is definitely very obscure and ambiguous, even to Germans with a fair measure of philosophic literacy. What makes things more difficult is that he often altered the meanings he originally attributed to certain words. Perhaps the most obvious and important example of this occurs with the word Dasein. In *Being and Time* one of the primary meanings of Dasein is "being-there", in which "there" refers to (Being) *in-the-world*. When using this same term in his later writings, "there" refers to where Being actually *is*: the dwelling place of Being. He usually indicates this sense by hyphenating the word, *Da-sein*.

He defends these "inconsistencies", as well as his other unique, unclear linguistic constructions, by emphasizing the fact that language becomes dull and lifeless when it is merely a fixed, unchanging, unambiguous tool for communicating information and classifying entities. Even relatively inventive, creative meanings are eventually reduced to "idle talk" once they have been spoken and thus there is a very real risk that their original communicative power – the understanding they are supposed to convey in the listener – will be lost.

Also, Heidegger sometimes felt forced to pioneer new and strange uses of language because the linguistic means to express his ideas did not exist. A typical and notable example of this occurred in one of his lectures when he declared: "Living in an environment, it means to me everywhere and always, it is all of this world, it is worlding" (GA 56/57: 71–3; Safranski 1998: 95). His listeners were struck by the phrase "*es weltet*": "it worlds" or "it is worlding". Via the "activity" contained in the term "worlding" it seems perhaps that Heidegger is attempting to convey in a single word the energetic aliveness – the *presencing* – of our environment, which is a process in constant flux that encapsulates and signifies our entire world of experience.

Ancient Greek and German

A major tool in Heidegger's renovation of language was his novel use of ancient Greek. He considered Greek the primordial, original language of Europe, most rooted in the experience of Being and thus paradigmatic for the thinking of Being. (This was a quite unfounded belief, but Greek, along with Latin and Hebrew, was once considered one of the three "sacred" languages of Christianity, so it was not such an utterly eccentric view as it might first seem.) Because of this special relation to entities and to Being, Heidegger asserts that Greek alone is *logos* – a language in which the words are inseparable from what they name: "[W]hat is said in it *is* at the same time in an excellent way what it is called ... What it presents (through its *legein*) is what lies immediately before us. Through the audible Greek word we are directly in the presence of the thing itself" (WIP: 45). According to Heidegger, German was directly descended from ancient Greek. (Again, his view was based on no etymological evidence, for Latin is really closer to Greek than German is.) He claimed that other European languages were either derivatives of German or contaminated by the "deforming conduit" of the dead language Latin, thus disconnected from their roots, the "umbilical cord" of Being. He believed this meant that Germany had a unique national asset of privileged access to this Greek experience of Being.

Heidegger claimed that through the audible Greek word we are directly in the presence of the thing itself, not first in the presence of a mere word-sign. He saw the Greek language as an extended memory of Being, where certain words were like a tape recording of the very first moment a human underwent a particular experience of existence. In reviving the usage of such words, he believed that the essence and energy of this original experience could be recaptured. He believed a resuscitation of this language could catalyse what he called "the other beginning": a new era of evolved thinking.

He also deeply explored his own language, searching out in particular earlier meanings of words that had connotations of "Being". For instance, "*bauen*" is the German verb meaning "to build", but he replaced this sense of the word with the Old German usage, which meant "nurturing, cultivating, preserving and caring", words more closely related to "Being" than to technical construction.

Talk: the basis of language

In his discussion of language in *Being and Time*, Heidegger maintains that Dasein's mode of understanding, and its moods (the way in which it is "attuned to the world" at any given moment) are always interacting to disclose the world, granting it intelligibility. Talking (discourse), which is equiprimordial with moods and understanding, is the expressive articulation of this intelligibility of the world, in the sense that discourse (talking) imparts a sense of structure – in terms of patterns of meaning – that differentiates and unites the multiplicity of separate, although connected, meanings that arise from, constitute and reveal the world. So discourse is *not* the same thing as language, for it is prior to grammatical properties or logic, and is thus the fundamental, ontological precondition for language, which, when "spoken out", naturally leads to language, and thus it is also a fundamental trait of Dasein's Being: "There is language, only because there is talk" (GA 20: 365), for "*The existential-ontological foundation of language is discourse or talk*" (BT: 203). (NB. Readers should note that the terms "discourse" and "talk" are synonymous and thus interchangeable. I prefer the translation "talk" since I feel that it facilitates an understanding of Heidegger's analysis.) Language, in terms of grammar, words, sentences and so on, is talk (discourse) manifested in the world in a ready-to-hand form that enables the articulation of intelligibility to be transmitted from one Dasein to another. First, there is the live action of talking. Relevant here is the identity and personality of speaker and listener, their relationship and the circumstances and nature of their interaction. The means used to express the talking is language, but *talk* is not necessarily (or fundamentally) linguistic, as Richard Dreyfus explains:

> *Rede* ordinarily means talk, but for Heidegger *Rede* is not necessarily linguistic, i.e., made up of words. So I shall translate *Rede* by "telling" keeping in mind the sense of telling as in being able to tell the time, or tell the difference between kinds of nails. We can make sense of Heidegger's use of both a linguistic and a non-linguistic sense of telling if we first see that both require a prior [expressive] structural articulation. (Dreyfus 1991: 215)

Later, when interpreted theoretically, language becomes words and sentences. Words and sentences are derived from a prior reality and as such do not carry with them the foundation of communication (which is talk). This was why Heidegger was fond of saying that statements may be "correct but not true". Any relevant authentic discussion of written language must take into account the complete circumstances of the original live action of *talking*.

Since "talk" is the basis of language, Heidegger considers the activities of "keeping silent" and of "hearing" as being of the greatest relevance since they are a fundamental part of the process of talking and therefore an indispensable part of the structure of language: "silence is one of talk's ways of being and as such it is a definite way of expressing oneself about something to others" (GA 20: 368). And silence plays a crucial role in conversation because true "hearing", which allows a genuine and close connection between people, depends on silence: "From such reticence stems the genuine ability to hear and in this ability to hear, genuine being-with-one-another is constituted" (GA 20: 369). Moreover, silence is also connected with the "silent call of Conscience" as it can "in being-with-one-another call and bring back Dasein to its very own Being", thereby awakening it from absorption in everydayness (*ibid.*).

Consequently, mere words and sentences cannot effectively represent language in terms of the original "live" process of talking. This is why, in the process of reading a novel, the skilled reader is not merely a viewer of the words on the page. He or she contributes their own "talk", which makes them feel like an active participant of the written content. This brings to life the events in the book via a filling-in of the unspoken components of the real-life circumstances being described. It is only when this existential mode of "talking" takes place that one really can gain some sense of the reality being expressed in words and sentences.

Language: our primary access to Being

In *Being and Time* Heidegger views and examines language as a means of interaction and communication between human beings, a process that evolves as a result of Dasein's significant commitments in an already-established world. Thus at this stage language is *not* primary in *Being and Time*, for prior to language, logically, although not temporally, is Dasein's *a priori* understanding of the significance of the world and the entities within it, and it is this which enables Dasein, during the process of interpreting, to disclose *meanings*, and on the basis of these meanings "is founded the Being of words and of language" (BT: 121). So at this point in Heidegger's thought he views language as the expression of a prior comprehension and interpretation of the world: "Discourse is the Articulation of intelligibility" (BT: 203–4); "To significations, words accrue" (BT: 204). However, in his later writings he regards this conception of language as untrue, for he now claims that the primordial and most important function of language is to name entities for the first time, thus giving us something that we can talk about, for if a thing has no name it clearly cannot be discussed. He calls this fundamental stage of language "projective language". According to Heidegger, projective language thus helps *found* the world in which we live:

> Language alone brings what is, as something that is, into the Open for the first time ... Language, by naming beings for the first time, first brings beings to word and to appearance. Only this naming nominates beings *to* their being *from out* of their being. Such saying is a projecting of the clearing, in which announcement is made of what it is that beings come into the Open *as*.   (PLT: 73)

In his later writings Heidegger strongly disputes the common view that we are the "creators" of language. For Heidegger, "projective language" is an impersonal force that establishes Dasein and its world, rather than a mere tool for communication. For it is "the word" that "first brings a thing into its 'is'" and "lets a thing be as a thing" (GA 12: 177, 220; Olafson 1993: 115). In other words, language *brings* "beings" into existence, in the sense that prior to "naming", entities may exist, but not in the same way as they exist after they have been named. By "establishing" and "preserving" beings through the action of "naming", language *enables* our primary access to Being. Thus Heidegger asserts: "Man acts as though he were the shaper and master of language, while in fact language remains the master of man … For strictly, it is language that speaks. Man first speaks when, and only when, he responds to language by listening to its appeal" (PLT: 215–16).

Language as the silent "saying" of the world

The language we are referring to here as "silent saying" has nothing to do with our conventional understanding of the word. Heidegger explains that all forms of conventional language can best be understood as the expression of a primordial language – a kind of "saying" that is not the same as speaking, for "someone can speak, speak endlessly, without saying anything. Conversely, someone is silent, he does not speak and can say a lot in his not speaking … 'Saying' means: to show, to let appear, to let be seen and heard" (OWL: 122). Saying is thus a "showing", which is the essence of language prior to all known forms of language and speech: "The essential being of language is saying as showing" (OWL: 123).

Heidegger explains how our familiar environment "shows us" things, in the sense that it allows us to understand and assimilate a knowledge of certain skills – for instance, fishing – without our needing to use speech, or language derived from speech. This indicates that there is meaning inherent in our world that exists prior to language. It is this process of transmission of meaning that he refers to when he speaks of the world "saying" something to us. This "saying" is obviously silent or mute because there is no perceivable "act" of communication. So Heidegger perceived the meaningfulness of the world as a kind of *silent saying* and he described the relation of human beings to that "saying" as one of "hearing".

In his later writings on language, Heidegger assigns great importance to this notion of hearing and claims that human speech is always, and necessarily, preceded by a "hearing". This is a "hearing" of the "saying" in which presence is realized; and because language in the widest sense *is* this presence and this saying, Heidegger states that "Language speaks. Man speaks in that he responds to language. This responding is a hearing. It hears because it listens to the command of stillness" (PLT: 210). So he is claiming that this language, which is prior to all human expression, is rooted *in* the world and "spoken" to us *by* the world. Later, he speaks of "Being" itself, as the fundamental voice of language.

In spite of this radical assertion that language is prior to human speech, he acknowledges that the relation is reciprocal, since without language man could not be man, any more than language could be language. He says that this "prior language" is dependent on human speech, but not created by human speech or under human control.

Heidegger characterizes the essential Being of language as an "echo" or response to the soundless voice of Being. The openness of Being, which eventually manifests as language, is itself the source of language. For language can potentially shed light on Being because it has its origin in the soundless voice of Being, the echo of silence, that is heard within the silence of stillness that precedes and is the essential and constant companion of language that illuminates the nature of Being. Within the silence of stillness we can "hear" the "noiseless sound" or "echo" of silence that is the essence and origin of language (OWL: 122).

Thus it is not *logos*, but silence as the "basic mood/voice" that encounters the wonder of the presencing of Being, being attuned to the silent voice of Being and responding from it (EH: 74). Therefore the noiseless sound or echo of silence that can be heard within the silence of stillness, even though it is the source and essential support of language, is not in itself "something linguistic". The sound of silence is an original announcement of the world-reality that can exist purely only inside silence; it is the silent *logos* of the ancient origin beyond the particular features of everyday-level language such as history, society or communication. For in silence the primordial reality of the world, the "unmanifested", which everyday language cannot access, keeps silently bubbling up.

Thus the language of historical Being originates from silence, which is the essence of language. In this sense, we can say that the true nature or essence of language can be characterized both as "not saying and at the same time saying", or "silent indication". Thus true thinking that strives to crystallize into living language the primordial phenomenon of Being requires a listening to the "sound of silence", which constantly emanates from the depths of the indescribable field of Being: a sound that, although it cannot be acoustically perceived, can be experienced, or "heard", through the entire embodied self and allowed to become the constant source of a new language of Being.

For the language of the true self arises from and is nourished by this silence, for the true self is an echo or pure manifestation of the silence and stillness of unmanifested reality and, as such, it potentially can become the positive ground for the production of a language that can illuminate the world.

Later, influenced by the poetry of Hölderlin, Heidegger begins to use a "language of metaphor" unique to him, attaching new meanings to simple words such as *sky* and *earth*. His philosophic speech becomes what linguists call an "ideolect": the idiom of an individual. At this stage, Heidegger's conclusion is that the essence of Being is never conclusively sayable, since only in silence one can appropriately think about Being and about the grounding of its "truth", *Ereignis*. However, the linguistic mode closest to Being is that expressed by the poet who, hearing what is said in the silent Saying of language, can compose it into poetry to awaken a renewed experience of the truth of Being.

CHAPTER EIGHT

Heidegger on poetry, poets and Hölderlin

Poetry: the primordial essence of language

Heidegger uses the term "*Poesie*" to refer solely to verse or poetry. He also sometimes employs the German word "*Dichtung*" (from "*dichten*", "to write, invent, compose verses"); it can be used to refer to poetry or verse, as well as to the entire field of creative writing, including novels. He normally uses this word in a wider sense, to refer to the act of invention, creation or projection, but he also sometimes uses *Dichtung* (and *dichten*) in a narrow sense, to refer purely to poetry or verse.

Heidegger points out that "Language itself is poetry [*Dichtung*] in the essential sense" (OWA: 74); his use of *Dichtung* here refers to the wider sense of the word – "creative projection". Heidegger means here that language is not only a means of communicating what we already know, but also serves another far more important purpose. The essence of language – its primordial, most important function – is "projective saying" (*ibid.*), the *naming of things for the first time* that opens up a new realm of communication through bringing what is, as something that is, into the open for the first time. "Language, by naming beings for the first time, first brings beings to word and to appearance. Only this naming nominates beings *to* their being *from out of* their being" (OWA: 73). In other words, "beings" are only really *seen* – only able to come forth into the open space of perception – when they are named. Thus it is "projective" language that predetermines the nature of what can or cannot be spoken about in ordinary communication.

Although projective language does not *literally* bring entities into being – does not *create* beings – it nevertheless names beings and assigns to them their status, function and overall significance, allowing beings to be discussed. So, in this sense, projective language *founds* the world in which we live, for the naming of beings discloses, establishes and preserves their existence, thus enabling our primary access to Being.

So Heidegger makes a clear differentiation between language whose function is merely to communicate that which has already been disclosed and *creative* language – projective language – which first names things. Furthermore, he asserts that "*Poesie* [poetry or verse] is the most original form of *Dichtung* [i.e. projective language]" (OWA: 74). In other words, Heidegger views the linguistic art of poetry or verse (*Poesie*) as the highest, purest expression of language as "projective saying".

According to Heidegger, poetry or verse is the essence and basis of "projective saying", which is the primordial, most important function of language. Moreover, he asserts that "*Poesie* takes place in language because language preserves the original essence of poetry [which is 'projective saying']" (*ibid.*). Thus Heidegger regards the poetic word as the exemplification of the essential nature of language: "'every genuine word is, as word, already poetic" (GA 52: 55; Pattison 2000: 174). In other words, the primordial essence of language, which is the saying of Being, is poetry. So true poetry is a mode of speaking that lets the essence of language itself be seen. As the essence of language, poetry is foundational for all language in its manifold workings.

Poetry: the deepest expression of Being

Heidegger's view of poetry recalls early Romantic ideas of poetry as the original language of ancient peoples that became desecrated and, in time, degenerated into everyday prose. In his lecture "Language" he discusses and explains language via his interpretation of a poetic work (PLT: 194ff.). Heidegger regards the question of language as intricately enmeshed with the question of human existence – with the question of Being itself:

> For in language man ventures furthest, putting himself altogether at risk by venturing out into Being. In language there occurs the revelation of beings ... In the power of language man becomes the witness of Being (*Seyn*). (GA 39: 61–2)

> The poet, as the paradigmatic speaker of language is "the founder of Being (*Seyn*)". (GA 39: 214)

Although Heidegger acknowledges that *Poesie* – poetry in the narrow sense – is "only one mode of the lighting projection of truth" (OWA: 73) that takes place in all art, he adds that "the linguistic work, the poem in the narrow sense, has a privileged position in the domain of the arts" (*ibid.*).

Poetry (*Poesie*) is the most important art of all because the disclosure of truth that takes place in the "projective saying" of poetry is prior to, and thus more fundamental than, the disclosure of truth that takes place in all the other arts. Architecture, painting and sculpture, for instance, operate in a realm already opened up by the "poetic" essence of language as "projective saying".

This is why Heidegger asserts that the poet, as the paradigmatic speaker of language, is "the founder of Being (*Seyn*)" (GA 39: 214). For, through the words of poetry, the essential Being, or worldly character, of the world is unconcealed and allowed to shine forth; poetry lets beings appear in their Being, *as* what they *are*. For poetry is "the saying of the world and earth, the saying of the arena of their conflict and thus of the place of nearness and remoteness of the gods" (OWA: 74). Thus Heidegger regarded poetry as intimately connected with truth and the deepest revelation of what is. He asserts that it is not the individual poet who speaks in poetry, but the essence of language speaking through the poet, who merely channels this "impersonal force".

For Heidegger, practical communication is definitely not poetry. To be poetry, language must take the form of a flow of "essential" words that are "tuned in to" and responsive to Being. He points out that in ordinary prose, words are "used up", whereas in poetry, words remain as things to be enjoyed, appreciated and understood in their own right. When someone speaks to us in everyday language, we attend to what is communicated; the words are simply there as vehicles of thought.

When a great poet speaks, however, we not only hear the "information" or message conveyed *by* the words, but we simultaneously notice and hear the actual *sounds* of the words – the *means* of communication – and we care about this as the disclosure of what is being expressed. So in poetry each word is disclosed as part of the listener's experience of truth.

Unlike the worn-out language of everyday communication, which has lost its disclosive power, poetry recalls language as it was, when it carried the energy inherent in language during the Presocratic era, at the very beginnings of Western thought, when the ancient Greek language first named entities: when there was the recognition that *there is* Being. At that time, all language was poetry. Language that recaptures this illuminating power that secretly resides in ordinary words lets us see the world as if for the first time, and it is *this* that is true poetry.

Art, poetry and the founding of truth

Heidegger also asserts that "All art, as the letting happen of the advent of the truth of what is, is, as such, *essentially poetry* [*Dichtung*]" (OWA: 72). There are ways in which both the "wide" (e.g. "invention" or "projection") and "narrow" (e.g. "poetry") connotations of *Dichtung* are applicable in this usage. In the wider sense, all true art involves an inventive "projection" of truth that reveals the Being, or essence, of things, and this transports us out of our usual everyday state of mind into a new dimension of awareness, which can sometimes alter entirely our perception of the world around us.

However, there is another way in which the narrower sense of "poetry" seems to be implied. First, the truth of art, like the truth of poetry, arises from its "composition", but more importantly, the disclosive power of all art forms is rooted in, or grounded upon, a prior disclosure of existence provided by the "projective saying" of language. Since *Poesie* is considered by Heidegger to be the essence of language as projective saying, all art is thus founded on poetry, and in this sense *is* poetry. Heidegger further explains:

> Art, as the setting-into-work of truth, is poetry. Not only the creation of the work is poetic, but equally poetic, though in its own way, is the preserving of the work; for a work is in actual effect as a work only when we remove ourselves from our commonplace routine and move into what is disclosed by the work, so as to bring our own nature itself to take a stand in the truth of what is. The nature of art is poetry. The nature of poetry, in turn, is the founding of truth. (OWA: 74–5)

On such occasions, art radically transforms our understanding of Being, and history takes an entirely new direction. This first occurred in the Western world when the ancient Greeks came to understand "Being" as "presence" (*Anwesenheit*).

Later, in medieval times, a new founding of truth arose: the perception of all beings as the creation of God. According to Heidegger, the third founding of truth in the West, still current today, is our conception of beings merely as "objects" to be manipulated for mankind's benefit, and this notion underlies our technological approach to existence.

Whenever an entirely new perception of the world has arisen, beings have been revealed or "unconcealed" to us in a brand new light that has transformed our whole manner of living and working, shifting history in an entirely different direction, a direction inspired and propelled by art.

There are three essential senses intended in Heidegger's use of "founding" (*Stiftung*), and art satisfies all of these. The first is "bestowing", which indicates that the truth of a work of art is not derived from a previous truth, and in this sense the truth is like the bestowal of a gift, a gift that accompanies a complete shift in perception and experience of reality: ordinary perception and experience are replaced by extraordinary perception; the ordinary is transformed into the extraordinary.

> The setting-into-work of truth thrusts up the unfamiliar and extraordinary and at the same time thrusts down the ordinary and what we believe to be as such. The truth that discloses itself in the work can never be proved or derived from what went before ... What art founds can therefore never be compensated and made up for by what is already present and available.   (OWA: 75)

The second meaning contained in "founding" is "grounding": truth is always in reference to human beings and so truth is "grounded" in people who are the "preservers" of truth. When a new truth arises it is always influenced by, adapted to and grounded upon a people's "endowment". This includes their physical environment and language of communication, their everyday customs and beliefs, and their movement towards their appointed destiny, for instance the advent of Christianity in a society.

The final meaning contained in "founding" is "beginning": a "beginning" (*Anfang*) that "already contains the end latent in itself"; a "genuine beginning", which "is always a leap forward, in which everything to come is already leaped over even if as something disguised" (OWA: 76). In other words, hidden or "disguised" in this "beginning" is an implicit plan, a "blueprint" that can be decoded to make a people's destiny explicit by defining and anticipating future possibilities and tasks for the historical unfolding of that society: "This foundation happened in the West for the first time in Greece. What was in the future to be called 'Being' was set into work setting the standard [for what was to come]" (OWA: 76–7, trans. mod.).

Thus the arrival of a great work of art can potentially enable a society to understand and integrate its overall way of life into a focused, future-directed, life-orienting new historical "beginning". Heidegger also asserts that the *origin* of the work of art – which is also the origin of the creators and the preservers (the audience) of true artwork and therefore the origin of the existence of a historical people – is *art*. For instance, the epics written by Homer implicitly reflect the tragedies that influenced the unfolding and development of the Greek city-states, because "art is in its essence an origin: a distinctive way in which truth comes into being, that is, becomes historical" (OWA: 78). (The reader should note, however, that this view of the early Greeks is not universally accepted.)

179

Poetry as a linguistic art derives its creative inspiration from the background "saying" (*Sagen*) of a people, that is, from their stories, legends, histories and proverbs, as well as their rituals and customs. It transforms all this into an arrangement that artistically expresses for a society their understanding of reality: "transforms the people's saying so that now every living word fights the battle and puts up for decision what is holy and what unholy, what great and what small, what brave and what cowardly" (OWA: 43). The greatest poetic works of a historical community serve an important role in "founding" the way of life of that community. A poetic work is a bequest, an "endowment", that can define the obligations and demands that need to be fulfilled by the future "preservers" of that community, whose world has been disclosed by the work.

Heidegger also regards it as our obligation to act as "preservers", by continuing the undertaking commenced at the dawn of our civilization, so that we can bring to realization its latent possibilities. In his *Introduction to Metaphysics* lectures, Heidegger describes the various influential trends that stand in the way of the "new awakening" to Being (*Seyn*). Central to his diagnosis of the times is what he calls the "emasculation of spirit" (IM: 45); the spirit is reduced to what Heidegger terms "intelligence" – instrumental reasoning only interested in the calculation and examination of given things and their transformation and reconstitution, which is placed in service of an ideological doctrine. As examples he cites Marxism, obsession with technology and racism. As a consequence, mankind's spirit loses its "openness" to the demands of "Being", which results in the "darkening of the world, the flight of the gods, the destruction of the earth, the transformation of men into a mass, the hatred and suspicion of everything free and creative" (IM: 38).

Heidegger encounters Friedrich Hölderlin

According to Heidegger, what is now required to overcome the forgetfulness of Being that pervades our modern life is a new poet who can construct a poetic framework or setting that will catalyse a transition to a new beginning founded on an authentic remembrance of Being, just as the earliest Greek philosophers and poets had done in the first "beginning". Heidegger found this poet in Friedrich Hölderlin (1770–1843), a German Romantic who unsuccessfully attempted a synthesis of Hellenic paganism and Christianity before collapsing into madness in 1806. In the early twentieth century, Hölderlin's poetry finally became very popular in Germany, making him, with Goethe and Nietzsche, one of the best-loved writers for German soldiers in the First World War.

Hölderlin's late hymns, when first published, struck Heidegger and other readers "like an earthquake" (OWL: 78). It has been claimed that Heidegger's reading of Hölderlin is rooted in an interpretation by Norbert von Hellingrath, who first published Hölderlin's hymns in 1914. This interpretation asserts that Hölderlin's later poetry is characterized by the attempt to bring to language "hidden or secret German ... that, though it does not exist, defines the essence of the Germany yet to come" (Edler 1990: 208). Although Heidegger was also inspired by other German poets such as Johann Peter Hebel, Gottfried Benn, Stefan George, Rilke and Trakl, he saw the essence of poetry most clearly in the works of Hölderlin, whom he viewed as the potential founder of new paths for Germany and the West.

Heidegger presented his first lecture on Hölderlin in 1934, and from then on the work of this poet remained a continual reference point in Heidegger's thought. When Heidegger first focused his attention on this poet, Hölderlin was viewed by the German public as the poet of the Germans: a genius of the heart who, with his yearning for a new wholeness of life, became a role model especially for those seeking a new understanding of that which is sacred in existence. The following lines from Hölderlin's novel *Hyperion* were frequently quoted:

> It is a harsh word and yet I utter it, for it is the truth: I cannot think of a nation that is more torn than the Germans, you see workmen but no human beings, thinkers but no human beings, masters and servants, young people and sedate, but no human beings – is this not like a battlefield, where hands and arms and all limbs lie about each other mutilated while the shed lifeblood seeps into the sand?
> (Hölderlin 1992–94: 738; Safranski 1998: 283)

Heidegger describes Hölderlin as a not-yet-emerged "power in the history of our nation that needs to be embraced if the German nation wishes to find itself" (GA 39: 214). He viewed Hölderlin as the poetically articulate witness to our lack of Being, a messenger of our potential ability to triumph over this lack. He also hoped to achieve, through readings of Hölderlin, a clearer understanding of his own endeavours to comprehend the thinking of thinking.

In his lectures on Hölderlin, Heidegger examines two of Hölderlin's hymns, "Germania" and "The Rhine". He quotes an aphorism by Hölderlin:

> Poets have mostly arisen at the beginning or at the end of a world period. With song the nations step out of the heaven of their childhood into active life, into the land of Culture. With song they return into original life.   (GA 39: 20)

181

Heidegger sees poets as the true inventors of a nation's culture, the providers of its sense of identity; for instance, Homer along with Hesiod defined the Olympian gods for subsequent Greeks. Heidegger also considers poetry in relation to other great creative acts, such as thinking and politics, which can also be "works" of great power. He asserts that:

> The fundamental mood, and this means the truth of a nation's *Dasein*, is originally donated by the poet. The thus revealed Being of that-which-is is comprehended as Being ... by the thinker, and the thus comprehended Being is ... placed into determined historical truth through the fact that the nation is brought to itself as a nation. This is accomplished by the creation ... of the state by the state creator.   (GA 39: 144)

Poets, thinkers and statesmen, according to Heidegger, determine human destiny through their work. Heidegger calls this creativity "battle", and in his series of lectures titled *An Introduction to Metaphysics* he writes:

> It is this conflict that first projects and develops what had hitherto been unheard of, unsaid and unthought. The creators, poets, thinkers, and statesmen then sustain the battle. Against the overwhelming chaos they set the barrier of their work, and in their work they capture the world thus opened up.   (IM: 62)

Because Hölderlin made poetry's potential to create culture the theme of his poems, Heidegger called him the "poet of making poetry".

Heidegger claims that the poet's calling is integrally related to the people (*Volk*), for poetry is fundamentally linked with "the basic happening of man's historical Dasein" (GA 39: 40). It is concerned with man's relation to beings-as-a-whole and with the nature of time itself, the primordial temporality in which that relation occurs, characterized, as it is, by the specific features of a particular period in history. This primordial time "is the time of poets, thinkers and the founders of states, i.e., of those who essentially found the historical Dasein of a people and give them their fundamental character. These are the authentic creators" (GA 39: 51).

Thus, to understand the truth of poetry we must understand what it is to be an entity that exists in time (GA 39: 48ff.). This "existing in time" does not refer to chronological time or to the particular epoch in which our lives take place but to the fact that we are essentially temporal creatures (GA 39: 48–9).

In the 1930s and 1940s, Heidegger delivered three lecture courses on Hölderlin's poetry (GA 39; GA 52) and *Hölderlin's Hymn "The Ister"*.

He also contributed a series of short essays on Hölderlin between the years 1936 and 1938. Largely influenced by these readings of Hölderlin, Heidegger's later thinking now became far more poetical in style. Indeed, in his lectures on the poet he frequently alludes to the relation between thinking and poetry, even describing the art of thinking as "co-poetizing". Heidegger came to view great philosophy as being both creative and poetic, asserting that our most authentic relation to language is poetic, and therefore language should be valued primarily as a rich source of poetic revelation rather than as a tool for representation.

In his later writings, rather than analysing, reasoning or arguing, he tended to propose, imply or entice, and thus ambiguous, vague or even enigmatic statements are considered by him as compatible with authentic philosophical thinking. One secondary source on Heidegger's later writings effectively encapsulates the essence of his new approach to thinking during this later period of his life.

> His writings on language and poetry do not represent the unfolding of a theory. They are rather a lingering with a subject matter, where lingering means holding back, not seeking advancement or mastery, refusing to determine the subject conceptually, acknowledging Parmenides' judgment "that everything that lies before us is ambiguous".
>
> (Bruns 1981: 150)

In his later writings on Hölderlin, Heidegger strives to highlight the lack of divine in contemporary existence, and to point the way to the dimension of the sacred as a realm where divinity might one day again reappear. It is not atheism that he regards as the enemy, but the attitude of complete indifference to the question of the holy, a godlessness that is not merely the absence of gods, but one in which their presence or absence makes absolutely no difference to us in our lives. Heidegger wants us to realize that a society's relation to the divine elements of existence plays a crucial role in its relation to Being.

Heidegger wrote more about the work of Hölderlin than about any other writer or philosopher except Nietzsche. Many important references to the poet appear throughout his later works, and his writings on him fill four volumes of Heidegger's collected works. Also of significance is Heidegger's belief that his lectures on Hölderlin and Nietzsche were evidence of his intellectual resistance to Nazism. Although his interest in Hölderlin pre-dates his involvement with the Nazis, his most intense studies of the poet took place after the resignation of his rectorship at Freiburg in 1934, when he sought to redefine the significance of German nationhood in a manner that would potentially offer a counter-movement to the modern technological approach to the planet (he had originally hoped that National Socialism would achieve this objective).

In his poetry, Hölderlin emphasizes the openness of the early Greek world to the intoxicating, captivating presence of their gods, and their direct experience of the powers of nature in demi-gods such as Heracles and Dionysus. The whole bias of his understanding of the Greeks is determined by his conviction that the gods have fled, and his work can be characterized as a poetic pursuit of a harmony that he envisioned as a return to the radiant presence of the Greek gods, but on German soil: a fusion of the Romantic view of nature with the striving for political freedom.

Whereas Nietzsche is regarded by Heidegger as the paramount voice of metaphysics – the last great thinker of the West in whom the misinterpretations and danger of metaphysics find their highest articulation – Hölderlin, in contrast, is promoted as a decisive alternative to Nietzsche, for he heralds a new non-metaphysical vision of human beings' place in the world – a new beginning that overthrows and transcends metaphysics (GA 52: 143). But Hölderlin, unlike Heidegger, was torn between his love for the Christian God and ancient Greece and its gods (in "Patmos" and in other later poems he strove desperately to reconcile Christianity with Hellenism). He was profoundly concerned about the nature of poetry and the poet's role in the cosmic order.

Heidegger saw Hölderlin's continual engagement with the Greeks as reflecting his own efforts to understand and elucidate early Greek thought. Heidegger strove to grasp the essence of early Greek thinking in order to gain insight into what is essential for the present situation and for the decisions we need to make for the future, and he assigns a crucial role to Hölderlin in the recovery of Being: "The historical destiny of philosophy culminates in knowledge of the necessity of giving a hearing to Hölderlin's word" (GA 65: 422).

Heidegger's way of understanding poets and their work

Because true poetry is a mode of unconcealment, it shares fundamental common ground with philosophy, and thus philosophers are often attracted to poetry. However, according to Heidegger, the philosopher does not approach poetry as a literary critic, nor is he concerned with conceptualizing poetry, or penetrating its pictorial language to find out exactly "what" is being expressed by it. Instead, he is interested in that which enables poetry to be revelatory of truth – the *essence* of poetry – so that he might learn and improve the art of thinking Being, for "Thinking is almost a co-poetizing

[*Mitdichten*]" (GA 52: 55; Pattison 2000: 162). The poet as much as the thinker (philosopher) is engaged in a questioning of existence (GA 52: 134). The poet speaks what the philosopher is to think.

Heidegger emphasizes that poetry is *not* philosophy for they use language in fundamentally different ways. The language of philosophy since Plato has been increasingly adapted to the requirements of formal logic, at times reducing language to a mere tool used for unambiguous self-expression and communication (GA 52: 14ff.). Far from seeing this as an advance, Heidegger regards this rigorously logical type of language as on a par with the most banal aspects of modern everyday existence (GA 52: 10).

In saying this, Heidegger is not suggesting that poetry itself lacks rigour (GA 52: 26), nor implying that the imagery of poetic language merely camouflages the "true" significance of the poem (GA 52: 29). He asserts, however, that the language of true poetry cannot be explained logically, psychologically or philologically, and that the meaning of the poetic word overreaches the personal circumstances, viewpoints and understanding of the poet. Therefore we must focus on the poem itself: on the words that belong solely to this unique linguistic construct, whose message transcends the human channel through which it came, and whose truth lies not only in what is said but also in what is left in silence (GA 39: 41; GA 52: 39). For, according to Heidegger, it is from silence that the primordial reality of the world arises; silence is the essence and origin of language (OWL: 122), the essential and constant companion of all language that strives to illuminate the nature of Being. Thus the essence of poetic language can be seen as a "silent indication" that originates from and expresses the silent voice of Being.

The following passage further clarifies what Heidegger is trying to communicate regarding the leap in thinking that is required to truly understand poetry:

> The poem is now no longer an even text, endowed with an equally flat "meaning", but this linguistic construct is in itself a vortex that snatches us away. Not gradually, but ... suddenly ... But to where does this vortex snatch us? Into speech [*das Sprechen*], of which the poem is the linguistic construct. What sort of speech is that? Who speaks to whom with whom about what? We are forcefully drawn into a conversation [*Gespräch*] that language [*Sprache*] brings to speech [*Sprache*], and indeed not just any casual or accidental speech ... (but one that concerns) naming and speaking.
>
> (GA 39: 45)

So there is a clear division and boundary that separates the poet from the thinker (GA 39: 129ff.). This assertion is especially important in the case of Hölderlin's poetry, for he was not only a close friend of Hegel when both were students in Tübingen, but also was philosophically literate and in addition wrote prose that ranks as philosophy. Heidegger acknowledges the strong affinity between Hölderlin and Hegel, but stresses that in order to understand this, it is also essential to recognize the fundamental differences between thinker and poet. In the case of Hölderlin and Hegel, the difference is that Hegel is basically a metaphysical thinker, but Hölderlin is not.

Thus, despite Heidegger's interpretation of Hölderlin as a philosopher and thinker, he makes it clear that he regards him first and foremost as a poet. Also, Heidegger draws a sharp distinction between poetry that merely expresses a person's experiences or culture, and "true" poetry, in which the words of the poet transcend his private opinions and experiences (GA 52: 6–7). It is always this latter sense that applies to Hölderlin's work. According to Heidegger, in reading this "true poetry", the aim is not to reconstruct the original intuition of the poet. This would be futile since the poet's words transcend his private views and psychological state, as well as his personal history and social circumstances. One should also resist being overwhelmed by the beauty of the poem (GA 52: 21). Instead, Heidegger asserts that the work of a true poet can be understood only in the light of the poetic work itself, for "only the poem itself can teach us what it is about" (GA 52: 2–3) and thus it cannot be "explained" by referring to its historical context, nor by comparing it with comparable citations from the author's own work.

So, according to Heidegger, faced with the specific purpose of interpreting Hölderlin's poetry, the personality and life of Hölderlin become irrelevant, for Hölderlin is significant to the interpretation only "insofar as the author brings the whole poem as a linguistic production into language" for "the poem as a whole is language and speaks" (GA 39: 42). Heidegger is once again emphasizing – this time in reference to Hölderlin – that in true poetry it is *language itself* that is expressing itself in the poem, rather than the particular character of the poet, for the word of the poet "overreaches itself and the poet in its poetic achievement" (GA 52: 12).

Further, just as Heidegger identifies the essence of the thinker with that single thought that determines his whole intellectual activity, so similarly he refers to the poem – in spite of its numerous words – in the singular, as the "poetic word" (GA 52: 33). This approach follows the pathway of Heidegger's fundamental and distinctive philosophical strategy of meditating on the "basic words" that, in his view, define the course of thinking.

Most importantly, Heidegger points out that the serious thinker is always ruled by what is *unthought*, since he strives to reach beyond that which is already familiar, to that which has not yet been understood, aiming to find answers to the various puzzling questions on existence that are the motivating force behind his philosophical thinking. Heidegger thus asserts that what is *unthought* should govern the interpretation of philosophical texts, for when a great thinker interprets another's work, he does not seek merely to grasp the essence of what the other thinker is saying, so as to re-express the content in a new manner; instead, he endeavours to penetrate *beyond* the work to discover the unanswered questions that were and are the original inspiration behind the thinker's search for truth.

Heidegger asserts that the serious thinker should adopt a similar approach when interpreting a poetic work. Instead of analysing the subject matter and style of the poem, the thinker's primary aim should be to ascertain what the poet did not think or say in the poem: to think what is *unsaid* and *unthought* by the poet. Moreover, since the full meaning of the poetic word overreaches the poet's own understanding, the thinker can understand the poet's works better than the poet himself.

But Heidegger points out that the *unthought* is immeasurably deep and that, when interpreting, every disclosure is simultaneously a concealing: truth is untruth. Thus one can never arrive at an ultimate or final unequivocal "truth" that is the essential or "true" meaning of a work because there can exist no final stage in an interpretative process that is infinite; thus all interpretations must be considered only provisional.

Heidegger is by no means implying here that one should therefore cease believing in the possibility of meaning, and therefore end one's search. On the contrary, he is suggesting that one should allow the process of thinking to be drawn onwards and never give up the effort to make sense of existence, because there is always something more to be thought about and understood in all true works of art, indeed in all human experiences.

In relation to the self-concealment of the poetic word, Heidegger asserts that the interpreter's role is that of hearing or attending to the poetic word while remaining in a "waiting" state of mind with a willingness to risk oneself, because there can never be any guarantee either that there actually *is* anything worth attending to or that the interpretation reached is in fact "correct"; the ever-present ambiguity, hinting and allusion in true poetry mean that every act of interpretation is unavoidably a leap into the unknown. So Heidegger sees the task of understanding the poet and the poem as requiring no historical, literary or any other type of prior knowledge: just the simple willingness to allow the poetic word to speak to us.

According to Heidegger, Hölderlin's poetry, like all great poetry, reveals itself only to those who are resolute, to those who immerse themselves entirely, without restraint or resistance, in the full force of the truth expressed in poetry. For such individuals, true poetry (and also great politics and profound thinking) can produce a radical transformation of awareness: a revolutionary event that can catalyse a total transformation of Being. But Heidegger points out that few are willing to surrender in this way to the poetic word. Instead, people tend to employ various tactics to maintain a safe distance or detachment from the true power of poetry. For instance, poetry is often understood merely as an expression of experiences or fantasy that entertain and broaden one's intellectual outlook, or, alternatively, as an ideological superstructure that conceals real conditions, or even, according to Nazi ideology, "as a biologically necessary function of a people" (GA 39: 27). Heidegger regards this detachment from the inherent meaning of things as a "liberalist" attitude: "If anything should bear the much-abused title of 'liberalist', then it is this mode of thinking. Because it, on principle and in advance, steps out of what it means and thinks, making it the mere object of its meaning" (GA 39: 28). In other words, in this "liberalist" approach, instead of surrendering to the inherent meaning of things, by allowing a direct experience of, or merging with, the "presence" of an entity, there is instead a methodical attempt, devoid of all feeling, to get "above, under, or behind" the thing that is encountered.

The significance of Hölderlin's poetry

Hölderlin observed that people today have scientific knowledge but have lost their ability to directly experience life's fullness and aliveness. While our telescopes penetrate the universe, we simultaneously "precipitate the festive ascent" of the emerging world. Nature has been forced to submit to human will. Our "cunning generation" has turned the "love bonds" between man and nature into "ropes" and it has "mocked" the boundaries of the human and the natural. Thus we have lost contact with the "divine". In other words, "spirit" no longer exists in our world and as a result nature, human relationships and everything else in existence are no longer truly understood or experienced. Consequently, humans no longer truly *see* the earth or *hear* the cry of the bird, and our language has "withered". Heidegger sums up this neediness of the time that inspires Hölderlin's poetry:

> For Hölderlin's historical experience, the appearance and sacrificial death of Christ mark the beginning of the end of the day of the gods. Night is falling. Ever since the "united three" – Heracles, Dionysus, and Christ – have left the world, the evening of the world's age has been declining towards its night. The world's night is spreading its darkness. The era is defined by the god's failure to arrive, by the "default of God" … Not only have the gods and the god fled, but the divine radiance has become extinguished in the

world's history. The time of the world's night is the destitute time, because it becomes ever more destitute. It has already grown so destitute, it can no longer discern the default of God as a default.

(PLT: 91–2)

This negative condition of mankind is, for Hölderlin, the "night of the gods". Hölderlin suggests that it is the task of the poet to re-establish mankind's lost connection with the divine, living presence of things: to revive his sense of his own significance and his true relation with nature and everything in existence.

When Hölderlin uses the word "divine" he is referring to man's authentic relation to nature and the world, which is characterized by an intense, wide-awake state of receptive awareness and celebration of being-in-the-world. In the 1920s Heidegger's word "authenticity" closely reflected this concept of the divine, but now he uses the term "relation to Being" (*Bezug zum Seyn*). In *Being and Time*, Heidegger explains that Dasein always stands in relation to Being (*Bezug zum Sein*), but this relation to Being also includes Dasein's evasion into inauthenticity. However, when Dasein's relation to Being becomes authentic, *Bezug zum Sein* becomes *Bezug zum Seyn*. So from this point onwards in Heidegger's writings, whenever he is referring to Dasein's "authentic" or "divine" relation to Being he uses the spelling *Seyn*.

In *Being and Time* this authentic relation to Being is depicted as predominantly the achievement of the individual resolute Dasein. In Heidegger's later writings, this individualism lives on in the guise of the poet and thinker, who are seen as heroic figures endowing entire nations with their gods and divinity. At this stage in his thought – and closely echoing his observation in *Being and Time* that some ages are more prone to authenticity than others (BT: 167) – Heidegger suggests that there are certain periods of history that facilitate an authentic relation to Being, and others that make it far more difficult, or even unattainable.

The latter, which Hölderlin calls the "night of the gods" and Heidegger terms "the darkening of the world", overwhelms entire epochs in the history of mankind. According to Heidegger, the *sheltering* of the truth of Being takes place only during periods of historical "greatness", and in his opinion we are currently suffering from an "oblivion of Being". As a consequence of this, "beings" are *not* sheltering Being, because they have been reduced to "unbeings". Heidegger claims that, as a result, we have become indifferent to the difference between beings and Nothing, and thus, for us, the universe is turning into a wasteland (CTP: 47).

According to Heidegger, Hölderlin's greatness stems from his birth amid the decline of an epoch when the "old gods" had abandoned the world and the new ones had not yet arrived. His poetry reflects both the suffering he

189

endured as a result of what had been lost, and also the violence of what was to come.

Heidegger discusses a closely interrelated complex of themes in Hölderlin's poetry. These include motifs such as "the rivers", "time", the "Between", "wandering", "place", the "feast", "measure", the "event of appropriation" and "remembrance". There is no hierarchical arrangement to these motifs, and Heidegger does not present them in a particular order, but only as they turn up in the course of interpreting Hölderlin's poetry. Their meanings are interdependent – the significance of each can be understood only by reference to all the others – and, therefore, it would be an error to single out any one theme as the most important or as *the* key to all the other motifs. These themes represent only a limited selection from Hölderlin's poetry but give the reader some further sense of Heidegger's understanding of Hölderlin and, in turn, the nature of poetic language.

Unlike ordinary, everyday Dasein that is always already in a world with pre-established values and customs, Heidegger sees the true poet as *extra*ordinary, since he cannot make use of what is already known in order to envisage in advance the world he is to establish. Influenced by his readings of Hölderlin, Heidegger sometimes spoke of the poet as being like a demigod: a mediator between humankind (mortals) and the gods, situated in a no-man's-land in between humans and the gods, conveying what the gods are hinting to the people, the identity and destiny of mankind being determined in this no-man's-land (HEP: 293ff.). "Thunder and lightning are the language of the gods and the poet is he whose task is to endure and to gather up this language and to bring it into the Dasein of the people" (GA 39: 31). The poet, standing between the "beckoning of the gods" and the "voice of the people", is also an "outcast – cast out into that in-between world between the gods and man" (EH: 47).

The location where the mediating role of the poet takes place is represented by the demi-gods, who are "above" mortals but "beneath" the gods. This place is referred to by Heidegger as "the Between" (GA 39: 285). Heidegger describes the mediating role played by Hölderlin as being connected with his preoccupation with the Greek demi-gods Dionysus and Heracles and the personified rivers, demi-gods of the German countryside. These demi-gods are messengers of meaning and truth that transcend their own understanding.

Heidegger sees the artist as being the vehicle of an impersonal force, which is "art", or the truth of Being itself. In reference to a line from Hölderlin, in which Hölderlin writes that "hints are, from of old, the language of the gods", Heidegger adds that the language of poetry is hinting and allusive; it is spoken on behalf of, and in front of, the people, but it is also veiled, for it is more like a sign than an assertion (GA 39: 32). Heidegger also reminds us that "What must be thought about, turns away from man. It withdraws from him" (WCT: 8). However, the slipstream produced by this withdrawal pulls us forwards and we are not merely guided by the clues and ambiguous signs of what is waiting to be thought, but in the process of being drawn towards that which is pulling away from us we ourselves become signs or indicators of what is to be thought:

> Man is not first of all man, and then also occasionally someone who points. No: drawn into what withdraws, drawing toward it and thus pointing into the withdrawal, man first *is* man. His essential nature lies in being such a pointer. Something which in itself, by its essential nature, is pointing, we call a sign. As he draws toward what withdraws, man is a sign. (WCT: 9)

The "Between" not only symbolizes the meeting point and dividing line betwixt gods and mortals, but also represents the absolute limits of human potential that are attained by the poet; it is a location in space and time where the most crucial, urgent enquiry is represented by the transcendental question "What or who exists 'beyond' humanity?" (GA 39: 167). Thus it is also the "Middle" of Being, "from out of which the whole realm of beings, gods, men, earth are to be newly brought out into the open" (GA 39: 183). This "Between", or "Middle" of Being, can also be viewed as representing the midpoint between Being and non-Being, and thus equivalent to potential or possibility, "the possibility that belongs to actuality" (GA 52: 118) in the sense of that which potentially can be accomplished through the freedom of action.

This realization of the existential possibilities available to mankind is represented by Hölderlin in his image of the "golden dream", "terrible but divine" (GA 52: 121). The "Between" also represents the transition point between past and future: the middle of time. Further, it is the region that discloses the movement of coming-into-being as the counter-movement to non-existence and the fleeting nature of human existence. It *restrains* time, thereby allowing us a *sense of presence* amid ceaseless change (GA 52: 146). In Hölderlin's poetry, this present moment is exemplified by the river (the river Ister), which is a becoming-in-the-midst-of-flux, and, like the eternal "now", preserves its identity in spite of its perpetual flowing and constant state of flux (e.g. the river Ister is always the river Ister; this present moment is always this present moment).

The river, a common motif in Hölderlin's poems, is central to Heidegger's commentary on Hölderlin. It is described as a "being-between" and it is regarded as a demi-god (GA 39: 163–4) because it originates in the mountains, which are considered to be the dwelling place of the gods, and it comes down from the mountains to water the land, thus making it fit to be inhabited by mortals. Heidegger strongly emphasizes, however, that the poetic motif of the river is not merely an image of Heraclitean flux, for the river is *in itself* the meaning it embodies; it is not an image "of" or a symbol "for" something, but an exemplification of becoming-in-the-midst-of-flux in the sense that the river's natural arrangement and layout, its stability and continuity, arise out of and are founded on its constant state of change.

Heidegger equates the river with the act of wandering: not a random purposeless wandering, for it is dependent on, and thus obliged to remain connected with, its source, which infuses its entire length. Hölderlin alludes to this when he comments that the river Ister seems to flow backwards to its source. A thread or memory of this source permeates the entire body of the river, and its umbilical link with its place of origin enables it to transform the landscape it encounters into dwelling places for mortals (GA 39: 93).

Heidegger states that this "state of wandering defines what it is to make oneself at home on earth"; namely, that "The river bears 'place' within itself. The river itself dwells" (GA 55: 36). Heidegger warns against seeing the river as merely a symbol for time and place. Instead, he favours the identification of the river with the poet himself: "the rivers are the poets who establish the poetic as the basis upon which man dwells" (GA 55: 183). Hölderlin also speaks of poets as being sailors seeking riches at sea, where the riches sought belong to the origin (GA 55: 59), for the river flows into the sea and in this sense the sea also retains a memory of the river's source.

Heidegger views the poet as a sign that hints at that which calls for thinking: "the sign, the demi-god, the river, the poet – all this poetically names the one and only basis of historical humanity's making itself at home and its being founded by the poets" (GA 55: 192). According to Heidegger, the poet defines his place precisely in between past and future in the "now" and so "founds what abides in the midst of flux" (GA 4: 45: Pattison 2000: 179) and "The poet is the founder of Being [*Seyn*]" in the sense of the historical oneness of earth, gods, humanity and all other entities (GA 39: 214).

Heidegger also speaks of authentic Dasein as being "a sign" in his "new thinking of Being" because this new thinking takes place in the practical world of human existence, embodied in man's moment-by-moment existence. If thinking is not embodied, it fails to enter and transmute the patterns of daily life. Thus Heidegger viewed Dasein as the primary bearer or "sign" of the new thinking.

The poet, like the river, remains connected with, and constantly retains, a memory of its source of Being, amid, and in spite of, life's temporal changes. But the way to the source is arduous and the destiny of the poet involves immense existential tensions. The source of a river lies upstream.

Similarly, to make the journey towards the source of Being, the poet is required to go against the stream, facing all the difficulties associated with this (GA 52: 170). For only through wandering far from home can one communicate what lies at the place of origin (GA 4: 32-4). The source of Being cannot be unequivocally named, but only hinted at through the enigmatic and ambiguous, hinting sign of the poetic word.

The river naturally wanders far from its source and, in doing so, brings new life to the landscape. Again, the journey away from the source is the precondition for the coming into existence of gods and mortals in their interrelatedness. For "humanity in its historicity is from the very beginning not at home but because its thinking and meditation seeks what is homely its supreme concern is joy" (GA 52: 189). Hölderlin thus affirms the inescapability of mankind's ontological homelessness, viewing humanity's journey away from the ancient Greek proximity to the source of Being, not as an error but as a "destining" that comes from Being itself.

True poetry, however, transcends the individual awareness of the poet, reaching out into the "Between", creating a time and space where mortals and gods can meet, reaffirming each other's respective spheres of existence. Such poetry is in essence festal, for the feast is also an occasion at which Gods and mortals meet one another, mutually acknowledging their individual realms of existence and their interrelatedness. Like the poetic word, the festival is ruled by ambiguity: potentially, it can serve either as an indolent fleeing from the monotonous routine of work or as an opportunity for focusing on what is most appropriate and authentic for mankind, which Heidegger alleges "is always out of the ordinary" (GA 52: 65); for in its most elevated form, the festival is a wedding feast of mortals and gods (GA 52: 69), an occasion for celebration – for fun, dance, for illuminating the darkness (GA 52: 66). The festival awakens our most sublime feelings: a pure, virtuous, spiritual ecstasy that calls for thinking (GA 52: 146–7).

Further, the festival, like the poetic word, provides order and measure, for it organizes our time by establishing the calendar (GA 52: 66) and thus in this sense the festival is "the ground and essence of history" (GA 52: 68). Heidegger also asserts that "The festival is that in which the initial event of appropriation occurs that bears and permeates everything that is involved in mutual encountering in its encounter" (GA 52: 69) and "The event of appropriation is what is festal in the feast" (GA 52: 77). In other words, for Heidegger, the festival is both an event (*Ereignis*) in the sense of an "occurrence" and also an event in the sense of an "appropriation", for it is in the setting of the festival that we appropriate our own essence: make our own what is most proper to us.

Heidegger is playing here on the meaning that is hinted by the structure of the word *Ereignis*: "*eigen*" (one's own), as in "*eigentlich*" (authentic).

The sense of "occurrence" or "happening" that is communicated by the everyday sense of the word *Ereignis* additionally suggests that although the individual subject is active in the act of appropriation, he is not independent of the larger context of what simply happens. For it is only during specific allotted times when the festival takes place, and only thanks to the grace and favour of the festival itself, that the human being is granted the opportunity of entering the state of awareness that enables his encounter with the gods. This way of thinking is comparable with Heidegger's dual understanding of "destining", in which something is simultaneously a consequence of destiny and also an adaptation of Being to human aptitude.

Heidegger adds, however, that the event of appropriation in the modern age exists only in the mode of "remembrance" – the title of one of Hölderlin's poems – because the festival in poetry takes place only under the condition of the poetic word being spoken now, in our godless, destitute, current times of planetary homelessness.

Hölderlin's influence on Heidegger's later thought

In 1951, inspired by Hölderlin's poeticizing of the early Greek world, Heidegger developed a new way of hinting at the nature of Being – what it means *to be* – envisaging the world through his poetic vision of existence as a unified interplay or "happening together" of the fourfold of earth, sky, gods and mortals: "This appropriating mirror-play of the simple onefold of earth and sky, divinities and mortals, we call the world" (PLT: 179). Heidegger's later writings are a poetic encountering of our planet as a world that deserves reverence, for he is attempting to draw our attention to the lack of any sense of the divine in contemporary existence and the fact that in the dimension of the sacred lies our hope for the future of the planet. He does not regard atheism as the danger, but rather our complete indifference to divine mystery and the sacred question of Being.

This "fourfold" conception of existence is fundamental to Heidegger's new categorial schema of reality, for it provides an alternative means of envisaging and comprehending beings that is, according to Heidegger, radically different from our current technological mode of understanding reality.

In this conception of reality, everything in our world is inextricably immersed in the unified interplay of the fourfold. Thus in his later writings, Heidegger's question "What is a thing?" brings the entire world into play, for he now regards "a thing" as something that "assembles" or "gathers" the fourfold, and this gathering together of the fourfold is the source of a thing's presence: "how does the thing presence? The thing things. Thinging gathers" (PLT: 174). Thus a jug's essential nature, its "presencing", "is the pure, giving gathering of the one-fold fourfold into a single time-space, a single stay. The jug presences as a thing" (*ibid.*). In other words, during its finite lifespan a thing "gathers together" – is constituted by – the fourfold of earth, sky, gods and mortals and this fourfold constitutes its presence or "presencing". So a thing's "presence" is or reflects the fourfold and thus Heidegger asserts that "The jug's essential nature, its presencing, so experienced and thought of in these terms, is what we call *thing*" (*ibid.*). Heidegger adds, "The jug is a thing insofar as it things. The presence of something present such as the jug comes into its own, appropriatively manifests and determines itself, only from the thinging of the thing" (PLT: 177).

The world of the fourfold as articulated in "The Thing" is essentially a Presocratic Greek world ruled by myth: the oldest and earliest world. But Heidegger's thinking does not merely speak of its recurrence for, according to Heidegger, the oldest things survive in a hidden manner in the present age, as "having been" (*Gewesen*). Thus, from Heidegger's perspective, that which is oldest (and currently concealed) is simultaneously the beginning and the origin: the truth of Being itself. To "think" the truth of Being, we need to evoke the past (*das Gewesene*): to "pre-think" (*Vordenken*) the arrival (as *Ereignis*, Event) of the earliest origins again in the future.

So the world that is implied by *Ereignis* – the Event – is grounded on the past and pre-thought to be in the future and thus, in one sense, it is only a *possible* world, not the real world of experience. Thus Heidegger states: "I don't know if this will ever happen or not! But within the essence of technology, I see the first glimmer of a much deeper mystery, of what I call the 'Event'" (Wisser 1970: 73). Heidegger's pre-thinking is not towards the world of the fourfold, but rather towards unifying Greek and modern thought.

An excellent example of the influence of the fourfold on Heidegger's understanding of reality can be seen in the following phenomenological description of an everyday earthenware jug, in which he reveals the jug to be enmeshed in a web of interconnected beings and events that span the totality of human existence and understanding, a realm of being that exists within the fourfold of earth, sky, gods and mortals. This brings to mind the well-known quote from John Muir (1838–1914), America's most famous and influential naturalist and conservationist. "When we try to pick out anything by itself, we find it hitched to everything else in the Universe" (Muir 2011: 104).

> The twofold holding of the void rests on the outpouring ...
> ... The outpouring gives water, it gives wine to drink.
> The spring stays on in the water of the gift. In the spring the rock dwells, and in the rock dwells the dark slumber of the earth, which

receives the rain and dew of the sky. In the water of the spring dwells the marriage of sky and earth. It stays in the wine given by the fruit of the vine, the fruit in which the earth's nourishment and the sky's sun are betrothed to one another … In the jugness of the jug, sky and earth dwell.

The gift of the pouring out is drink for mortals … But the jug's gift is also at times for consecration … The outpouring is the libation poured out for the immortal gods. …

In the gift of the outpouring earth and sky, divinities and mortals dwell *together all at once*. These four, at one because of what they themselves are, belong together. Preceding everything that is present, they are enfolded into a single fourfold.   (PLT: 172–3)

It is interesting to note at this juncture that the things to which Heidegger devotes most attention are made by human beings (i.e. the jug, various works of art, etc.). When he does allude to things that are not *made*, he passes them by without comment. Thus it might be interesting to offer the following as an example of the type of phenomenological description that Heidegger might have offered in order to reveal the manner in which an animal such as a deer in a forest is enmeshed in the realm of being that exists within the fourfold.

The deer is intrinsically a part of the forest in which it lives. Its being is sustained by the plants, bushes and trees that provide it with food and shelter. Its presence gathers the forest of which it is a part and, simultaneously, the earth beneath it whence the forest arises towards the sky. The forest growth that offers it food, shelter and safety reaches upwards towards the sky, absorbing the light from the sun and the rain, which falls from the clouds, which becomes part of the deer via its food and drink. Thus the deer is a site of "gathering" or "assembly", which encompasses the earth and the sky and the forest in which it lives, which is also a "thing" in the sense of this "gathering"; it assembles earth and sky and the multitude of living beings that inhabit its tranquil presence, and which also gather the earth and sky while taking care of their daily survival.

The "gathering" in the above description seems to be missing the "mortals" and "divinities". However, if we regard human existence as being an intrinsic, inseparable part of the entire context of our planet that exists within the framework of the fourfold, we could reasonably assert that the "gathering" of the deer, the forest and everything that exists within it also includes human existence – "mortals" – in the sense that we are an inextricable part of nature, and in our assumed role as "guardians" of this planet it is our duty to watch over the earth and all that it comprises, to protect it from exploitation and destruction. Perhaps, with a small stretch of the imagination, the "divinities" can be seen in this context (although Heidegger might disagree) as the guiding light behind the ecological awareness that is urging mankind to protect the planet.

In Heidegger's conception of the fourfold he seems to be forging a type of "secular theology" expressed in philosophical yet poetic language. This seems strange, as it would appear to contradict his lifelong view that theology should play no role in any authentic discussion of philosophy.

CHAPTER NINE

Heidegger on art

The Origin of the Work of Art

One of Heidegger's chief concerns in the mid-1930s was the key role played by art in mankind's relation to Being. In his analysis of the subject, he is not interested in examining it in the narrow sense, as part of aesthetics, since, like metaphysics, he regards aesthetics as defined and constrained by the spirit of "enframing", which has resulted in our destructive modern-day technological approach. Instead, his insights into art are an integral part of his fundamental philosophical exploration of the nature of Being.

His longest discussion of art, *The Origin of the Work of Art*, first published in 1950 in the collection *Holzwege*, was derived from material initially delivered in a public lecture to the Art-Historical Society of Freiburg-im-Breisgau on 13 November 1935. He repeated the lecture in Zurich in January 1936, and during the same year revised and expanded the content, presenting it as a three-part lecture in Frankfurt on 7 and 24 November and 4 December. Until then, Heidegger had paid little attention to art, which had hardly been mentioned in *Being and Time* (and, perhaps strangely for a German, Heidegger also showed relatively little interest in music, a field in which Germans had for long excelled).

Although the focus in both of these works is on "Dasein and its world", the emphasis in each is different. *Being and Time* examines Dasein's nature, or Being, in an already-established world, whereas *The Origin of the Work of Art* enquires as to *how* the world was first established. As the title suggests, Heidegger's treatment of art focuses on its origin, which he argues is *prior* to "art" as we normally use the word, in reference to what we call the fine arts, and even prior to the division between science and art that characterizes our civilization. *The Origin of the Work of Art* can be read as a key to the origin not only of art but also of humanity's historical existence and destiny, so the emphasis is very different from the emphasis in *Being and*

Time, for the former focuses on the role played by art in founding Dasein's world, rather than on Dasein's Being, in an already-established world.

From a more current perspective, *The Origin of the Work of Art* can also be read as a "thinking confrontation" with humanity's reaction to the advent of planetary technology. For Heidegger believed strongly that a truly artistic outlook on life allows us a more fundamental, *direct experience* of things, which can create a genuinely caring, authentic way of living that is in complete contrast to the destructive technological approach to existence that is prevalent today; thus in his "Addendum" to *The Origin of the Work of Art*, he writes that art "belongs to the *disclosure of appropriation* by way of which the 'meaning of Being' (cf. *Being and Time*) can alone be defined" (OWA: 86).

It is clear from *The Origin of the Work of Art* and its "Addendum", written some fifteen years later, that Heidegger's long search for truth had led him to the firm belief that truth cannot be captured in theoretical propositions. He concluded that it is principally through art (especially the art of poetry), that the elusive nature of "truth" or "Being" discloses itself.

Artworks and other things

In the text that follows, I have endeavoured to make my clarifications of *The Origin of the Work of Art* follow as closely as possible the twists and turns of Heidegger's original work. Thus, instead of offering the reader concise explanations of Heidegger's final conclusions, my text attempts to remain in accordance with the spirit of Heidegger's original essay by guiding the reader along its convoluted paths, which will lead them in circles and steer them down dead-ends: a journey that undoubtedly will at times be frustrating and perplexing.

I have chosen this approach in an attempt to provide the reader with a *direct experience* – a genuine "taste" – of Heidegger's basic method of philosophical analysis, which he views as part of the fundamental nature of thinking. His approach entails embracing the well-known "hermeneutical circle" in which we always already begin with a vague and general understanding of that which we are enquiring about prior to beginning the enquiry. The task of interpretation then is not to seek to avoid the circle but to *enter into it* and make the pre-theoretical and pre-objective understanding of Being thematic (see "The Origin of the Work of Art", in BW: 144; BT: 193–5, 362). The "dead-ends" that the reader is led down will allow them potentially to "see" Heidegger's thoughts as they evolve – to experience and learn from his distinctive, highly original process of thinking – so that "Thinking along with the essay functions as a kind of apprenticeship" (Braver 2009: 40–41). This approach seems especially fitting here, since the subject we are dealing with is art.

Heidegger believed that the most important role of all true art was the disclosure of the Being of beings. Unlike other "things", he believed that art can serve to show us what a "thing" *is*, and thus, in one sense, it potentially can be more real than reality itself, for it can disclose the essence of "ordinary" things that usually goes unnoticed by us in everyday life.

In the opening paragraph of *The Origin of the Work of Art* it immediately becomes clear that one of Heidegger's aims in this lecture is to dethrone the creator-artist from the privileged position granted him by Romanticism. He intends to undermine what he regarded as the common misunderstanding of art that focuses solely on the artist: the idea that "the work arises out of and by means of the activity of the artist" (OWA: 17).

This viewpoint regards art as purely an expression of the artist's vision, its meaning rooted in the subjectivity of the artist. He calls this the "usual view" and at the beginning of the lecture makes it clear that this is an incomplete and inaccurate understanding of art. For he argues that the artist and his artwork are mutually dependent: "it is the work that first lets the artist emerge as a master of his art. The artist is the source of the work. The work is the source of the artist. Neither *is* without the other" (*ibid.*). He adds that the artist and the artwork both owe their existence and identity to a third factor that is prior to both: art. In other words, art is the source of both artist and artwork.

He then asks whether the significance attributed to the word "art" depends on the existence of artists and artworks or whether the converse is true: "Do works and artists exist only because art exists as their origin?" (OWA: 18). Heidegger responds that whatever the answer to this might be, "the question of the origin of the work of art becomes a question about the nature of art" (*ibid.*).

To discover the essential nature of art, Heidegger focuses on the *artwork* (in which art is undoubtedly present), rather than the artist, because we should be able to deduce what art *is* – the essence or true nature of art – through studying and ascertaining the essential nature of actual artworks. However, he now makes the seemingly illogical "circular" statement that to reach this understanding of artworks requires a prior knowledge of the essential nature of art. Without a prior understanding of the essence of art we cannot examine artworks for the purpose of ascertaining their essential nature (in order to deduce what art is) because, if we do not already know what art actually *is*, we cannot be sure that what we are examining is indeed an artwork. For the qualification required to make this judgement is knowledge of the essence of art (*ibid.*). In other words, it is my implicit prior knowledge of art that enables me to recognize clear cases of works of art.

Having accepted such circular thinking as inescapable in such an investigation, Heidegger continues his analysis of what a work of art actually *is*, in an attempt to discover the essence of art that is the source of all artworks. He begins by pointing out one basic characteristic of all artworks: they are "things".

For instance, a painting, like a mirror or a clock, is some*thing* that one often hangs on a wall, and just as things like sacks of cement or building bricks are transported for delivery from one place to another, paintings and various other forms of artwork are moved from one exhibition to another, or shipped from one country to another. Even music, an apparently intangible art form, is also still a "thing", for when not audibly expressed as music, the musical scores of "Beethoven's quartets lie in the storerooms of the publishing house like potatoes in a cellar" (OWA: 19) and when such musical works are being performed they still express their "thingly element" as sound vibrations in air.

But Heidegger points out that although those working in jobs such as shipping, or as cleaners in museums, may indeed regard works of art as mere objects or "things", normally art is considered to be an aesthetic experience. However, according to Heidegger, even during the aesthetic experience of art one cannot escape this "thingly aspect", which is always present in all artworks, a fact often reflected in our speech by comments such as "the architectural work is *in stone*, the carving is *in wood*, the painting *in colour*" (*ibid.*).

Perhaps, Heidegger suggests, any enquiry into the thingly nature of artwork is irrelevant and confusing, since that which constitutes the artistic element of artwork differs from, overshadows and transcends its thingly nature. Although an artwork is obviously a fabricated thing, what it signifies to the observer is very different from its mere thingly presence, since the artwork contains symbolic significance.

Heidegger then points out that the thingly feature of the artwork is created by the craftsmanship of the artist, and may be an essential "substructure into and upon which" the symbolic, artistic essence is built. Thus, to directly and fully experience and understand the living presence of the work of art in order to discover the presence and essence of art that lies within it, we must first identify and understand its thingly nature. We need to understand clearly what a thing actually *is*, as "only then can we say whether the artwork is a thing ... to which something else adheres" or "at bottom something else and not a thing at all" (OWA: 20).

In order to distinguish between entities "that have the mode of being of a thing" and entities "having the mode of being of a work" (OWA: 21),

Heidegger's investigation now attempts to reach an understanding of what he terms the "thing-being", "thingness" or "thingly character" of the thing: the essence of what a thing *is*.

Heidegger points out that, according to Kant, in the language of philosophy "all beings that in any way are, are called things" (*ibid.*). Even that which does not show itself – God himself – is regarded as a thing, so "On the whole the word 'thing' here designates whatever is not simply nothing. In this sense the work of art is also a thing, so far as it is not simply nothing" (*ibid.*). So this concept of a thing does not differentiate between artworks and all other things. However, in our intuitive understanding of the word we tend not to use "thing" in reference to God, or for entities such as humans, animals, insects or plants; in other words, we do not connect this word with living entities, but instead normally use the word to refer to "Lifeless beings of nature and objects of use" (*ibid.*), that is, inanimate objects such as hammers, shoes, a stone or a piece of wood.

Heidegger points out that although objects of use are indeed "things", they are not "mere things" in the strict sense of the word. Only such things as a stone or a lump of earth or piece of wood can be called a "mere thing", so this excludes all things that are animate entities as well as all utensils. He now suggests that if we can discover the thingly character of this category of "mere things", which "count as things in the strict sense" (OWA: 22), we shall then be able to identify and characterize the thingly essence that resides in all things including artworks. Perhaps then we can identify, understand and characterize the essence of great art: "the almost palpable reality" (*ibid.*) that exists aside from its thingly essence.

To demonstrate that artworks are qualitatively very different from other things, Heidegger assesses the validity of different interpretations of "the thingness of things" applied to equipment, "mere things" and artwork. In Heidegger's view, the most appropriate overall definition of a "thing" is "a composite of form and matter". He chose this description out of three traditional definitions of the thing that have long been regarded as axiomatic in the West. The other two conceptions that he disregarded as being inaccurate are: (i) a bearer of properties; and (ii) the unity of perceptual sensations.

The first of these two, "a bearer of properties", has been widely accepted as an all-encompassing definition both in our everyday understanding of things as well as in the West's mostly Latin-based philosophical vocabulary. It is applied to the entire range of known entities in the universe, from inanimate entities such as stones, to gods and their qualities.

Heidegger regards this conception as inappropriate because he asserts that the distinguishing features of a thing, for example, the physical properties of a block of granite, do not shed light on its "core" around which these features are assembled. A knowledge of the properties of a block of granite will not enable us to see in the block of granite what the stone carver sees in it when he experiences the immediate "undisguised presence of the thing" (OWA: 25). Thus the definition "a bearer of properties" "does not hit upon the thingly element of the thing, its independent and self-contained character" (*ibid.*).

Although this definition can be applied to anything, it cannot capture the true *essence* of a thing – its individual "Being" or "presencing" – but merely "assaults" it: "To be sure, the current thing-concept always fits each thing. Nevertheless, it does not lay hold of the thing as it is in its own being, but makes an assault on it" (*ibid.*). Also, since this definition of a thing applies not only to "mere things" but also to any being whatsoever, it cannot be used to differentiate "thingly beings from non-thingly beings".

Heidegger also rejects the conception of a thing as "the unity of perceptual sensations" – that is, the sum total of received sensory information in terms of colours, sounds, smells, touch sensations and so on – because he points out that we do not *first* receive, and *then* interpret and transform a variety of sensory stimuli into our experience of a thing; rather, we simply experience things *immediately*, as they are in their completeness: "We hear the Mercedes in immediate distinction from the Volkswagen" (OWA: 26). In other words, in normal perception, sense data – the characteristics or qualities perceived by our senses – are only noted later, after our primary, immediate experience of the thing in its totality.

Thus, out of the three traditional conceptions of a thing, Heidegger asserts that the description "composite of form and matter" is the most popular and appealing, the dominant interpretation of the thing. This definition applies equally to things of nature as well as to objects of use, where form is regarded as that which is imposed on matter for a particular purpose, for Heidegger observes that what exists as useful is, or invariably appears to be, "the product of a process of making. It is made as a piece of equipment for something" (OWA: 28). He also points out that everything in existence is a synthesis of form and matter, in other words "formed matter", and that this feature is the source of an entity's colour, degree of hardness or softness, size, strength and density: the source of an entity's appearance.

"Form and content are the most hackneyed concepts under which anything and everything may be subsumed" (OWA: 27). So this definition is applicable both to equipment and to "mere things" such as rocks. It also seems equally applicable to artwork in the sense that all artwork is indeed "formed matter"; it consists of "material" "formed" by the artist. The thingly element in the work of art is "the matter of which it consists" (*ibid.*). Moreover, Heidegger admits that "The distinction of matter and form is *the conceptual schema which is used, in the greatest variety of ways, quite generally for all art theory and aesthetics*" (*ibid.*). Yet he adds that

"This incontestable fact, however proves neither that the distinction of matter and form is adequately founded, nor that it belongs originally to the domain of art and the artwork" (*ibid.*). Since the form–matter interpretation can be, and has long been, applied to all beings, how could it be employed to discriminate between the thingly essence of "mere things" (entities that are neither useful nor made) and the thingly essence of artwork, equipment and all remaining entities?

Heidegger continues his investigation of the form–matter definition of things by explaining that the intended purpose of a piece of equipment (i.e. a shoe) determines its shape (form) and material composition (matter) and, conversely, the shape and material composition of a piece of equipment (its form–matter structure) determines, and in this sense *is*, its usefulness. Since "usefulness" is the obvious and fundamental feature of – and therefore *is* – the "Being" of equipment, this means that the form–matter structure of a piece of equipment determines and *is* the very essence of its Being (which is its usefulness or function). However, Heidegger concludes that "matter and form have their proper place in the essential nature of equipment. This name designates what is produced expressly for employment and use. Matter and form are in no case original determinations of the thingness of the mere thing" (OWA: 28).

Heidegger now analyses the relation between equipment, "mere things", and the artwork, and concludes that equipment takes an intermediate place between the other two, for equipment is "self-contained like the mere thing but it does not have the character of having taken shape by itself like the granite boulder … equipment displays an affinity with the art work insofar as it is something produced by the human hand. However, by its self-sufficient presence the work of art is similar rather to the mere thing … Thus the piece of equipment is half thing, because characterized by thingliness, and yet it is something more; at the same time it is half art work and yet something less" (OWA: 29). Further, since the form–matter structure of equipment is its essential Being or "thingness", and equipment occupies an intermediate place between mere things and artworks, this implies that the form–matter structure – the Being of equipment – holds the key to understanding the constitution or *essence* of all beings: "the suggestion is that nonequipmental beings – things and (art)works and ultimately everything that is – are to be comprehended with the help of the Being of equipment (the matter–form structure)" (*ibid.*).

According to Heidegger, this dominion of the form–matter definition as constituting every entity in the universe received support historically from medieval Christian theology, where it was applied to the totality of the relationship between God and the world, all "things" being created or "made" by God.

In the text of *What is a Thing?*, Heidegger points out that Kant's concept of *pure reason* constitutes a mathematical predetermination of the whole field of possible experience, the entire realm of knowable beings. "What is a thing must be decided in advance from the highest principle of all principles and propositions, i.e. from pure reason, before one can reasonably deal with the divine, worldly, and human" (WT: 110–11). On this basis, Heidegger asserts that Kant is not concerned with "the question of the thingness of the things that surround us" but with "the thing as an object of mathematical-physical science" (WT: 128). So the form–matter definition of the thing ultimately results in the "form" of mathematics or pure reason projecting itself onto the "matter" of the world.

According to Heidegger, the consequence of this view of things is that the mystery of the world is ignored and instead everything is understood, explained and laid bare by modern science merely in terms of what is mathematically knowable, which results in the entire planet being reduced to and treated as a resource for technological exploitation for the supposed benefit of mankind. However, in *The Origin of the Work of Art*, owing to the fact that equipment occupies a uniquely intermediate position between the "mere thing" and artwork, Heidegger chooses to continue his investigation into the Being of things in general by first investigating the Being or "equipmental character" (i.e. usefulness) of equipment, because "Perhaps this will suggest something to us about the thingly character of the thing and the workly character of the work" (OWA: 32).

He takes for his example an everyday piece of equipment – a pair of peasant shoes – and he discusses these as depicted in a well-known painting by Van Gogh, asking "But what is there to see here?" He quickly indicates that knowledge of the various possible materials, mode of construction and functions of equipment – in this case shoes – is not sufficient for comprehending the essential character or usefulness of equipment. Instead, he assumes that to encounter and understand the usefulness or essential being of equipment we need to observe the equipment, in this case peasant shoes, while the equipment is being used.

However, Heidegger's discussion of Van Gogh's painting of peasant shoes not only proves that this assumption is erroneous, but also indicates that the form–matter definition does not in fact allow us to understand the being of equipment, artwork or "mere things". Instead, Heidegger reaches the conclusion that it is only through artwork that we can we discover the *essential nature* of equipment, in this instance, the true "Being" or usefulness of a pair of peasant shoes and their inextricable involvement with the world of the peasant and the earth on which they rest.

He convincingly demonstrates, through his analysis of Van Gogh's painting, that "the equipmentality of equipment first genuinely arrives at its appearance through the work" (OWA: 36). In contrast to this, the form–matter definition, as well as the other two aforementioned traditional conceptions of thingness, serve only to obstruct our attempts to discover the essence or Being of "mere things", equipment and, especially, artwork.

Earth and world

Before looking at Heidegger's analysis of Van Gogh's painting and other artworks, it helps to understand two ontological categories used by Heidegger – *earth* and *world* – that are central to his discussion of art. Heidegger asserts that the truth concealed in all genuine works of art arises out of a tension or conflict between opposing forces: between two distinct "realms" that exist in the "clearing" from where the truth of all Being arises. He identifies these realms as "earth" and "world", and sees them as essentially and always in conflict. Heidegger states that when he uses the term "earth", this word:

> is not to be associated with the idea of a mass of matter deposited somewhere, or with the merely astronomical idea of a planet. Earth is that whence the arising brings back and shelters everything that arises without violation. In the things that arise, earth is present as the sheltering agent. (OWA: 42)

> Upon the earth and in it, historical man grounds his dwelling in the world. (OWA: 46)

> Earth shatters every attempt to penetrate it. It causes every merely calculating importunity upon it to turn into a destruction. (OWA: 47)

In *Being and Time*, Heidegger treats nature merely as something available for practical human purposes or as a present-at-hand object that can be studied by natural science. But in *The Origin of the Work of Art*, Heidegger's usage of the term "earth" aims at escaping traditional ways that science and philosophy have thought about nature. Earth is a more fundamental term that opens the possibility of a new, more profound way of relating to nature We can respect it as something that existed long before we arrived on this planet: as an entity that is far more significant and powerful than us, and resistant to all our manipulations and interpretations (an approach enthusiastically adopted by today's "deep ecology" movement). Heidegger's label "earth" can be interpreted as the mysterious source from which humans and all other beings arise. It is the natural foundation on which our world rests and it supplies our world with the raw materials required for manufacturing the things we use in our daily life. Earth encompasses the entire realm of nature, a domain that follows its own laws and cannot be truly tamed by man. It is the realm of animals, plants, soil and rock that extends far beyond, and exists independently from, human history. In Van Gogh's painting, for example, Heidegger describes the earth as revealed in its "quiet gift of the ripening grain" in the summer and its "unexplained self-refusal" in winter (OWA: 34). Indeed, this resistance to interpretation is the essential nature of earth: "The earth appears openly cleared as itself only when it is perceived and preserved as that which is by nature undisclosable … The earth is essentially self-secluding" (OWA: 47).

In reference to "world", Heidegger states: "World is never an object that stands before us and can be seen. World is the ever-nonobjective to which we are subject as long as the paths of birth and death, blessing and curse keep us transported into Being" (OWA: 44). A practical way of reaching a better understanding of Heidegger's conception of world is to view it as a more fundamental term than "culture" or "society" for referring to the human environment that determines our values and way of life. He describes world as being the ever-changing realm of decision and work, of action and responsibility. World is that which creates the structure and significance of human existence; it is the context that determines what matters in our lives and what does not. Heidegger describes it as the place where "all things gain their lingering and hastening, their remoteness and nearness, their scope and limits" (OWA: 45). "The world is the self-opening openness of the broad paths of the simple and essential decisions in the destiny of a historical people" (OWA: 48). "World" shapes our sense of identity and our activities by providing a system of meanings and motives that make it possible for us to reach a deeper understanding of ourselves and our environment, and thus our purpose in life.

Heidegger saw world and earth as taking opposite sides in the play of *alētheia*, constantly locked together in what he views as essential *strife* (as in Presocratic thinking). The world of human products and activities is established by taming and utilizing the earth on which it rests. The earth, however, which cannot be truly tamed, fights back, overgrowing, consuming and reclaiming our creations if we do not look after and protect them. But earth and world are mutually dependent: they need and sustain one another. The human world rests on the earth, reliant on it for its materials and shelter. The earth in turn is made visible by the constructions of the world, which display the rock of the earth on which they rest as well as earth's stormy weather that is reflected in the scars of erosion that appear in them. The outcome of this strife is an apparently stable reality: "The world, in resting upon the earth, strives to surmount it. As self-opening it cannot endure anything closed. The earth, however, as sheltering and concealing, tends always to draw the world into itself and keep it there" (OWA: 49).

In other words, world (society and culture) arises from earth, and tries to understand that from which it arises. For human culture instinctively recoils from, and fears, the realm of the unknown; it strives for clarity and thus tries to *unconceal*, to display openly the sense of identity of its people and their surroundings and to illuminate and understand nature. But the character of earth (nature) is to hide or *conceal* its inner workings.

In *Being and Time* Heidegger points out that human understanding is intrinsically finite; we can never gain total knowledge of, or complete mastery over, anything. Our depth of understanding of earth, of nature's mysterious power, will always be very limited and thus we shall never be in a position to fully understand existence. Thus no truth or interpretation of reality is absolute, because understanding always remains a never-perfected process of interpretation. No matter how much progress we make towards fathoming the nature of beings and Being, there will always remain dimensions that are utterly inaccessible to interpretation. All unconcealment necessarily involves both world and earth, with their numerous illuminations and limitations.

Further, according to Heidegger, the truth sheltered in and revealed by authentic artwork arises out of, and depends on, the conflict or tension within the artwork that is caused by the opposing forces of earth and world. Consequently, in any genuine work of art neither one of these realms can exist without the other. So Heidegger asserts that in "setting up a world and setting forth the earth, the work is the fighting of the battle in which the unconcealedness of beings as a whole, or truth, is won" (OWA: 55). He regards works of art as belonging simultaneously to the realms of earth and world, but in a special way. For artworks are not natural things such as clouds or rocks, which belong to the realm of earth; nor are they practical things such as shoes, which are part of the human world. Instead, art somehow manages to merge both earth and world, simultaneously allowing each to maintain its independence.

Heidegger asserts that the genuine work of art can open up a world by revealing universally important human issues in a manner that conveys a particular community's mode of understanding itself at a specific juncture in history. Thus the genuine work of art has the potential to be a world-transforming event that opens up a "clearing" in which things become accessible and intelligible. It can shape and crystallize a society's comprehension of Being, thus providing it with a common and coherent focus and direction in life. Simultaneously, true artwork allows the earth to display itself as it really is: as something concealed. It reveals the fact that the earth does *not* show itself and, thus, artwork also displays the infinite mystery of existence. Artworks disclose the conflict between world and earth, reminding us of the fact that every culture and political system – the entirety of human life – is founded on insecurity and uncertainty, and thus our existence is a mystery that can never be fully comprehended.

To deepen our understanding of Heidegger's conception of the role of art, let us now look at his analysis of the Van Gogh painting of shoes, which is the first work of art discussed in the text of *The Origin of the Work of Art*.

Heidegger in Van Gogh's shoes

In 1930 in Amsterdam Heidegger saw one of Van Gogh's eight paintings of shoes. His discussion of the painting implies that the shoes belonged to a poor peasant woman working the fields, and the secondary literature on Heidegger often assumes that this was the case. However, according to the critic Meyer Schapiro, there are no grounds for presuming that the shoes in fact belonged to a peasant woman. It is more likely that the shoes belonged to Van Gogh himself. Although the painting is employed in his evocation of the world of the peasant woman, nowhere in the text does Heidegger actually claim that Van Gogh's painting *is* a painting of her shoes, for at no time does he discuss their ownership. He just says that the shoes are *like* those of a peasant. Thus there seems no justification to the assertion that Heidegger is indeed claiming that the Van Gogh painting *is* a painting of a pair of peasant woman's shoes.

More importantly, it seems clear from the following rhetorical question, asked by Heidegger with reference to the shoes, that he considers the historical identity and precise appearance of the shoes that were used as a "model" for Van Gogh's painting irrelevant for understanding the work of art as a work of art:

> Is it our opinion that the painting draws a likeness from something actual and transposes it into a product of artistic – production? By no means. The work, therefore, is not the reproduction of some particular entity that happens to be present at any given time; it is, on the contrary, the reproduction of the thing's general essence.
>
> (OWA: 37)

In other words, Heidegger certainly does not intend artworks to be evaluated as faithful imitations of reality. Instead, in Heidegger's analysis of the shoes in the painting, he contrasts what such shoes might have meant to a peasant woman wearing them with what the painting of those shoes allows us to see. He implies that, although common sense might suggest otherwise, we can perhaps discover what a piece of equipment truly *is*, in other words, reach a deeper understanding of the nature of the usefulness of a piece of equipment – in this case shoes – not in the process of actually using the equipment, but through simply viewing a pictorial representation of unused equipment, as shown in the painting by Van Gogh, which depicts a pair of empty, inactive, peasant shoes suspended in bare, undefined space.

> The equipmentality of equipment first genuinely arrives at its appearance through the work and only in the work ... Van Gogh's painting is the disclosure of what the equipment, the pair of shoes, *is* in truth. This entity emerges into the unconcealedness of its being. The Greeks called the unconcealedness of beings *Aletheia* ... In the work of art the truth of an entity has set itself to work ... Some particular entity, a pair of peasant shoes, comes in the work to stand in the light of its Being ... The nature of art would then be this: the truth of beings setting itself to work.   (OWA: 36)

Heidegger explains that when the shoes are fulfilling their true function, worn by the peasant woman in the field, they are inconspicuous to her; she just wears them without reflecting on or even noticing them. For there is a fundamental distinction between art objects, and non-art objects such as tools or clothing, which have a function. The latter are presented or "framed" as "ready for use" and the raw matter that the item comprises blends and disappears into its form, which is why the *material* becomes completely inconspicuous to its user. In the work of art, however, the material used is *apparent* to the observer, as it has not been "used up" and made unnoticeable via classification as an item of utility, and it is also conspicuous on account of the tension it manifests, caused by the opposing forces of unconcealment and concealment that exist in all true works of art. So for the peasant woman, the shoes simply serve their basic function, allowing her to stand, walk and work in the field. In contrast, Van Gogh's painting discloses to the observer the "living presence" of the shoes as well as the life of hard labour that their presence reveals. Expressed in oil paint, one can see their essential "shoeness": the full context of the "truth of their Being" in the world of the peasant.

Heidegger points out that in the painting we can sense in the various details and texture of these worn-looking, rugged, heavy shoes, the intense hardships, sufferings and worries that make up the way of life – the *world* – of their hardworking owner, who struggles through cold windy fields for miles every day, coming home in them exhausted each night. One also can sense these shoes' inextricable relation to the mysterious earth: the changing seasons, the richness of the summer soil and the desolate winter landscape.

> On the leather lie the dampness and richness of the soil. Under the soles slides the loneliness of the field-path as evening falls. In the shoes vibrates the silent call of the earth, its quiet gift of the ripening grain and its unexplained self-refusal in the fallow desolation of the wintry field ... This equipment belongs to the *earth* and is protected in the *world* of the peasant woman.   (OWA: 34)

Heidegger sees the painting as revealing the *essential Being* of the shoes, which he says is their "reliability". He explains that the usefulness of the shoes is entirely dependent on their reliability, because usefulness cannot exist without the presence of reliability. It is this reliability that provides the peasant woman with access to the realm of nature, or earth – its agricultural gifts and hardships – that enable her to cope with the demands of her world and that contribute to any security that exists in her world. For the functioning of the peasant's world and earth depends utterly on the reliability of the equipment she uses to survive. By showing us the *truth* of peasant shoes, the Van Gogh painting provides us with an insight into the significance of the peasant world, not always readily apparent to someone actually living such a hard life.

So Heidegger regards the shoes as belonging both to the earth and to the human world. He saw this painting as clearly expressing the "essential strife" between earth and world. In great paintings such as this one, the clash between the forces of hiddenness and those of unconcealment is further revealed by the conflict between "presence" and "absence": the absence of the actual object depicted and yet, simultaneously, its intense "presence" via the artist's representation.

And in all great art we also find this coexistence of unconcealment and concealment – the presence or "Being" that they embody is "concealed" or "hidden" in the sense that we cannot externalize it or extract it from any of the materials used in its construction. Yet at the same time it is disclosed or manifested via the radiant projection of Being perceived by the observer. Heidegger now offers another example of the forces of conflict between earth and world, in a very different art form.

Heidegger's Greek temple

In his description of the Greek temple as a work of art, Heidegger rejects what is often seen as Plato's view that art is merely an imitation of reality.

211

The temple is not art as *imitation* of reality: it *is* reality, as a work of art. In choosing the temple as an example of artwork, Heidegger demonstrates that a work of art has the potential not only to *disclose* a world, but also to *set up* a world by revealing its structure.

Such artwork does not predetermine, or "enframe", the world in the way that, according to Heidegger, mathematics does, but instead allows the world to shine forth as what it actually *is*. Unlike the Van Gogh painting, which *discloses* but does not "set up" or belong to the world of the peasant, the temple reveals and helps to establish the world for the Greeks by giving them direction and constantly reminding them of what is important.

> It is the templework that first fits together and at the same time gathers around itself the unity of those paths and relations in which birth and death, disaster and blessing, victory and disgrace, endurance and decline acquire the shape of destiny for human being. The all-governing expanse of this open relational context is the world of this historical people. (OWA: 42)

The temple not only reflected the early Greek way of life, but also contributed to it, for it acted as a unifying, cohesive force that structured daily existence by drawing people together for communal matters. It founded for the Greeks their moral space of heroes, slaves and gods, defining their "measure" or standards for ethical conduct, just as the medieval cathedral helped Christians establish and maintain their different world and lives, guided by Christian values, with its images of temptation versus divine reward, saints versus sinners.

The temple thus clearly illustrates for Heidegger the fact that some works of art not only reveal the true meaning or essence of a thing, but also serve to establish and maintain the particular world to which a people belongs by defining and limiting the cultural and social possibilities for that particular society. This provides the community as a whole with common meanings and references – a model or ideal example of how to live and understand themselves and their fellow man within a shared existence: "The temple, in its standing there, first gives to things their look and to men their outlook on themselves" (OWA: 43).

But the temple does not just establish and set up a world, but also sets forth the *earth* on which the world is grounded. The temple has quite literally arisen *from* the earth, for it is built on foundations of rock, with earthy, natural materials, and it is also encircled by nature, battered by storms. The temple thus reveals earth *as* earth and simultaneously shows how the human world is rooted in earth as the necessary setting of the human world and the provider of all our raw materials.

It draws our attention to the mystery and majesty of the earth on which the world rests, for the temple is the product of the conflict between earth and world and through its embodiment of this strife it contains the two features essential for revealing the truth of Being – openness and conceal-ment – and thus the temple shelters the truth of Being. The sky is the place of openness. The earth is the site of concealment. The temple conceals the earth beneath it while linking the earth to the sky. Inside the temple there is simultaneously the presence and absence of a god (he is invisible to the eyes but manifest in faith). The columns of the temple enclose or *conceal* an area that is simultaneously open to the outside.

Although in *The Origin of the Work of Art* the disclosure of Being and beings that arises from the strife between world and earth is discussed only in relation to artworks, in *Contributions to Philosophy* Heidegger makes it clear that this same disclosive process can be seen at work in any entity that shelters the truth of Being (CTP: 269). For instance, if perceived in a certain manner, a mountain may be seen as sheltering the truth of Being and we shall then experience its "Beingness" or "Thereness" more deeply while also becoming more aware of the entire realm of "Being". For exam-ple, some mountains can be viewed as entities deeply enmeshed with, and important to, our existence; perhaps they serve as a mountaineering chal-lenge, or a winter resort, a source of important minerals or even the resi-dence of a god. In such cases, the mountain will no longer be ignored or taken for granted as a relatively insignificant thing that just happens to be situated there.

Instead, the mountain is now seen as a place where various meaning-ful dimensions of our existence are gathered and displayed. More impor-tantly, we shall now realize and accept that the mountain shelters truths that challenge and transcend human interpretation; it will always in some way remain a mystery to us that can never be completely understood, and by acknowledging and respecting this mystery we shall experience the way in which this mountain sets forth not only the earth but also the world. For Heidegger, however, *art* is regarded as being the *principal* way in which truth happens.

The fundamental nature of true artwork: a summary

It is important to note at this point that Heidegger's discussion of art does not in any way apply to *low*-quality artworks, such as propaganda art or kitsch, where the full meaning is immediately apparent and potential ques-tions are unambiguously answered. Instead, he is only concerned with "true" works of art. True artworks are not inspired or influenced by consumer expectations and they have a captivating presence that is enduring, whereas inferior forms of art – even if they happen to be rather clever or innovative, perhaps stimulated by new fashions or trends – may attract our curiosity or interest only momentarily, and then rapidly become *passé*. In stark contrast, a genuine work of art holds our interest and demands time and silent reflection to be truly appreciated, for it is a never-ending source of disclosure. Each encounter with artwork of this calibre can potentially provide fresh insights and new depths of experience that change our way of viewing the world. The *Being* of such works of art touches our *own Being*, in a manner that connects us with the truth of Being itself. This is because in all great art, both the artist and the artwork are the products of the truth of Being, and thus in great artwork the truth of Being is at work and remains *in* the work.

In the true work of art, the process of creation by the artist is described by Heidegger as a drawing up to the light from the well of Being; it is the expression of an impersonal force, which uses the artist to actualize itself. The artist serves as a "passageway that destroys itself in the creative process for the work to emerge" (OWA: 40). In other words, according to Heidegger, genuine art does not result from the artist initially having a clear plan of his intended creation that he subsequently externalizes in the production of the artwork. Instead, the truth of Being disclosed to the artist (and to us) is revealed *in* the artwork itself and not prior to it. So, according to Heidegger, Van Gogh did not envisage or "see" the shoes in the way they appear in his painting before he painted them, but only *during* the painting of them as they emerged on the canvas: "the opening up of the Open, and the clearing of beings, happens only as the openness is projected" (OWA: 71). It is the existence of this impersonal force – the truth of Being, which is the source of all true artwork – that makes the presence of artists and "preservers" (the audience) of art *possible*.

In addition, great works of art are communal; they help to define and establish our relationships with others and strengthen our sense of who we are by stimulating fresh insights into our own and our fellow men's existence. For true artwork lifts its audience or "preservers" "out of the realm of the ordinary" by suspending their normal habits and values and modes of knowing and perceiving things (OWA: 66).

> Preserving the work does not reduce people to their private experiences, but brings them into affiliation with the truth happening in the work. Thus it grounds being for and with another as the historical standing-out of human existence in reference to unconcealedness. (OWA: 68)

Although Heidegger acknowledges that *all* things, or beings, have the capacity to indicate Being, if experienced in the appropriate manner, he claims that certain beings such as artworks can potentially *shelter* the truth of Being to a far higher degree. This concept of *sheltering* is mentioned frequently in his *Contributions to Philosophy*:

> Sheltering belongs to the essential unfolding of truth … The clearing must ground itself in what is open within it. It requires that which it contains in openness, and that is a being, different in each case (thing – equipment – artwork). But this sheltering of what is open must also and in advance be such that openness comes into beings in such a way that self-concealment, and thereby Being, essentially unfolds in it. (CTP: 243)

Heidegger saw the "clearing" – the open region of unconcealment, in other words the realm of Being – as necessarily "grounded" in beings. For the occurrence of Being cannot take place without beings, for the *truth of Being* needs to be *sheltered* in *beings*. So there can be no Being without beings and no beings without Being. And "beings" have the potential to "shelter" the truth of Being in their "Beingness" because in and through their "Beingness" one also potentially can sense the entire realm of Being. He asserts that works of art "make unconcealment as such happen in regard to beings as a whole" (OWA: 56). This "sense" of Being, however, never approaches a complete revelation of Being because, as Heidegger states on many occasions, Being is intrinsically mysterious.

According to Heidegger, our everyday familiarity with beings is shallow and banal, but artworks serve to "transport us out of the realm of the ordinary" (OWA: 66). They potentially can make us genuinely aware of the Being of beings, so that we do not simply take them for granted. "The more essentially the work opens itself, the more luminous becomes the uniqueness of the fact that it is rather than is not" (OWA: 65–6).

Is art still an essential source of the truth?

In the epilogue of *The Origin of the Work of Art* (OWA: 79–81) Heidegger asks whether art is still today a source of eternal, essential truth, a "necessary way in which that truth happens which is decisive for our historical existence"? He cites Hegel's proposition that art has ceased to be valued by us as the highest mode in which truth finds expression, that it is no longer the highest need of spirit.

215

Heidegger asserts that the validity of Hegel's verdict cannot yet be determined because it has arisen out of a truth of beings that has *already happened*, a truth that has influenced Western thought since the time of the early Greeks. Thus we are not in a position to evaluate Hegel's claim because we are too deeply enmeshed in old conceptions of reality. However, one could perhaps argue, compatible with Heidegger's conception of true art, that the phenomenon of rock and roll music is one recent example of "great art" that has played a decisive role in determining our historical existence. For according to Heidegger's definition, true art radically transforms our understanding of Being, causing history to take an entirely new direction. Such art is not influenced or determined in any way by the world of consumers for it is not rooted in pre-existing truths: "The truth ... in the work can never be proved or derived from what went before ... by what is already present and available" (OWA: 75), but instead it founds a new "beginning", which "thrusts up the unfamiliar and extraordinary and at the same time thrusts down the ordinary and what we believe to be as such ... it also contains strife with the familiar and ordinary" (OWA: 75–6).

Rock and roll music, when it first burst on the ears of our society, was certainly not created by popular demand. Although rock and roll emerged from rhythm and blues in the southern US in the 1950s, the "truth" of rock and roll was still, in a sense, a "bestowing", characterized by a paradigm shift that took the music world completely by surprise: an extraordinary musical revolution that gave birth to new values in society that were in conflict or "strife" with the "familiar and ordinary" standards of the day. It altered entirely not only the manner in which the general public understood and appreciated music, but also the way in which people viewed the world and their role in it. The essence or "truth" of rock and roll was "grounded" by its "creators" and "preservers" – the musicians and their appreciative audience – and this "new beginning" contained within itself a blueprint for mankind's future modes of questioning Being as well as the forces within society and government that control us. In other words, it shifted mankind's historical existence in an entirely new direction. As such, it does not seem unreasonable to cite the event of rock and roll as possible evidence *against* Hegel's proposition.

216

CHAPTER TEN

Heidegger on technology

One of the dominant themes of Heidegger's later writing is his critique of modern technology. Heidegger never liked modern cosmopolitan life, with its consumerism, shallow values and disregard for nature, but from the 1950s onwards this feeling intensified greatly. He wrote: "Everywhere we remain unfree and chained to technology, whether we passionately affirm or deny it" ("The Question Concerning Technology", in BW: 311).

He saw mankind as obsessed with production and profit, irrespective of the current or future consequences, and this calculating, mercenary behaviour governed all decisions. What most horrified Heidegger was his realization that these were only the earliest symptoms of a "diseased" way of thinking that set itself no limits, the prognosis being infinite technological expansion that would eventually eradicate all other ways of thinking. Human existence would finally become completely subordinate to technological dictatorship.

He observed the mesmerizing power of television as one of the most visible signs of the dominion of technology, and asserted that human beings are, strictly speaking, no longer "at home" where, seen from outside, they live. In other words, you may *appear* to be seated in your lounge but in fact, thanks to your television and home entertainment system, you have been "teleported" and are now a "spectator" in a football stadium or the voyeur of a sex scene. He saw this as an example of humanity's collective "migration" into a condition of homelessness; radio, television and other modern modes of communication are today much closer to man than the traditions of his native world.

> Hourly and daily they are chained to radio and television ... All that with which modern techniques of communication stimulate, assail, and drive man – all that is already much closer to man today than his fields around his farmstead, closer than the sky over the

earth, closer than the change from night to day, closer than the conventions and customs of his village, than the tradition of his native world.   (DT: 50)

However, what is most important to Heidegger in discussing technology is not technology itself. He considered the debate over the atom bomb (which began after the bombs were dropped on Japan in 1945) a mere "journalistic footnote" to a crisis whose real source is rooted in "the forgetting of Being".

This forgetfulness arose from the substitution of rationalist scientific thinking for the insight of true penetration into Being. As a result of this, 2000 years of egotistical philosophical thinking has completely obscured our true relation with Being and thus we place ourselves – individually and collectively – at the centre of an existence that exists *for* us, and *because* of us. Heidegger saw the many physical expressions of technology as an inevitable outcome of this arrogant delusion, which he saw as the real danger.

Enframing: the "mindset" of technology

Humanity's egocentrism, which Heidegger viewed as a symptom of modern metaphysics, gave rise to the "mindset", a way of understanding beings as a whole, that not only underlies modern technological developments, but also influences the way we approach virtually every other aspect of our lives. Heidegger called this attitude "*Gestell*", which means "enframing". Enframing describes our restricted understanding of ourselves and all things in existence in terms of "resources" and, as a consequence of this, humans now tend to view the whole planet merely as a vast stockpile of potential products for extraction and manipulation for our desires and goals. Heidegger believed that this fundamental misunderstanding has ruled our development since the time of Plato and that it has become the disclosure of Being that defines the modern epoch.

The process of enframing seeks to make everything more accessible for the pursuit of our objectives, motivating us to create the artificial boundaries that divide land into continents, countries, states, cities and communities. It causes us to define cultural and racial differences that allow us, when we are powerful, to exploit those "not like us".

Enframing has caused us to treat the creatures of our natural world as mere resources for our use or entertainment; we hunt and kill them for the sake of "sport" or vanity clothing, and make them "homeless", abducting them from their primordial, essential contexts, to place them in zoos or in our own homes as exotic pets. And the rest of existence is treated in the same way. Trees, for instance, are regarded by this enframing state of mind mainly as a material resource for building houses, making furniture or producing paper. Or we see forests as useful because they absorb carbon dioxide and release oxygen, and their roots prevent erosion of the land in areas that would otherwise be uninhabitable.

Thus we relate to nature as if it is simply a massive energy supply for the benefit of mankind: "Agriculture is now the mechanized food industry. Air is now set upon to yield nitrogen, the earth to yield ore, ore to yield uranium and uranium is set upon to yield atomic energy" ("The Question Concerning Technology", in BW: 320). In other words, "Nature becomes a gigantic gasoline station, an energy source for modern technology and industry" (DT: 50).

Heidegger contrasts this confrontation, forceful coercion and harnessing of nature for the sake of "maximum yield at the minimum expense'" ("The Question Concerning Technology", in BW: 321), with modes of existence that take advantage of the power of nature in a non-destructive manner that is compatible with its way of Being. For instance, the windmill *reveals* wind energy, but does not attempt to take possession of the wind's energy or stockpile it as a resource for future use: "the windmill does not unlock energy from the air currents in order to store it. In contrast, a tract of land is challenged in the hauling out of coal and ore" (*ibid*.: 320). And in traditional rural life, "The work of the peasant does not challenge the soil of the field. In sowing grain it places seed in the keeping of the forces of the growth and watches over its increase" (*ibid*.). In contrast to this, there is the technological abuse of our rivers exemplified by the hydroelectric plant on the Rhine river: "What the river is now, namely, a water-power supplier, derives from the essence of the power station" (*ibid*.: 321).

The enframing mindset is evident not only in science and technology, but pollutes nearly every aspect of human existence, from atomic physics to the content of glossy magazines. We reveal its influence on our way of thinking in popular expressions such as "the culture industry", "the leisure industry" or "the horse racing industry", and in phrases such as "quality time". Natural things are labelled "natural resources" and artworks and books are often viewed as "information resources". Even the act of writing is now called "word-processing", suggesting that our very language is now seen as just another resource for manipulation.

Heidegger also observed enframing in the arts and sciences, where teaching and research has been "institutionalized" in terms of a predetermined area of enquiry that *dictates* and *precludes* various methods and topics. Education and research, rather than being an induction into a humanistic way of life, has been reduced to just another resource and object of consumption.

For the "enframed" technologically minded Dasein, "to be" simply means to be the manipulator and exploiter of other beings, or to be personally available for manipulation and exploitation, for humans too have been reduced to exploitable manpower: "does not man himself belong even more originally than nature within the standing-reserve? The current talk about human resources, about the supply of patients for a clinic, gives evidence of this" (*ibid.*: 323). And the influence of enframing reaches far beyond the boundaries of our planet, where the moon and the planets are viewed as potential "stock" in the form of an available supply of commodities or material resources.

Even the "human potential movement" is a symptom of this attitude of "enframing", with its concern for a total mobilization and enhancement of everything, *including* us. A piece of dialogue from the film *2001: A Space Odyssey* epitomizes this current situation: when the robot computer HAL is asked if he is happy on the mission, he replies, "I am using all my capacities to the maximum. What more could a rational entity want?"

According to Heidegger, this outlook is destroying the intrinsic value or importance of everything around us, and to compensate for our resultantly impoverished lives we desperately seek experiences in the form of superficial stimulation: ever-more brutal thrills that leave us fundamentally "untouched". So we consume never-ending entertainment and information and interact with representations of reality rather than reality itself. The epitome of this is the "virtual reality" provided by computers.

Heidegger suggests that the ultimate purpose of all this manipulation of life is simply "the will to will": self-assertion for the sake of more power. We are gripped by the compulsion to control things. The destructive results of this surround us and, if we continue on this course, our future could fit that explained by O'Brien, George Orwell's totalitarian ideologist: "Power is not a means; it is an end" (Orwell 1961: 217); "if you want a picture of the future, imagine a boot stamping on a human face – forever" (*ibid.*: 20).

Technē, poiesis and the essence of technology

In spite of this bleak outlook on the future, the problems of environmental destruction and the threat of nuclear and/or chemical and biological warfare, Heidegger does not suggest taking any practical action for dealing with the negative effects of technology. Instead, he urges the need to reflect on the essence of technology. He claimed that only an understanding of this essence can prepare us for an adequate response to the actual physical problems caused by modern technology.

Towards this end, Heidegger began researching all possible "lost meanings" of the word "technology". This term originally derives from the ancient Greek *technē*, but since the 1830s it has come to mean "the application of scientific knowledge and thinking to manufacturing". In its original sense, the word *technē* encompassed several possible meanings. It could mean the fine arts, the "arts of the mind", the skills and activities of a craftworker, and it also contained a sense of what Heidegger called *"poiesis"*, which means "to bring into presence", or "bring forth": exactly what happens in all arts and crafts ("The Question Concerning Technology", in BW: 318). According to Heidegger, this etymological research therefore indicates that *technē*, with its sense of *poiesis*, belongs to the same realm of truth as *alētheia*: fundamental truth as unconcealment. So *technē*'s original Greek meaning includes connotations lost to our modern understanding and expression of technology. In its original sense, *technē* was not merely a practical aptitude or way of making, but more importantly a mode of knowing and revealing as the "truth" of *alētheia*. That is why the word *technē* was used in reference to art, for the essence of art lies not in the act of making, but in the process of *disclosing the truth*: things as they really are.

Heidegger concludes, therefore, that "Technology is a mode of revealing. Technology comes to presence in the realm where revealing and unconcealment takes place, where *alētheia*, truth, happens" (*ibid.*: 319). Heidegger ascribed the loss in modern technology of the original sense of *technē* to Plato's demeaning of entities and to the Aristotelian–Cartesian utilitarian use of knowledge for mastering nature. For, according to Heidegger, the metaphysical understanding of Being that has prevailed in the West from the time of Plato and Aristotle onwards has been conducted within the paradigm of enframing. Consequently, for Heidegger, science and technology are not in opposition to, but are the outcome of the disclosure of, that truth of Being that first arose from Greek metaphysics.

Thus, although modern technology still "discloses", it does so in a highly restricted manner that wipes out *poiesis*: the revealing of the "presence" or "being" of an entity. The kind of revealing that occurs in modern technology is, therefore, very different from that which takes place in a work of art. Whereas art allows things to be revealed, technology forces things to fulfil a specific purpose, so that things are "disclosed" only within their particular type of usefulness. This mode of revealing, or enframing, is the essence of modern technology: "The essence of modern technology lies in enframing" (*ibid.*: 330).

Enframing: danger or source of awareness?

So Heidegger claims that it is not technology but the coming to presence of enframing that is the (real) danger hanging over our world. And although enframing is the essence of technology, it is not *itself* anything technological; it sustains technology, but exists independently from it. "Enframing means the way of revealing that holds sway in the essence of modern technology and that is itself nothing technological" (*ibid.*: 325). "It is the way in which the actual reveals itself as standing-reserve" (*ibid.*: 329).

Enframing is thus intrinsically connected with the world of technology, in that the technological outcome is what the mode of enframing itself demands; technology is the logical and unavoidable consequence and conclusion of enframing, for enframing "challenges man and puts him in position to reveal the actual, in the mode of ordering, as standing-reserve. As the one who is challenged forth in this way, man stands within the essential realm of enframing" (*ibid.*).

Theoretical science, the outcome of the mode of disclosure of the enframing mindset of metaphysics, is the most refined expression of revealing the world in terms of its calculability. Thus it unavoidably establishes the world as a resource for technological manipulation.

As Heidegger understands it, because enframing is rooted in Being itself, it *precedes* man; humans are not the *cause* of enframing but an indispensable part of its expression. Enframing is clearly not something we do, since it already influences and defines who we are and the nature of the world in which we live: we function *within it*; our actions are guided by it. "Modern technology, as a revealing that orders, is thus no mere human doing" (*ibid.*: 324). It is a phase of our destiny sent by Being, which is happening to us as part of the mystery of existence: "Enframing, as a challenging-forth into ordering, sends into a way of revealing. Enframing is an ordaining of destining, as is every way of revealing. Bringing-forth, *poiesis*, is also a destining, in this sense" (*ibid.*: 330).

When Heidegger uses the term destiny (*Geschick*) he is simultaneously implying that enframing is a way in which Being synchronizes itself with mankind's potential to comprehend Being; enframing is thus a manifestation of one of the potential modes of interpreting Being that are available to mankind.

The essence of modern technology, enframing, not only plays a key role in determining our identity, actions and understanding of the world, but we also serve it, sustain it and continually strengthen and extend its control over us. In his 1950 lecture "The Turning", Heidegger asserts: "it seems time and time again as though technology were a means in the hand of man. But in truth, it is the coming to presence of man that is now being ordered forth to lend a hand to the coming of presence of technology" (QCT: 37). So, in Heidegger's understanding of technology, man is not the "subject" who is turning nature into an object of exploitation but, rather, "both the subject and the object are sucked up as standing-reserves" (QCT: 173). According to this way of thinking, when we travel, for instance, we are not "subjects" using a transportation system but, rather, we are used by the transportation system to occupy the space provided by its various modes of transport: "Whatever stands by in the sense of standing-reserve no longer stands over against us as object" ("The Question Concerning Technology", in BW: 322).

We can see the truth of Heidegger's words evidenced by the never-ending, highly rapid evolution of new generations of computer technology and in the explosion of new genetic engineering enterprises. Mankind has been drawn into serving technology, and has become the *primary resource* of technology, thus "lending a hand" to the coming to presence of technological developments. Further, we are not in a position to control the speed or direction of our technological development because such control is an intrinsic property of enframing and its *modus operandi*, and thus it is beyond our influence.

So, for Heidegger, the *essence* of technology is part of the question of the essence or meaning of Being and the essence of Dasein, and as such it belongs to the realm of truth, so it is not simply a misconception of the world, but an unconcealing of the world in a certain aspect or dimension of its Being. Thus enframing, although highly limited in terms of its world-disclosure, is a mode of the coming to presence of Being and thus an intrinsic part of Being, and beyond our control. This is why Heidegger emphasizes that since the essence of technology is Being itself, man can never achieve dominion over the realm of technology.

> If the essence, the coming to presence of technology, Enframing as the danger within Being, is Being itself, then technology will never allow itself to be mastered, either positively or negatively, by a human doing founded merely on itself. Technology, whose essence is Being itself, will never allow itself to be overcome by man. That would mean, after all, that man was the master of Being.
>
> (QCT: 38)

Since the origin of enframing does not lie in any human act, but emerges as an expression of the truth of primordial Being, where is the danger? Heidegger's response is that – in accordance with the way *alētheia* operates – the action of revealing one facet of Being conceals others. Consequently, the view of existence provided by enframing automatically blocks our awareness of the remaining potential modes of Being. And since enframing is always the source of our worldview, we remain *permanently* closed off from all these other ways of Being, and thus lose contact with the deeper essence or meaning of our own Being:

> [A]s a destining, it (enframing) banishes man into the kind of revealing that is an ordering. Where this ordering holds sway, it drives out every other possibility of revealing. Above all, enframing conceals that revealing which, in the sense of *poiesis*, lets what presences come forth into appearance.
>
> ("The Question Concerning Technology", in BW: 332)

Thus, although Heidegger acknowledges the many successes of science and technology resulting from our enframing perspective on existence, he points out that this outlook is an extremely limiting, one-sided approach to reality.

More importantly, although the action of enframing allows us to develop a very valid type of practical and theoretical knowledge of the world, what is *not* valid is its false belief in its own totality. For enframing is definitely not the only kind of unconcealment contained in *technē*. There is also the way of unconcealment exemplified, for example, by authentic works of art. By viewing everything through this single filter of enframing, and mistaking this one-sided view of reality for "omnicompetence", we live an impoverished existence that denies the rich variety of other experiences and understandings of Being that are potentially available to us.

The result is that Being remains forever shrouded in oblivion, its deeper and richer meaning neglected and forgotten, for while enframing rules our outlook, it "not only conceals a former way of revealing (bringing-forth) but also conceals revealing itself and with it that wherein unconcealment, i.e., truth, propriates. Enframing blocks the shining-forth and holding sway of truth" (*ibid.*: 333).

However, Heidegger asserts that although our enframed, technological understanding of Being is a "destiny" of mankind, which since the time of Plato has caused us to increasingly understand everything in the world, including ourselves, in terms of resources to be organized, enhanced and efficiently used, this does not mean that this outlook needs to be our fate, where "'fate' means the inevitableness of an unalterable course" (*ibid.*: 330):

> [D]estining is never a fate that compels. For man becomes truly free only insofar as he belongs to the realm of destining and so becomes one who listens, though not one who simply obeys ... freedom

stands in the closest and most intimate kinship to the occurrence of revealing, i.e., of truth ... when we consider the essence of technology we experience enframing as a destining of revealing. In this way we are already sojourning within the free space of destining, a destining that in no way confines us to a stultified compulsion to push on blindly with technology, or what comes to the same, to rebel helplessly against it and curse it as the work of the devil. Quite to the contrary, when we once open ourselves expressly to the *essence* of technology we find ourselves unexpectedly taken into a freeing claim.   (*Ibid.*)

Further, Heidegger points out that in the very fact that the process of enframing *is* rooted in Being lies the key to dealing with it; the antidote to the dangers associated with enframing lie within it. He expresses this view by quoting a line from his favourite poet, Hölderlin: "But where danger is, grows / The saving power also" (Hölderlin 1966: 462–3). To begin with, we can see this apparent paradox (on a somewhat superficial level of analysis) in modern technology itself. In spite of the serious problems technology is creating for our civilization and the whole planet, the solutions to these same problems often exist in their *source*: the science and technology that created them. Biologists, botanists, chemists and other members of the scientific establishment have played a key role in alerting us to the dangers of many industries, and orbiting satellites have alerted us to various hazards such as ozone depletion. Cleaner cars, energy-saving systems, wind farms, solar panels and other "green" initiatives all depend on the *application* of science, rather than its rejection.

However, Heidegger points out that no matter how sophisticated our science, it will not be able to solve the difficulties caused by technology if we continue to view the planet through our "enframed" way of thinking. Instead, we need to see ourselves as the "custodians" rather than the "users" of the world in which we live, and to reach this state of awareness requires accessing the "saving power" contained in enframing. To do this, we should pay close attention to the essential unfolding of this mode of revealing and, in doing so, we shall become increasingly aware of the extreme danger connected with this understanding of Being, and "The closer we come to the danger, the more brightly do the ways into the saving power begin to shine and the more questioning we become. For questioning is the piety of thought" ("The Question Concerning Technology", in BW: 341).

For the danger – oblivion of Being caused by mankind's enframed understanding of Being – when truly grasped *as* the danger, potentially can become that which saves us: "We look into the danger and see the growth of the saving power" (*ibid.*: 338). However, Heidegger also observes that:

Human activity can never directly counter this danger. Human achievement alone can never banish it. But human reflection can ponder the fact that all saving power must be of a higher essence than what is endangered, though at the same time kindred to it.

(*Ibid.*: 339)

So, focusing on the essence of technology and the dangers associated with this outlook can make us deeply aware of the danger of the oblivion of Being, which in turn can motivate us to focus our attention more closely on the question of Being. So, paradoxically, in the danger of enframing lies the potential motivation and source of our awareness of Being: "Thus the essential unfolding of technology harbors in itself what we least suspect, the possible rise of the saving power" (*ibid.*: 337). So, according to Heidegger, to escape from our forgetfulness of Being (*Seinverlassenheit*) we must first *become fully aware of its existence.*

[It] must be experienced as the basic happening of our history ... And this requires: 1. that *Seinverlassenheit* be recollected in its long and concealed, self-concealing history ... 2. that *Seinverlassenheit* also be experienced as the need that looms across into the transition and lights it up as the way into the future.   (GA 65: 112)

Heidegger felt that "forgetfulness of Being" conceals itself – is hidden from us – behind our intense concern with beings and, as a consequence of this, we do not usually experience any "distress" or "neediness" (*Notlosigkeit*) as a result of it. He regarded this "lack of distress" as being the greatest distress of human existence: "*Seinverlassenheit* is the innermost ground of the distress of lack of distress ... Is there ever a way out of a distress of the sort that constantly denies itself as a distress?" (GA 65: 119). However, if we become fully aware of this distress, if we experience forgetfulness of Being in its most acute, intense manifestations, then forgetfulness of Being itself will disclose Being to us (GA 65: 410ff.)

Heidegger's response to technology

Heidegger considers that seeing technology as a problem for us to fix is yet another example of technological thinking. For instance, in our efforts to protect the environment from industry we shout for laws to preserve the rainforests, proclaiming that they contain thousands of useful natural products, such as possible cures for cancer. So even this worthy attempt to protect the ecology of our planet is entrapped within the same mind-set that it is fighting. Indeed all efforts to control and manage the planet are merely further examples of technological thinking: "The instrumental conception of technology conditions every attempt to bring man into the right relation to technology ... The will to mastery becomes all the more urgent the more technology threatens to slip from human control" ("The Question Concerning Technology", in BW: 313). Thus Heidegger asserts: "No single man, no group of men, no commission of prominent states-men, scientists, and technicians, no conference of leaders of commerce and industry, can brake or direct the progress of history in the atomic age" (DT: 52). Rather, instead of direct action, he believes the key to this dilemma may be found through reflective attunement to Being, which "lets beings Be".

This "letting-be" involves waiting and listening in an open, receptive manner to the "voice" of Being. We must no longer take Being for granted; instead, we must realize that it is a gift, an "event" (*Ereignis*) that should be appreciated, not a resource that is available for manipulation. Implied here seems to be the idea that if we allow ourselves to remain open to Being, there may arise an understanding of another way of Being that will spontaneously guide us in the right direction. This view is shared by many followers of "deep ecology", who believe that saving the planet and all that it "houses" requires a raising of awareness; otherwise all direct action is taking place on unstable foundations that will ultimately crumble.

The threat of technology, therefore, is not a problem that needs a solu-tion, but an *ontological condition* that requires a transformation of our understanding of Being. "The issue is the saving of man's essential nature. Therefore, the issue is keeping meditative thinking alive" (DT: 56), by remaining receptive to the possibility of other modes of understanding Being that may become available to us. For, "If releasement towards things and openness to the mystery awaken within us, then we should arrive at a path that will lead to a new ground and foundation" (*ibid.*).

This "releasement" that Heidegger refers to is an intensely alert, non-excluding openness, an "awaiting" that is free from all expectation: a state of consciousness that is fully open and attuned to the "voice" of Being and thus utterly receptive to the arrival of new modes of understanding Being that become available to us. Heidegger's hope is not that we get rid of technology, but that once we recognize that the technological understand-ing of Being is a "clearing", a historical understanding that is a destining of Being, we shall be in a position to achieve a healthier, balanced, "free" relation with it, based on an enthusiastic awareness of other ways of Being. He suggests that we can make use of technology without letting it affect our inner and real core:

> We let technical devices enter our daily life, and at the same time leave them outside, … as things which are nothing absolute but remain dependent on something higher. I would call this comportment to technology which expresses "yes" and at the same time "no," by an old word, *releasement towards things.*   (DT: 54)

He also recommends that we strive to protect the "endangered species" of pre-technological activities from being mobilized as resources. These are activities that have now become marginal practices in our culture. He is referring to simple natural pleasures, such as genuine friendship, quiet walks through the countryside, sitting and gazing at the starlit sky: anything *not* motivated by the desire for "efficiency", "productivity" or "personal improvement". He hoped that such a lifestyle might help to establish a more meaningful direction to our existence in which non-technological practices were *central*, and technology *marginal*. (Interestingly, he detested using a typewriter and composed all his texts by hand, but employed his brother to type, and although he had no television set, he still took pleasure in watching sports on other people's sets; see Petzet [1993: 209–10].)

The greatest danger, according to Heidegger, is that "the approaching tide of technological revolution in the atomic age could so captivate, bewitch, dazzle, and beguile man that calculative thinking may someday come to be accepted *as the only way* of thinking" (DT: 56). This is why Heidegger, controversially, thinks that even if we resolve all the negative expressions and consequences of technology, and use it only in "positive" ways, the outcome *may* still be disastrous. The planet, potentially, could be transformed into a peaceful place, with nature perfectly controlled and providing food for everyone. Humans may achieve apparent "harmonious satisfaction" with abundant entertainment offered by a plethora of pleasure-oriented hi-tech innovations. However, Heidegger points out the real danger here of becoming entrapped and entranced by our technological lifestyle, so that we are merely part of a system that no one controls but that moves towards the total recruitment and enhancement of all beings, including us. In the process we lose all awareness of more meaningful and natural ways of living that allow us contact with the mystery of nature and the wonder of the meaning of Being. In the vice-like grip of our "enframed" technological understanding of Being, we shall mistakenly believe that this is all there is. Life will have lost its depth, and we shall have lost our true freedom.

It is clearly Heidegger's hope that true thinking will help prepare the other beginning and save us from being reduced to "mechanized animals" by technology (CTP: 275). The key to this saving power may be found in the creative arts, which are related to, and yet different from, technology.

Via their shared roots in *technē*, he saw art as capable of revealing a new, more "poetic" form of technology:

> Because the essence of technology is nothing technological, essential reflection upon technology and decisive confrontation with it must happen in a realm that is, on the one hand, akin to the essence of technology and, on the other, fundamentally different from it. Such a realm is art. ... Could it be that the fine arts are called to poetic revealing? Could it be that revealing lays claim to the arts most primally, so that they for their part may expressly foster the growth of the saving power? ... Whether art may be granted this highest possibility of its essence in the midst of the extreme danger, no one can tell.
>
> ("The Question Concerning Technology", in BW: 340)

However, for art to play this role requires us to question and acknowledge the truth of our current situation, to:

> bear witness to the crisis that in our sheer preoccupation with technology we do not yet experience the essential unfolding of technology, that in our sheer aesthetic-mindedness we no longer guard and preserve the essential unfolding of art. Yet the more questioningly we ponder the essence of technology, the more mysterious the essence of art becomes.
> (*Ibid.*: 340–41)

CHAPTER ELEVEN

Tao, Zen and Heidegger

Over the past two decades, a number of authors on Heidegger have recognized that his work has a certain affinity with East Asian thinking, notably with Taoism and Zen Buddhism, especially in his later thought. The fact that the Japanese have published seven translations of *Being and Time*, and that Heidegger is probably the most-studied modern philosopher in Asia, may well reflect this similarity between his own and East Asian thinking. On various occasions, Heidegger himself spoke of this connection. Otto Pöggeler, an eminent commentator on Heidegger's work, writes that Heidegger "gladly acknowledged to visitors the closeness of his thinking to the Taoist tradition and Zen Buddhism" (1987: 49). William Barrett related that when reading one of D. T. Suzuki's books on Buddhist thought, Heidegger said that Suzuki expressed what he himself had always tried to say (1956: xi).

The parallels between Heidegger and East Asian thinking are indisputable, which is why readers with a prior understanding of Asian philosophies will find themselves in familiar territory when they first encounter Heidegger's writings. What is not certain, however, is whether his thought was consciously influenced by East Asian philosophy, or whether the similarities are merely an example of what has been called "the universality of truth" expressing itself in a variety of ways.

Commentators on Heidegger's work who are sceptical about a direct East Asian influence on his thought emphasize his assertion that the modification of our technological approach to existence "cannot happen because of any takeover by Zen Buddhism or any other Eastern experience of the world … Thinking itself can only be transformed by a thinking which has the same origin and calling" (OGSU: 281). In other words, Heidegger claims that the "new beginning" he envisages for the West can only spring from the West itself, because the "first beginning", which has culminated in the modern technological disclosure of human beings and all other entities as "raw materials", originated in ancient Greece. Consequently, it is only via the European tradition that a transformation in thinking can come about. He further adds that linguistic differences have forced the Western and Eastern races to live in different "houses of Being".

Moreover, the thinkers and poets discussed in his writings (such as Anaximander, Heraclites, Parmenides, Sophocles and Hölderlin, and mystical Christian thinkers such as Meister Eckhart) and his extremely rare references to East Asian philosophy, certainly give the impression that his intellectual roots lie solely in the West: with the ancient Greeks and various figures in the Judaeo-Christian tradition. However, in his pioneering but highly controversial work *Heidegger's Hidden Sources*, Reinhard May investigates – through close textual comparisons between selections from Heidegger's major works and passages from German translations of Taoist and Zen texts – the possibility that Heidegger drew on these sources for at least *some* of the major ideas in his philosophy.

May concludes from his analysis that Heidegger's work was indeed influenced by East Asian thought to a hitherto unrecognized extent and that, without acknowledging his sources, Heidegger on occasion borrowed, even appropriated, key themes of central importance to his work, primarily from German translations of Taoist classics and, to a lesser extent, from German translations of Zen Buddhist texts as well. These "borrowed" themes include his thoughts on Being, Nothing and the clearing, as well as the complex relations between language, Way and Saying. May also suggests that this appropriation of East Asian thinking continued for some years via Heidegger's numerous discussions with Chinese and Japanese scholars.

If these non-metaphysical philosophical traditions did indeed strongly influence Heidegger's thought, and May's revolutionary conclusions became accepted in Western academe, this could have far-reaching implications for future interpretations of Heidegger's work, especially in regard to the orientation of forthcoming comparative studies of his philosophy.

While most Heidegger scholars do *not* accept that even Heidegger's later thinking was heavily indebted to Eastern thought, the connection cannot be totally ruled out. (There is perhaps a parallel here with Schopenhauer, who claimed to have reached his conclusions about the noumenal and phenomenal quite independently of Indian thought, but who is known to have read a translation of *The Upanishads* while working on his masterpiece *The World as Will and Representation*. This knowledge has not undermined later appreciation of Schopenhauer's thinking.)

A single chapter obviously cannot thoroughly investigate the connection between Heidegger's thinking and East Asian philosophy, but the following discussion should inspire the reader to explore further this important aspect of Heideggerian scholarship. Although, admittedly, the content of this chapter is not *mainstream* Heidegger in terms of Western academic work, it is nevertheless absolutely relevant for anyone who wants to get a broad perspective on his work. The chapter provides a general overview of some similarities between Heidegger's thought and ideas from Taoism and Zen, and this is followed by a small selection of textual comparisons of passages from Heidegger's major works and translations of Taoist and Zen texts.

Finally, it must be stressed that this chapter does not challenge the acceptance of Heidegger's thinking as among the most profound, elaborate and influential contributions to Western philosophy. It simply questions whether the origins of his thinking are *exclusively* Graeco-Teutonic.

Taoism and Heidegger

Heidegger took no formal courses in Eastern philosophy, nor did he talk to any great extent about meditation, spiritual training or enlightenment. Nevertheless, Heidegger spent several months during the summer of 1946 working with a Chinese scholar, Paul Shih-yi Hsiao, on a translation into German of the *Tao Te Ching*, although they completed only eight of the eighty-one chapters (Hsiao 1987). The degree to which this collaboration consciously influenced Heidegger's thought is clearly debatable, but there are certainly some obvious parallels between aspects of Taoism and Heidegger's thinking. In one essay, for instance, he acknowledges resonances between the *Tao* and his conception of *Ereignis* as the "event of appropriation" (OWL: 92).

In Taoism, the *Tao* (often translated "Way") encompasses both the cosmic and human realms of experience. The "Way" is described as the source of the cosmos and everything in existence: the weather, mountains, rivers, plants, animals and human beings. Similarly, Heidegger cites "Being" as the essence of Dasein: the primordial or fundamental basis of Dasein's ability to encounter and understand itself and the universe of entities it engages with in the world.

The *Tao* points to "natural laws" of the universe and nature, and indicates ways of living that synchronize with these. Similarly, Heidegger alludes to modes of being-in-the-world that are in harmony with and reflect the mystery of existence. The creative works of "true" poets and artists are exceptional examples of this, and pre-technological activities that are not motivated by the desire for "efficiency", "productivity" or "personal improvement", such as quiet walks through the countryside or gazing contemplatively at the star-lit sky, can also tune us into the incredible wonder of existence.

The *Tao*, like Heidegger's account of existence, allows for a far more temporalized understanding of the world and our way of Being than does classical Western metaphysics. For the *Tao* is always in the midst of change and can be understood in this context only. Similarly, Heidegger describes "Being" as a continually evolving phenomenon, and Dasein's structure as temporal. Thus, according to Heidegger, Being – the sense of what it means *to be* – can be explored and understood only in relation to, or in the context of, time.

Taoist philosophy explains that the *Tao* cannot be expressed in words or concepts. In *Being and Time*, dissatisfied with the results of his discussion of Being, Heidegger asserted that words cannot explain the "isness" of Being, which is intrinsically mysterious and self-concealing, and that attempts to define it, or subject it to logical analysis, are like "reaching into a void": "the essence of Being is never conclusively sayable" (GA 65: 460). Thus we can only speak of it tautologically: "a being has its being in Being, and Being persists as the Being of a being" (WCT: 221).

The *Tao* can be sensed only through direct experience, or hinted at figuratively through such means as imagery. George Pattison (2000: 203) notes the prominence of water imagery, used to hint at aspects of the "Way" in Taoist philosophy (e.g. "the highest good is to be like water"), which parallels the images of Nature used in Heidegger's lectures on Hölderlin, such as the poetic motif of the river. Further, the ideal Taoist state of mind described as *wu wei*, one of contemplation defined by "letting things be as they are", seems to correspond closely with Heidegger's description of "releasement" (*Gelassenheit*), in which one adapts to the way things are, without consciously "willing" anything, while in a state of totally alert "openness" that is free from all expectation.

In the Taoist work *Chuang-tzu*, the models offered of people who live according to the *Tao* are not wise "sages" who live and meditate in isolation from the world, but frequently artisans and craftsmen as well as others who have attained consummate mastery of various psycho-physical skills. For in Taoism, sensitive, smooth and seemingly effortless manual dexterity rather than intellectual development is considered to be the outer sign of a developed inner strength that is aligned with the *Tao*: a sign that one's power (*Te*) has become fully integrated. Thus the message behind many Taoist fables is that we have a "*body* of knowledge" that needs no help from the thinking mind, for when we are detached from the grip of discursive thought the "wisdom of the body" can express itself, allowing the hands to do their own kind of "thinking". One could perhaps call this "body-thinking": a thinking that takes place through and in the hands. Similarly, in the early 1940s Heidegger alluded to a relation between thinking and the hands by calling "authentic thinking" a *Handeln*, meaning "activity". Later he describes such thinking as a *Hand-Werk* (literally, "a work of the hand"), which means "craft": "We are trying to learn thinking. Perhaps thinking, too, is just something like building a cabinet. At any rate, it is a craft, a 'handicraft'. 'Craft' literally means the strength and skill in our hands" (WCT: 16).

According to Heidegger, this type of thinking is not analytical or exploitive thinking confined to the brain, but a sensitive, meditative thinking, a "reaching and receiving, holding and carrying, pointing and gesturing" (*ibid.*) that expresses a person's entire Being: an expression that allows artists such as Cézanne and Klee to depict things on canvas in a way that captures the essential nature of their Being. Heidegger asserts that:

> The gestures of the hand pervade the whole of language and in fact most purely when man speaks in being silent … All the work of the hand is rooted in thinking. Therefore, thinking itself is man's … hardest handiwork, if from time to time it would be accomplished properly … Socrates is the purest thinker of the West. Therefore he wrote nothing. (WCT: 16–17)

Heidegger is certainly not implying here that the hand is rooted in the "thinking of the *mind*", but rather that our hands possess a pre-conceptual ontological understanding or awareness: an *a priori* understanding of Being. For pre-ontologically, that is, without any need for reflective awareness and understanding, we are, through our hands, *always and already in a relation* with the Being of beings. There seems to be a natural understanding of this fact in our daily vocabulary: we talk about a *tactful* way of handling things. The good craftsman is deeply *in touch* with the materials he uses: with the *Being* of that which he is crafting.

Thus the hand is not just an "extension" of the body; it *is* the lived body. It responds to our five senses and, most importantly, it embodies our "kinaesthetic sense". We shape our world through the activity of our hands, and thus Heidegger seems to be suggesting that, by evolving our awareness in a manner that transforms our effort-filled, desire-driven grasping, seizing and holding into a releasing, letting-go and letting-be, that is grounded on an authentic sensing of Being, perhaps we can escape the tyranny of our technological worldview.

In "The Turning" (*Die Kehre*), Heidegger observes that "thinking is genuine activity, genuine taking a hand, if to take a hand means to lend a hand to … the coming to presence of Being" (QCT: 40). So the origin of technology and the solution to the problem of nihilism is "in our hands". By altering our way of relating to the things we touch and handle we can alter our world:

> "Using" does not mean utilizing, using up, exploiting. When we handle a thing, for example, our hand must fit itself to the thing. Use

234

implies fitting response. Proper use does not debase what is being used – on the contrary, use is determined and defined by leaving the used thing in its essential nature. But leaving it that way does not mean carelessness, much less neglect. On the contrary; only proper use brings the thing to its essential nature and keeps it there ... safe in its essence. (WCT: 187)

According to Heidegger, we are appropriately caring when we relate "to the thing in hand according to its nature, thus letting that nature become manifest by the handling" (WCT: 195). This experience of touching or handling a thing can reveal the illusory nature of subject–object duality, since ontologically the touching and the touched are a single event occurring in a unified tactile field of energy.

Heidegger's way of thinking about the hands, while highly compatible with Taoist thought, is very different from the metaphysical viewpoint, which traditionally believes that the human body is incapable of thinking. Thinking is supposed to take place only in the "mind" located in the brain, and this mind is treated as being completely separate from the body; thus the *bodymind* and its innate wisdom is completely ignored. Nietzsche realized that this mode of understanding fuels moral and spiritual dysfunction.

Finally, Heidegger's understanding of death as a constant presence within life, rather than a state beyond and opposed to life, closely resembles the Taoist standpoint. For in Taoism life and death are not viewed as opposing one another but simply part of the natural cycle of continual change, like the seasons of the year. Thus death is neither desired nor feared, and the Taoist attitude is one of serene acceptance.

Zen and Heidegger

A certain affinity with elements of Buddhism, especially Zen, and also with Taoism has long been the subject of comment in connection with the later Heidegger. There is a substantial history of Heidegger-reception in Japan that explores these affinities.
(Pattison 2000: 201)

If your mind is empty, it is always ready for anything; it is open to everything. In the beginner's mind there are many possibilities; in the expert's mind there are few. (Suzuki 2010: 2)

This fundamental view of the "beginner's mind" in Zen Buddhism is clearly echoed in a letter written by Heidegger, in 1928, to the former prefect of the clerical seminary in Constance, which Heidegger had formerly attended as a student. In the letter, Heidegger asserted: "Perhaps philosophy shows most forcibly and persistently how much Man is a beginner. Philosophising ultimately means nothing other than being a beginner" (Safranski 1998: 1). Furthermore, in his search for an understanding of the question of Being, Heidegger turned to the *beginnings* of philosophy in Greece, while searching in the present for the place in which philosophy is always being born anew. He also often talked in terms of "the new beginning" with reference to the change in thought that he hoped could emerge as a result of his new approach to thinking.

Heidegger's description of the experience of authenticity has much in common with Zen Buddhist enlightenment. Both arise from insight into the non-dualistic nature of existence. From the perspective of Zen, "salvation" can be found in the experience of the Nothingness that lies at the ground of our being. Thus Zen speaks of "pure experience" or the "experience of Nothingness" as *satori* or enlightenment. Similarly, Heidegger describes how intense anxiety can open us to a profound awareness of Nothingness that, in turn, potentially can lead to an authentic mode of existence.

A famous Zen story about the "stages" of enlightenment states: "Before enlightenment occurs, mountains are mountains; at the moment of enlightenment, mountains cease being mountains; but then mountains become mountains again" (Zimmerman 2006: 298). "Zen enlightenment, *satori*, involves direct insight into one's radical groundlessness … In the light of such a revelation, everyday practices … lose their meaning. Afterward, however, one reenters these practices, but in a way no longer burdened by ignorance about what it means to be human" (*ibid.*). The similarity to Heidegger's thinking seems clear. For Heidegger, prior to living authentically one exists according to everyday practices. When we allow anxiety to reveal to us that we are "being-towards-death", rooted in "Nothingness", everyday practices slide away into meaninglessness; afterwards, one resumes everyday practices, but this time guided by an awareness of our *own* possibilities that allows us to *choose* our *own* way of life, rather than a way of living dictated by the expectations of the They (Zimmerman 2006: 298).

Like Zen enlightenment, Heidegger's state of authenticity requires no faith in, or experience of, God. Both Zen and Heidegger maintain that the "self" is not any sort of "thinking thing". It is not an ego that exists in separation from the "external" world, but rather the Nothingness or openness in which the continual play of phenomena can arise. Especially in his later thought, Heidegger resembles Zen in his adoption of the idea that the achievement of authenticity requires *Gelassenheit*, which implies "release from the will and the abandonment of all effort"; one cannot simply *resolve* to become authentic. In Zen Buddhism (particularly in the *Soto* tradition) it is likewise maintained that enlightenment can never be "willed" but can only be cultivated by learning to "let things be" in everyday life. "In holding fast, or grasping, the whole universe vanishes. In letting go, or releasing, the individual world appears, in which everyone asserts his true existence" (Sekida 1977: 329). Also, as Pattison points out: "Zen enlightenment ... is not understood simply in personal terms. It does not just give an answer to the question 'How must I live?' but also to the question 'How is it with the world?' In this regard, Zen experience is understood as ontological disclosure" (2000: 203).

Although Heidegger and Zen accept that one cannot actually *resolve* to become enlightened or authentic, each recommends a variety of procedures to encourage a state whereby one is more likely to be "willing not to will": a state that increases one's chances of experiencing this non-willed "letting go" or "release", which allows one to experience the truth of Being for the first time. In Zen, there is an emphasis on the importance of sitting meditation, proper breathing and working with paradoxical *koans*. This parallels the later Heidegger's claims that releasement (*Gelassenheit*) may be cultivated by proper breathing, meditative practices and through the contemplation of paradoxical questions.

Heidegger believed that the mind is more receptive to the "astonishing mystery of Being" when it is completely absorbed in questions that ultimately are unanswerable, such as "Why is there something rather than Nothing?", or "What is the meaning of Being?" For, according to Heidegger: "If the power of the intellect in the field of inquiry into the Nothing and into Being is thus shattered, then the destiny of the reign of 'logic' in philosophy is thereby decided. The idea of 'logic' itself disintegrates in the turbulence of a more original questioning" ("What is Metaphysics?", in BW: 105). This is reminiscent of the *koan* approach to enlightenment, used in the *Rinzai* sect of Zen, where the student meditates on a question that has no logical answer, such as "What is the sound of one hand clapping?" Out of such practices can arise the experience of utter stillness and complete silence: an awareness of the Nothingness or openness of Being pervading all things (see Zimmerman 1983).

Heidegger's authentic approach to life thus shares many qualities with the Zen way of life, for both arise in the absence of any "conscious willing", following a "spontaneous" realization of the non-dualistic nature of existence that "releases" the individual from the illusion that they are a separate independent ego, living in a world disconnected from all other apparently independent entities. The division between observer and world – between subject and object – normally experienced by the awareness of "everyday

Dasein", melts into an overwhelming sensation of complete unity with all existence.

In this state of awareness, reality is now experienced directly "as it is", untainted by "everyday language", and liberated from the judging mind, which divides and rigidifies the world with its linguistic segmentation. *Authentic* Dasein and Zen masters live in a "fluid" universe where the illusory distinctions and boundaries that seem to separate entities are no longer experienced; all dualisms are shattered, including the one between presencing and absencing, Being and Nothingness. Thus both Heidegger and Zen "attempt to think past the conceptualisation of the experience in terms of dualistic categories, the relativisation of Being and Nothingness, and the concern for 'place' or 'site' of thinking and experience" (Pattison 2000: 203).

Life is now experienced as a "spontaneous arising" in which there is a mutual interconnection – an interpenetration – of all entities in a unified field of awareness or Being that is inseparable from the womb of Nothingness from which all arises. This experience is epitomized by the "all is one" realization of Zen. Similarly, in Heidegger's thought, the unity of all things in existence is clearly hinted at in *Being and Time,* in the concept of "equipment totality", which recognizes the interconnectedness of everything in Dasein's world of practical and personal concerns, which constitute Dasein's primary way of "being-in-the-world" and "being-with-others".

The Zen recognition that the apparent "solidity" of the things we encounter in the world is illusory since all things in reality are "empty" and impermanent finds an echo in Heidegger's praise of Socrates, who remains continually in the "powerful draught" of ever-changing direct experience, which constantly undermines the presumed solidity of the familiar everyday world.

> All through his life and right into his death, Socrates did nothing else than place himself into this draft, this current, and maintain himself in it. This is why he is the purest thinker of the West. This is why he wrote nothing. For anyone who begins to write out of thoughtfulness must inevitably be like those people who run to seek refuge from any draft too strong for them.
>
> ("What Calls for Thinking?", in BW: 382)

Also, just as Zen is aware of the suffering created as a result of our futile attempts to make the Nothingness or emptiness that we are into something enduring, Heidegger regards this same condition as "inauthentic living" and points out that liberation from this is possible only when Dasein finally realizes that it is intrinsically a being-towards-death.

Both Heidegger's "authentic understanding" and Zen enlightenment increase the intensity of our experience of Being. Freed from dualism, humans can now experience a new, non-domineering relation with all entities in existence. Heidegger describes a full flowering of the state of "care", and in Zen there is the emergence of spontaneous, deepened compassion. In both cases, there is a profound transformation in the person's approach to existence. In Zen Buddhism, the enlightened human being exhibits compassion *equally* for all beings, human and non-human alike and, similarly, Heidegger, in his later writings, calls for humanity to let "*all* beings be". Further, in both Zen and Heidegger, "letting beings be" does not arise from any ulterior motive, but from a profound sense of identification, or "oneness", with everything in existence.

Heidegger and Zen have much in common: "in both we see, for example, the use of everyday objects ... as a means of awakening us to the truth of how things are" (Pattison 2000: 203). Both assign great importance to ordinary actions of everyday life. Such actions are seen to be a potential source of "authentic understanding", or "awakening", that may arise spontaneously when there is an unselfconscious *practical* interaction with our world and the entities in it.

Practical interaction with the world is Dasein's *primordial* way of relating to, and understanding, reality, a way that potentially can reveal that human existence is intimately and inextricably linked to all things. For instance, according to Heidegger, we cannot truly know the nature of a hammer by analysing it in a detached, objective manner, but only via our wholehearted *use* of it. Similarly, in the Zen way of life, giving full attention to ordinary daily activities such as cleaning our shoes, sweeping the floor or making a cup of tea is regarded as a potential means of awakening us to the truth of how things are: the nature of Being. Heidegger's reverence for everyday activities is epitomized in the Zen "tea ceremony", where the act of making a cup of tea is transformed into a meditative art.

Finally, both Heidegger's later writings and Buddhist thought share a common belief that the ontological event of *appearance* of humans and all other entities is uncaused. In other words, the arising, or coming into Being, of universal phenomena – the self-manifesting or presencing of entities – cannot be explained by any sort of religious, metaphysical, mythical or scientific narrative, since reason cannot possibly give "ground" to that which is "groundless".

Concepts of causality are thus relevant only as part of a conceptual scheme for relating or describing phenomena after they have already come into Being as "things". According to Buddhist and Heideggerian accounts of reality, everything in existence arises spontaneously and simultaneously and is inextricably linked. In Buddhism this is seen as the moment-by-moment co-production of self-luminous phenomena emerging from the inexhaustible field of Absolute Nothingness. In later Heidegger, it is described as the dance of earth, sky, gods and mortals in which all things manifest themselves in the event (*Ereignis*) of mutual appropriation – a dance in which entities impart to one another their appropriate place in the universe.

Text similarities between Heidegger's work and Taoist and Zen classics

The striking similarity between certain key ideas in Heidegger's thinking and central themes in Taoism and Zen becomes evident if we compare extracts from Heidegger's texts in which he discusses "the Nothing" (*das Nichts*), "Being" and "the *thing*", with extracts from classic Taoist and Zen works covering these same topics. According to May (1996), the results of these textual comparisons suggest that Heidegger's understanding of these topics, extensively elaborated in his later writings, was indebted to Taoist and Zen Buddhist thought. This claim directly conflicts with the views of most Heidegger scholars, who have assumed without question that Heidegger's revolutionary understanding and explanations of Being and Nothingness emerged solely from his creative "destruction" of the history of Western ontology. Even if the parallels between Heidegger's terminology and Taoism cannot in themselves prove any direct influence, they certainly provide interesting ground for further investigation.

"Nothing" and "Being"

The most fundamental, distinctive theme of East Asian thought is visible in Taoism in the ancient insight, expressed in chapter 2 of the *Tao Te Ching* of Lao Tzu, which states that *yu* (Being) and *wu* (Nothing) mutually produce one another. In the Victor von Strauss translation, the passage reads: "Being and non-being give birth to one another" (Lao-Tse 2009: 58; May 1996: 26); Richard Wilhelm translates it as: "Being and non-being engender one another" (Dschuang Dsi [Chuang Tzu] 1972: 42; May 1996: 26). Compare this with Heidegger's assertion: "Being and Nothing are not given beside one another. Each uses itself on behalf of the other" (QB: 97). The topic is expanded in chapter 40 of the *Tao Te Ching*, which states that all things originate from Being (*yu*), and that Being originates from Nothing (*wu*). In the von Strauss translation: "All beings originate from being, / Being originates from non-being" (Lao-Tse 2009: 111).

This description of the relation between Being and Nothing is fundamental to East Asian understanding of the *Tao*. Zen Buddhism adopted and further developed this insight: "Being is none other than Nothing, / Nothing is none other than being" (Shinjin-mei 1925: 70). Compare this with Heidegger's version: "Nothing as 'Being'" ("What is Metaphysics?", in BW: 106) and, "Nothing and Being the Same" (*ibid.*: 115).

Thus, in Heidegger's later writings, "Nothing" and "Being" are considered to be equiprimordial: "to think *that* Nothing that is equiprimordially the same as Being" (QB: 101).

The "thing"

Heidegger's analysis of the essential nature of the *thing* brings to light yet further textual similarities between his own thinking and Taoist philosophy. In the classic Taoist work *Chuang Tzu* it is written that "What gives things their thingness is not itself a thing" (Dschuang Dsi [Chuang Tzu] 1972: 233; May 1996: 29). In a remarkably similar statement, Heidegger writes: "the thingly character of the thing does not consist in its being a represented object, nor can it be defined in any way in terms of the objectness ... of the object" (PLT: 167).

The *Tao Te Ching* also emphasizes the important relation between usefulness and emptiness, or Nothing (*wu*), via the example of three different kinds of "thing": a cartwheel, a jug and a room. In each case it is shown that the "usefulness" (or, in more Heideggerian terminology, the "ready-to-hand" nature) of these things depends on the emptiness, or Nothingness, that they contain: the wheel depends on its hub, the jug on its hollowness, and the room on its openings. Thus chapter 11 of the *Tao Te Ching* states: "The work of pitchers consists in their Nothingness" (Laotse 1980: 51; May 1996: 30). Von Strauss translates this as: "The use of the container accords with its non-being" (Lao-Tse 2009: 68; cf. 204–6; May 1996: 30).

Compare this Taoist explanation of the "thingly character" of the container with the one that Heidegger provides in his 1950 lecture, "The Thing": "The thingly character of the container does not in any way consist in the material of which it is made, but rather in the emptiness that does the containing" ("The Thing", in PLT: 169). (Note that Heidegger also asserts that "emptiness is ... the same as Nothing" [WT: 19].)

For both Heidegger and the *Tao Te Ching*, the essence of the jug's "Being", or "usefulness", is its "emptiness" or "Nothingness", which allows the jug to express its true function of containing and pouring liquid.

Conclusions on Heidegger's East Asian influences

That Heidegger's later thinking *might* have been strongly influenced by Taoist philosophy is not difficult to believe, for a fundamental motive behind his work is to overcome the influence of Western metaphysics, which he regards as being fundamentally onto-theo-logical (ID: 59). Taoist philosophy, therefore, would have been an attractive field of study, since metaphysics was never developed in ancient China (see Needham 1975: 37). Consequently, Taoist philosophy has no roots in Aristotelian logic, it has no use for any ontology involving dualistic thinking and, most importantly, it has not been influenced by theology. Thus it is refreshingly free from the assertion of so-called "eternal truths", which, according to Heidegger, as the residue of Christian theology, still pollute metaphysical thinking. Further, since Heidegger was deeply moved by poetry, and the great philosophers of classical Taoism were *poets* as well as thinkers, these philosophers (like Western poets such as Rilke, Trakl and Hölderlin) represented potentially helpful "models" for his own approach to philosophy.

However, in the summer of 1949, during an exchange of letters with Jaspers, once a close friend, there is a flat denial by Heidegger of any such Asian influences. Instead, he emphasizes *exclusively* Western sources. The exchange commenced with a letter sent by Jaspers, thanking Heidegger for sending three recently published books: the new edition of "What is Metaphysics?" and the second editions of "On the Essence of Truth" and the "Letter on Humanism". In this letter, Jasper writes:

> Many questions arise for me. I have still not managed to get to the mid-point of the whole thing. It helps somewhat to think of Asian ideas, which I've been interested in for years, knowing well that I lack a penetrating understanding, and yet finding myself wonderfully stimulated from that direction. Your "Being", the "clearing of Being", your reversal of our relation to Being into Being's relation to us, the remainder of Being itself – I seem to have perceived something of the sort in Asia. That you are driving toward that at all, and – according to your interpretation of *Being and Time* – always have done, is extraordinary. (*Briefwechsel*: 178)

In the letter replying to Jaspers's suggestion that his writings "resonate" Asian thinking, Heidegger asserts that "The resonances presumably have a quite different root: since 1910 I have been accompanied by the master of learning and life Eckhardt"; Heidegger further adds that Parmenides, and "the lack of the subject–object relationship in the Greeks", in combination with his "own thinking", are the true source of his new approach to thinking (*ibid.*: 280).

Taking into account May's findings (and the emphasis in Heidegger's thought on the value of "authenticity"), this clear denial by Heidegger of any "resonances with Eastern thinking" is rather surprising and also, perhaps, very revealing. In his subsequent reply to Heidegger, Jaspers actually specifies Lao Tzu, but since this extracts no additional commentary from Heidegger, he does not take the discussion further.

The possibility that the close parallels between Heidegger's thinking and East Asian philosophy might be purely coincidental – perhaps simply a consequence of the "universality"of truth – is rejected by May on the basis of the large number of close textual correlations that he uncovered (of which this chapter has offered only a very few). According to May, examples of such correlations in Heidegger's writings increased significantly in number after his joint enterprise with Hsiao on translating the *Tao Te Ching* in the summer of 1946.

Based on the information provided here, one can reasonably conclude that Heidegger's interest in, and familiarity with, East Asian thought is indisputable. Moreover, on the basis of May's findings, it would seem that one cannot simply dismiss, without further investigation, the suggestion that Heidegger may have deliberately elaborated and incorporated East Asian thinking in his own approach to philosophy without ever providing the customary indications of his sources.

However, one could perhaps offer the following defence for such an omission: Heidegger asserts that "thinking" *has* to "poetize", in response to the enigma of Being (EGT: 58), and consequently, as a "philosopher-*poet*" he may have felt legitimately exempt from the academic custom of citing sources. Perhaps Heidegger held the same viewpoint, regarding art and poetry, that is concisely expressed in the following passage from *Death in Venice* by Thomas Mann:

> It is certainly good that the world knows only the beautiful work, and not also its sources, nor the conditions of its origination; for knowledge of the springs from which inspiration flowed to the artist would often confuse and shock people, thereby annulling the effects of what is excellent.   (Quoted in May 1996: 45)

Moreover, it is interesting to note that Pattison, having acknowledged highly significant affinities between Heidegger and East Asian philosophy, nevertheless concludes:

It is probably more fruitful, and certainly adequate for any attempt at philosophical interpretation, simply to note the affinities without attempting to track down their sources, especially as the elements that link Heidegger, Zen and Daoism also relate to other currents in his thought (e.g. the Presocratics).   (2003: 204)

If one believes that in the interpretation of philosophical text one should endeavour to reveal not only the thinker's concealed thoughts, but also their *source*, then this chapter should add to our understanding of Heidegger a new slant on his thought that it is hoped will inspire readers to a deeper knowledge of non-Western thinking, especially since Heidegger seems to have demonstrated, via his own approach, the validity of trans-cultural thinking.

CHAPTER TWELVE

Heidegger's politics

Heidegger's politics, and the debate as to whether his philosophy lends itself readily to Nazi ideology, is normally considered central to reading and interpreting his thought. Some thinkers, however, rejecting any suggestion of the "*ad hominem* argument" linking the life and work, suggest that Heidegger's personal political views and behaviour be regarded as philosophically insignificant, because a philosophy and moral character exist independently: "Being an original philosopher ... is the result of some neural kink that occurs independently of other kinks ... Philosophical talent and moral character swing free of each other" (Rorty 1998: 32–3). This standpoint tries to evaluate Heidegger's thinking on its merits while rejecting one of Heidegger's fundamental convictions – that thinking and meaning derive from one's concrete experience of being-in-the-world – which implies that "authentic" philosophizing arises from authentic existence (although this does not necessarily mean that others will view an "authentic existence" as *morally* acceptable).

Although Heidegger was *not* a political philosopher in the traditional sense, most people accept that we cannot completely segregate his life and work; first, because of the sheer enormity of the regime's crimes against humanity, and second, because after the war, even after the full horrors of the Holocaust had been exposed, Heidegger *still* never expressed openly real guilt or deep regrets over his actions. Indeed, he made great efforts to vindicate himself using a variety of highly questionable excuses, inspiring Polt to assert: "It is hard to avoid the conclusion that Heidegger's postwar self-interpretation is cowardly and self-deceptive. To speak the language of *Being and Time*: it is glaringly inauthentic" (1999: 159).

According to Heidegger, it was the *Nazis*, not Heidegger, who were ultimately at fault. The National Socialist state had failed to live up to its true historical potential, as he indicated in a 1935 lecture *Introduction to Metaphysics*: "'The works that are being peddled nowadays as the philosophy of National Socialism have nothing whatever to do with the inner truth and greatness of this movement [namely, the encounter between global technology and contemporary man]" (Wolin 1993: 103). But Tom Rockmore argues that although Heidegger soon broke away from the actual Nazi regime, he never renounced an *ideal* Nazism that preserves the "inner truth and greatness" of the movement (1992: 123–4).

When Heidegger first supported this totalitarian regime, however, he did not have the benefit of hindsight. He entered the Nazi Party at a politically feverish time, and his enthusiasm was shared not only by the many other "revolutionary conservative" intellectuals who supported Hitler, but also by 43.9 per cent of German voters in the last free election of March 1933. The Nazis' violent anti-Semitism was regarded by many merely as an odious but peripheral tactic to win the racist vote that would fade away once they were firmly in power. Further, although Hitler was clearly anti-Semitic, at that time anti-Semitism was not viewed, as it is today, as utterly unacceptable and instantly disqualifying a politician or political movement from serious consideration. At this stage, no one could have suspected that voting for Hitler would eventually entail the methodical murder of six million people.

Heidegger, like many German *völkischer* conservatives had, even during the Weimar Republic, longed for a more charismatic and nationalistic government. To such people the Nazis represented renewed order and national regeneration amid the poverty of the economic slump and the chaos of the collapsing Weimar democracy, which Heidegger despised. Most importantly, Nazism appeared at the time the only real safeguard against a communist revolution. Heidegger, at first, also genuinely believed in many Nazi policies. Leaving the League of Nations; unilaterally renouncing the Treaty of Versailles, which had pinned the blame for the First World War on Germany; rearmament; the attempt to achieve economic autarky and the concomitant abolition of unemployment: all these were, for Heidegger, evidence of the "nation's will to assert itself", the fulfilment of that primal demand of "Dasein" that it should preserve and save its own essence.

What is more disturbing to many is not his initial entry into the Nazi Party, but his later failure (after 1945) to acknowledge openly the extent of his error, once he was made fully aware of the Nazi atrocities. Even after the collapse of Germany in 1945, he implied that if the right influences had been applied to the movement in its early stages, the result could have been beneficial. What would have happened and what could have been averted if in 1933 all available powers had arisen, gradually and in secret unity, in order to purify and moderate the "movement" that had come to power?

He continued to believe that a philosophically idealized version of National Socialism was a political antidote to Western nihilism and its accompanying "decadent" values and that it could potentially save Western civilization from a technological and nihilistic downward spiral of self-destruction. To the end of his life he maintained this same view.

An in-depth discussion of this whole topic is clearly a formidable task that obviously cannot be dealt with adequately in one chapter. Consequently, my aim here is merely to introduce the reader to some of the key themes that have been vigorously debated at length in several excellent works, including: Hugo Ott's *Heidegger* (1993), Richard Wolin's *The Heidegger Controversy* (1993), Young's *Heidegger, Philosophy, Nazism* (1997) and Rudiger Safranski's *Martin Heidegger* (1998).

The facts and fiction of Heidegger's Nazism

Heidegger's version of his behaviour during this time has been challenged repeatedly. In 1962 Guido Schneeberger published all Heidegger's original rectorial speeches. In 1987, a decade after Heidegger's death, the French translation of a book by Victor Farías, *Heidegger and Nazism*, claimed that it proved unequivocally Heidegger's deep commitment to, and involvement with, National Socialism. Although the reliability of much of this book has since been questioned, the publication caused uproar, especially in France, stimulating a torrent of articles, conferences and new books debating this heated issue. Since the radical intelligentsia in France – from Sartre to Derrida – had based itself on the anti-rationalist philosophy of Heidegger, French intellectuals felt obliged to clarify their relation to Heidegger's work. More recently, key documents and letters have been published following research by Pöggeler and the Freiburg historian Ott, and the information contained in these casts significant doubt on the truth of Heidegger's "defence statement".

The facts suggest that far from being pressured into the job, Heidegger used the rectorship as a platform for an energetic attempted foray into the political arena. A group of Nazi professors and assistant professors, acting with Heidegger's full cooperation, had been working for his appointment since March 1933. Heidegger himself chose and organized the programme for his inauguration. It was attended by party officials and military representatives as well as the newly appointed Nazi Minister for Education and Culture. The ceremony included a Brahms overture, the flying of Nazi flags and the singing of the party anthem, *Horst Wessel*, accompanied by Nazi salutes and shouts of "Sieg Heil!" Thus, from the very beginning, the orchestration of cultural symbols unambiguously identified Heidegger's rectorship with the Nazi revolution: not what one might expect from a man *pressured* into becoming rector.

As rector, he cooperated with the new regime in numerous ways, helping to synchronize the administration, faculty and student bodies of the university with Nazi party political policies. He rapidly established the *Führerprinzip* (leader principle) at the university (1 October 1933), which meant the termination of democratic elections for rectorships, so guaranteeing his own position as head of Freiburg University. He also joined a Nazi coalition that forced the resignation of the board of the German Academics Association – the official representative body of university teachers – and later he called for the association's abolition. Further, he formed close alliances with radical party educational reformers to discuss the reformation of German universities on Nazi principles, even sending two telegrams to Hitler about this in late 1933.

On one occasion, Heidegger actively promoted the introduction of special military training work-and-study camps for students and professors, organizing one of them himself near his home in Todtnauberg in October 1933. Participants wore Nazi SA (Brownshirt) uniforms and the purpose of the camp was avowedly: "The lively inculcation of the aim of a National Socialist revolution in our university system" (Ott 1993: 229). In a letter to one of the participants Heidegger wrote: "The goal of the university revolution is the SA student" (Safranski 1998: 263).

Heidegger's lectures and speeches became increasingly polluted with Nazi political sentiment, unambiguously expressing the strident nationalism and rhetoric of favourite Nazi themes. In an address to "German Students", on 3 November 1933, on the same day that he enforced the Nazi "cleansing laws" within the university, which ended all financial aid for Marxists, Jews and other "non-Aryans", he urged the student body and faculty to willingly participate in the new National Socialist order:

> The National Socialist revolution is bringing about the total transformation of our German existence (*Dasein*) … Let not propositions and "ideas" be the rules of your Being (*Sein*). The Fuhrer alone *is* the present and future German reality and its law. Learn to know ever more deeply: from now on every single thing demands decision, and every action responsibility. Heil Hitler!
> ("Political Texts, 1933–1934", in Wolin 1993: 46–7)

A week later he spoke out, openly supporting Hitler's decision to withdraw Germany from the League of Nations. He also backed the Labour Service programme policy in which he ranked intellectual service in third place after military and labour service. In June 1933, after visiting him in Freiburg, his former close friend, Jaspers, had described him as being "like a man intoxicated, with something threatening emanating from him"

(Safranski 1998: 250). When Jaspers asked him how one could expect someone as uneducated as Hitler to rule Germany well, Heidegger's bizarre reply was: "Education is quite irrelevant … just look at his wonderful hands!" (*ibid.*: 232).

Heidegger also secretly denounced various colleagues to the Gestapo. In one case, he accused a professor of chemistry, Hermann Staudinger, of being a politically unreliable, former pacifist, and when his allegation was verified he urged, in a letter dated 10 February 1934, that Staudinger be fired immediately without any pension.

Heidegger had earlier enjoyed close friendships and relationships with many Jewish people, such as his teacher Husserl, who was Jewish by birth (although he had converted to Protestantism), his protégés Löwith and Helene Weiss, Jaspers's wife, and his lifelong friend and correspondent Elizabeth Blochmann. Most important was his intense three-year love affair with his Jewish student Arendt, which began in 1925. However, appalled at Heidegger's conduct when he became the National Socialist rector at Freiburg University, Arendt broke her friendship with him. (She resumed it again after the war, when she revisited Germany in 1950 and later became one of Heidegger's chief proponents, being instrumental in publishing translations of his work in the US.)

Nevertheless, Heidegger seemed to share the widespread anti-Semitism of the times, believing that Jewish people in some ways threatened German life. This is revealed in a letter to the German Science Scholarship committee in 1929, in which he recommended that they should give his *non-Jewish* assistant, Eduard Baumgarten, a grant rather than continuing financial support for "the growing influence of the Jews (Verjudung)". Ironically, several years later he denounced Baumgarten to a Nazi official for becoming "closely tied with the Jew Fränkel" (*ibid.*: 272).

In another letter, written by Heidegger in 1929, although not discovered until 1989, he told the acting president of the scholarship-granting organization German Science Scholarship committee:

> There is a pressing need for us to remember that we are faced with the choice of either bringing genuine autochthonous forces and educators into our German spiritual life, or finally abandoning it to the growing Judaization in the wider and narrower sense.
>
> (*Ibid.*: 255)

Indeed, as early as 1921 Heidegger was investigating the feasibility of eradicating the Hebraic root from the Western intellectual tradition (see PIA: 123–6; GA 63: 17–24). This idea grew into an obsession: to return to the horizon of Being that opened up with the Greeks and which was eclipsed by Christianity, Judaism and the fusion of the Jewish and Greek horizons in the Middle Ages. Thus it seems very possible that Heidegger also saw in National Socialism the opportunity for a new world order, liberated from Hebraic morality and religion.

In spite of this, Heidegger, unlike many other German philosophers of the time, was not prejudiced against German philosophy written by German Jews. Although he liked to emphasize the superiority of German philosophy to that of the French, English or Americans, he never differentiated between German and German-Jewish philosophers. In a lecture during the mid-1930s he proclaimed, in defence of Spinoza, that if one asserts that Spinoza's philosophy is Jewish, then all philosophy from Leibniz to Hegel was Jewish too (Safranski 1998: 256). Further, when he first became rector of Freiburg University, he banned Nazi students from distributing anti-Semitic posters and leaflets within the university, prevented a planned book-burning of "Jewish" and "Bolshevik" works and attempted to stop the purge of "undesirable" volumes from the university library. Also, when his Jewish associates Eduard Fränkel, professor of classical philology, and Georg Von Hevesy, professor of physical chemistry, were threatened with dismissal because of their Jewish origins, he wrote to the Ministry of Education, praising their "extraordinary scientific standing" and "irreproachable conduct" (Ott 1993: 108). In addition he arranged a research fellowship at Cambridge University for his Jewish research assistant and later editor Werner Brock, whose dismissal he could not prevent.

So although Heidegger's conduct at times was indisputably anti-Semitic, the fact that he also demonstrated behaviour to the contrary suggests that his attitude towards Jews was ambivalent. However, since Hitler's regime was obviously violently anti-Semitic, Heidegger's support of the Nazis suggests a total indifference to the welfare of German Jews in general. Moreover, as a prerequisite for taking office, Heidegger agreed to enforce at Freiburg University the anti-Jewish decrees of 1 April 1933 (the Law for the Reconstitution of the Civil Service). This meant the dismissal of Jews from university positions and the end of financial aid for them. In addition, he refused to accept Jewish dissertation students, passing them to a Catholic colleague, and formed close associations with anti-Semites such as Ernst Krieck (a populist of peasant origins) and Alfred Baümler, professor of philosophy at Berlin – linked to Alfred Rosenberg's national office for intellectual and ideological education – with whom he discussed the National Socialist reformation of German universities.

Yet there are no overtly anti-Semitic or racist remarks in Heidegger's lectures and philosophical writings. Most importantly, Heidegger never supported official Nazi doctrines of Aryan or Nordic biological, racial superiority. In his writings *Contributions to Philosophy* (1936–38) he insistently rejected the Nazis' biologically based racism and eugenics; it was symptomatic of the "reign of calculation", the technological forgetfulness of Being, and incompatible with the conception of Dasein of his 1920s writings. According to Heidegger, "Dasein" is far more fundamental than any such categories. Race is a non-historical, *biological* factor; it is Dasein's "history", not its "biology", that truly separates it from the lower animals. Also, in his *Logic* lectures he asserts: "Blood, bloodline, can be a fundamental determination of human beings only if it is determined by temperament. The voice of blood comes from the fundamental mood of a human being" (*Logica*: 84; Polt 1999: 155).

Does Heidegger's philosophy support National Socialism?

Heidegger often insisted that philosophy is the activity of questioning Being: that it is not a "worldview" – a *rigid representation* of beings. And yet he chose to adopt the National Socialist worldview. With such clear evidence of his Nazi commitment, the enquiry into his politics poses difficult questions for philosophy, and for readers who are drawn to Heidegger's thought.

In the reading of his works, can one ignore his known political allegiances? Are these two areas independent of one another's influence or are they connected in certain ways? If the latter is the case, then should Heidegger's thought be accepted as a significant philosophical resource to be widely circulated? If not, then what can one do about the already huge impact he has had on twentieth-century thought?

Opinions are extremely divided. Some claim that his philosophy lends support to a National Socialist ideology and thus entirely reject his work; others suggest the charges against him are primarily biographical and that his thought stands "autonomous" from his private actions and is in no way contaminated by, or even significantly related to, his political support of the Nazis (which, as mentioned earlier, is a highly questionable stance).

In accordance with Husserl's opinion that phenomenology endorses no particular system of values over another, Heidegger's intention was to exclude *all* ethical and political judgement from *Being and Time*, so as to provide a "pre-ethical" and "apolitical" analysis of being-in-the-world, and he attempted to achieve this by restricting his contributions exclusively to ontology and existential anthropology. But according to S. J. McGrath, the personal standards or ideology of a philosopher are always and unavoidably present in their work, for even when they are occupied with constructing an "ethically neutral" ontology or epistemology, their own unexamined values are being inscribed into the foundation. McGrath suggests that Heidegger's "alleged neutrality" provides him with a significant "tactical" advantage: "Heidegger's alleged ethical neutrality in *Being and Time* makes it possible for him to say whatever he wants about Dasein without having to worry about what the ethicists or political theorists might think about it" (2008: 79–80). Heidegger's political activities in the 1930s suggest to many that a particular ethics and politics are *implicit* in his writing. This being the case, McGrath asks: "if certain ethical-political applications of ontology are more suited than others, what becomes of the primacy of the question of Being?" (*ibid.*: 77–8).

Pierre Bourdieu is one of several authors who assert that *Being and Time* is a crypto-fascist text. Thus in his book *The Political Ontology of Martin Heidegger* he argues that the ontology of Dasein is in fact a "political ontology" that paves the way for Nazism. This would seem to be a reasonable interpretation given the fact that Heidegger, too, freely admitted that his support for National Socialism "lay in the essence of his philosophy" and that "his concept of 'historicality' was the basis of his political engagement" (Löwith 1993b: 142). Similarly, McGrath suggests that "The ontological foundation of Heidegger's politics is found in section 74 [BT: 434ff.] of *Being and Time*, 'The Basic Constitution of Historicity'" (2008: 96). And Pöggeler is also convinced that there is a definite connection between Heidegger's thought and his political actions: "Was it not through a definite orientation of his thought that Heidegger fell – and not merely accidentally – into the proximity of National Socialism, without ever truly emerging from its proximity?" (1993: 198).

Indeed, Heidegger saw his "existential decision" for National Socialism as a step towards "authenticity". In all Heidegger's political speeches, he uses the language of "Being", "existence", "decision", "essence" and "resolve" that had been developed in *Being and Time*. Habermas argues strongly that Heidegger's politics was grounded in his thinking – the singular form of *Dasein* becoming the *German Dasein*: no longer "unique" and "just-mine", it becomes the *National Dasein*, the "Being" of the German *Volk*. Dasein's struggle for authenticity becomes the German nation struggling to find its spiritual mission or destiny in the *Volk*, a unique, unified being. In November 1933 Heidegger declared:

> Freedom ... is the incorporation of historical Being into will that knows ... into the mastery of a structured order of a people. Care for the freedom of historical Being is in itself the empowerment of the power of the state as the essential structure of an historical mission. Because the Being of the historical Dasein of man is grounded in temporality, that is, care, therefore the state is essentially

necessary ... the state as the essential law of historical Being ... and this means the preservation of its mission and the struggle for its task. The state is the historical Being of the people. (*Logica*: 118)

Such views certainly do not *confront* dictatorship, but Heidegger was never a supporter of democracy. He often complained about the "democratized decay" of Germany's post-1945 institutions, and declared that he was unconvinced that democracy was the best political system for the modern age. He liked to cite Homer: "The rule of the many is not good; let there be one ruler, one king" (1999: 204). In 1966, during his interview with *Der Spiegel*, he asks: "How can a political system accommodate itself to the technological age, and which political system would this be? I have no answer to this question. I am not convinced that it is democracy" (OGSU, in Wolin 1993: 104–5). In 1974, just two years before his death, he declared to a friend: "Our Europe is disintegrating under the influence of a democracy that comes from below against the many above" (Petzet 1993: 222).

Further, that Heidegger should affiliate himself with radical right-wing politics and favour dictatorship over the principle of majority rule seems perfectly compatible with his contempt for the They. If, according to Heidegger, the public sphere is dominated by "averageness", characterized by "levelling" and resistance to excellence, with most people living their lives "in untruth", then why *not* abolish civil society as well as the democratic process, and instead, place *full* power in the hands of someone worthy, who has the courage to act?

However, Polt disagrees with all crypto-fascist interpretations of Heidegger's thought, asserting instead:

> [O]n the whole, I agree with Heidegger's claim in *Being and Time* that the text does not "discuss what Dasein *factically* resolves in any particular case" [BT: 434]. ... Nearly all the ontological claims in *Being and Time* are simply too general to be branded fascist, and defenders of (this) position have to rely on a heavy dose of suspicion and innuendo in order to find Nazism between the lines of what Heidegger actually wrote ... Even if we granted that fascism is the logical outcome of Heidegger's views, this would not count as a *refutation*. If one wants to reject *Being and Time*, one is still under the obligation of coming up with a better description of the human way of Being. There is no political shortcut around ontology. (Polt 1999: 163)

Paradoxically, Heidegger's work has also underpinned much political thought *opposed* to Nazism. Best known are the works of Derrida, Sartre,

Merleau-Ponty and Albert Camus, which employ Heidegger's *own thinking* to invalidate and *discredit* his Nazi beliefs. Sartre, for instance, believed that an "existential" politics was diametrically opposed to Nazism, and he wrote an article in defence of Heidegger's thinking (although not of Heidegger) in a 1944 edition of a pro-communist newspaper. Sartre attributed Heidegger's support for the Nazis to fear, conformity and careerism: unacceptable behaviour, but explained by the exceptional context of the times.

More recently, Young exonerated Heidegger's philosophy of *any* complicity with Nazism. He argues that *Being and Time* implies that to treat any Dasein as a "mere thing" would be an ontological error, and yet this is precisely what the Nazi regime did (see Young 1997: 102–8). Further, he claims that, in its unique authenticity, Dasein exists in a manner that is *entirely* incompatible with Nazi regimentation; the suggestion is that support for this standpoint is evidenced in the discussion of authentic and inauthentic "being-with" (BT: 153–8). Young, and others who hold this viewpoint, assert that when Heidegger fell for the allure of Nazism he behaved as a They-self, by following the masses rather than standing up for the individual conscience. However, one can reasonably argue against this position because, according to *Being and Time*, behaviour is authentic when it is resolutely chosen; thus whether a choice conforms with the masses or not is utterly irrelevant, as long as it satisfies this single requirement of resoluteness. And it is very possible that Heidegger's choice *may* have been resolute.

Thus, although Heidegger asserts that the essence of his philosophy did inspire his National Socialism, and there are those who argue, convincingly, that it does indeed lend support to a National Socialist ideology, his thinking also has been shown to support political values that are in direct opposition to all forms of fascism. So it seems that the wording of Heidegger's philosophy of existence has a certain "universal applicability" that enables its various proponents to adapt it to their particular prejudices or commitments.

"Heidegger's Silence"

Perhaps the most controversial aspect of Heidegger's involvement with the Nazis is his silence about the Holocaust during his post-war years of teaching and writing. That he never openly apologized nor spoke of the atrocities committed against the Jews and others has shocked and confused many, including some admirers. This refusal to discuss the Holocaust is known as "Heidegger's Silence" and at the time was especially conspicuous, given his assertion in *Being and Time* that silence can be a far more authentic and revealing mode of communication than speech (BT: 208). But if that is indeed the case, then what exactly was his silence trying to say to us? The most benevolent speculation one can offer is that it expressed his profound acknowledgement that the horrors of the Holocaust are *literally* unspeakable.

However, Safranski suggests a more ominous facet to this silence:

> [T]he problem of silence is not that he was silent on Auschwitz. In philosophical terms he was silent about something else: about himself, about the philosopher's seducibility by power. He too … failed to ask the one question: Who am I really when I am thinking? … In short: knowledge of self protects against seduction by power. (1998: 421)

McGrath also suggests that:

> To recant or apologize would have been to concede that the liberals were right all along and, because his politics was rooted in his ontology, reverse the direction of his thinking. Heidegger's refusal to recant is proof that his political actions had an essential relationship to his philosophy. (2008: 93)

In fact, Heidegger did not actually remain silent and he did acknowledge the negativity of National Socialism, although only as a symptom of an underlying problem with the entire world. He never gave up his belief in the potential of an ideal version of the movement. In 1943, in spite of the terrible destruction wreaked by the Nazis, Heidegger still regarded Germany as potentially the "saving power" – rather than the scourge – of Western humanity: "The planet is in flames. The essence of man is out of joint. Only from the Germans can there come a world-historical reflection – if, that is, they find and preserve their 'Germanness'" (GA 55: 123; Wolin 1993: 14).

In 1948, in a letter to Herbert Marcuse, once briefly his student, Heidegger wrote that in 1933 he had "expected from National Socialism a spiritual renewal of life in its entirety, a reconciliation of social antagonisms and a deliverance of Western Dasein from the dangers of communism" ("An Exchange of Letters", in Wolin 1993: 162). Much later, on 19 September 1960, in a letter replying to a former student, Hans-Peter Hempel, he acknowledged his error but – still entrenched in his *denial* of guilt – he tried to excuse his himself by referring to Hegel and Hölderlin, who, like Heidegger, had also "slipped up". He argued that greater men have made such mistakes: Hegel saw Napoleon as the World Spirit, and Hölderlin saw him as the prince of the feast to which the gods and Christ had been invited.

More importantly, the various notorious references he made about the Holocaust attempt to reduce German guilt via comparisons that seem to downplay the enormity of the horror. In 1947, in another letter to Marcuse, Heidegger wrote that the charge of genocide could only be justified if one simultaneously made the same charge against the victors' treatment of the East Germans (*ibid.*: 163; Ott 1993: 192–3). Two years later, in a lecture in 1949, "The Danger", he said:

> Hundreds of thousands die *en masse*. Do they *die*? They succumb. They are done in. They become mere quanta, items in the business of manufacturing corpses. Do they die? They are liquidated inconspicuously in extermination camps … but to die is to endure death in its essence.   (Quoted in Young 1997: 172)

Critics suggest that this statement seems to reduce the murdered concentration camp victims to mere items of mass production, thus justifying the executioners' dehumanization of their victims.

Heidegger's most infamous comment about the Holocaust appeared in his lecture "The Enframing" (1949). In it he compared, with shocking insensitivity, the methods of extermination used in the concentration camps with modern farming techniques. He asserts that mechanized industrial agriculture is "in essence the same as the manufacturing of corpses in gas chambers and extermination camps" (quoted in Young 1997: 172). This equation seems to many to be an attempt to reduce German guilt for these crimes against humanity by suggesting they are merely a consequence or symptom of an abstract process that is dominating the entire world: a consequence of the excesses of technological civilization. Attempting to defend his remark, Young argues that Heidegger's assertion does *not* trivialize the horrors of Auschwitz but is a declaration of the world-historical significance of this dreadful occurrence, as the *definitive embodiment* of the levelling, dehumanizing process of the mass production of modern technology that is rooted in our technological worldview (*ibid.*: 187).

Many years later, in 1966, in an interview with the German magazine *Der Spiegel*, Heidegger was still trying to defend his political involvement by claiming that at the time he had believed that it was the only way he could save the university, and science in general, from the anti-intellectualism of mainstream National Socialism. Further, he saw in the movement an "awakening" that he considered could rescue not only Germany but also the West.

One possible reason for Heidegger's refusal to discuss the horrors of the Holocaust might be found in his philosophy. If he were to speak of the evils committed, he would automatically be introducing a value-based ethics into his work, and he was strongly opposed to any attempts to derive ethical or theological principles from his work. It should be noted, however, that he did not mean that philosophers are required to deny the existence of God or human values; rather, that philosophical thinking should not be influenced by them. "I do not behave religiously in philosophizing, even if as a philosopher I can be a religious person" (GA 61: 197; Polt 1999: 165). It is interesting to note that, in spite of such comments, in *Contributions to Philosophy* he refers incessantly to "the gods", since although he can no longer accept the Christian version of God, he is allowing for the possibility of a new revelation of the divine whose presence can transform our lives.

Heidegger and the question of ethics

In *Being and Time* Heidegger's reticence to speak of justice and injustice, good and evil, and right and wrong was in part influenced by the general attitude among many philosophers of his era who felt that philosophy should not, and cannot, offer practical guidance on how to live or how to govern. Wittgenstein, Karl Popper, Russell and of course Husserl all shared this same belief. Thus, according to Heidegger, it is not the thinker's task to provide ethical rules for action ("Letter on Humanism", in BW: 255), even though rules are regarded as necessary in the technological approach to life, which strives to control the behaviour of all entities. The alternative to a rule-based ethics may be a value-based ethics. But Heidegger regarded the ontological status of values as extremely vague, since either philosophers define them as existing in some "eternal realm" (Platonism) or values are defined in terms of human concepts and desires (subjectivism) that ignore the true significance of the *Being* of beings. Heidegger emphasizes that:

> to think against "values" is not to maintain that everything inter-
> preted as "a value" … is valueless … Rather, it is important finally
> to realize that precisely through the characterization of something
> as "a value" what is so valued is robbed of its worth … Every valu-
> ing, even where it values positively, is a subjectivising. It does not
> let beings be … thinking in values is the greatest blasphemy imagi-
> nable against Being. (*Ibid.*: 251)

In other words, Heidegger questions the validity of values in society such as moral goodness, obligation, duty and justice, since he regards them merely as subjective distortions *imposed* on Being.

Instead, he asserts: "Only so far as man, ek-sisting into the truth of Being, belongs to Being can there come from Being itself the assignment of those directives that must become law and rule for man ... Otherwise all law remains merely something fabricated by human reason" ("Letter on Humanism", in BW: 262). To support this argument further, Heidegger offers some etymological "evidence" by pointing out that the *fundamental* meaning of "ethics" is contained in the term *ethos*, "abode": "If the name 'ethics,' in keeping with the basic meaning of the word *ethos*, should now say that 'ethics' ponders the abode of man, then that thinking which thinks the truth of Being as the primordial element of man, as one who ek-sists, is in itself the original ethics" (*ibid.*: 258). Thus, if ethics is understood in the sense of the original meaning of the term *ethos*, then Heidegger's thought can be regarded as the fundamental or "original" ethics: an ontology that prepares the "ground" for ethical work by uncovering the ontological structures at play in any ethical situation. For example, Heidegger points out that "ontological guilt" – an intrinsic part of Dasein's Being – is *prior to*, and the *foundation* of, ethics and morals, which emerge from an understanding of this guilt: "This essential being-guilty ... the existential condition for the possibility ... for morality in general and for the possible forms which this may take factically. Primordial 'Being-guilty' cannot be defined by morality, since morality already presupposes it" (BT: 332).

In this sense Heidegger's thought contains something analogous to a "transcendental ethics". So the *Dasein analytic*, potentially, could be viewed as presenting a formal structure of human existence – devoid of content or detail – within which various ethical standpoints could potentially be developed. For in thinking on the truth of Being, man's thinking becomes a channel through which the truth of Being can manifest and reveal itself as the essence of who we are. Such thinking is the highest form of action ("Letter on Humanism", in BW: 217), and the most fundamental source of our *ethos*. Heidegger emphasizes: "More essential than instituting rules is that man find the way to his abode in the truth of Being. This abode first yields the experience of something we can hold on to. The truth of Being offers a hold for all conduct" (*ibid.*: 262).

Thus Heidegger believes that externally imposed rules and ethics definitely are not the answer, for he suggests that if we stand in the truth of Being and listen to the voice of Being, we shall be provided with the necessary guidelines for existing in the appropriate manner:

> Along with "logic" and "physics," "ethics" appeared for the first time in the school of Plato ... Thinkers prior to this period knew neither a "logic" nor an "ethics" nor "physics." Yet their thinking

was neither illogical nor immoral. But they did think *physis* in a depth and breadth that no subsequent "physics" was ever again able to attain. The tragedies of Sophocles ... preserve the *ethos* in their sagas more primordially than Aristotle's lectures on "ethics."

(*Ibid.*: 256)

Heidegger intentionally avoids discussions of good and evil in his writings, and on the rare occasions that he does speak of these categories, he equates good with "healing" and evil with "rage", and regards them as having their source in the interplay of Being and nihilation:

With healing, evil appears all the more in the clearing of Being. The essence of evil does not consist in the mere baseness of human action, but rather in the malice of rage. Both of these, however, healing and raging, can essentially occur only in Being, insofar as Being itself is what is contested. In it is concealed the essential provenance of nihilation. What nihilates illuminates itself as the negative.   (*Ibid.*: 260)

Since any discussion of Nazism and the horrors of the death camps requires entering into an ethical debate, it should now be clear that, from Heidegger's standpoint, an examination of the Holocaust is beyond the range of his philosophy; moreover, his endorsement of Nazism would seem to disqualify him from contributing to ethical reflection.

However, the question as to whether or not his thought does contain or imply ethics is nevertheless still a strongly contested issue, as is indicated by the significant number of titles covering this matter. Michael Lewis, for instance, writes:

What is the place of ethics in Heidegger's thought; and of what relevance to this place is being-with (Mitsein)? The answer to the first question is simple and quite unwavering throughout Heidegger's long trek: the place of ethics is the ontological difference. Ethics in its most originary sense, means dwelling near to Being, seeking it and responding to it ... The answer to the second question is "everything".   (2005: 1)

Frederick Olafson also suggests an ethical component to Heidegger's writing and, again, it is related to Heidegger's account of "being-with" (*Mitsein*): "To be subject to the claim that presence makes is the greatest claim that a human being makes; it is what 'ethics' is" (Zollikon: 273). According to Olafson, this quotation:

explicitly connects presence with ethics, but it does not acknowledge the even more important connection of ethics with *reciprocal*
presence and thus with *Mitsein*. The trouble with this association
of presence (but not *reciprocal* presence) with ethics is that it issues
in a conception of the relation of thought to the truth of Being as
the "original ethic" without any reference to our relation to one
another. (1998: 1)

But even if the world has no moral signposts, there is still the question of whether our relation to one another can by itself yield standards of right and wrong ... My thought was that if that conception
could be developed beyond the very brief sketch [Heidegger] gave
of it in *Being and Time,* it might be possible to show that it has at
least a proto-ethical character and that this would be of fundamental importance for any inquiry into the ground of ethics. (*Ibid.*: 3)

Olafson further asserts that:

Heidegger invokes at least one other concept to which an unmis-
takeably ethical character attaches. This is the concept of *Fursorge*
– one human being's caring about another – and it is this caring
that he declares to be, in its several modalities, central to our being
with one another ... he is even willing to go so far as to state that
we are, as he puts it, "for the sake of others". (*Ibid.*: 4)

Joanna Hodge also strongly disputes the validity of Heidegger's denial
of an ethical component to his enquiries; she claims to have uncovered
a *repressed* ethical element in his writings, a "transformed ethics" that
Heidegger has failed to identify (an ethics that neither seeks nor offers any
abstract, universal moral standards), which is central to his understanding
of metaphysics and philosophy:

While for Heidegger the completion of metaphysics is not the occasion for the advent of ethics, his texts can also be read as opening
up a possible retrieval of ethics, as a textual tradition, especially
out of the writings of Nietzsche, Schelling, Kant, Aristotle and
Plato. The themes to be retrieved are *Gerechtigkeit*, responsibility,
evil, autonomy, and the relation between theoretical and practical
reason. (1995: 1)

I identify in Heidegger's thinking a kind of ethical articulation
which occurs before a division between the formation of individuals

and the formation of collective identity, in advance of any division into ethics and metaphysics, into moral and political philosophy. There is a kind of meta-ethics which takes place in advance of any division between ethics and politics, if these are understood as concerned with the formation respectively of individuals and of communities, as independent processes.   (*Ibid.*: 3)

And Young asserts that there is "a thesis fundamental to all phases of Heidegger's thinking: the inseparability of ontology and ethics, of 'being' and 'the ought', the necessity for the grounding of the latter in the former. (See especially the *Introduction to Metaphysics*, pp. 196–9 ...)" (2001: 24). For, according to Heidegger, modern thinking is controlled by the division between "fact" and "value" – between the "is" and the "ought" – and this is the way that most human beings experience the values of their particular culture.

The result is moral nihilism, which arises from the inevitable, continual conflict between the "facts" of Being/reality (that which we actually *discover* and *recognize* to be the case) and "reality-as-it-ought-to-be", which is determined by "fabricated" human values ("Letter on Humanism", in BW: 279). Heidegger clarifies that when I "fabricate" or *choose* my own fundamental values (as Sartre suggests), if circumstances subsequently make adhering to them difficult or impossible, then I can adjust them, or "unfabricate" them, and choose others; thus they lack any *genuine ethical authority*, as do values derived from someone else's fabrications, where the authority is simply "the power of the other".

Indeed, values, whether self-fabricated or from an outside "authority", say *nothing* about the world *as it is*, for they are merely expressions of the human will – desires/assumptions projected and imposed onto the world, and the outcome is the technological approach to existence that controls and exploits all beings, thereby ignoring our openness to Being and the true significance of "beings" and "Being" (*ibid.*: 251).

Heidegger also attacks the assertion that there exist fully objective (thus independent of personal choice) and yet *autonomous* "moral facts"; for instance, the idea that *killing is wrong* is something that is *intuitively* and *inherently* obvious, so we do not need to *choose* this value *or* be given it by an outside authority. Heidegger claims that such assertions are merely an attempt – by camouflaging the source – to lend authority to what, once again, are merely *fabricated* human values. He concludes from this analysis that only "the grounding of man's historical existence on beings as a whole" (Ni: 90) can establish an authoritative ethic.

Young thus points out that, for Heidegger:

A grounding in ontology is, then, necessary to a genuinely authoritative ethics. But Heidegger also claims that it is sufficient. Properly understanding one's world does not, he says, "consist in mere information and notions about something". Rather, "he who truly knows what is knows what he wills to do in the midst of what is" [PLT 67]. And again, he who properly understands the "truth of beings as a whole" knows his own "position in the midst of beings" [Ni: 88]. (2001: 26)

So it seems quite clear that Heidegger is completely convinced that truth and freedom cannot be contained in any system of ethics or morality constructed by human beings. Instead, when one is *attuned* to Being, appropriate behaviour (that in the conventional sense could be called "ethical") arises *spontaneously* from Being itself, independently of, and liberated from, the human will.

However, ethics, as previously suggested by Olafson (1998: 1–4), does not necessarily need to be based on rules or values – it can also be construed in terms of our responsibility to "the other". For example, Emmanuel Levinas presents this conception of ethics, in a manner that questions the validity of Heidegger's affirmation of the *priority* of Being over beings. Levinas suggests that to do this "is to subordinate the relation with *someone*, who is a being (the ethical relation), to a relation with the *Being of beings*, which is impersonal" (1969: 45).

Ethics can also be based on the concept of virtue and, in this sense, Polt asserts:

> In some ways, one can even argue that Heidegger himself is close to Aristotle, the great philosopher of virtue. For both, our highest purpose is to become what we essentially are by practicing our highest activity: the activity of openness to what is, and to Being itself. (1999: 170)

The various viewpoints presented here point to the obvious complexity of this controversial matter, and thus it should be evident that an in-depth presentation of the arguments offered clearly is *not* within the scope of this book. However, the aim has been only to alert the reader to the fact that this is an important topic for future investigation and discussion.

Glossary

alētheia Ancient Greek: "truth". Etymologically, *alētheia* means unconcealment (BT: 261). Heidegger believed that all other truths, for instance propositional truth, are superficial in comparison, for they depend on and are derived from this primordial truth of +words, all such truths must always already be grounded on a prior understanding of Being and beings, a more fundamental truth of unconcealment that is central to our existence.

Angst German: "anxiety", also sometimes translated as "dread". *See* **anxiety**.

anticipation Heidegger calls the "authentic" attitude towards death "*Vorlaufen*", which literally means "running forwards" or "to run on ahead" (BT: 306); the English translation is "anticipation". This is different from "expecting" death, which is imagining its realization, for in anticipating death, I relate to it *not* as an actuality or event but as a constant possibility: the continual anticipation of the possibility of the impossibility of any existence at all (BT: 307). In light of this indefinite yet constant threat of death, everyday relations and attachments cease to offer any security and thus lose their dominating influence over my life. "Resoluteness", the key feature of authenticity, requires a lucid and continual anticipation of death, and it is this "anticipatory resoluteness" – the *authentic* form of caring – that Heidegger uses to illuminate Dasein's temporality, which he claims is the "ultimate" basis for understanding Dasein (BT: 351).

anxiety Not about any particular being (BT: 231); rather, it is about beings as a whole and about my being-in-the-world as a whole (BT: 233). Consequently, when I am in its grip, it influences my entire outlook on existence. Heidegger regards anxiety as a potentially "enlightening" event: the royal road to authenticity that inspires Dasein to ask about the meaning of Being, the meaning of its own Being. The mood arises when we sense (consciously or subliminally) the inherent precariousness of our life: the "Nothingness" that lies at the heart of human existence, the constant possibility and inevitability of our own death. This alienates us from our everyday world, causing existence to appear senseless, for ambition now seems futile and all achievements insignificant. However, similar to the situation whereby great works of art can emerge from an artist's suffering, the overwhelming pain of anxiety potentially can expand our awareness into an authentic recognition of our freedom, an illuminated perception of existence that motivates us to choose our own possibilities in life rather than those offered by the "They" because we now realize that, since the "They-world" cannot protect us against death, we should not rely on it for our life. Heidegger sees this experience as absolutely essential to the philosopher, since the detachment it provides from worldly concerns and prejudices is essential to true thinking.

a priori Latin: "what comes before, earlier". Used by Heidegger to refer to our pre-reflective, pre-conceptional, rudimentary understanding of our own nature and the nature of the entities surrounding us, which allows us to make sense of our world. Our "*a priori*" understanding is the precondition of all further knowledge.

as-structure The identity and purpose of a thing that is instantly understood owing to our *a priori* comprehension of the environment. Thus when we encounter an entity, we immediately see it as something that is used for a certain purpose – "as a table" (BT: 190), as a tray used for serving meals; we instantly understand its practical significance in terms of the possibilities it opens up for us. Seeing this as-structure of things is the primary way we understand the nature of things in our daily reality. The interpretation of this as-structure is based on our primordial ready-to-hand relation with our everyday environment, where we experience entities as being in a contextual web of significant relations or involvements with other entities.

Augenblick *See* **moment of vision**.

authenticity When Dasein faces, during the identity crisis of deep anxiety, the inescapable fact that it may die at any time, it is provided with a vantage point from where it is able to grasp its life as a whole and understand its significance. This can inspire Dasein to enter an authentic mode of existence, where what it cares about most of all is the fact that it is a being-towards-death: that it is always, and inescapably, on a journey towards its own death, which may happen at any moment. No longer feeling at home in the world, Dasein becomes resolute (this is the essential and key feature of authenticity). Resolute Dasein frees itself from the all-pervasive domination of the They-self, through an awareness of its own self and own possibilities in the light of its own mortality and, in so doing, it "chooses to choose" its own way of life (BT: 313–14), for in accepting and assuming responsibility for its life and its death it achieves an authentic recognition of its own freedom mirrored in the realm of possibilities that are revealed when the influence of the They-world is undermined. Dasein's authentic choices may, or may not, result in an alteration of the actual content of Dasein's life, for the only pertinent matter here becomes the fact that Dasein now takes full responsibility for its own life, while basing its choices on an understanding and acceptance that all its possibilities are limited by death. In his later writings Heidegger tends to emphasize a much less "voluntary", "will-full", subjectivistic dimension to the essential precondition of authenticity than he does in *Being and Time*. Authenticity is now conceived of as *Gelassenheit*: a releasement from will. *See* **Gelassenheit**.

bauen German: "to build". Heidegger replaced this sense of the word with the Old German usage: "nurturing, cultivating, preserving and caring".

being A being (or beings) and its synonym "entity" (or entities) refer to any event or thing – animate or inanimate – that has an existence of some sort. Thus all things in existence – humans, animals, chairs, electric razors, stones, planets, atoms, molecules, chemical processes – can be called "beings" or "entities".

Being Translation of German "*Sein*" or, in Heidegger's later spelling, "*Seyn*". The original German term for Being is "*das Sein*". This noun is derived from the infinitive of the verb *sein*, "to be". The literal translation, therefore, of the noun *das Sein*, is "the to be". This should help to remind the reader that, whenever the term Being with a capital B is used, it also includes the sense "to be". So "the question of the meaning of Being" also means "to question what it means to be". Heidegger uses the word "Being" to refer to that which *determines* entities *as* entities: that on the basis of which entities are already understood as entities. Note that "determine" does not mean here to "create" or cause, for Being is not any kind of thing or process; it does not produce entities, since only entities produce entities and Being is neither an entity nor a class of entities. Thus Being should never be thought of as an abstract noun, or regarded as referring to God, the universe or anything in it. Instead, "determine" refers to the fact that Being enables us to encounter and understand the entities in our world. There are two basic ways of Being: being-human, which Heidegger calls Dasein, and non-human Being, which is expressed either as present-at-hand or ready-to-hand. It is the shared factor of "Being" that inhabits all entities, that makes our own existence inseparable from everything else. In this sense, all "beings" truly are the same.

being-in-the-world An *a priori* existential that refers to Dasein's pre-conceptual understanding of and indivisible unity with the world, which is an intrinsic part of Dasein's existence. Dasein has an *a priori* capacity to understand, relate to, care about and concern itself with the things in its surrounding world.

being-towards-death Dasein's mortality is described as a being-towards-death: "Factical Dasein exists as born, and as born it is already dying in the sense of being towards death" (BT: 373). Heidegger considers an authentic awareness of mortality as the fundamental means for Dasein to achieve authenticity. When Dasein faces and accepts, during the identity crisis of deep anxiety, the inescapable fact that it is always as a "being-towards-death" – that it may die at any time – it begins to care about its way of living in a far more intense and profound way. It now realizes and accepts that its existence is limited by death and bases its choices in life on this understanding. Dasein has now entered an authentic mode of existence in which it chooses its own way of life, rather than a way of life dictated by the expectations and values of the They.

being-with An *a priori* existential that refers to the social dimension of Dasein's existence, which is a fundamental feature of Dasein's being-in-the-world. This existential enables Dasein to relate to others, and directly or indirectly Dasein always and essentially experiences existence in relation to other people, for the world of Dasein is a "with-world": as long as I exist, I am always involved with others in some way, for it is ontologically impossible for me to exist as Dasein without depending on some shared communal norms.

the "Between" Heidegger sometimes spoke of the poet as being like a demi-god: a mediator between humankind (mortals) and the gods, situated in a no-man's-land between humans and the gods, conveying what the gods are hinting to the people, the identity and destiny of mankind being determined in this no-man's-land (HEP: 293ff.). "Thunder and lightning are the language of the gods and the poet is he whose task is to endure and to gather up this language and to bring it into the Dasein of the people" (GA 39: 31). This location, where the mediating role of the poet takes place, is referred to by Heidegger as "the Between" (GA 39: 285). The Between not only symbolizes the meeting point and dividing line betwixt gods and mortals, but also represents the absolute limits of human potential that are attained by the poet. It is a location in space and time where the most crucial, urgent enquiry is represented by the transcendental question: "What or who exists 'beyond' humanity?" (GA 39: 167). Thus it is also the "Middle" of Being "from out of which the whole realm of beings, gods, men, earth are to be newly brought out into the open" (GA 39: 183). This Between, or Middle of Being, can also be viewed as representing the midpoint between Being and non-Being, and thus equivalent to potential or possibility, "the possibility that belongs to actuality" (GA 52: 118), in the sense of that which potentially can be accomplished through the freedom of action. The Between also represents the transition point between past and future: the middle of time. Further, it is the region that discloses the movement of coming-into-being as the counter-movement to non-existence and the fleeting nature of human existence. It restrains time, thereby allowing us a sense of presence amid ceaseless change (GA 52: 146).

care Care is the primordial condition of Dasein, its most fundamental feature: the most basic characteristic of the human condition. Dasein's Being is care, in the sense that it is care that makes human existence meaningful and makes a person's life matter to them, and it is care that ultimately directs us to the mystery of Being itself. Heidegger asserts that all the features that constitute Dasein's being-in-the-world in its average everydayness – fallenness (its absorption in the They-world), being-with (its social context), thrownness (its living past), moods and understanding have their roots in, and are unified by, this fundamental state of care. Thus care underlies and constitutes all our experiences and involvements in the world. For even when Dasein is neglectful of others, or unconcerned or uncaring in his actions, Heidegger asserts that care is still active, but in a "deficient mode" (BT: 83). Towards other people (being-with-one-another), care takes the form of solicitude: taking care of, or providing for, the welfare of those in need of help (BT: 158). There are two types of solicitude: "dominating", inauthentic solicitude helps in a manner that reduces others to dependency, whereas "authentic" solicitude helps others to take responsibility for their own lives, to stand on their own two feet and take care of themselves (GA 21: 223; BT: 159). During the practical activities of our jobs and daily lives, in our use of machines, computers, tools or any other objects employed to achieve our aims, care becomes concern (*Besorgen*) in the sense of "attending to" or "taking care of" the way we handle things that are ready-to-hand ("equipment") However, the aspect of Dasein's way of being-in-the-world that it most cares about is the fact that it is alive. When Dasein faces, during the identity crisis of deep anxiety, the inescapable fact that it may die at any time, it begins to care about its way of living in a far more intense and profound way. Care now makes Dasein a unified, autonomous self (BT: 366ff.); Dasein enters an authentic mode of existence, where what it cares about most of all is the fact that it is a being-towards-death. Although in *Being and Time* "care" appears to apply specifically to Dasein's way of Being, later on Heidegger asserts that care is "solely 'for the sake of beyng', not the beyng of man, but the beyng of beings as a whole" (GA 65: 16).

categories/categorical Heidegger calls the fundamental structures of Dasein's Being "existentials". He contrasts these with *categories*, which refer to the fundamental structures of the Being of entities other than Dasein. Similarly, Heidegger uses the term "existential" in reference to Dasein's mode of Being, but employs the term "categorical" in reference to the way of Being that characterizes those beings or entities that Dasein encounters in the world. However, as a consequence of Dasein's fallenness, Dasein's awareness has become so completely absorbed in the beings it encounters and interprets that it has come to interpret itself and think of itself in the same way, and thus Dasein mistakenly views itself as also having a categorical mode of Being. The categorical way of Being has formed the basis of ontology since the time of Aristotle and it is this way of Being that Heidegger overturns in *Being and Time*. For since the time of Aristotle ontology has erroneously attempted to reach an understanding of the existential meaning of Being – an understanding of the existential meaning of Dasein's Being – by asking categorical questions, which is an approach that is only appropriate for reaching a *categorical* understanding of the categorical mode of Being, a mode of Being that belongs to entities *other* than Dasein. As a result, this philosophical tradition has reinforced Dasein's self-misunderstanding that arises from its mistaken identification with categorical Being. A fundamental aim in Heidegger's analysis is to free us from this ontological tradition, which is impeding us from experiencing an authentic sense of who we really are.

circumspection Describes the type of "involved" (rather than detached or objective) "looking around" one's environment that is guided by the demands of practical interests or activities. Circumspection recognizes how the things we use in our daily existence relate to one another.

clearing The site where Being spontaneously reveals itself. It is owing to the fact that Dasein *is* a "clearing" that it always already has a pre-reflective understanding of Being and the beings it encounters in the world. Normally Dasein is not aware of the "clearing", but only the beings that are unconcealed in it. However, if it explicitly attends to the clearing itself, it does not just experience unconcealed beings, but simultaneously it becomes aware of the fact that there *are* beings and that it is *aware* of them. Heidegger refers to this "awareness of awareness" as "standing in the clearing". Since Dasein is the "clearing" or "open space" for the occurrence of Being, this means that without Dasein there is no Being (*Sein*). Equally, without *Sein* (Being) there is no Dasein. In his later writings,

Heidegger concludes that it is Dasein's destiny to become the receptive site or clearing in preparation for the possibility of a historical transformation, a "new beginning" arising from the "propriative event" of *Ereignis*.

Conscience When Heidegger speaks of Dasein's Conscience, he is not referring to the traditional, ethical or religious conception of conscience, but instead offers a fundamental, existential interpretation that sheds further light on our way of Being. Not everyone has a "conscience" (lower-case "c"), in terms of our conventional understanding of the word, but everyone has a "Conscience" (capital "C") in Heidegger's more fundamental, existential sense. This fundamental Conscience – unlike conscience in the traditional sense – does not have an inner voice that judges, commands, forbids, condemns or excuses actions on moral grounds. He claims that only when we respond to the special moments of insight offered by our Conscience can we develop the authentic understanding necessary for a genuine "conscience" (in the traditional sense). Like "traditional" conscience, Heidegger's fundamental Conscience also involves a division of Dasein into a caller and a called. The "call" of Conscience focuses on and highlights the conflict between Dasein's two contrasting ways of Being: (i) the They-self in which Dasein is absorbed in the present, preoccupied with the worldly concerns of everyday reality, where the choices it makes, the way it thinks and all its behaviour is under the influence of the They; (ii) the "homeless" self, which has been thrown naked into a bare, meaningless world. This "homeless" part of Dasein's Being also functions as Dasein's primordial, ontological Conscience, which silently calls out to the They-self, summoning this fallen inauthentic self to turn away from the influence and restricted possibilities of They and to contemplate instead its own possibilities and, from among these, to make its own resolute choices in life, in the light of its own mortality. It is the They-self's background awareness of its potential for authenticity that motivates the primordial Conscience to call out, and that allows the They-self potentially to respond. In appealing to the fallen They-self to become an individualized authentic self, the call of Conscience reveals to Dasein its own primordial guilt.

correspondence theory The standard definition of truth used today, in which judgements, statements or propositions are correct or true only if they factually "match" the object or situation they are referring to. A proposition is either true or it is not.

da/*das Da* German: "there", "here"; the There.

Dasein/Dasein In English books on Heidegger's work, this German word is usually left untranslated. Heidegger uses it to refer exclusively to *us* and our *way of Being*, in place of the standard German terminology for human beings. The word has no plural so it can refer to a single human being as well as all human beings.

He selected this "ontological" term "Dasein" because he felt that it best encapsulated, emphasized and expressed the fact that we are unique beings, qualitatively very different from all other entities, because the essence of who we are is contained in our way of Being, and thus cannot be grasped via a description of our ontic characteristics because Dasein's Being has no "fixed" nature that exists independently of its way of Being. "The essence of Dasein lies in its existence … So when we designate this entity with the term 'Dasein', we are expressing not its 'what' (as if it were a table, house, or tree) but its Being" (BT: 67). The characteristic in our way of Being which most differentiates us from other beings is our unique capacity for understanding Being and for *choosing* our way of Being, for Being is an issue for us, our own Being as well as the Being of other beings, and Being is not revealed *except* in relation to Dasein.

datability The primordial time references "then", "ago" (i.e. on that former occasion) and "now", which derive from the existential modes of awaiting, retaining and making present, belong to the basic way in which Dasein relates to its worldly activities and to entities in the world in the mode of ready-to-hand. Heidegger calls the structure of this existential "datability". Fundamentally, time is experienced and datable in terms of significant events: "now", "(a not-yet) then" and "on that former occasion" are worldly events that can be "dated" by reference to specific things or events – "on that former occasion *when* you fell over"; "then, when the post arrives"; "now that you have finished eating". In other words, Heidegger demonstrates that my "time" has a content or *datability* that relates to my practical activities of everyday existence.

deep ecology The ecological movement that emphasizes raising mankind's consciousness as the primary means for saving the planet.

destiny For Heidegger, "destiny" is different from fate in the sense that it is something that is shared – it is the destiny of an entire community – and thus it is not something that individual Dasein can have on their own. Destiny arises, or "becomes free", only when the fates of individual Daseins are unified through social interaction in a common world with a shared history; the historizing of each individual Dasein then becomes a "co-historizing" that determines or creates this single shared destiny. Under such circumstances, each individual Dasein has a destiny, which is simultaneously the shared destiny of the entire community (BT: 436).

destruction Heidegger refers to his interpretation of the history of philosophy as "The destruction of the history of ontology" (BT: 44). But he uses "destruction" strictly in the sense of "de-construction": the destructuring or peeling away of layers of tradition "structures piled on top of each other that make the sense of Being unrecognizable" (GA 15: 337, GA 24: 31; Inwood 2000b: 183). Therefore "destruction" should not be viewed in the "*negative* sense of shaking off the ontological tradition" (BT: 44), since from Heidegger's standpoint to forget or ignore this heritage is the best way to ensure that its influence over us still holds sway. So his intention is "to *destroy* the traditional content of ancient ontology until we arrive at those primordial experiences in which we achieved our first ways of determining the nature of Being – the ways which have guided us ever since" (*ibid.*). Thus, "The destruction of the history of ontology is essentially bound up with the way the question of Being is formulated" (*ibid.*), and must be guided by this at all times. He regards this deconstructive process as particularly vital to his investigation of the question of Being because "Dasein 'is' its past in the way of *its* own Being" (BT: 41). Our sense of who we are, our perceptions of the world and the way we behave, are not only inherited – a synthesis of interpretations of existence and modes of living as they have evolved throughout the centuries – but they are what *make* us Dasein. Moreover, "all philosophical discussion … is pervaded by traditional concepts … and traditional angles of approach" (BPP: 22), and Heidegger wants us to recognize the limitations of these rigid, conceptual, inherited interpretations so that we see clearly that our current perceptions are not the only way of understanding Being.

Towards this end, he attempts to retrieve the hidden possibilities contained in Western thinking by deconstructing its dominant influences via meticulous analysis and criticism. His intention is to shatter the brittle outer structures that tradition has frozen around the concepts of many of these great thinkers in order to uncover that which might be relevant to the investigation of Being, since a particular thinker may, implicitly, have said many things that potentially could advance and enrich our understanding. He also shows how the texts of these influential philosophers sometimes undermine and subvert themselves, thereby indicating further concealed possibilities and alternative ways of thinking that are pertinent to the question of Being. Heidegger believed that as a philosopher one is *obliged* to "do violence" to the history of thought, the violence being the great force required to make the words of a thinker from the past relevant to one's present concern (in this case, the question of Being) while remaining "faithful" to the style of thinking and spirit of the particular thinker one is dealing with. Thus Heidegger never alters the actual words of a philosopher in his discussions, but instead forces them to yield a meaning that previously had not been apparent. He proceeds in reverse chronological order from Kant and Descartes to Aristotle and, finally, to the Presocratic philosophers in order to demonstrate, first, the particular way in which each of these thinkers fails to recognize the "ontological difference": the fundamental distinction between Being and things that exist ("beings"). Heidegger felt that many of these philosophers wanted to investigate Being but, owing to this basic confusion of traditional understanding, instead found themselves exclusively investigating "beings". Unsurprisingly, his treatment of philosophers varies considerably: he resonates with, and applies far more critical attention to, thinkers such as Nietzsche, Kant and Plato than he does with others such as Hegel. From the former thinkers, he manages to extract insights into the being-question that no tradition had previously seen. Most importantly, Heidegger noted that the belief "that Being is always to be understood in terms of the present" has, since the time of Aristotle, been handed down throughout the history of ontology: "Entities are grasped in their Being as 'presence'; this means that they are understood with regard to a definite mode of time – the '*Present*'" (BT: 47). This assumption, according to Heidegger, prioritizes our *theoretical* grasp of things rather than our actual existence, which he claims cannot be understood if we prioritize the present. For unlike other entities that are encapsulated exclusively in a present moment and position, Dasein is "temporal": deeply rooted in a past heritage while occupying the present and looking towards future possibilities. Since answers to the meaning of Being can be found only through *our* existence, this means that the traditional ontology of time, and thus the entire approach to the being-question, has to change radically. Heidegger also demonstrates how Kant's ontology (in spite of Kant's claim that his thought marks a new beginning in the history of philosophy) is in many aspects simply a repetition of Descartes' standpoint, since Kant's subject is still the subject of the *cogito*, and not Dasein. Similarly, Heidegger discloses how Descartes' ontology is merely a repetition of Scholastic thought, whose ontology has its basis in Aristotle.

Dichtung German: from *dichten*, "to write, invent, compose verses". *Dichtung* can be used to refer to poetry or verse, as well as to the entire field of creative writing, including novels. Heidegger normally uses this word in a "wider sense", to refer to the act of invention, creation or projection, but he also sometimes uses *Dichtung* (and *dichten*) in a "narrow sense", to refer purely to poetry or verse.

discourse In his discussion of language in *Being and Time*, Heidegger maintains that Dasein's mode of understanding, and its moods (the way in which it is "attuned to the world" at any given moment) are always interacting to disclose the world, granting it intelligibility. *Talking* (discourse), which is equiprimordial with moods and understanding, is the expressive articulation of this intelligibility of the world, in the sense that *discourse* (talking) imparts a sense of *structure* – in terms of *patterns of meaning* – that differentiates and unites the multiplicity of separate, although connected, meanings that arise from, consitute and reveal the world. So discourse is *not* the same thing as language, for it is prior to grammatical properties or logic, and is thus the fundamental, ontological precondition for language, which, when "spoken out", naturally leads to language, and thus it is also a fundamental trait of Dasein's Being: "There is language, only because there is talk" (GA 20: 365), for "*The existential-ontological foundation of language is discourse or talk*" (BT: 203). Language, in terms of grammar, words, sentences and so on is talk (discourse) manifested in the world in a ready-to-hand form that enables the articulation of intelligibility to be transmitted from one Dasein to another.

dualism The theory or philosophical viewpoint (strongly defended by Descartes) that mind and matter are two distinct things, that reality consists of independently existing irreconcilable principles or contrasting features.

dwelling See pages 111–13.

ecstatic Heidegger uses the term "ecstatic" (from the Greek, meaning "standing outside of itself") to describe Dasein's temporality. For the essence of temporality, which is also the essence of Dasein, is its expansion or stepping outside itself into the unity of the "ecstases" of future, present and past, each of which expands into the others. The ordering of these three ecstases of time is prior to and independent of any temporal chronology (BT: 375–6). Thus the ecstatic future is not "later" than the ecstatic present, for at any moment of my life I am vulnerable to the power of death, thus my vulnerability is always an actual, living issue for me. Nor is my future later than my past, because my past, as "thrownness", is currently shaping and giving meaning to my present and future experiences. Further, my present is always enmeshed with and influenced by my future possibilities and my living past. In other words, the present moment simultaneously comprises the past and future and, in this sense, it goes beyond, or "transcends", the merely present, so we can never occupy exclusively, or merely, a "punctual" here and now moment, because in our understanding, and in our mode of being-in-the-world, we always already exist in three temporal dimensions at once (BT: 370 ff.)

eigentlich German: "authentic" or "real". The noun is *Eigentlichkeit*.

Eigentlichkeit German: "authenticity". These words are related to the adjective *eigen*, which means "personal" or "own"; being "authentic" means being true to one's "own self" by doing one's "own thing".

enframing From the German *Gestell*. Enframing refers to the technological "mindset" or attitude that is characterized by a narrow, restricted understanding of ourselves and all things in existence as "resources" for exploitation. According to Heidegger, it is this attitude that has caused mankind to treat nature as "a gigantic gasoline station, an energy source for modern technology and industry" (DT: 50). Enframing is the essence or source of the modern understanding and approach to technology, but exists independently from it. It sustains technology, but is not itself anything technological: "Enframing means the way of revealing that holds sway in the essence of modern technology and that is itself nothing technological" ("The Question Concerning Technology", in BW: 325). Enframing is thus intrinsically connected with the world of technology, in that the technological outcome is what the mode of enframing itself demands. In other words, technology is the logical and unavoidable consequence and conclusion of enframing. This is why Heidegger emphasizes that it is not technology, but the "coming to presence" of enframing that is the (real) danger hanging over the world. Furthermore, Heidegger asserts that enframing is rooted in Being itself; it precedes man and thus it is beyond our control. So enframing is clearly not something we do, since it already influences and defines who we are and the nature of the world in which we live. We function within it; our actions are guided by it. It is a phase of our destiny sent by Being that is happening to us as part of the mystery of existence. Humans are not the cause of enframing but an indispensable part of its expression, thus "Modern technology, as a revealing that orders, is thus no mere human doing" (*ibid.*: 324), since the essence of technology is Being itself. Heidegger thus emphasizes that man can never achieve dominion over technology. The threat of technology, therefore, is not a problem that needs a solution, but an ontological condition that requires a transformation of our understanding of Being.

entity *See* **beings**.

epistemology From the Greek "*epistēmē*", meaning knowledge. Any systematic exposition of the grounds of and means to knowledge constitutes an epistemology. Its central questions include the role of experience and reason in the accumulating knowledge; the relationship between knowledge and certainty; and how new conceptualizations of the world affect the transformation of knowledge and all such issues are connected to the philosophical concerns about the nature of truth, experience and meaning. Nearly every great philosopher has contributed to the epistemological literature. According to Wilhelm Dilthey (who strongly influenced Heidegger), unlike the natural sciences, which produce knowledge, the human sciences instead produce understanding. Thus we cannot effectively employ the techniques used in the natural sciences to understand meaningful human behaviour and its linguistic expressions and symbols, because the natural sciences seek to explain natural events by providing general laws that are universally applicable at all times, whereas human behaviour is "place and time sensitive". Indeed, in *Being and*

Time, Heidegger asserts that our mode of Being only makes sense in terms of its historical, social and cultural context, and importantly, it also only *is* what it is in terms of this
context. *Being and Time* can be viewed as a critique of previous ontological approaches
that ignore this.

equipment In everyday life, we encounter equipment of numerous sorts for writing, sewing,
working, transportation, measurement and so on. Heidegger defines equipment as,
essentially, something that is "in-order-to". Structurally, this "in-order-to" describes what
Heidegger calls an assignment, which is the process of employing X (a piece of equipment) to achieve Y (a task). The term "assignment" indicates that a piece of equipment is
made visible in its ontological genesis, thus one could reasonably assert that there is no
such "thing" as a piece of equipment, since equipment achieves the status of equipment
only while it is being used; so a hammer becomes equipment only while it is being used
as such. Heidegger describes the mode of being of equipment as "ready-to-hand" (*see*
ready-to-hand).

equipment totality When Dasein relates to a ready-to-hand item, it understands the item as
fundamentally existing within a network of other entities. Thus "one tool is ontologically
impossible"; a tool is always part of an implicit network of inter-referential equipment
in Dasein's place of work. For instance, a hammer exists within the network of other
related tools, raw materials, the job it is used for, its end result or product and so on.
This complete network of instruments and materials related to a ready-to-hand item
Heidegger calls "equipment totality" (BT: 98).

equiprimordial Equally original or basic: neither is derivable from, based on, or reducible
to, the other.

Ereignis German: "event" or "occurrence". In *Being and Time*, the word "*Ereignis*" is used
for an event that happens to Dasein; it can apply to "a storm, refurbishing one's house or
the arrival of a friend, hence to things that are present-at-hand, ready-to-hand or there-
with-us" (BT: 294). Later, Heidegger's use of the word alters. For instance, he refers
to nihilism as a long-drawn-out *Ereignis* in which truth about beings as a whole gradually changes, moving towards a conclusion determined by nihilism. Another *Ereignis*
to which he refers is the beginning of metaphysics. Indeed, Heidegger views the entire
history of Being as having been determined by various *Ereignis* that send the different
modes of Being or "presencing" that have shaped Western history into its Greek, Roman,
medieval, modern and technological epochs. Heidegger also frequently uses the term
in reference to the initial revelation of Being – the "supreme event" that constitutes
the *Anfang*, "the beginning" or essencing of Being – the initial disclosure of Being that
first let human beings have meaningful access to the Being of entities. In this usage of
Ereignis, Heidegger is referring to the occurrence in which mankind was first appropriated by Being, the result being a complete transformation of man's essence from "rational
animal" to Da-sein, the "there" of Being: the site of Being's revelation or disclosure. In
other words, this supreme event of Being makes man into the "property" of Being; man
is now owned by Being.

essence Understood as "what-ness", this refers to the ontical properties of an entity. For
example, the essence of a tree consists of the physical properties that constitute the
physical make-up of a tree. However in reference to Dasein, essence does not refer to its
"what-ness" (ontical constitution) but to Dasein's "ontological" constitution, to Dasein's
distinctive mode of being, which makes it the unique entity that it is. "The 'essence' of
Dasein lies in its existence" (BT: 67). In his later thinking Heidegger asserts that *dwelling
in the world* is the "essence" of Dasein's mode of Being.

existence Heidegger uses the word "existence" (*Existenz*) *not* in the traditional sense of
referring to the fact that an entity "exists", but in a narrow, unusual sense to indicate
Dasein's *unique* "essence", which is *fundamentally* different from the "essence" or
"nature" of all other entities; so he *only* applies the term to Dasein. "*The essence of*

Dasein lies in its existence" (BT: 67). By "existence" Heidegger means Dasein's "mode of Being" (and never the fact that Dasein *is*: "exists"). Further, Heidegger wants us to understand that Dasein's essence is rooted in its mode of Being. For Dasein's self is not any sort of thing or entity, or unchanging centre of our Being that remains the same throughout our lives. Rather, it is a *way of existing* (BT: 152–3).

existentials English translation of Heidegger's term *"existentialia"*. The term is used in reference to Dasein's ontological characteristics. Each of Dasein's "existentials" refers to a specific *a priori* mode of Dasein's way of Being and way of understanding the world. Heidegger analyses all these existentials, which together constitute Dasein's complete *a priori* way of understanding and being-in-the-world that forms the basis of Dasein's capacity to question and investigate the meaning of Being.

existential Pertaining to our (Dasein's) way of Being. An existential analysis is an investigation of our mode of Being. Existential questions are questions pertaining to Dasein's way of Being such as "How does Dasein relate to its past?"

existentialism Philosophical and literary movement inspired by Kierkegaard (the term was coined after his demise by the French philosophers Sartre and Marcel), who rejected the abstract rationalism of Hegel's philosophy as well as other systematic philosophical approaches that attempted to develop an all-embracing "objective" understanding of existence that could reconcile all oppositions and satisfy everyone's interests and needs. Existentialism, instead, focuses on the uniqueness of each existing individual's personal perspective on existence and concern for their own life. Human existence is not determined by a "fixed" human essence but rather by our practical personal engagements and goals, since for each of us our own Being is the fundamental issue and it is the mode in which we deal with this issue that shapes the nature of our life.

facticity The sum total of Dasein's current situation and future possibilities, which are the consequence of Dasein's "thrownness": the totality of what I have been, what I am and on the basis of this what I can be in terms of my possibilities.

falling/fallenness The fundamental feature of inauthentic living as the They-self. According to Heidegger, "falling" characterizes Dasein's general mode of existence in which it lives mostly, or even entirely, as the They-self, absorbed in its everyday dealings with the world. Falling is defined by shallow, short-lived curiosity, empty talk or gossip, and submission to the values, interpretations and interests of the anonymous general public. In falling, one drifts along with the fads and trends of the crowd, caught up in the mindless busy-ness, lulled by feeling that everyone else is doing the same; Dasein becomes blind to all its possibilities, and tranquillizes itself with that which is merely "actual".

fate Heidegger calls the resolutely chosen possibility to which Dasein steadfastly commits itself "Dasein's fate". Heidegger does not use the term "fate" in the ancient Greek sense of "predetermination beyond our control", however: our freedom to choose our fate is necessarily limited because it must be derived from our own heritage in the face of the constant possibility of death, which can happen at any time (BT: 436). Thus Dasein's self-chosen fate is rooted in an act of authentic resoluteness "in which Dasein hands itself down to itself, free for death, in a possibility which it has inherited and yet chosen" (BT: 435).

fore-conception Refers to our capacity to interpret things, which is dependent on our prior familiarity with that which is to be interpreted. In other words, although I may see something as a tool, I will be unable to see it as a "monkey wrench" if I have no concept of a "monkey wrench".

fore-having Refers to our general understanding of entities and the complete context in which they are involved. For example, the fore-having of a mechanic will be his global understanding of all the tools in his workshop, whereas the fore-having of a psychologist would be his broad understanding of human nature.

fore-sight Refers to the act of focusing the attention on what is to be interpreted (or a specific feature of it). The mechanic will focus his attention on an engine, or a specific mechanical fault in it, whereas the psychologist might construct a personality profile of an individual or focus on one specific behavioural dysfunction.

fore-structure Our prior awareness of the web of significant relations that defines the existence of a "ready-to-hand" entity. Our awareness of this fore-structure is a prerequisite to all interpretation and understanding. Heidegger divides this fore-structure into three separate parts, although all are simultaneously active during any given act of interpretation. He emphasizes that interpretation is always guided by this fore-structure.

founding There are three essential senses intended in Heidegger's use of "founding" (*Stiftung*), and art satisfies all three. The first is "bestowing", which indicates that the truth of a work of art is not derived from a previous truth and, in this sense, the truth is like the bestowal of a gift, a gift that accompanies a complete shift in perception and experience of reality. Ordinary perception and experience are replaced by extraordinary perception; the ordinary is transformed into the extraordinary. The second meaning contained in founding is "grounding": truth is always in reference to human beings and so truth is "grounded" in people, who are the "preservers" of truth. When a new truth arises it is always influenced by, adapted to and grounded upon a people's "endowment". This includes their physical environment and language of communication, their everyday customs and beliefs, and their movement towards their appointed destiny, for instance the advent of Christianity in a society. The final meaning contained in "founding" is "beginning", a "beginning" (*Anfang*) that "already contains the end latent in itself", a "genuine beginning" that "is always a leap forward, in which everything to come is already leaped over even if as something disguised" (OWA: 76). In other words, hidden or "disguised" in this beginning is an implicit plan, a "blueprint" that can be decoded to make a people's destiny explicit by defining and anticipating future possibilities and tasks for the historical unfolding of that society.

the fourfold In 1951, inspired by Hölderlin's poeticizing of the early Greek world, Heidegger developed a new way of hinting at the nature of Being – what it means to be – envisaging the world through his poetic vision of existence as a unified interplay or "happening together" of the fourfold of earth, sky, gods and mortals. This fourfold conception of existence is fundamental to Heidegger's new categorial schema of reality, for it provides an alternative means of envisaging and comprehending beings that is, according to Heidegger, radically different from our current technological mode of understanding reality. His aim is to bring our attention to the lack of any sense of the divine in contemporary existence and the fact that in the dimension of the sacred lies our only hope for the future of the planet. In this conception of reality, everything in our world is inextricably immersed in the unified interplay of the fourfold. Thus, in his later writings, Heidegger's question "What is a thing?" brings the entire world into play, for he now regards "a thing" to be something that "assembles" or "gathers" the fourfold and this gathering together of the fourfold is the source of a thing's presence. An excellent example of the influence of the fourfold on Heidegger's understanding of reality can be seen in his phenomenological description of an everyday earthenware jug, in which he reveals the jug to be enmeshed in a web of interconnected beings and events that spans the totality of human existence and understanding: a realm of being that exists within the fourfold of earth, sky, gods and mortals.

fundamental ontology The term used by Heidegger to emphasize his unique approach to ontology, which investigates Being by focusing its investigation primarily and directly on the nature of Being itself rather than on the consequences of Being: entities and their associated characteristics or ontical features. Heidegger's fundamental ontology attempts to answer the most fundamental of all questions: what is the meaning of Being?

Gelassenheit *Gelassenheit* is the central feature of authenticity in Heidegger's later writings. He adopted this term from Meister Eckhart, the fourteenth-century German mystic and theologian, who used it to describe the state of divine peace arising from an absence of self-will. The root of the word "*Gelassenheit*" is "*lassen*", meaning "letting" or "allowing", but in Heidegger's usage the term is perhaps best translated as "releasement". It refers to a state of awareness characterized by a "let it be" attitude, a surrendering to Being that is free from all conscious willing. Heidegger describes *Gelassenheit* as a kind of waiting. This "waiting" is qualitatively very different from the usual kind of human waiting, in that it has no concrete objective. It is not a "waiting for", which expects or hopes for something in particular to arrive or happen in the future, but is a totally alert "openness" that is free from all expectations; the awareness is entirely immersed in the moment, in a state of wide-open, non-excluding presence that is utterly receptive to whatever arises. This state of consciousness closely resembles the Taoist condition of *wu wei*, which refers to the release of "conscious willing", with the awareness open and attuned to the "Way". According to Heidegger, Dasein's freedom lies in being attuned to Being and the presence of beings in this state of *Gelassenheit*, which simply "lets Beings be". This approach to life can serve to provide a potential remedy or counterforce to *Gestell*, the essence of technology. "Higher acting", he writes, "is concealed in releasement than is found in all the actions within the world and in the machinations of all mankind" (PLT: 61). According to Heidegger, "releasement" allows us to remain fully open and attuned to the "voice" of Being and thus receptive to the arrival of any new modes of understanding Being that become available to mankind.

Gestell   German: stand, "enframing". *See* **enframing**.

ground   The foundation or "basis of".

guilt   The guilt Heidegger is interested in has nothing to do with our normal understanding and use of the word, which is connected with ethics and morals that assert that we are guilty of either doing something that we should not have done, or not doing something that we should have done. Instead, Heidegger is referring to an ontological guilt that is prior to the foundation of ethics and morals, that presupposes or emerges from an understanding of this guilt rather than the other way round: "The primordial 'Being-guilty' cannot be defined by morality, since morality already presupposes it for itself" (BT: 332). Heidegger's "authentic", ontological guilt refers to a non-specific, unconditional, existential guilt, which is a primordial part of our essential way of Being as "care": "entities whose Being is care … are guilty in the very basis of their Being" (BT: 332). It is the call of Conscience that informs me that I am guilty in the very basis of my Being; the very fact of my existence automatically makes me guilty. To deny one's primordial guilt is to ignore the call of Conscience, and this is the basis of inauthenticity. In everyday existence Dasein is absorbed in the present and does not acknowledge its guilt. Only authentic Dasein realizes its guilt and acts in full awareness of it. So when Conscience calls us, it is asking us to own up to our authentic guilt and to make our actions our own. By doing this we can exist authentically. Heidegger asserts that, when we own up to guilt, we gain resoluteness, which is the fundamental mindset of authenticity. The accusation of guilt understood in this "primordial ontological meaning" is addressed to Dasein in so far as it fails to respond to the task of shaping its life within a thrownness that it cannot and never will master and control. The realization of our primordial existential guilt arises from the understanding that our existence is rooted in "Nothingness", and that we can never be all that we can be.

hermeneutics   Hermeneutics is the philosophical enquiry into how we make interpretations. Heidegger regarded the process of interpretation in general as being circular in nature, in the sense that prior to beginning any enquiry we always already begin with some understanding of that which we are enquiring about. For in order to investigate the meaning of a text, of a concept, of a pattern of behaviour and so on, the interpretation of any part requires some prior understanding of the whole to which that part belongs, and, similarly, the interpretation of a whole requires a prior understanding of its parts.

For instance, to comprehend the words or sentences (the parts) of an essay requires some understanding of the topic of the essay and the cultural or literary tradition to which that essay belongs (the whole). So hermeneutic analysis does not endeavour to discover something completely new, but focuses its attention on that which is *already* understood or sensed to some extent. It is circular in nature because it begins from an overall general sense of what is being analysed and then proceeds to specific parts of this whole and then once again returns back to the overall picture. Heidegger's approach to the question of Being entails embracing this "hermeneutical circle". So when he asks the question of Being, he does so on the basis that we already understand Being *in general*, for it is this that allows us to raise questions about it in the first place. He regards Dasein's essential nature as fundamentally hermeneutical: always requiring meaning and always making meaning possible (GA 21: 151), for Dasein has an *a priori* understanding of its own Being and of the Being of other entities in its world. So in our dealings with the world "we always conduct our activities in an understanding of Being" (BT: 25). In other words, we possess a pre-reflective, rudimentary understanding of our own nature and that of the entities surrounding us that allows us to make sense of our world. It is Dasein's aware-ness of the ever-present possibility of death (for the sense of our own life beginning and ending is what gives our life-span its sense of "wholeness" and meaning) that provides it with a prior awareness of its existence *as a conceptual whole*, and it is this that enables Dasein to investigate what it means to be. According to Heidegger, the true role of the philosopher is to interpret this pre-reflective understanding of being-in-the-world and make it explicit in a conceptually articulate, thematic form, in an ontological theory. Although the investigation is described as being circular it would be more accurate to describe Heidegger's method as having a continually deepening spiral structure, since his enquiry does not simply repeat itself, but instead, each circular movement penetrates to a deeper level. He begins with a preliminary, general understanding and analysis of existence, which leads to insights that result in a revision and deepening of this previous analysis, which in turn leads to further insights and so on (BT: 193–5). In this manner he *continually reinterprets* the facets of our existence on increasingly deeper levels that provide a more profound understanding of our own Being – the truth of who we are - thus getting closer to an understanding of the meaning of Being as a whole.

histriology Macquarrie and Robinson's translation in *Being and Time* of Heidegger's word "*Historie*". It refers to history in the ordinary sense, as the systematic, scientific study and narration of the "dead" past.

historicality Macquarrie and Robinson's translation in *Being and Time* of Heidegger's word *Geschichlichkeit* (the Stambaugh translation is "historicity"). Heidegger uses the word to refer to the fundamentally "living" historical nature of human existence; it is used exclusively in reference to Dasein's unique mode of being-in-the-world as a historical being. Heidegger asserts that it is only because of Dasein's historicality, which is rooted in Dasein's temporality, that we have any interest at all in past events and an ability to study them scientifically in a way that is meaningful to us. Thus, there would be no such thing as history in any sense of the word if Dasein were not historical, since Dasein's historicality provides an *a priori* understanding, or sense of history, that discloses the historical past, and in doing so provides the basis for histriology. Dasein's historicality depends on the structure of its "historizing".

historizing This term refers to the unique and peculiar way in which Dasein's being-in-the-world stretches itself between its birth and its death (BT: 425, 427). Dasein's histor-izing is not something that happens automatically. Historizing occurs when Dasein runs ahead to its own death, returns back to its own birth, or beyond, and rebounds into the authentic present to resolutely choose and adhere to one of its possibilities in a "moment of vision".

inauthenticity This refers to the normal way we live (as the They-self), which is charac-terized by a lack of awareness of our *own* possibilities and a lack of awareness of our authentic Self. This condition arises from our absorption in ways of living provided by others. When Heidegger uses the term "inauthenticity" he is definitely not suggesting that it is any less real than "authenticity", since he emphasizes that Dasein's inauthentic existence, characterized by "falling" and the They-self, is not a consequence of wrong choices or moral weakness, but is part of the structure of normal everyday existence in the world. *See also* the They-self and falling/fallenness.

intentionality   This term refers to a concept that forms the central core of Husserl's phe-nomenonology: "*Intentio* literally means directing-itself-toward. Every lived experience, every psychic comportment, directs itself toward something. Representing is a representing of something, recalling is a recalling of something, judging is judging about something, presuming, expecting, hoping, loving, hating – of something" (HCT: 29). So according to Heidegger, consciousness is never self-contained, since throughout all its modes of expression it is always extending beyond itself *towards* something. Heidegger (unlike Husserl) believes that this fact is only of secondary relevance, since what is of primary importance here is our *intentional comportment* towards that which we are perceiving, since this comportment embraces the entirety of lived experience within which we encounter any objects of perception. So when I perceive an entity, simultaneously I see it *as* something – I relate to it *instantly* – for my intentional comportment towards it derives from my prior understanding of the totality of the world surrounding me, which automatically determines *how* things are disclosed to me, the nature of my perception: "interpretation is never a presuppositionless apprehending of something presented to us" (BT: 191–2). Heidegger differentiates two modes of intentionality: "intentional presuming" and "intentional fulfilment". The former is active; if I tell my brother "there is a dog outside the front door", in spite of understanding me he will not be able to predict *how* he will experience the dog when he opens the door – whether he will perceive it as beautiful, frightening or friendly, say – because he has not yet experienced it in its *concrete reality*. Heidegger would describe intentionality as being "fulfilled" only when my brother actually sees the dog for himself, "so that what is at first only emptily presumed in it demonstrates itself as grounded in the matter" (HCT: 49). In *Being and Time* and, more specifically, in *History of the Concept of Time* (1985), Heidegger demonstrates how Husserl's highly theoretical presentation of intentionality fails to take into account the fact that Dasein's primary relation to the world is one of concern. In contrast to Husserl, Heidegger does not view intentionality as a structure of *consciousness*, but as a structure of *Dasein*, for it is Dasein's understanding of Being that makes intentionality possible; Dasein comports itself to entities, and is the "bearer" of intentionality. Whereas Husserl considers theoretical modes of intentionality, especially the intentionality of perception, as being *primary*, with *practical* modes of intentionality being based on them, for Heidegger the reverse is true: it is "concern" (*Besorgen*), as concernful-having-to-do-with practical everyday reality, that constitutes the *basic* mode of intentionality (which is influenced by Dasein's mood). The "mere perception" of something is, for Heidegger, a *deficient* mode of this "concerned" intentionality.

interpretation   The immediate understanding of the "as-structure" and "fore-structure" of the entities around us, which means that we experience entities in their completion rather than in terms of their characteristics. So when we see a motorcycle, we do not see a shape and some colours and hear some noises, and then infer that we are seeing a motorcycle. Instead, we first see a motorcycle, and only then we may possibly abstract its properties.

irresoluteness   Refers to Dasein's mindless absorption in the present as the They-self, in which it is ignorant of its own self and its own future possibilities.

logos   Greek: saying, word, proposition. Heidegger's term for a language in which the words are inseparable from what they name. Through the audible Greek word we are directly in the presence of the thing itself, not first in the presence of a mere word-sign.

marginal practices These are non-technological activities that have now become merely marginal practices in our culture. He is referring to simple natural pleasures, such as genuine friendship, quiet walks through the countryside, sitting and gazing at the starlit sky: anything not motivated by the desire for "efficiency", "productivity" or "personal improvement". Heidegger hoped that such activities might help to establish a more meaningful direction to our existence in which non-technological practices are central, and technology marginal.

meaning "Meaning" is what one arrives at when "understanding" becomes aware of the as-structure of entities. To comprehend the meaning of something is to understand its function, while seeing its significant purposive relations with other entities. According to Heidegger, Dasein possesses an *a priori* understanding of its being-in-the-world that provides it with a sense of the practical potential of the things in its environment. Because of this, Dasein experiences its own existence as part of a network of meaningful relations to other beings; thus it is able to understand its own Being and its own possibilities, in relation to its being-in-the-world as part of a significant whole. It is our *a priori* comprehension of existence that first discloses to us, and gives meaning to, our surrounding world and the entities within it.

metaphysics Philosophical study of the fundamental nature, constitution and structure of reality, which is concerned with the existence of non-physical entities such as God, time and space.

moment of vision Authentic Dasein makes decisions in the authentic present, which Heidegger calls *der Augenblick*, "the moment (of vision)", a moment of resolute decision where Dasein seizes the authentic possibilities presented by its "situation" (BT: 388). Only resolute Dasein has experiences of an authentic present, characterized by the "moment of vision". This moment of vision is therefore of exceptional significance to Heidegger, for it is an expression of resolute Dasein's sharpened sense, and authentic understanding, of the "moment", the pulsing heartbeat of time. For in Heidegger's understanding, the "moment" is not simply the passing of time through a moment-point of the present; it is not a mere occurrence, something that is automatically "given" to Dasein; rather, it has to be discovered because our normal inauthentic relation to time conceals the moment. In other words, the moment of vision is an achievement derived from Dasein's authenticity, a manifestation of Dasein's return to itself from dispersal in fallenness: "The moment of vision is nothing other than the look of resolute disclosedness in which the full situation of an action opens itself and keeps itself open" (FCM: 149). To acknowledge and face up to the moment – which compels one to decision – is what Heidegger regards as a "fundamental possibility of Dasein's existence proper" (FCM: 149).

moods Although Heidegger uses the unusual word "*Befindlichkeit*" to express the concept of mood (meaning roughly "how one finds oneself" or "how one is doing"), the more usual German word for mood is *Stimmung*. This word also means the tuning of a musical instrument. Heidegger exploits this association. He views "being in a mood" as being "tuned to" life in a certain way and this influences our general attitude to the totality of things and the nature of our understanding at any given moment; moods can enhance or reduce our clarity of perception. Moods, often ignored by philosophy, are a primordial part of Dasein's essential character and way of Being, for Dasein is never moodless. So we are always attuned in some way to things in general – to our overall situation, our "Being-in-the-world as a whole" (BT: 176), permanently in some kind of mood, which in turn influences our feelings and behaviour and our general outlook on the world, for mood "has always already disclosed being-in-the-world as a whole, making it first possible to direct oneself towards something in particular" (*ibid.*). Heidegger asserts that intense moods such as anxiety, and also deep existential boredom, can reveal fundamental truths of existence for they can disclose with intensity the bare nature of existence as it is, without the "trappings" of job, house or personal social life. They are therefore potentially a vital source of insight into the nature of our being-in-the-world. Heidegger also asserts that there is a basic philosophical mood that is a prerequisite for true understanding. In the absence of this mood, ideas that previously have been deeply grasped are now experienced as a tiresome jumble of "word husks" and "forced" concepts: "All essential thinking requires its thoughts and propositions to be dug out like ore, each time anew, from the basic mood. If the mood fails, then everything is a forced clatter of concepts and word-husks" (GA 65: 21).

nihilism Generally used in reference to the abandonment or collapse of all forms of tradition and authority, all moral, religious and philosophical values and interpretations of reality. In the nihilistic state of mind there seems to be no purpose or significance to the universe; no sense of any unity that gives life meaning; no eternal truths or values. It is one of the key concepts in Nietzsche's philosophy, and his ideas on the subject influenced Heidegger's own understanding of the topic. A fundamental motive behind Heidegger's questioning of Being is his wish to overcome this condition of nihilism, which he believed could have catastrophic consequences for the future of humanity. Heidegger states as early as 1935 what nihilism essentially means for him: "to concern oneself only with beings in forgetfulness of Being" (IM: 203) He describes the "getting over" of nihilism as requiring a pressing of "the inquiry into Being expressly to the border of Nothing and to incorporate it (Nothing) into the question of Being" (*ibid.*).

Nothing The "Nothing", in Heidegger's usage, does not refer to the negation "not any-thing", for he regards Being and the Nothing as equi-primordial, mutually dependent and indivisible like two sides of a coin: "to think that Nothing that is equi-primordially the same as Being" (QB: 101). "The Nothing ... reveals itself as belonging to the Being of beings" ("What is Metaphysics?", in BW: 108). Thus "Nothing" is not the negation of Being, the "Nothingness" of nihilism as it has been often understood since Nietzsche. Indeed, Heidegger asserts that the overcoming of nihilism requires "the inquiry into Being expressly to the border of Nothing and to incorporate it (Nothing) into the question of Being" (IM: 203). We normally suppress our awareness of the Nothing, but the mood of anxiety sometimes reveals it, thereby deepening our understanding of beings, for it is against the background of Nothing that every being presents itself as not Nothing, that is, as something: "In the clear night of anxiety the original openness of beings as such arises: that they are beings – and not Nothing ... The essence of the originally nihilating Nothing lies in this, that it brings Dasein for the first time before beings as such" ("What is Metaphysics", in BW: 103). Thus, according to Heidegger, "Being" is meaningful only because it lives constantly in the shadow of the Nothing: "Without the original revelation of the Nothing, there is no selfhood and no freedom" (*ibid.*). According to Heidegger, we currently live in an age characterized by an "oblivion of Being" and, as a consequence of this, "beings" are not sheltering Being, because they have been reduced to "unbeings". As a result, we have become indifferent to the difference between beings and Nothing and thus, for us, the universe is turning into a wasteland (CTP: 47).

nullity Heidegger's ontological analysis reveals that at the basis of human existence there is nothing. Thus Dasein's very Being is "Being-the-basis of a nullity" (BT: 329). For, owing to the chance event of its *throwness*, which determines its birth, "Dasein is not itself the basis of its Being" (BT: 330). In other words, since Dasein has in no way whatsoever determined the life situation and circumstances into which it has been "thrown", this means ultimately that, aside from the fact that it is a being-towards-death, it has *no possibilities that are truly its own*, because its past, which it cannot control owing to its throwness, must serve as *basis* for the entirety of its existence (BT: 329–30), since it is Dasein's past that provides the currently available possibilities that it chooses to determine its future. It is the realization of its own mortality (the fact that it is a being-towards-death), revealed during mood of anxiety, that discloses to Dasein its essential nullity: that its existence stands on nothing – "The 'Nothing' with which anxiety brings us face to face, unveils the nullity by which Dasein, in its very *basis*, is defined; and this basis itself is as thrownness into death" (BT: 356). Thus in this state of consciousness, Dasein's normal sense of identity in terms of its personal attributes and accomplishments can no longer be maintained, since Dasein now realizes that the entirety of its existence is grounded on nothing.

ontic knowledge Knowledge about things in existence and their characteristics without any regard for their actual Being: the primordial fact of their existence. In other words, knowledge about that which exists as a consequence of Being rather than knowledge of the actual nature of "Being" itself.

ontic truth Factual information. Refers to truth that has been "proved" by verifiable "facts".

ontological Information, statements, remarks or observations pertaining to Being itself, or the Being of entities.

ontological difference Being, unlike beings, does not have any measurable properties since "the Being of entities 'is' not itself an entity" (BT: 26). The term "ontological difference" refers to this fundamental distinction or dissimilarity between Being and beings.

ontologist Philosopher who investigates the nature of Being.

ontology Philosophical speculation on the nature of Being is known as ontology. It began in fifth-century BCE Greece, with the Presocratic thinkers who became intrigued by, and questioned, the seemingly inexplicable fact of existence. According to Heidegger, however, Plato and all philosophers who came after him made the grave mistake of adopting a "theoretical stance" for their interpretation of Being. This gave rise to the "oblivion of Being" that still persists today. As a result, ontology has largely been preoccupied with investigating "things" in existence rather than Being itself. Heidegger calls his approach a fundamental ontology because it asks *directly* about Being itself, what "Being" actually *is*: "the meaning of Being".

onto-theology Any philosophical approach that searches for an origin of Being in some type of substance or transcendental super-Being (God). Heidegger considered all such approaches to be an evasion of the fundamental question of Being.

phenomenology Phenomenology, founded in the early years of the twentieth century by Edmund Husserl, attempts to describe the experience of phenomena *directly*, free of all influence from previous interpretations and theories of existence. The term derives from the Greek *phainōmenon*, which Heidegger interprets as meaning "*that which shows itself in itself*, the manifest" (BT: 51) and *logos* as essentially meaning *making something manifest* (BT: 56). Thus Heidegger presents the formal definition of phenomenology as "to let that which shows itself be seen from itself in the very way in which it shows itself from itself" (BT: 58). For Heidegger, "*Only as phenomenology, is ontology possible*" (BT: 60). There are, however, important and crucial differences between Husserl's and Heidegger's approaches. For instance, "evidence" is Husserl's term for a state in which a phenomenon reveals itself to consciousness. When something is entirely unconcealed (revealed), this is described as perfect or "adequate" evidence. This concept of truth strongly influenced Heidegger, but, unlike Husserl, who completely disregards the temporal structure of phenomena, Heidegger asserts that unconcealment occurs only because we are *historical* and he considers *complete* unconcealment to be impossible, since truth and untruth always arise simultaneously. Husserl observed that our relation to things is determined by intention (*see* **intentionality**) for I always see things *as* something: a tree *as* a tree (in *Being and Time* this phenomenological *as* is shown to be an important feature of Dasein's mode of interpreting the world). However, pertaining to this, Heidegger also asks the more important question: what *determines* this relation of intentionality to the world in the first place? Husserl merely *presupposes* this question of Being, so instead of investigating the *Being* of consciousness, he simply takes for granted the Being of that being which is consciousness, in spite of the fact that without Being it could not function at all. So whereas Husserl's phenomenology focuses on the intentional structures of consciousness, and the way things are constituted in consciousness, Heidegger is interested in the phenomenological conception of the phenomenon, fundamentally in terms of "that which is concealed in what shows itself and thereby enables what shows itself to show itself". In other words, it is not merely the letting be seen and description of *entities* as they show themselves to us in our direct experience of them that concerns Heidegger, but the letting be seen of an entity in terms of the "extraction" and "interpretation" of that which lies *hidden*, which *belongs* to an entity "so essentially as to constitute its meaning and its ground" (BT: 59). Heidegger is referring here to the "Being" of entities: that on the basis of which entities are always already understood. So, in contrast to Husserl's approach, which is exclusively a *reflective* phenomenology of *consciousness*, Heidegger's is essentially an interpretive, hermeneutic phenomenology: a laying bare or exhibiting of Dasein and the structures of its Being as well as the structures of the Being of other entities (since understanding other entities is an innate feature of Dasein's Being). (See BT: 49–63 for Heidegger's discussion of phenomenology.)

Poesie For Heidegger, language is not merely a means of communicating what we already know. The essence of language, its primordial, most important function, is "projective saying" (OWA: 74): the naming of things for the first time. Language as "projective saying" predetermines the nature of what can or cannot be spoken about in ordinary communication, and thus it founds the world in which we live, since the naming of beings discloses, establishes and preserves their existence, thereby enabling our primary access to Being. Heidegger's term "*Poesie*" refers solely to verse or poetry, which he regards as the highest, purest expression of language as "projective saying", the essence and basis of projective saying. So according to Heidegger, *Poesie*, the linguistic art of poetry, is a mode of speaking that lets the essence of language itself be seen and therefore it is foundational for all language in its manifold workings. Heidegger asserts that *Poesie* is the most important art of all because the disclosure of truth that takes place in the "projective saying" of poetry is prior to, and therefore more fundamental than, the disclosure of truth that takes place in all the other arts; architecture, painting and sculpture, for instance, operate in a realm already opened up by the "poetic" essence of language as "projective saying". Thus Heidegger regarded poetry as being intimately connected with truth and the deepest revelation of what is.

poiesis Ancient Greek: making, creating, "to bring into presence" or "bring forth".

present-at-hand Describes entities for which Dasein has no use, or for which Dasein has merely a detached objective interest. Science treats entities as present-at-hand when it observes and studies their physical properties. Also, the same object – depending on the way we relate to it – can be present-at-hand or ready-to-hand.

primordial That which is prior to everything, which has existed from the beginning and therefore cannot be derived from anything else.

projection I am *thrown* out of the past and into the present while projecting from within my thrownness towards the future. The term "projection" refers to Dasein's efforts to fulfil its own possibilities.

ready-to-hand Entities that are experienced by Dasein as having a useful practical function for human purposes. Relating to things as "ready-to-hand" is Dasein's fundamental way of being-in-the-world.

repetition Heidegger claims that, to be fully authentic, the possibilities Dasein projects for its future have to be drawn from its past in terms of its *heritage*, which serves as a stockpile of currently available "inherited" possibilities for living authentically, possibilities that can then be questioned, interpreted and adapted to Dasein's own circumstances and potentials (BT: 435). This heritage, which Dasein shares with others, provides Dasein with many possible self-interpretations accumulated over thousands of years. Thus according to Heidegger, authentic existence always "repeats" (in the sense of "retrieves") some inherited possibility, which serves as a model or point of reference that Dasein uses to guide its own life: *"Repeating is ...* going back into the possibilities of the Dasein that has-been-there ... The authentic repetition of a possibility of existence that has been ... By repetition, Dasein first has its own history made manifest" (BT: 437–8).

resoluteness The key feature of authenticity, which describes Dasein's total commitment to the fundamental path it has freely chosen in life. Resoluteness requires a clear awareness of the totality of one's existence and the constant possibility of death.

the river The river, a common motif in Hölderlin's poems, is central to Heidegger's commentary on Hölderlin. It is described as a "being-between", and it is regarded as a demigod (GA 39: 163–4). Heidegger strongly emphasizes, however, that the poetic motif of the river is not merely an image of Heraclitean flux, for the river is in itself the meaning it embodies; it is not an image "of" or a symbol "for" something, but an exemplification of "becoming-in-the-midst-of-flux" in the sense that the river's natural arrangement and layout, its stability and continuity, arise out of and are founded on its constant state of change. In Hölderlin's poetry, the present moment is exemplified by the river (the river Ister), which, like the eternal "now", preserves its identity in spite of its perpetual flowing and constant state of flux (e.g. the river Ister is always the river Ister; this present moment is always this present moment).

Sein German: "Being", derived from the verb "to be".

Seyn Archaic German spelling of *Sein* (Being). In Heidegger's writing, whenever he is referring to Dasein's "authentic" or "divine" relation to Being, he uses the spelling *Seyn* (an old spelling used centuries earlier).

technē Ancient Greek: from which "technology" derives. In its original sense, the word encompassed several possible meanings. It could mean the fine arts, the "arts of the mind", the skills and activities of a craftworker, and it also contained a sense of what Heidegger called *poiesis*, which means "to bring into presence" or "to bring forth": exactly what happens in all arts and crafts. According to Heidegger, this etymological research therefore indicates that *technē*, with its sense of *poiesis*, belongs to the same realm of truth as *alētheia*: fundamental truth as unconcealment. So *technē*'s original Greek meaning includes connotations lost to our modern understanding and expression of technology, since in its original sense *technē* was not merely a practical aptitude or way of making, but more importantly a mode of knowing and revealing as the "truth" of *alētheia*. Heidegger ascribed the loss in modern technology of the original sense of *technē* to Plato's demeaning of entities and to the Aristotelian–Cartesian utilitarian use of knowledge for mastering nature. For, according to Heidegger, the metaphysical understanding of Being that has prevailed in the West from the time of Plato and Aristotle onwards has been conducted within the paradigm of enframing. Thus, although modern technology still "discloses", it does so in a highly restricted manner that wipes out *poiesis*: the revealing of the "presence" or "being" of an entity. The kind of revealing that occurs in modern technology is therefore very different from that which takes place in a work of art. Whereas art allows things to be revealed, technology forces things to fulfil a specific purpose, so that things are "disclosed" only within their particular type of usefulness. This mode of revealing, or enframing, is the essence of modern technology: "The essence of modern technology lies in enframing" ("The Question Concerning Technology", in BW: 330).

temporality Heidegger uses the term "temporality" specifically and exclusively in reference to Dasein's mode of existing, to the way Dasein experiences and lives as, through and in time: its fundamental way of being simultaneously spans, and is constituted by, the three dimensions of time. Thus, according to Heidegger, "to be" is always "to be temporal", and since temporality determines the primordial meaning of Dasein's Being and Dasein's sense of what it means to be, this further suggests that the appropriate horizon or context for understanding Being must be time. In other words, it is Dasein's temporality that makes Being accessible to us. There are two main notions of temporality: authentic (primordial) temporality, which is exemplified by resolute Dasein; and inauthentic temporality, the temporality of everyday and/or fallen Dasein.

the They Dasein's primordial state of being-with (the social context of its world) includes a fundamental and necessary feature of our Being, called the They. The They is Heidegger's term for the anonymous general public and its social and cultural customs, expectations and interpretations of life, which are a part of the particular world that Dasein inhabits. When Dasein exists inauthentically as the They-self, it simply accepts the "way of the They", allowing it to structure and guide its mode of existence.

the They-self Heidegger's term for the inauthentic mode of the self, which lives according to the range of social and cultural customs, expectations and interpretations of life offered by the particular world it inhabits. From birth onwards most of us live our complete lives as the They-self, completely absorbed in the ways of living that others provide us, while ignoring our own unique individuality.

thrownness The event of being thrust into an existence not of our choice that has been determined by the random forces of chance or destiny. Thrownness is a central feature of Dasein, always fundamentally influencing and shaping its entire existence; it determines what Dasein has been, where Dasein always already is, who Dasein always already is and Dasein's options for the future. In other words, my thrownness means that I have a past I always carry with me that must serve as a foundation for my present existence, and which defines and limits my future possibilities, because the choices I make, and all I create, must be made on the basis of what I already am at the moment, which is influenced by my past: the continuing momentum of my thrownness. So I can never create myself anew, as I have to work with what I have been and what I am now in order to become what I want to be in the future. Thus, ultimately, everything I am and do has been made possible by the "already given" situation into which I was thrown.

transcendence Heidegger asserts that "Every disclosure of Being ... is transcendental knowledge" (BT: 62). His use of this term is intended to communicate his understanding of Being, as that which lies "beyond" all entities (BT: 22, 62). This crucial distinction between Being and beings underlines the emphasis of his search, which is for ontological knowledge of Being. He also sometimes describes Dasein's being-in-the-world as transcendence (BT: 415). Transcendence, in this instance, refers to the state or locus by which, or from which, Dasein can reflect on the totality of human experience; by maintaining a critical distance or detachment from the world, Dasein is able to understand entities not merely in terms of their sheer actuality but, more importantly, in terms of their possibilities. For example, Dasein's past is significant not merely in terms of what it has been but, more importantly, for the possibilities it provides for Dasein's present and future existence. Similarly, for Dasein, a particular tool is not merely actual but rather it is something that Dasein has the potential to use for a purpose that transcends the hammer and its actual use of it. This capacity for transcendence, which is rooted in Dasein's ecstatic temporality, is what enables and inspires Dasein to ask about the source of all creation: to ask "Why is there anything at all rather than Nothing?" Without this ability Dasein would be incapable of providing the account of entities that is given in *Being and Time*, because Dasein's potential for transcendence is the fundamental basis for philosophy.

understanding Dasein's *a priori* pre-conceptual understanding of its everyday world, the things in it and how it fits into this world. This pre-conceptual grasp of existence, which is a fundamental feature of Dasein's being-in-the-world, inspires, directs and enables Dasein to question existence and make interpretations of its surroundings. Heidegger asserts that all understanding is circular, in the sense that any interpretation that is to contribute to understanding must already have understood what is to be interpreted.

So all interpretations are based on a prior context of intelligibility. The most important function of understanding is to project or see things in terms of their future possibilities. To understand myself and thus find meaning in myself is to be aware of my own possibilities and to realize that I not only have possibilities but also am my possibilities, for my Being includes my "can be" (*Seinkönnen*) (BT: 183), my "potentiality-for-Being". In other words, I am not just what I am, I am also who I am not yet (BT: 185).

unready-to-hand Heidegger's term for the "present-at-hand" condition of equipment ("ready-to-hand" items) that is broken or rendered unusable.

world Heidegger's conception of Dasein describes its Being as a "being-there" in which "there" refers to the world. The "world", in Heidegger's usage of the word, is not a *physical* space but a context of meaning: a domain of possibilities that is inhabited by Dasein's *active* understanding, which manifests as Dasein's knowing *what* to do and *why* it makes sense to do it. Heidegger's usage of "world" in this sense of *possibilities* refers to the entire circumstances or context that influence a particular Dasein's total existence: "that 'wherein' a factical Dasein as such can be said to 'live'" (BT: 93) (what Husserl terms the "life-world"). This includes the entire circumstances or context of Dasein's life: birthplace, country of residence, culture, social environment, education, family, friends, career, pastimes and so on.

worldhood The basic underlying infrastructure of a Dasein's world. In other words, the totality of all our practical and functional relations with everything in the particular world we inhabit.

worlding A word coined by Heidegger to refer to the dynamic presence of the world. The sense of "activity" contained in the term "worlding" expresses the energetic aliveness – the presencing – of an environment that is a process in constant flux. The term "worlding" suggests that each environment in which we find ourselves simultaneously embraces, encapsulates and signifies our entire world of experience. This explains why a single item, even from the past – perhaps just the fleeting memory of a toy robot we owned – can dredge up a whole world of associated memories and emotions; the toy robot "is worlding".

Further reading

The best concise introduction to Heidegger's own works is the revised and expanded edition of Martin Heidegger's *Basic Writings*, Krell (ed.) (1993). This anthology contains an introduction to *Being and Time* as well as ten key essays by Heidegger, published between 1927 and 1964, that include "What is Metaphysics?", "On the Essence of Truth", "The Origin of the Work of Art" and "The Question of Technology". The most well-known and reliable English translation of Heidegger's magnum opus, *Sein und Zeit*, is *Being and Time*, Macquarrie & Robinson (trans.) (1962).

The most thorough, comprehensive biographical study of Martin Heidegger is Rüdiger Safranski's *Martin Heidegger: Between Good and Evil* (1998). It includes an insightful account of Heidegger's personality, actions and intellectual development, and some perceptive observations on his philosophy. An excellent account of Heidegger's life and his political involvement with fascism is Hugo Ott's *Heidegger: A Political Life* (1993). It sheds light on numerous negative features in his personality and behaviour.

A useful collection of important original documents by Heidegger, as well as essays and letters by Heidegger's colleagues, is *The Heidegger Controversy: A Critical Reader*, edited by Richard Wolin (1993). The essays provide contemporary context and testimony to his political ties and there are further interpretive evaluations by critics in France and Germany.

For an excellent and fully comprehensive guide to Heidegger's thought and the complexities of Heidegger's unique use of vocabulary, consult *A Heidegger Dictionary* by Michael Inwood (2000). This easy-to-use dictionary traces the history of one hundred words or concepts (from "*alētheia*" to "world") through Heidegger's entire career from his earliest lectures up to his later essays and seminars. A useful examination of Heidegger's basic concepts, each chapter compiled by a leading scholar in the field, is *Martin Heidegger: Key Concepts*, edited by Bret W. Davis (2010a).

On the link between Heidegger and East Asian thought, I recommend *Heidegger and Asian Thought*, edited by Graham Parkes (1987), Reinhard May's *Heidegger's Hidden Sources* (1996) and Michael E. Zimmerman's *Eclipse of the Self: The Development of Heidegger's Concept of Authenticity* (1986).

A highly readable and useful commentary on *Being and Time*, written in straightforward everyday language, is Michael Gelven's *A Commentary on Heidegger's Being and Time* (1989).

A thought-provoking survey of the full range of Heidegger's thought is Richard Polt's *Heidegger: An Introduction* (1999), and Michael Inwood's *Heidegger: A Very Short Introduction* (2000) is another compact survey and introduction. *The Cambridge Companion to Heidegger*, 2nd edn, edited by Charles Guignon (2006), provides a stimulating overview of all the major themes of Heidegger's thought via a collection of essays by leading scholars.

Heidegger's Later Writings: A Reader's Guide, by Lee Braver (2009), offers an accessible introduction to eight of Heidegger's most important essays, which cover many of the central topics of his later thought. It provides a useful companion to Heidegger's *Basic Writings*, which features the original essays. Another useful discussion of Heidegger's later writings can be found in George Pattison's *The Later Heidegger* (2000).

An intelligent defence of Heidegger's thought is provided by Julian Young in *Heidegger, Philosophy, Nazism* (1997).

Heidegger's Being and Time by William Blattner (2009) and *Being-in-the-World: A Commentary on Heidegger's Being and Time, Division 1*, by Hubert L. Dreyfus (1991) are both highly recommended.

Bibliography

Works by Heidegger

An Introduction to Metaphysics, (i) R. Manheim (trans.). New Haven, CT: Yale University Press 1959. (ii) G. Fried & R. Polt (trans.). New Haven, CT: Yale University Press, 2000. Original lectures 1935, revised and first published 1953.

Aristotle's Metaphysics θ, 1–3: On the Essence and Actuality of Force, W. Brogan & P. Warnek (trans.). Bloomington, IN: Indiana University Press, 1995. Published in the *Gesamtausgabe* as *Aristoteles, Metaphysik θ, 1–3: Von Wesen und Wirklichkeit der Kraft*, H. Hüni (ed.). Frankfurt: Klostermann, 1981. GA 33.

Basic Concepts, G. E. Aylesworth (trans.). Bloomington, IN: Indiana University Press, 1933. Original lecture 1941. Published in the *Gesamtausgabe* as *Grundbegriffe*. Frankfurt: Klostermann, 1981. GA 51.

The Basic Problems of Phenomenology, A. Hofstadter (trans.). Bloomington, IN: Indiana University Press, 1982 [written 1927]. GA 24.

Basic Writings, D. F. Krell (ed.). London: Routledge, 1993.

Being and Time, J. Macquarrie & E. Robinson (trans.). Oxford: Blackwell, 1962 [written 1927].

Briefwechsel: 1920–1963 (with Karl Jaspers). Frankfurt: Klostermann, 1990.

"Briefwechsel mit einem japanischen Kollegen", 1963. Published in the *Gesamtausgabe* as "Brief an Takehiko Kojima" in GA 11, *Identität und Differenz*. Translated in *Identity and Difference*, J. Stambaugh (trans.). New York: Harper & Row, 1969.

Contributions to Philosophy (From Enowning), P. Emad & K. Maly (trans.). Bloomington, IN: Indiana University Press, 1999. Original lectures 1936–38. Published in the *Gesamtausgabe* as *Beitrage zur Philosophie (Vom Ereignis)*, F.-W. von Herrmann (ed.). Frankfurt: Klostermann, 1979. GA 65.

Discourse on Thinking, J. M. Anderson & E. H. Freund (trans.). New York: Harper & Row, 1966 [written 1944–45, 1955].

Early Greek Thinking, D. F. Krell & F. Capuzzi (trans.). New York: Harper & Row, 1975 [written 1935–53].

Elucidations of Hölderlin's Poetry, K. Hoeller (trans.). Amherst, NY: Humanity Books, 2000. *Erläuterungen zu Hölderlins Dichtung*. Frankfurt: Klostermann, 1981 [written 1936–68]. GA 4.

The Essence of Human Freedom: An Introduction to Philosophy, T. Sadler (trans.). London: Continuum, 2002. Original lecture 1930. Published in the *Gesamtausgabe* as *Vom Wesen der Menschlichen Freiheit: Einleitung in die Philosophie*, H. Tietjen (ed.). Frankfurt: Klostermann, 1983. GA 31.

Feldweg-Gespräche. Frankfurt: Klostermann, 1995 [written 1944–45].

The Fundamental Concepts of Metaphysics: World, Finitude, Solitude, W. McNeill & N. Walker. Bloomington, IN: Indiana University Press, 1995 [written 1929–30]. GA 29/30.

Gesamtausgabe [Collected Works]. Frankfurt: Klostermann, 1975– .

Grundbegriffe der aristotelischen Philosophie. Frankfurt: Klostermann, 2002 [written 1924]. GA 18.

Heraklit. Frankfurt: Klostermann, 1979 [written 1943–44]. GA 55.

History of the Concept of Time: Prolegomena, T. Kiesel (trans.). Bloomington, IN: Indiana University Press, 1985. Original lecture, 1925. Published in the *Gesamtausgabe* as *Prolegomena zur Geschichte des Zeitbegriffs*, Frankfurt: Klostermann, 1979. GA 20.

"Hölderlin and the Essence of Poetry", D. Scott (trans.). In *Existence and Being*, W. Brock (ed.), 270–91. Chicago, IL: Henry Regnery, 1949. Original lecture given in Rome, 1936.

Hölderlins Hymne "Andenken". Frankfurt: Klostermann, 1976 [written 1941]. GA 52.

Hölderlins Hymnen "Germanien" und "Der Rhein", S. Ziegler (ed.). Frankfurt: Klostermann, 1980; 2nd edn 1989. Original lectures 1934–35. GA 39.

Holzwege, F.-W. von Herrmann (ed.). Frankfurt: Klostermann, 1978 [written 135–46]. GA 5.

Identität und Differenz. Pfullingen: Neske, 1990 [written 1955–57]. GA 11.

Identity and Difference, J. Stambaugh (trans.). New York: Harper & Row, 1969 [written 1956–57].

Logic: The Question of Truth, T. Sheehan (trans.). Bloomington, IN: Indiana University Press, 2010. Lectures of 1925–26. Published in the *Gesamtausgabe* as *Logik: Die Frage nach der Wahrheit*, W. Biemel (ed.). Frankfurt: Klostermann, 1976. GA 21.

Logica: Lecciones de M. Heidegger (semester verano 1934) en el legado de Helene Weiss, V. Farías (intro. & trans.). Barcelona: Anthropos, 1991. [German and Spanish]

Logik als Frage nach dem Wesen der Sprache, G. Seubold (ed.). Frankfurt: Klostermann, 1998. GA 38.

The Metaphysical Foundations of Logic, M. Heim (trans.). Bloomington, IN: Indiana University Press, 1984 [written 1928]. GA 26.

Die Metaphysik des deutschen Idealismus (Schelling), G. Seubold (ed.). Frankfurt: Klostermann, 1991. GA 49. Original lectures 1941.

Nietzsche I: The Will to Power as Art, D. F. Krell (trans.). San Francisco: Harper & Row, 1979 [written 1936–37].

Nietzsche II: The Eternal Recurrence of the Same, D. F. Krell (trans.). New York: Harper & Row, 1984 [written 1937, 1953].

Nietzsche III: The Will to Power as Knowledge and as Metaphysics, J. Stambaugh, D. F. Krell & F. A. Capuzzi (trans.). New York: Harper & Row, 1987 [written 1936–40].

Nietzsche IV: Nihilism, F. A. Capuzzi (trans.). New York: Harper & Row, 1982 [written 1940–46].

Nietzsche Seminare 1937 und 1944, P. von Ruckteschell (ed.). Frankfurt: Klostermann, 2004. GA 87.

Nietzsches II: Unzeitgemässe Betrachtung, H.-J. Friedrich (ed.). Frankfurt: Klostermann, 2003. GA 46.

On the Way to Language, P. D. Hertz (trans.). New York: Harper & Row, 1971 [written 1950–59].

On Time and Being, J. Stambaugh (trans.). New York: Harper & Row, 1972 [written 1962–64].

"Only a God Can Save Us: *Der Spiegel's* Interview with Martin Heidegger", M. P. Alter & J. D. Caputo (trans.). *Philosophy Today* 20 (Winter 1976): 267–84.

Ontology and the Hermeneutics of Facticity, J. van Buren (trans.). Bloomington, IN: Indiana University Press, 1999 [written 1923]. GA 63.

"The Origin of the Work of Art". In *Poetry, Language, Thought*, A. Hofstadter (trans.), 17–87. New York: Harper & Row, 1975 [written 1935–37]. Originally published in *Holzwege* (Woodpaths) (1950).

"Overcoming Metaphysics". In *The End of Philosophy*, J. Stambaugh (trans.), 84–110. Chicago, IL: University of Chicago Press, 2003 [written 1938–39].

Parmenides, A. Schuwer & R. Rojcewicz (trans.). Bloomington, IN: Indiana University Press, 1992. Published in the *Gesamtausgabe* as *Parmenides*, M. S. Frings (ed.). Frankfurt: Klostermann, 1982. GA 54.

Pathmarks, W. McNeill (ed.). Cambridge: Cambridge University Press, 1998 [written 1919–61].

Phänomenologische Interpretationen zu Aristoteles. Einführung in die phänomenologische Forschung, W. Bröcker & K. Bröcker-Oltmanns (eds). Frankfurt: Klostermann, 1985. GA 61.

"Phenomenological Interpretations in Connection with Aristotle: An Indication of the Hermeneutical Situation", J. van Buren (trans.). In *Supplements from the Earliest Essays to Being and Time and Beyond*, J. van Buren (ed.), 111–45. Albany, NY: SUNY Press, 2002 [written 1922].

The Phenomenology of Religious Life, J. A. Gosetti-Ferencei & M. Fritsch (trans.). Bloomington, IN: Indiana University Press, 2004 [written 1918–21].

Plato's Sophist, R. Rojcewicz & A. Schuwer (trans.). Bloomington, IN: Indiana University Press, 1997 [written 1924–25]. Published in the *Gesamtausgabe* as *Platon: Sophistes*. Frankfurt: Klostermann, 1992. GA 19.

Poetry, Language, Thought, A. Hofstadter (trans.). New York: Harper Perennial, 1975 [written 1935–51].

The Principle of Reason, R. Lilly (trans.). Bloomington, IN: Indiana University Press, [1957] 1991. Original lectures 1956.

The Question Concerning Technology and Other Essays, W. Lovitt (trans.). New York: Harper & Row, 1977.

The Question of Being, W. Kluback & J. T. Wilde (trans.). London: Vision, 1959 [written 1955].

Der Satz vom Grund, P. Jaeger (ed.). Frankfurt: Klostermann, 1997. GA 10.

Seminare (1915–1973), C. Ochwadt (ed.). Frankfurt: Klostermann, 1986, 2nd rev. edn 2005. GA 15.

Unterwegs zur Sprache. Pfullingen: Neske, 1965 [written 1950–59]. Published in the *Gesamtausgabe*, F.-W. von Herrmann (ed.). Frankfurt: Klostermann, 1985. GA 12.

Vom Wesen der Wahrheit: Zu Platons Hohlengleichnis und Theatet, H. Mörchen (ed.). Frankfurt: Klostermann, 1988. GA 34.

Vorträge und Aufsätze, F.-W. von Herrmann (ed.). Frankfurt: Klostermann, 2000. GA 7.

Wegmarken, F.-W. von Herrmann (ed.). Frankfurt: Klostermann, 1976. GA 9.

What is a Thing?, W. B. Barton Jr & V. Deutsch (trans.). Chicago, IL: Henry Regnery, 1967 [written 1935].

What is Called Thinking?, F. D. Wieck & J. G. Gray (trans.). New York: Harper & Row, 1968 [written 1951–52].

What is Philosophy?, W. Kluback & J. T. Wilde (trans.). New Haven, CT: College & University Press, [1955] 1958.

Zollikon Seminars: Protocols – Conversations – Letters, M. Boss (ed.), F. Mayr & R. Askay (trans.). Evanston, IL: Northwestern University Press, 2001 [written 1963–66].

Zur Bestimmung der Philosophie, B. Heimbuchel (ed.). Frankfurt: Klostermann, 1987. GA 56/57. Original lectures 1919.

Zur Sache des Denkens, 3rd edn. Tübingen: Niemeyer, 1988 [written 1962–64].

Zur Seinsfrage. Frankfurt: Klostermann, 1946.

Other works

Agamben, G. 2004. *The Open: Man and Animal*. Stanford, CA: Stanford University Press.

Arendt, H. 1995. *Heidegger and Modern Philosophy*, M. Murray (ed.). New Haven, CT: Yale University Press.

Ayer, A. J. 1984. *Philosophy in the Twentieth Century*. London: Unwin Hyman.

Barrett, W. 1956. "Introduction". In *Zen Buddhism*, D. T. Suzuki. Garden City, NY: Doubleday.

Beistegui, M. 2003. *Thinking with Heidegger: Displacements*. Bloomington, IN: Indiana University Press.

Beistegui, M. 2006. *The New Heidegger*. London: Continuum.

Bernasconi, R. 1985. *The Question of Language in Heidegger's History of Being*. Atlantic Highlands, NJ: Humanities Press.

Biemel, W. 1976. *Martin Heidegger: An Illustrated Study*, J. L. Mehta (trans.). New York: Harcourt Brace Jovanovich.

Blattner, W. 2009. *Being and Time*. London: Continuum.

Bloch, E. 1969. *Spuren*. Berlin: Suhrkamp.

Braver, L. 2009. *Heidegger's Later Writings: A Reader's Guide*. London: Continuum.

Bruns, G. 1981. *Heidegger's Estrangements: Language, Truth, and Poetry in the Later Writings*. New Haven, CT: Yale University Press.

Calarco, M. 2004. "Heidegger's Zoontology". In *Animal Philosophy: Ethics and Identity*, M. Calarco & P. Atterton (eds), 18–30. London: Continuum.

Coleridge, S. T. 1825. "Aphorisms on Spiritual Reflection". In *Aids to Reflection in the Formation of a Manly Character on the Several Grounds of Prudence, Morality, and Religion*, 141–9. London: Taylor & Hessey.

Davis, B. W. (ed.) 2010a. *Martin Heidegger: Key Concepts*. Durham: Acumen.

Davis, B. W. 2010b. "Introduction: Key Concepts in Heidegger's Thinking of Being". See Davis (2010a), 1–16.

Davis, B. W. 2010c. "Will and *Gelassenheit*". See Davis (2010a), 168–82.

Derrida, J. 1989. *Of Spirit*, G. Bennington & R. Bowlby (trans.). Chicago, IL: University of Chicago Press.

Derrida, J. 1991. "'Eating Well', or the Calculation of the Subject: An Interview with Jacques Derrida". In *Who Comes After the Subject?*, E. Cadava, P. Connor, J.-L. Nancy (eds), 98–119. London: Routledge.

Derrida, J. 1992. *Points de suspension, Entretiens*. Paris: Galilée.

Derrida, J. 1993. *Aporias: Dying – Awaiting (One Another at) the Limits of Truth*, T. Dutoit (trans.). Stanford, CA: Stanford University Press.

Derrida, J. 1995. *Points ... Interviews, 1974–1994*, E. Weber (ed.), Peggy Kamuf *et al.* (trans.). Stanford, CA: Stanford University Press.

Derrida, J. 2006. *L'Animal que donc je suis*. Paris: Galilée.

Dreyfus, H. 1991. *Being-in-the-World: A Commentary on Heidegger's Being and Time, Division 1*. Cambridge, MA: MIT Press.

Dschuang Dsi (Chuang Tzu) 1972. *Das wahre Buch vom südlichen Blütenlan*, R. Wilhelm (trans.). Dusseldorf: Diedrichs Verlag.

Edler, F. 1990. "Philosophy, Language and Politics: Heidegger's Attempt to Steal the Language of the Revolution in 1933–1934". *Social Research* 57(1): 197–238.

Elden, S. 2006. "Heidegger's Animals". *Continental Philosophy Review* 39(3): 273–91.

Farías, V. 1989. *Heidegger and Nazism*, J. Margolis & T. Rockmore (eds), P. Burrell, D. di Bernardi & G. R. Ricci (trans.), Philadelphia, PA: Temple University Press.

Franck, D. 1991. "Being and the Living". In *Who Comes After the Subject?*, E. Cadava, P. Connor, J.-L. Nancy (eds), 135–47. London: Routledge.

Gadamer, H.-G. 1985. *Philosophical Apprenticeships*, R. R. Sullivan (trans.). Cambridge, MA: MIT Press.

Gelven, M. 1989. *A Commentary on Heidegger's* Being and Time, rev. edn. DeKalb, IL: Northern Illinois University Press.

Glendinning, S. 1998. *On Being With Others: Heidegger–Derrida–Wittgenstein*. London: Routledge.

Guignon, C. (ed.) 2006. *The Cambridge Companion to Heidegger*, 2nd edn. Cambridge: Cambridge University Press.

Haar, M. 1993. *The Song of the Earth: Heidegger and the Grounds of the History of Being*, R. Lilly (trans.). Bloomington, IN: Indiana University Press.

Hawking, S. 1988. *A Brief History of Time: From the Big Bang to Black Holes*. London: Bantam.
Heraclitus. *The Complete Philosophical Fragments*, W. Harris (trans.). http://community. middlebury.edu/~harris/Philosophy/Heraclitus.html (accessed March 2011).
Hodge, J. 1995. *Heidegger and Ethics*. London: Routledge.
Hölderlin, F. 1966. *Poems and Fragments*, M. Hamburger (trans.). Ann Arbor, MI: University of Michigan Press.
Hölderlin, F. 1992–94. "Hyperion". In his *Sämtliche Werke und Briefe*, vol. 1, J. Schmidt (ed.). Frankfurt: Deutscher Klassiker.
Homer 1999. *Iliad, Volume II, Books 13–24*, 2nd edn, A. T. Murray (trans.), W. F. Wyatt (rev.). Cambridge, MA: Harvard University Press.
Hsiao, P. S. 1987. "Heidegger and our Translation of the Tao Te Ching". See Parkes (1987), 93–103.
Inwood, M. 2000a. *Heidegger: A Very Short Introduction*. Oxford: Oxford University Press.
Inwood, M. 2000b. *A Heidegger Dictionary*. Oxford: Blackwell.
Inwood, M. J. 2005. "Heidegger, Martin". In *Oxford Companion to Philosophy*, T. Honderich (ed.), 371–5. Oxford: Oxford University Press.
Jaspers, K. 1993. "Letter to the Freiburg University Denazification Committee, December 22, 1945". In *The Heidegger Controversy: A Critical Reader*, R. Wolin (ed.), 144–151. Cambridge, MA: MIT Press.
Laotse 1980. *Tao te king: Das Buch des Alten vom Sinn und Leben*, R. Wilhelm (trans.). Dusseldorf: Diedrichs Verlag.
Lao-Tse 2009. *Tao Te Ching*, V. von Strauss (trans.). Charleston, SC: BiblioBazaar.
Large, W. 2010. *Heidegger's Being and Time*. Edinburgh: Edinburgh University Press.
Lawlor, L. 2007. "Animals Have No Hand: An Essay on Animality in Derrida". In *This is not Sufficient: An Essay on Animality and Human Nature in Derrida*, 39–70. New York: Columbia University Press.
Levinas, E. 1969. *Totality and Infinity*, A. Lingis (trans.). Pittsburgh, PA: Duquesne University Press.
Lewis, M. 2005. *Heidegger and the Place of Ethics*. London: Continuum.
Long A. & D. Sedley, 1987. *The Hellenistic Philosophers*, vol. 1. Cambridge: Cambridge University Press.
Löwith, K. 1993a. *My Life in Germany Before and After 1933*. London: Athlone.
Löwith, K. 1993b. "My Last Meeting with Heidegger in Rome, 1936". In *The Heidegger Controversy: A Critical Reader*, R. Wolin (ed.), 130–43. Cambridge, MA: MIT Press.
May, R. 1996. *Heidegger's Hidden Sources: East Asian Influences on His Work*, G. Parkes (trans.). London: Routledge.
McGrath, S. J. 2008. *Heidegger: A (Very) Critical Introduction*. Grand Rapids, MI: Eerdmans.
McNeill, W. 1999. "Life Beyond the Organism: Animal Being in Heidegger's Freiburg Lectures, 1929–30". In *Animal Others: On Ethics, Ontology, and Animal Life*, H. P. Steeves (ed.), 197–248. Albany, NY: SUNY Press.
Muir, J. 2011. *My First Summer in Sierra*. New York: Houghton Mifflin Harcourt.
Needham, J. 1975. *Science and Civilization in China, vol. 2: History of Scientific Thought*. Cambridge: Cambridge University Press.
Neske, G. & E. Kettering (eds) 1990. *Martin Heidegger and National Socialism: Questions and Answers*. New York: Paragon House.
Nietzsche, F. 1974. *The Gay Science*, W. Kaufmann (trans.). New York: Vintage.
Olafson, F. 1993. "The Unity of Heidegger's Thought". In *The Cambridge Companion to Heidegger*, C. Guignon (ed.), 97–121. Cambridge: Cambridge University Press.
Olafson, F. 1998. *Heidegger and the Ground of Ethics: A Study of Mitsein*. Cambridge: Cambridge University Press, 1998.
Orwell, G. 1961. *1984*. New York: New American Library.
Ott, H. 1993. *Heidegger: A Political Life*, A. Blunden (trans.). New York: Basic Books.
Parkes, G. (ed.) 1987. *Heidegger and Asian Thought*. Honolulu, HI: University of Hawaii Press.

Pattison, G. 2000. *The Later Heidegger*. London: Routledge.

Petzet, H. W. 1993. *Encounters and Dialogues with Martin Heidegger, 1929–1976*, P. Emad & K. Maly (trans.). Chicago, IL: University of Chicago Press.

Pöggeler, O. 1987. "West–East Dialogue: Heidegger and Lao-Tzu". See Parkes (1987), 47–78.

Pöggeler, O. 1993. "Heidegger's Political Self-Understanding". In *The Heidegger Controversy: A Critical Reader*, R. Wolin (ed), 198–244. Cambridge, MA: MIT Press.

Polt, R. 1999. *Heidegger: An Introduction*. London: UCL Press.

Polt, R. 2005. "Ereignis". In *A Companion to Heidegger*, H. L. Dreyfus & M. Wrathhall (eds), 375–91. Oxford: Blackwell.

Polt, R. 2010. "Being and Time". See Davis (2010a), 69–81.

Regan, T. 1999. "Foreword". In *Animal Others: On Ethics, Ontology, and Animal Life*, H. P. Steeves (ed.), xi–xiii. Albany, NY: SUNY Press.

Rockmore, T. 1992. *On Heidegger's Nazism and Philosophy*. Brighton: Wheatsheaf.

Rorty, R. 1981. *Philosophy and the Mirror of Nature*. Princeton, NJ: Princeton University Press.

Rorty, R. 1998. "Taking Philosophy Seriously". *New Republic* (11 April): 31–4.

Russell, B. 1989. *Wisdom of the West*. New York: Crescent Books.

Safranski, R. 1998. *Martin Heidegger: Between Good and Evil*. Cambridge, MA: Harvard University Press.

Schatzki, T. 1992. "Early Heidegger on Being, the Clearing, and Realism". In *Heidegger: A Critical Reader*, H. L. Dreyfus & H. Hall, 81–98. Oxford: Blackwell.

Scruton, R. 2001. *A Short History of Modern Philosophy: From Descartes to Wittgenstein*. London: Routledge.

Sekida, K. 1977. *Two Zen Classics: Mumonkan and Hekiganroku*. New York: John Weatherhill.

Sheehan, T. (ed.) 1981. *Heidegger: The Man and the Thinker*. Chicago, IL: Precedent.

Sheehan, T. 2010. "The Turn". See Davis (2010a), 82–101.

Shinjin-mei 1925. "The Seal of Faith", S. Ohasama (trans.). In *Zen: Der lebendige Buddhismus in Japan*, A. Faust (ed.). Gotha: Perthes.

Suzuki, S. 2010. *Zen Mind, Beginner's Mind*. Boston, MA: Shambhala Publications.

Tenzin Gyatso 2005. *Essence of the Heart Sutra: The Dalai Lama's Heart of Wisdom Teachings*. Somerville, MA: Wisdom Publications.

Vallega-Neu, D. 2010. "*Ereignis*: The Event of Appropriation". See Davis (2010a), 140–54.

Warnek, P. 2010. "The History of Being". See Davis (2010a), 155–67.

Wisser, R. 1970. *Martin Heidegger im Gespräch*. Freiburg: Alber.

Wisser, R. 1990. "Martin Heidegger in Conversation with Richard Wisser", L. Harris (trans.). In *Martin Heidegger and National Socialism: Questions and Answers*, G. Neske & E. Kettering (eds), 81–7. New York: Paragon House.

Wolin, R. (ed.) 1993. *The Heidegger Controversy: A Critical Reader*. Cambridge, MA: MIT Press.

Wrathall. M. 2005. *How to Read Heidegger*. London: Granta.

Young, J. 1997. *Heidegger, Philosophy, Nazism*. Cambridge: Cambridge University Press.

Young, J. 2001. *Heidegger's Philosophy of Art*. Cambridge: Cambridge University Press.

Young, J. 2002. *Heidegger's Later Philosophy*. Cambridge: Cambridge University Press.

Zimmerman, M. 2006. "Heidegger, Buddhism and Deep Ecology". In *The Cambridge Companion to Heidegger*, 2nd edn, C. Guignon (ed.), 293–325. Cambridge: Cambridge University Press.

Zimmerman, M. 1983. "Heidegger and Heraclites on Spiritual Practice". *Philosophy Today* 27(2): 87–103.

Zimmerman, M. 1986. *Eclipse of the Self: The Development of Heidegger's Concept of Authenticity*, 2nd edn. Athens, OH: Ohio University Press.

Index

Printed in Great Britain
by Amazon